Visual Cognition and Action

Visual Cognition and Action

An Invitation to Cognitive Science

Volume 2

edited by Daniel N. Osherson,
Stephen Michael Kosslyn, and John M. Hollerbach

The MIT Press
Cambridge, Massachusetts
London, England

Second Printing, 1990

This book was set in Palatino by Asco Trade Typesetting Ltd., Hong Kong and printed and bound by Halliday Lithograph in the United States of America.

Library of Congress Cataloging-in-Publication Data
(Revised for vol. 2)

An Invitation to cognitive science.

  Vol. 2 edited by Daniel N. Osherson, Stephen Michael Kosslyn, and John M. Hollerbach.
  Includes index.
  Contents: v. 2. Visual cognition and action.
  1. Cognition. 2. Cognitive science. I. Osherson, Daniel N. II. Kosslyn, Michael Stephen.
III. Hollerbach, John M.
BF311.I68   1990   153   89-30868
ISBN 0-262-15036-0 (v. 2)
ISBN 0-262-65034-7 (v. 2: pbk.)

Contents

List of Contributors

Irving Biederman
Department of Psychology
University of Minnesota

E. Bizzi
Department of Brain and Cognitive
Sciences
Massachusetts Institute of
Technology

Fred Dretske
Department of Philosophy
Stanford University

Henrietta L. Galiana
Department of Biomedical
Engineering
McGill University

Alvin Goldman
Department of Philosophy
University of Arizona

John M. Hollerbach
Department of Brain and Cognitive
Sciences
Massachusetts Institute of
Technology

Stephen Michael Kosslyn
Department of Psychology
Harvard University

F. A. Mussa-Ivaldi
Department of Brain and Cognitive
Sciences
Massachusetts Institute of
Technology

Daniel N. Osherson
Department of Brain and Cognitive
Sciences
Massachusetts Institute of
Technology

Elizabeth S. Spelke
Department of Psychology
Cornell University

S. Ullman
Department of Brain and Cognitive
Sciences
Massachusetts Institute of
Technology

Charles E. Wright
Department of Psychology
Columbia University

A. L. Yuille
Division of Applied Sciences
Harvard University

Foreword

The book you are holding is the second of a three-volume introduction to contemporary cognitive science. The thirty chapters that make up the three volumes have been written by thirty-one authors, including linguists, psychologists, philosophers, computer scientists, biologists, and engineers. The topics range from arm trajectories to human rationality, from acoustic phonetics to mental imagery, from the cerebral locus of language to the categories that people use to organize experience. Topics as diverse as these require distinctive kinds of theories, tested against distinctive kinds of data, and this diversity is reflected in the style and content of the thirty chapters.

As the authors of these volumes, we are united by our fascination with the mechanisms and structure of biological intelligence, especially human intelligence. Indeed, our principal goal in this introductory work is to reveal the vitality of cognitive science, to share the excitement of its pursuit, and to help you reflect upon its interest and importance. You may think of these volumes, then, as an invitation—namely, our invitation to join the ongoing adventure of research into human cognition.

The topics that we explore fall into four parts: "Language," whose nine chapters are found in volume 1, along with an introductory chapter for the volumes as a whole; "Visual Cognition" and "Action," which make up volume 2; and "Thinking," whose seven chapters belong to volume 3, along with an epilogue devoted to three supplementary topics. Each volume ends with a listing of the chapters in the other two.

Since each part is self-contained, the four parts may be read in any order. On the other hand, it is easiest to read the chapters within a given part in the order indicated. Each chapter concludes with suggestions for further reading and questions for further thought.

The artwork at the beginning of each chapter was provided by Todd Siler. We hope that it enhances your enjoyment of the work.

Paul M. Churchland

Fred Dretske

K. Fowler

H. L. Galianno

Merrill F. Garrett

Alvin I. Goldman

Innis Hara

James Higginbotham

John M. Hollerbach

Keith Holyoak

[signature]

Richard K. Larson

Howard Lasnik

Richard Lewontin

Joanne L. Miller

Fentinell Venknli

Daniel N. Osherson

Steven Pinker

Mary C. Potter

Paul Horni

Edward E. Smith

Elizabeth Speke

Stephen P. Stich

Shimon Ullmann

Charles E. Wright

Al Ville

Edgar Zurif

Visual Cognition

Visual Cognition: Introduction

Stephen Michael Kosslyn

It is difficult to overstate the importance of vision in our lives. We use vision not only to help us recognize food when we are hungry and a bed when we are sleepy but also to read, to observe a friend's facial expressions, to appreciate the beauty of a potential mate or a work of art, to navigate, and to track a shooting star. Indeed, vision has permeated even our language, which is replete with visual metaphors (as you will immediately see, or at least catch a glimpse of). Visual perception guides us in our daily commerce with the environment and provides much of our knowledge about the world.

Thus, it is important to understand vision if we are to understand the nature of the mind. Such an understanding will have many other benefits as well. For instance, if we knew how human vision works, we would be in a position to endow machines with similar capabilities. This accomplishment would benefit many segments of society, ranging from the blind to the mentally retarded, who would enjoy reading machines and "seeing-eye" automobiles. We would also be able to design visual displays that play to our strengths and avoid our weaknesses. As anyone who has read national news magazines knows, there is plenty of room for improvement in even simple charts and graphs—let alone displays used in nuclear powerplants and the like.

The five chapters in "Visual Cognition" outline the high points of this field. In these chapters we will focus on how information is stored and processed during vision, asking questions such as these:

> How do we detect depth, given that the back of the eye is a two-dimensional sheet and that depth information is thus not directly preserved from the outset?
> How do we register shape in a way that allows us to recognize objects under varying circumstances, including when parts are missing or added?
> What is the relationship between vision and visual mental imagery?
> What aspects of visual perception are learned?
> What does it mean to "see" something?

Chapter 1 deals with low-level vision, focusing on how we organize the world into units that are likely to correspond to objects and their parts, and how we register various properties (such as depth and movement) of these units. (For readers with a background in mathematics, technical details are provided and set off by rules.) Chapter 2 explores how we recognize these units as corresponding to objects, focusing on the nature of the mental representations used to store shape. Chapter 3 builds on these two chapters to consider another function of visual representations, namely, their role in forming and using mental images. Chapter 4 addresses the development over age of visual perception, summarizing new information about ancient controversies. Finally, chapter 5 takes a hard look at the philosophical foundations of the assumptions made in the preceding chapters.

The tour through visual cognition offered in these chapters is by no means complete (for example, it does not examine the biochemical events that underlie visual processes); but it does give more than a glimpse of the peaks of some very substantial mountains. It is intended to provide an in-depth sense of key points in the different areas and of how varied types of research fit together. Even more than that, it is intended to give a sense of how the essential interdisciplinary nature of cognitive science is allowing modern investigators to make headway on problems that have plagued thinkers for thousands of years.

Chapter 1

Computational Theories of Low-Level Vision

A. L. Yuille and S. Ullman

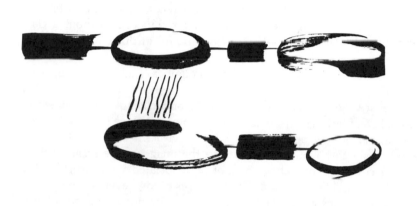

Vision appears to be an immediate, effortless event. To see the surrounding environment, it seems we need only open our eyes and look around. However, this subjective feeling disguises the immense sophistication of the human (or animal) vision system and the great complexity of the information-processing tasks it is able to perform in an apparently effortless manner.

The study of vision has progressed in recent years within a number of disciplines, in particular, neurophysiology, neuroanatomy, psychology, psychophysics, and computational vision. In this chapter we will review some of the main directions in computational vision, which is the study of vision from an information-processing point of view. This itself is a vast subject, and we will limit discussion here to the stages of the visual process known collectively as "early" or "low-level" vision. In particular, we will look at the characteristics of low-level vision, examples of the visual tasks involved, the methodology of the computational approach, and the fundamentals of contemporary theories, especially as they apply to the analysis of visual motion.

1.1   The Scope of Low-Level Vision

The term *low-level vision* refers to the first processing stages in the analysis of the incoming visual information. Although there is no clear, well-accepted delineation of the domain of low-level vision, it can be characterized as dealing primarily with problems related to the recovery of physical properties of the visual environment. These properties include depth to different points in the visual field, surface orientation of objects, boundaries of objects, material properties, motion in space, and the like. In contrast, the *high-level* processes of visual perception discussed in chapter 2 use the representations produced by the early processes for tasks that are no longer purely visual in nature, such as object recognition. The distinction between "low-" and "high-level" vision is a rough one, without a clear dividing line, but it has nevertheless been useful in discussions of visual perception.

The processes of low-level vision have a number of additional properties and goals.

Low-level vision is believed to act in a manner almost independent of the domain and task. That is, when we view a given scene on two different occasions, performing perhaps two different visual tasks, the set of low-level processes that would be applied to the image of the scene, such as extracting edges or computing the motion associated with objects in the field of view, would be identical. The processes of low-level vision may use general assumptions about the surrounding environment, but not object-specific knowledge. Thus, processes such as motion perception may incorporate some knowledge or assumptions about the continuity or rigidity of objects in general, but not knowledge specific to, say, telephones or elephants.

Many of the processes of low-level vision are believed to be applied by the visual system in parallel to large portions of the visual field. For example, the extraction of edges and their orientations, and the short-range computation of direction and speed of motion in the image, appear to be performed simultaneously across the visual field, or large parts of it. This is in contrast to object recognition, for instance, which appears to operate sequentially, one object (one or small group of objects) at a time.

One of the main goals of early vision is to organize the raw intensity data into a representation that describes the significant events, such as edges, in the image. This can be achieved by applying a number of processes to the image to detect these events. For example, *intensity edge detection* locates places where the image intensity has a sharp discontinuity. The boundaries of objects usually give rise to such discontinuities. *Texture boundary detection* identifies places where the texture of the images changes sharply—for example, at the boundary between a lawn and a road. *Motion segmentation* uses the difference in speed between objects to locate boundaries between objects that cannot be detected in static images.

A second general goal of low-level vision is to estimate depth or surface orientation. A number of different processes contribute to this task. *Binocular stereo vision* matches the images of the object in the two eyes and then obtains the depth of the object, perhaps by triangulation. If the surface of the object is known to have regular texture, then *shape from texture* can determine its orientation. For example, the shape of a golf ball can be estimated from the projection of its dimples. If the reflectance function (the disposition to reflect light) of an object is known, then *shape from shading* can find its orientation, provided the light source direction is known. Sometimes the silhouette of an object gives a strong perception of shape. This is an example of *shape from contour*. *Structure from motion* can estimate the depth and three-dimensional structure of objects.

Finally, low-level processes also compute the material properties of objects. *Color* can help distinguish between different objects, and *texture* can also give clues to their properties.

1.2   Methodological Considerations: The Levels of Explanation

Vision can be studied at different levels of abstraction. Marr (1982) describes three distinct levels: the *mechanism level*, the *algorithmic level*, and the *computational level*.

The mechanism level is the most basic of all. It describes what the physical elements of the brain (or computer) are doing. For the brain, we want to find out which neurons are involved in the process, what they are doing, and how they influence other neurons. In a computer, we need to know the structures and states of the logic elements. Any process can be described in terms of the mechanism level; however, this description is usually too complicated to be useful.

The next level of abstraction describes the algorithm for the process, which then controls the activity of the hardware. There are an infinite number of ways a particular algorithm could be implemented; the most efficient way depends, in part, on the available hardware.

The highest level of abstraction is the computational level. This involves analyzing problems in terms of an information-processing viewpoint, to determine what is being computed and why, and supplying mathematical models for them. Algorithms can then be designed to implement these models. The computational level is the most abstract and is largely independent of the other levels. Thus, although the hardware systems of a computer and a brain are very different, since the computational visual tasks for a robot and a human are very similar, the computational level theories should be similar.

An interesting illustration of the similarity of biological and artificial systems at the computational level has been provided by Dawkins (1986). Dawkins describes how the problems that engineers and physicists experienced in attempting to build radar systems just before World War II paralleled the problems that zoologists experienced in attempting to understand the echolocation mechanisms of bats. For example, a radar system must send out a strong wave pulse, or else its range will be very limited. If it does this, however, it risks damaging its ultrasensitive receivers, which are waiting for echoes from the pulse. The engineers designed a periodic system in which a strong pulse signal was sent out with the receivers desensitized; then the pulse was shut off and the receivers switched on. Meanwhile, the zoologists were independently discovering that a very similar method is used by bats.

The computational approach provides rigorous theoretical discipline by insisting that theories are specified mathematically and implemented algorithmically. These implementations help "keep the theorist honest" by ensuring that all the assumptions of the theory are made explicit. They also make it easier to test the theories and see how they perform with different types of input.

Computational theories and models can often be compared to human performance by *psychophysical* experiments, in which experimental subjects are shown visual stimuli and asked to perform visual tasks. Although existing theories are not able to duplicate the abilities of humans, some of these theories are consistent with a large range of experiments. When evaluating a theory, it is important to determine the range of conditions under which it works, and when and why it breaks down. A theory that agrees with a range of experiments does not become useless if it disagrees with new experimental data. Indeed, the reasons why the theory fails are often helpful in designing subsequent theories.

It is also desirable, but usually more difficult, to try to determine whether, where, and how methods similar to the computational models are implemented in the brain. For a review of the neuroanatomy or neurophysiology of the visual system from a computational perspective, see Ullman 1986.

The three-level distinction is important for clarifying problems and avoiding the confusion of issues from different levels. It is unclear, however, how independent the levels actually are. In particular, the hardware of the brain may place strong constraints on the algorithms that can be implemented. Some theorists therefore start by assuming network models for the brain and then investigate what computations can be "naturally" performed by different types of hardware (Rumelhart and McClelland 1986).

1.3   The Fundamentals of Contemporary Theory

1.3.1   The Ill-posedness of Vision and the Need for Natural Constraints

Too little information arrives at the retina to recover unambiguously the full three-dimensional world. The light emitted by an object depends on a number of unknown factors such as the orientation of the object and the scene illumination. Moreover, the information in the image is usually insufficient to separate these individual contributions and determine them uniquely.

To understand the difficulties involved, imagine watching a sphere rotating in space. The sphere has some textured patches on it, so that as it moves, it reflects different amounts of light to your retina. Your brain is able to interpret this moving pattern of light on your retina as a rigidly moving sphere in space, and this is what you "see." Now suppose that the texture elements of the sphere move independently in space, in such a way that their projections exactly coincide with the first situation. Your brain receives the same input stimulus as before, and so you again see a moving sphere. Finally, suppose that you see a movie of the rotating sphere. The texture elements all lie in a single plane, the screen on which the movie is being shown. Still, the perception is the same.

This example is rather extreme, but it illustrates the point that different physical events in the world can give rise to the same pattern of light on the retina. In this sense vision is ill-posed and it needs to make assumptions about the world to interpret the data. Finding and describing these assumptions is one of the main goals of the computational study of early vision. These assumptions reflect the regularities of the world and hold true most of the time (in a statistical sense). Situations in which these assumptions do not hold may then give rise to misperceptions and visual illusions.

The assumptions used in low-level vision are primarily general in nature and not domain-dependent. They do not involve first identifying the context of a scene and then making deductions. Typically they are very simple, such as assuming that moving objects are rigid.

These assumptions can be investigated by psychophysical experiments, which find out how humans perceive visual stimuli. For example, subjects can be shown simple stimuli for which there is not enough information to specify a unique percept. By systematically varying the stimuli, it is sometimes possible to find which assumptions are used. It is also possible to produce visual illusions by finding stimuli for which the assumptions are incorrect. The use of these general assumptions is also believed to be largely innate or to appear at a very early stage, following only limited visual experience. There is some evidence, for example, that the use of rigidity in motion perception is already present by the age of 5 months

(Gibson, Owsley, and Johnston 1978). Similarly, binocular stereo vision seems to develop at about the age of 2 to 3 months (Held 1987). (For more on the origins and development of visual knowledge, see chapter 4.)

1.3.2   Modules and Representations

The complexity of vision suggests that it is too diffcult to be performed in a single stage. Following standard engineering practice, which recommends breaking down an overall process into a number of subprocesses as much as possible, current vision theory suggests decomposing vision systems into a number of semi-independent modules. These modules combine to compute representations of the visual scene of differing degrees of abstractness. An example of such a theory is described by Marr (1982). The simplest version of this theory involves a large number of modules and three stages of representations. The overall layout is illustrated in figure 1.1.

The first representation stage is called the *primal sketch*. This is a symbolic representation obtained directly from the image by detecting and describing significant features in ᵗhe image, such as intensity edges and texture boundaries. It also involves more global processes that group the features.

The primal sketch is the input into a number of different modular processes that together compute a viewer-centered representation of the

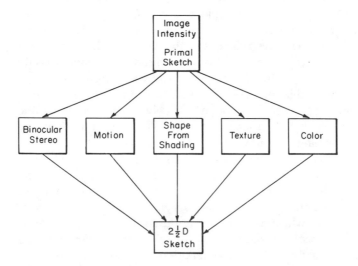

Figure 1.1
The organization of Marr's theory. The modules (for instance, binocular stereo) act on the image and the primal sketch to produce the 2½-D sketch.

world called the $2\frac{1}{2}$-D *sketch*. This representation describes the surrounding surfaces and their properties, such as their depth, surface orientation, color, and texture. The modular processes are believed to work relatively independently. Some of the modules, such as binocular stereo and structure from motion, extract three-dimensional information, and others compute color and texture information.

The final, and most controversial, representation is the full *3-D representation*. This is an object-centered representation used for recognition. It is constructed "on top of" the $2\frac{1}{2}$-D sketch and is used to describe three-dimensional objects in terms of volumetric primitives.

Low-level vision is only concerned with the first two levels of representation. Aspects of the 3-D representation are discussed in chapter 2. In sections 1.4 and 1.5 we will consider the processes that compute the primal sketch and the $2\frac{1}{2}$ D sketch.

1.4   Toward the Primal Sketch

1 4 1   Edge Detection

The most basic problem of low-level vision is *edge detection*. This problem concerns the initial organization of the input image into units that are both meaningful and more convenient for subsequent processing stages. The input to this computation is the raw intensity image. This can be thought of as a large array of time-dependent values, representing the light intensity of points in the visual field, sampled regularly. An edge map of this image is a set of contours that mark the locations where the image intensity changes significantly from one level to another.

We first consider one-dimensional "images." An edge occurs when the image intensity changes significantly, or where there is a steep intensity gradient. *Differentiation* is the mathematical operation used to detect change. Edges can therefore be located at points where the first spatial derivative of the image intensity will be a positive maximum or a negative minimum. This implies mathematically that the second spatial derivative of the intensity is zero (see figure 1.2). Thus, we could look for edges at places where the first derivative of the image is an extre..num (a maximum or a minimum) or where the second derivative of the image is zero. However, not all extrema of the derivative of the image will correspond to significant edges; many will be due to small random fluctuations of the intensity, or *noise*.

To avoid responses due to fluctuations, the image is usually first smoothed to attenuate the noise. One way to do this is to take a local average of the image by replacing the value of the image intensity at a

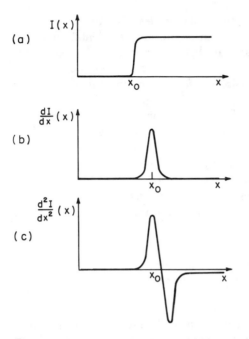

Figure 1.2
Edge detection can be performed by finding either maxima of the first derivative or zero crossings of the second derivative. (a) A step edge at x_0 without noise. (b) The first derivative of the image. Note the maximum at x_0. (c) The second derivative of the image. Note the zero crossing at x_0.

point by a positive weighted average of the intensities of its neighboring points. Mathematically this corresponds to *convolving* the image with a *filter*. The amount of smoothing depends on the weights of the sum and the size of the neighborhood. If only the nearest neighbors are chosen, then limited smoothing will be performed, and only small fluctuations will be eliminated. In general, the broader the filter, the more smoothing is done.

After the image has been smoothed to reduce the noise, it can be differentiated and edges can be marked at the extrema of the first derivative or at the zeros of the second derivative. Mathematically the two steps of smoothing and then differentiating twice can be combined into a single step, in which the image is convolved with a single filter. This new filter has a positive center and a negative surround, unlike the original smoothing filter, which was always positive (see figure 1.3).

The filter that combines smoothing and differentiation can be extended to two dimensions using similar ideas. The resulting two-dimensional filter

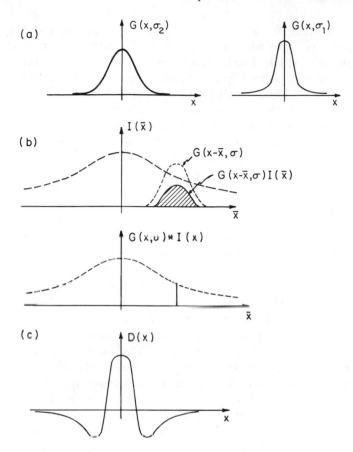

Figure 1.3

Filtering, smoothing, and differentiation. (a) The Gaussian filter $G(x, \sigma)$. The filter becomes broader as σ increases and therefore performs more smoothing. (b) The convolution of an image function $I(\bar{x})$ with a Gaussian filter. The averaging is done with the filter centered on a point $\bar{x}$ and yields a value equal to the area of the shaded region. The filter is then moved and the new average computed. (c) The filter obtained by combining the smoothing and differentiation operations. A two-dimensional version of this filter, obtained by rotating the filter about the vertical axis, has the form of a "Mexican hat."

looks rather like a Mexican hat, with a positive central region and a negative surround. The filter has the shape of the Laplacian of a two-dimensional Gaussian function. The application of this filter to the image means that the image is smoothed by a Gaussian filter of a fixed standard deviation σ and the second-order spatial derivatives are taken in both in x and y direction and added. This filter is convolved with the image, by the local averaging process, and the zeros are labeled as edges.

It is interesting that neurons have been found in the early processing stages of the visual system (retinal ganglion cells and cells in the lateral geniculate nucleus of the thalamus) whose receptive fields closely match the shape of this filter. The shape of these receptive fields is often described as the *difference of Gaussians* (DOG).

In the above filter one parameter was left unspecified: the value of the spatial constant σ, which controls the size of the operator. This is an important choice. If σ is small, then the image will only be smoothed a little and edges due to small noise fluctuations will be detected. If it is too large, the image will be smoothed too much and significant edges will disappear.

One way of resolving this problem is to first attempt to estimate the noise in the image and then deduce an approximate value for σ. This can be done, although noise estimation requires assumptions about the type of noise, which may not be universally valid. The optimal scale of analysis also depends on the structure of the image: sharp, closely spaced edges require a smaller operator than isolated, gradual edges. Since structure of interest may occur at a variety of scales, there may not be a single optimal scale of analysis (optimal σ). A photograph of a cat, for example, will have a large-scale structure corresponding to the outline of the body and a small-scale structure corresponding to the fur.

An alternative method is to use not a single operator but a number of operators of different sizes, and then combine the results in an integrated edge map (Marr and Hildreth 1980). The optimal way of integrating results from different scales of analysis is still an open problem in the area of edge detection. One possible method of using multiple scales for distinguishing significant from insignificant edges is by identifying edges that appear in a similar position at more than one scale. If an edge is signaled in the smallest channels but disappears for the larger ones, then it is considered a noise effect and rejected. Intuitively, only strong edges can resist substantial smoothing and exist at coarse scales, so we expect the number of edges to decrease as σ increases. In fact, there are mathematical theorems showing that this is always the case for the Laplacian of a Gaussian operator: no new edges can be created as σ increases. Figure 1.4 shows the results of convolving an image with a DOG filter and extracting the zero crossings at different values of σ.

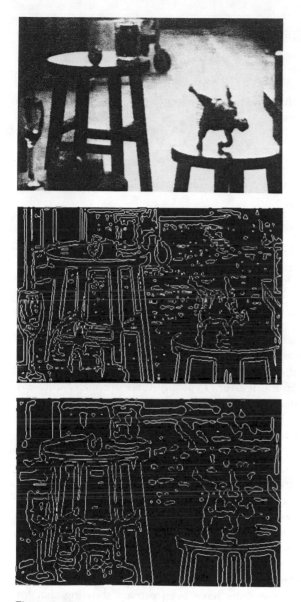

Figure 1.4
The edges of an image at different scales. (a) The original image. (b) The edges of the image at scale $\sigma = 2.0$. (c) The edges of the image at $\sigma = 4.0$.

The Gaussian filter is given by

$$G(x, y, \sigma) = \frac{1}{2\pi\sigma^2} \exp\left(-\frac{(x^2 + y^2)}{2\sigma^2}\right),$$

where σ controls the width of the filter. The larger σ is, the broader the filter. The Laplacian operator is

$$\nabla^2 = \frac{\partial^2}{\partial x^2} + \frac{\partial^2}{\partial y^2}.$$

The Laplacian of the convolution of the Gaussian with the image is

$$\nabla^2 G * I(x, y) = \int \int \nabla^2 G(x - w, y - z) I(w, z) \, dw \, dz.$$

The zeros of this function are marked as intensity edges. As σ increases, noise fluctuations in the image get smoothed out, and the number of edges decreases.

There are two main reasons for using a symbolic edge map rather than the image itself as a basis for further processes. The first, and most important, reason is that the lighting for a given scene is relatively arbitrary and is usually unknown to the viewer. Typically there are many different sources of illumination and often multiple reflections from objects. The scene itself—the objects in it and its geometrical layout—is invariant under these lighting fluctuations. Intensity edges in the image usually correspond to features in the scene, such as boundaries of objects and surface markings, and therefore also tend to be invariant. The second reason is that the edge maps contain far fewer bits of information. For example, systems are being designed (Pearson and Robinson 1985) to extract caricatures of faces and hands, by edge detectors, and send this information down telephone lines in real time as an aid to deaf people and for long-distance conference calls. It might be thought that this reduction in the number of bits representing the image means that some important information from the image is being thrown away. Surprisingly, however, a number of mathematical theorems have been proved showing that for large classes of images the edges uniquely specify the image (Logan 1977; Curtis, Oppenheim, and Lim 1985; Yuille and Poggio 1985). It is unclear how robust these theorems are if noise is added to the image, but they show that the edges contain a significant amount of information. Thus, edge detection serves the dual purpose of lighting invariance and data reduction.

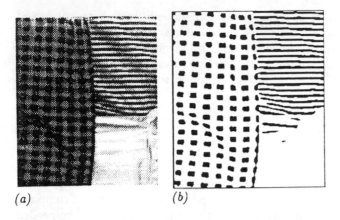

(a)   *(b)*

Figure 1.5
Texture boundaries between two pieces of clothing (a) There is only a small intensity change between the two regions, but the perception of a boundary is strong because of the differences in texture. (b) The textons, dark blobs in this case, detected by Voorhees and Poggio. The boundary can be detected from the change in texton properties. These images are courtesy of Voorhees and Poggio (1987).

1.4.2   Texture Segmentation

There is another type of boundary that cannot be found by the methods described above. This is the *texture boundary*, illustrated in figure 1.5, where the texture differs significantly across the boundary but the illumination does not. Such boundaries can be found by defining a set of *descriptors* for a texture and a rule for deciding how different the descriptors for two textures must be before the boundary between them is quickly detectable. Julesz (1981) argues that there is a distinction between boundaries that can be detected within a couple of hundred milliseconds, or *preattentively*, and those that require *visual attention*. Low-level vision restricts itself to pre-attentive processes.

Two general types of descriptors have been proposed. In the first approach textures are described by statistical properties. In the second approach a class of primitive elements, or *textons* (Julesz 1981), described by a small set of properties, is defined. These textons are extracted from the image and their properties are determined. For example, a texton might be a blob and its properties could include its orientation, its shape, and the mean intensity difference between it and the background. Boundaries between regions would then be detected either if there were significant differences between the statistics of the regions or if the texton properties, including perhaps the density of textons, differed significantly in the two regions. Voorhees and Poggio (1987) describe a theory that extracts textons from natural images and segments a scene using the textons' properties.

A large number of psychophysical experiments have been conducted (Julesz 1981) to find out what texture boundaries are preattentively detectable—in other words, what texture boundaries can be found by the low-level processes we are considering in this chapter. The results of these experiments are inconclusive, although they rule out some simple conjectures.

1.4.3   The Primal Sketch

The primal sketch was originally proposed by Marr (1976) to produce a symbolic representation of the image using processes like those discussed in this section. Exactly how it should be constructed is an open question, however, and few attempts have been made to implement it in a computer program. It was originally thought that the primal sketch would be needed as an input to the modules that compute the $2\frac{1}{2}$-D sketch. In the next section, however, we will see that it is possible to design reasonable binocular stereo and motion systems whose input is just the positions of the intensity edges.

1.5   Toward the $2\frac{1}{2}$-D Sketch

We will now deal with the modules that act either on the primal sketch, or on the edge map, or directly on the image intensity values. The output of these modules can then be combined to give the $2\frac{1}{2}$-D representation.

Several modules have been used to estimate depth, including binocular stereo, motion, shape from shading, shape from texture, and shape from contour. Here we will mainly concentrate on two modules, binocular stereo (how we use two eyes to extract depth information) and structure from motion.

1.5.1   Binocular Stereo: The Correspondence Problem

Binocular stereo is one of the most important modules for obtaining depth (see figure 1.6). This module exploits the fact that each eye sees a slightly different view of the world. More precisely, points in space that are projected on the two eyes are matched and the depth to the points in space can be computed by triangulation.

For binocular stereo two images of a scene are given (one for each eye). If corresponding primitives in the images can be found, then the depth of the point can be determined by simple trigonometry, assuming that the imaging geometry is fully known. (See figure 1.6a.) The matching is aided by an important geometrical constraint, *the epipolar line constraint* (figure 1.6b), which ensures that a primitive in the left eye can only be matched to

(a)

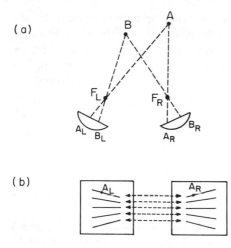

(b)

(c)

Figure 1.6

The geometry of binocular stereo, assuming a pinhole camera model for each eye. (a) Points A and B in space are projected through the foci F_L and F_R to the points A_L, B_L, A_R, and B_R on the two retinas. If the stereo system can compute that A_L and A_R correspond, then the depth of A can be found by triangulation. However, if A_L is matched to B_R, then the wrong depth is computed. (b) The epipolar line constraint. A point A_L in the left image can only be matched to a point A_R in the right image on the corresponding epipolar line. (c) The importance of the direction of gaze (the relative orientation of the eyes). If the eyes are oriented with foci F_L^1 and F_R^1, then the centers of the eyes will correspond to a depth D_1. If the eyes are rotated so that the foci move to F_L^2 and F_R^2, then the eyes will fixate at a depth D_2.

a primitive lying on a specific line in the right eye. If the two eyes are parallel to each other focusing at infinity, then this constraint means that only points at the same height in the two images can be matched. Thus, a key part of binocular stereo is to solve the correspondence problem between primitives in the two images. The difficulty of this problem depends on the complexity of the primitives that the system tries to match. If the system matches low-level primitives, such as image intensity or edges, then the correspondence problem is hard since there are many possible matches. If the system matches more complicated primitives, such as edges of buildings, then the correspondence problem is straightforward but the system must work hard to extract these primitives. Moreover, the number of matching primitives tends to be small, so the resulting depth map is sparse.

There are binocular stereo theories that match image intensities between the images. It is likely, however, that the intensity of a point in space is slightly different in the two eyes. Thus, systems using this approach introduce errors, compared to systems using edges as primitives. On the other hand, binocular stereo systems using edge maps only give depth values on the edge maps and need to be interpolated if depth values are to be obtained elsewhere.

Julesz (1971) invented *random dot stereograms* to demonstrate that binocular stereo is possible using only low-level primitives and no scene-dependent information (see figure 1.7). These stereograms are comprised of two images, one for each eye. The images consist of dots arrayed

Figure 1.7
A random dot stereogram. The central square is displaced in the right image. When the two images are fused, the square is perceived to lie in front of the background.

randomly so that the images have no structure. The central square in the left image is shifted by a small amount in the right image. If such images are fused (viewed stereoscopically), however, they give a strong three-dimensional percept. The central square is perceived to lie at a different depth from the rest of the image. This suggests that the matching primitives are fairly simple. It also highlights the enormous complexity of the task faced by the visual system: despite the huge number of possible matches between the dots in the two images, the correct answer is almost always obtained.

1.5.2   Binocular Stereo: An Algorithm

One of the most influential binocular stereo theories was invented by Marr and Poggio (1979) and extended and implemented by Grimson (1981). This theory has also been proposed as a plausible model of some aspects of the human visual system. Like the edge detectors proposed by Marr, it makes critical use of the concept of multiple scales. The input is the edge maps in the two eyes obtained at four or five different scales. The key point is that at the coarsest scale, which underwent the most smoothing, few edges will be detected and the correspondence problem will be comparatively simple (see figure 1.8). To solve the correspondence problem at this scale, imagine placing the left and right eye edge maps under one another. The *disparities* are the differences between the positions of the corresponding edges in the two edge maps. If these disparities are small, compared to the average distance between edges in each of the images, then the correspondence problem is easy to solve: it is simply a matter of picking the closest match (see figure 1.9).

Marr and Poggio give a statistical argument to determine how far one should search before expecting errors due to random noise effects in the two images. If the disparities are bigger than the average distance between edges in the eyes, then this method will fail. There are two ways to deal with this problem. The first is to do the matching at an even coarser scale, where there will be even fewer edges. The second is to alter the relative positions of the left and right edge maps, perhaps by changing the relative directions of gaze of the two eyes, by *verging*. If the two eyes are verging at approximately the depth of the stimuli (see figure 1.9), then the edges in the two eyes will be almost exactly aligned and the disparities will be small. The idea of altering the vergence is critical when we consider the finer, less smoothed edge maps. One possibility is that the coarsest channels can be used to guide the vergence for the finer channels.

Marr and Poggio based their algorithm on a computational analysis of the problem. Theoretically, the correspondence problem is combinatorially explosive and constraints are needed to resolve it. The main constraint

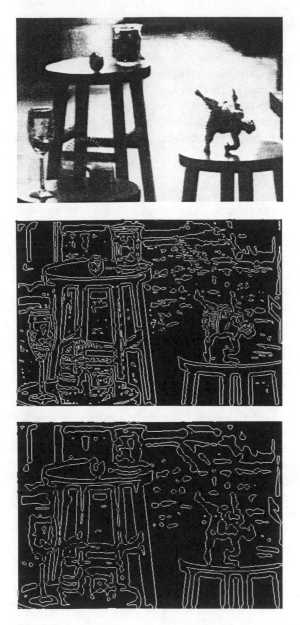

Figure 1.8
The edges for a pair of stereo images. (top) The two stereo images. (middle) The edges computed in both images at $\sigma = 2.0$. (bottom) The edges computed at $\sigma = 4.0$. At the coarsest scale there are few edges, so the correspondence is usually simple; the closest match is usually correct. This correspondence can be used to guide the matching at the finer levels. The epipolar lines are approximately horizontal for these images.

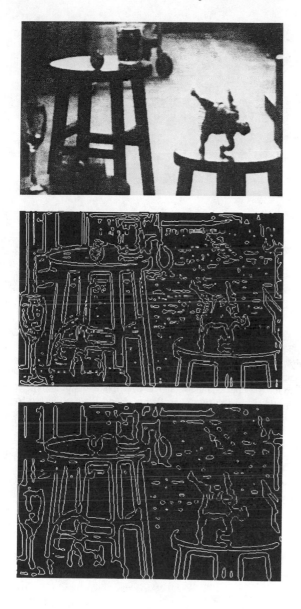

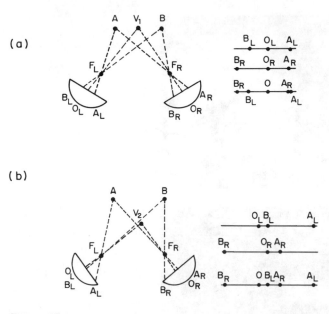

Figure 1.9
The importance of the direction of gaze. If the direction of gaze changes, then the disparities also change. The disparities will be smallest, and hence the correspondence will be simplest, if the eyes are fixating directly at the object. Marr and Poggio's theory suggests that the coarse-level correspondences can cause the eyes to fixate near the object, thereby simplifying the correspondence problem for the finer channels. (a) The eyes fixate at a point V_1, so it is projected to the centers O_L and O_R of the two eyes. Points A and B are projected to points A_L, A_R, B_L, and B_R. The disparities are computed by comparing the relative positions of the features in the two images. Since A and B are at roughly the same depth as V_1, the disparities are small. It is straightforward to solve the correspondence problem to match B_L with B_R and A_L with A_R. (b) The eyes change their direction of gaze and fixate at V_2, with A and B unchanged. The disparities are now much larger and the correspondence problem is therefore harder. In this situation many binocular stereo theories would incorrectly match B_L to A_R, leaving B_R and A_L unmatched.

they suggested was that surfaces tend to be smooth, except at their boundaries, and hence the disparities at neighboring positions in the image tend to be similar. This constraint can be used to justify the algorithm described above. An example where this assumption is violated can be found by looking through a dirty window at a scene outside. Edges may be due either to the dirt on the window or to objects in the scene. These two edge types will be at very different disparities and, unless the system is able to distinguish between them, it will make mistakes and match scene primitives to dirt primitives. In this situation the algorithm breaks down.

Psychophysicists had observed that there was a limit, *Panum's area*, to the size of disparities that could be fused without eye movements (Julesz 1971). (Note that large disparity gradients correspond to steep depth gradients.) It had also been observed that eye movements, changes in vergence, were sometimes needed to fuse two images. Marr and Poggio's model suggested a prediction for the size of Panum's area, based on their noise analysis, and a role for eye movements, based on their coarse-to-fine strategy. The experimental evidence suggests that their predictions are only roughly correct and that the true binocular stereo system is more complicated.

So far this system only gives depth values for the edge points, and yet binocular stereo produces the perception of continuous surfaces. Grimson (1981) proposed solving this problem by surface interpolation, essentially passing a smooth surface near the depths given at the edge map. He could justify this interpolation by arguing that any significant changes in the object's geometry would give rise to edges in the intensity. This argument can be supported by mathematical theorems, termed informally "no news is good news," which state that between zero crossings the variation in surface orientation is limited. He could also demonstrate by referring to psychophysical experiments that humans perceive smooth surfaces from binocular stereo in depth even with sparse stimuli, such as dots, provided there is sufficient density, and hence some interpolation must be involved (see also Collett 1985).

1.5.3   Color Vision

The extraction of color and material properties is another important task of low-level vision. The visual system has three color channels that operate under normal lighting conditions and a fourth channel that operates mostly at low illumination levels. These channels might be used to aid edge detection. For example, the edge between two objects of similar image intensity but different colors—say, red and green—might be detected by comparing the outputs of the red and green color channels. Surprisingly, this information does not seem to be used much, and edges of this type are

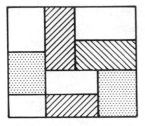

Figure 1.10
A mondrian. The different patches of the mondrian have different colors. The perceived color of each patch is relatively independent of the illumination but does depend on the color of the other patches.

often perceptually weak and difficult to localize. Some work has attempted to find rules for using color information to detect material changes between objects. These theories, though interesting, are as yet inconclusive.

The color system nevertheless shows an important ability to filter out irrelevant lighting conditions. This is emphasized most strongly by Land's (1964) experiments on color perception. In these experiments the subject is shown a picture made up of rectangular patches of different colors, a *mondrian* (see figure 1.10). The mondrian is illuminated by light sources of different color, and yet the perceived colors of the patches do not change much as the illumination is varied. The spectral distribution of the light from an object that arrives at the eye is a function of the color of the light incident on the object and the surface reflectance function of the object, the intrinsic color of the object. The perceived color of a patch of a mondrian, however, is relatively independent of the spectrum of the incident illumination. It does, however, seem to depend on the color of the neighboring patches.

The color constancy effect is clearly useful as a way of preserving the properties of objects as lighting conditions change. Without this effect the perceived color of a red London bus would change strongly whenever the bus turns a corner from a shady side street into the sun.

A number of theories have attempted to explain the color constancy effect. Some of these theories (see, for example, Land 1964; Horn 1974) exploit the different characteristic spatial behaviors of the reflectance functions of mondrians: the reflectance function is essentially constant inside the different color patches and then has sharp discontinuities at the boundaries of these patches. Moreover, the incident illumination can be assumed to vary smoothly with position. These regularities can be used to determine the reflectance function of the surface in the three different color channels, up to an arbitrary scaling factor in each channel. Thus, the relative colors of patches can be found by this method, but to find their absolute color requires normalizations of the three color channels. There are a number of ways to do this—for example, by assuming that the average color of the whole mondrian is white—but none are fully satisfactory.

1.5.4   The $2\frac{1}{2}$-D Sketch

Marr (1982) proposed that the outputs of these modules are used to create a representation of the world, the $2\frac{1}{2}$-D sketch, in terms of surfaces whose properties such as depth and color have been made explicit (see also Barrow and Tennenbaum 1981). Although considerable work has been done on the individual modules, it is unclear exactly how the information from different modules should be combined to construct such a representation.

1.6   The Analysis of Visual Motion

To gain further insight into the computational approach, let us consider some experimental studies in more detail. We will focus on visual motion and, for reasons of space, concentrate on work by Ullman (1979, 1984) and Hildreth (1984). Although this work does not provide the final solutions to these problems, it is hoped that it contains some of the necessary ingredients for such a theory. Considerable work has been done in this area; for more references, see the suggestions for further reading at the end of the chapter.

One of the most important modules of early vision is motion analysis. This problem includes two subproblems: (1) Motion measurement. The input to this computation is a temporal sequence of images, or an intensity image changing as a function of time. The desired output is some representation of the velocity field, specifying the speed and direction of motion of elements in the image. This can be used, for instance, to detect motion boundaries. (2) The recovery of structure from motion. Motion information is used at this stage to recover the three-dimensional structure of moving objects.

The ability of humans to perceive the structure of a moving object on the basis of motion information alone was demonstrated by the classic experiments of Wallach and O'Connell (1953). In these experiments an unfamiliar object was rotated behind a translucent screen, and the shadow of its projection was observed from the other side of the screen. In most cases the observers spontaneously perceived the correct three-dimensional structure and motion of the hidden object, even when each static view was unrecognizable and contained no three-dimensional information. Similar experiments have been performed using unconnected dots presented on a computer-controlled screen. For example, in an experiment carried out by

(a)

(b)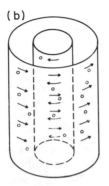

Figure 1.11
The rotating cylinder experiment. (a) A single transparent cylinder rotates. Its structure is quickly perceived from the motion of the dots. (b) Two transparent cylinders rotate in opposite directions. The structure of both cylinders can be perceived from the motion of the dots.

Ullman (1979) dots were painted on the surface of a transparent cylinder (see figure 1.11a). This configuration was simulated on a computer screen (so that no binocular stereo information was available) by computing the projection of the dots on the two-dimensional plane. Observers were then shown a sequence of frames, simulating the rotation of the cylinder. Although each individual frame consisted merely of a random collection of dots, observers of the dynamic scene perceived it spontaneously as a three-dimensional cylinder rotating in space. The visual system is able to solve the correspondence problem between dots at different times and then solve for the structure. The correct perception was also obtained for the more complex stimulus shown in figure 1.11b, although it was less stable. This stimulus consisted of two concentric transparent cylinders rotating in opposite directions. In the central region observers perceive dots belonging to each cylinder.

Ullman (1979) proposed that the recovery of structure from motion should be decomposed into two stages. In the first stage features are tracked, or matched, over time (solving the correspondence problem) and in the second stage the structure of the object is recovered. Ullman described a number of experiments suggesting that these two stages are independent.

1.6.1   Motion Measurement

The problem of motion measurement has received considerable theoretical and experimental attention in recent years. The problem consists of finding which features in an image correspond as the image varies over time. Potentially, many matches could be made, and the visual system of a human, or of a robot, will need to make a good choice. The correspondence problem is worse for motion than for binocular stereo, since binocular stereo can exploit the epipolar line constraint.

Many of the experimental studies have dealt with the phenomenon of apparent motion, where the observer samples at discrete time intervals and yet perceives smooth, continuous motion. Cinema films (with 24 image frames per second) demonstrate how easily people see smooth movement in these situations. In the simplest experiments of this type the images consist of dots and only two frames are used. The problem is then to find which dots match between the two frames. Braddick (1973, 1974) created random dot images, by analogy with random dot stereograms, and made the distinction between long-range and short-range motion. For short-range motion the dots move very little between frames and the correspondence problem is relatively simple. For long-range motion the dots can move large distances between frames. Braddick described a number of experiments, illustrated in figure 1.12, that showed significant differences between long- and short-range motion and suggested that they are mediated by different processes and used for different purposes.

One of Braddick's experiments consisted of using two frames of random dots, uncorrelated except for a central region, which could be a horizontal or vertical rectangle. The displacement between these regions was small for short-range motion and large for long-range motion. The observer's task was to determine whether the rectangle was horizontal or vertical.

A second experiment consisted of a vertical line in the first frame and two vertical lines in the second frame. The task was to find the perceived motion of the line in the first frame. Did it move smoothly to one of the lines in the second frame, or did it split into two lines?

Braddick varied the experimental conditions by changing the interstimulus interval (ISI), flashing a strong light during the ISI, and altering the amounts of displacement. He found that the first task could only be accomplished if the displacements were small (less than 15 minutes of visual angle), the ISI was about 100 milliseconds, and no flashing lights appeared during it. By contrast, the second task could be performed with larger displacements (up to several degrees of visual angle), large ISI (over 300

(a)

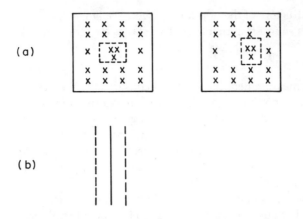

(b)

Figure 1.12
Braddick's motion experiments. (a) The central rectangle in the random dot pattern in the first frame is displaced in the second frame. The task is to determine whether the rectangle is horizontally or vertically oriented. The experiment investigates over what range of displacements this distinction can be made correctly. (b) There is one bar in the first time frame and two bars (marked by dotted lines) in the second frame. The experiment tests which bar in the second frame is perceived to correspond to the bar in the first frame.

milliseconds), and with a flash during the ISI. These, and other, differences suggested that short-range and long-range motion are quite different processes. A similar dichotomy between a long-range correspondence process and a short-range intensity-based process has been suggested in the context of computer vision. These two motion measurement processes are discussed in the next two sections.

1.6.2   Long-range Motion Correspondence

Many experiments have been done on the phenomena of long-range motion correspondence. Ullman (1979) analyzed the experiments and proposed a theoretical model for motion correspondence for features between two time frames. This was based on a cost function minimization scheme called *minimal mapping*. A cost is assigned to each possible way of matching features between the two frames based on the distance traveled by the features, so that short distances are preferred. The *cover principle* is used to require that features in each frame have at least one match. The theory predicts the correspondence that minimizes the cost function while satisfying the cover principle.

More precisely, suppose we have N dots in the first frame and M dots in the second. Let $\mathbf{x}_i$, $i = 1, \ldots, N$, and $\mathbf{y}_a$, $a = 1, \ldots, M$, represent the

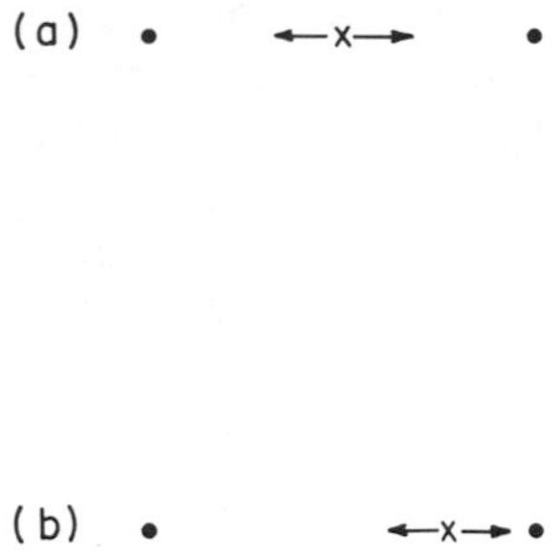

(a) •   ←—x—→   •

(b) •   ←—x—→ •

Figure 1.13
Dots and minimal mapping theory. (a) The dot in the first time frame (marked by a cross) is equidistant from the dots in the second frame (marked with dots). The single dot is perceived to split into two dots. (b) The dot in the first frame is close to one of the dots in the second frame. It is perceived to move to this dot.

positions of the features in the two frames. We define a matching matrix V_{ia} so that $V_{ia} = 1$ if the feature at x_i in the first frame goes to the feature at y_a in the second frame, and $V_{ia} = 0$ otherwise. The energy is defined by

$$E(V_{ia}) = \sum_{i=1,a=1}^{i=N,a=M} V_{ia}d_{ia},$$

where d_{ia} is a measure of the distance between the points x_i and y_a in the two frames. For example, d_{ia} might correspond to the distance between the points, in which case $d_{ia} = |x_i - y_a|$. The matches are found by minimizing $E(V_{ia})$ over all possible correspondences satisfying the cover principle. In mathematical terms, we must find the $N \times M$ matrix V_{ia} with binary entries that minimizes the engergy $E(V_{ia})$ subject to the constraint that each row and column in the matrix contains at least one nonzero term.

There are efficient ways of minimizing the cost function; it is unnecessary to calculate the energy for possible correspondences. Ullman showed that energy functions of this type can be minimized using standard algorithms from linear programming theory.

Minimal mapping theory can be tested by experiments with a small number of dots. Particularly interesting cases occur when the first frame has one dot and the second frame has two. If the single dot lies equidistant from the pair of dots, then the perception is of one dot splitting into two dots. Otherwise, the dot appears to move to the dot in the second frame closest to it and the cover principle is violated (see figure 1.13).

Although Ullman's minimal mapping theory was successful in explaining a wide range of experiments, a number of phenomena suggest that the theory needs some modifications. Perhaps the most dramatic of these is the motion capture phenomenon demonstrated by Ramachandran and Anstis (1985). In one of these experiments dots were superimposed on a moving sine wave grating. The presence of this grating affected the matching of the dots; it appeared that the dots were "captured" by the grating. It seems that minimal mapping theory does not reward motion coherence sufficiently strongly to account for some of these effects (Yuille and Grzywacz 1988).

Motion inertia is another phenomenon that needs explanation. If a scene is viewed over more than two frames, the matching between frames is found to have a weak dependence on the previous motion of the dot. There is a tendency for the dot to continue moving in a straight line (Ramachandran and Anstis 1985; Grzywacz 1987).

In conclusion, it appears that minimal mapping theory can account for the long-range correspondence process under simple conditions (well-separated features, two-frame presentations), but extensions are needed to account for the full range of long-range correspondence phenomena.

1.6.3   Motion Measurement: Short Range

Short-range motion correspondence is simple if we consider stimuli that consist only of dots and if the motion of the dots between frames is small compared to the average spacing between dots. In this case correspondence can be achieved by simply matching each dot with its nearest neighbor in the subsequent frame. A problem still exists, however, if we consider more complicated stimuli. In some theories of motion edges are extracted from the image and the edges must be matched between different time frames. Here the correspondence problem becomes the *aperture problem*; although the component of the velocity field perpendicular, or *normal*, to the contour is known, we have no knowledge of the tangential component (see figure 1.14a). For example, we are unable to tell if a circular line is rotating. Most attempts to solve these problems involve appeals to smoothness of the velocity field.

Hildreth (1984) described such a theory for matching contours. The problem is ill-posed, and a natural constraint is needed to solve it. Hildreth observed that neighboring elements in a rigidly moving object tend to move with similar velocities. Thus, the velocity field of such an object will tend to be smoothly varying in space. Hildreth defined a mathematical measure of smoothness and proposed that the perceived velocity field should be the smoothest velocity field consistent with the data. Notice that if the object is moving in a straight line, the velocity of all of its elements will be constant. In this case the smoothest velocity field consistent with

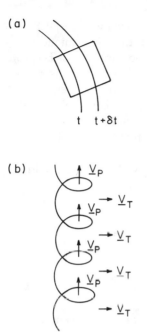

Figure 1.14
The aperture problem and the barberpole illusion. (a) The aperture problem. The contour is shown at times t and $t + \delta t$. By just considering the motion of the contour inside the aperture, it is impossible to solve for the exact correspondence between the two contours. (b) The contour lies on the surface of a cylinder (the barberpole). As the cylinder rotates about its axis, the perceived velocity of the contour, V_P, is vertical. However, the true velocity of the contour, V_T, is horizontal.

the data will be constant, so the algorithm obtains the correct motion. If the object is rotating, the algorithm is not guaranteed to find the correct solution. It is interesting that for these situations the human visual system makes similar mistakes.

Hildreth's theory is described by an energy function $E(\mathbf{v}(s))$. The energy function is made up of two parts,

$$E(\mathbf{v}(s)) = \int \mathbf{v}(s)) \cdot \mathbf{n}(s) - u(s))^2 ds + \lambda \int \frac{\partial \mathbf{v}(s)}{\partial s} \cdot \frac{\partial \mathbf{v}(s)}{\partial s} ds.$$

Here s denotes the arc-length along the contour, $\mathbf{n}(s)$ is the normal to the contour, $u(s)$ is the observed normal component of the velocity field, λ controls the strength of the smoothing, and $\mathbf{v}(s)$ is the velocity field on the contour to be determined. The function is minimized with respect to the velocity field. It is straightforward to show that there is a unique minimum. This has the important advantage that the minimum of $E(\mathbf{v})$ can be found by standard steepest descent algorithms. The minimum is interpreted to be the estimated velocity field. The first part of the energy function ensures that the normal component of the estimated velocity is near the observed normal velocity (because of noise in the data strict equality is not desirable). The second part ensures that the velocity field is smooth.

The simplest method of steepest descent is to give the velocity field $\mathbf{v}(s)$ an initial value and then update it by the following rule:

$$\frac{d\mathbf{v}(s)}{dt} = -\frac{\partial E}{\partial \mathbf{v}(s)}.$$

For Hildreth's energy function this reduces to

$$\frac{d\mathbf{v}(s)}{dt} = -2\mathbf{n}(s)(\mathbf{v}(s) \cdot \mathbf{n}(s) - u(s)) + 2\lambda \frac{\partial^2 \mathbf{v}(s)}{\partial s^2}.$$

The velocity field will then converge to the minimum of the energy function as t increases.

There are several visual illusions that seem to be consistent with Hildreth's theory. In the barberpole illusion (see figure 1.14b) the contours on the pole rotate, but the observer perceives vertically upward motion, which Hildreth's theory predicts. Another illusion is caused by rotating an ellipse. The observer perceives either an ellipse rotating with deformation or a circle rotating in three dimensions. Hildreth's theory predicts the former. An advantage of Hildreth's theory is that mathematical analysis can be done showing when it predicts the correct motion and when it fails.

Smoothness of the velocity field is a natural constraint to use to solve the aperture problem, but it needs more justification. Although the velocity field generated by a smooth object will usually be smooth, it does not immediately follow that the smoothest velocity field should be the preferred solution. Ullman and Yuille (1987) have shown statistical considerations in support of the smoothest velocity field solution.

1.6.4   Structure from Motion

For any set of moving dots in the image plane there is an infinite number of possible objects moving in space. Thus, solving the correspondence problem, or measuring the motion, is only half the battle in recovering structure from motion. The problem is still ill-posed, and further assumptions are needed to recover the depth. Ullman (1979) proposed that rigidity was the assumption needed to produce a unique, and correct, three-dimensional percept.

Consider the rotating cylinder experiment again. After solving the correspondence problem and obtaining the motion of the dots on the image plane, we still need to recover the structure. Ullman and others have proved theorems showing, for example, that if four points are moving rigidly in space, then it is possible to determine their relative positions from three views of them. Moreover, it is possible to tell from the motion of the points in the image whether they are moving rigidly or not.

These theorems enable us to recover the structure of moving objects. For each set of four points we can obtain three views, by watching over time and applying the theorems. If the points lie on the same object, we recover the relative depths. If some points lie on different objects, then the theorems show there is an inconsistency. Thus, we do not even need to know which object the individual points lie on.

This approach is elegant and has some successes, but it has three drawbacks. First, it is unclear how stable the results are if there is noise in the data; that is, a small mistake in the position of one point might significantly alter the result. Second, this theory suggests that structure from motion can be found almost instantaneously, yet experiments show that structure develops over time. Third, the theory assumes that the motion is strictly rigid, yet experiments show that humans can perceive the structure of objects even for nonrigid motion.

For these reasons Ullman (1984) proposed an alternative approach called *incremental rigidity*. This scheme assumes that the system incrementally constructs an internal model of the object being viewed. The model is specified by a number of feature points in the image and initially assumes that the object is flat. The correspondence problem between these features is assumed to be solved, by one of the methods described in the previous section. We assume the image lies on the x, y plane so that the x and y coordinates of the feature points are known and the z component, or height, is unknown. The system now maintains an internal model of the object containing estimates of the positions of the feature points. The system updates the model between different time frames by choosing new z coordinates so that the change in rigidity of the model is minimized.

There are several possible measures of the change in rigidity. The simplest is to define it to be

$$M(z_i(t + \delta t)) = \sum_{i,j=1}^{i,j=N} (d_{ij}(t + \delta t) - d_{ij}(t))^2.$$

Here $d_{ij}(t)$ and $d_{ij}(t + \delta t)$ are measures of the three-dimensional distances between the ith and j^{th} points at times t and $t + \delta t$, respectively. For example, we can set

$$d_{ij}(t) = (x_i(t) - x_j(t))^2 + (y_i(t) - y_j(t))^2 + (z_i(t) - z_j(t))^2.$$

If the object is moving rigidly, then the distances between the points (in three dimensions) will not change and so $M = 0$ and there is no change in rigidity.

Thus, at time $t + \delta t$ the x, y components of the feature points are determined by measurements on the image plane and the z components are estimated by minimizing $M(z_i(t + \delta t))$ with respect to $z_i(t + \delta t)$, for each of the N points. This can be done by standard steepest descent algorithms. The initial values of the z components are set to zero.

The object is initially estimated as being flat, and the perception of its three-dimensional structure develops over time as more information becomes available.

Although there is no mathematical proof that this scheme will always converge to the correct result, computer simulations have shown that it works well. In fact, psychophysical experiments (Grzywacz et al. 1987) suggest that it does better than humans for stimuli containing four dots. The convergence time (the number of time frames needed to see the structure) was similar for this model and for the experimental observers. Unlike the algorithm, however, the observers did not converge to exactly the right structure but instead tended to underestimate the depth of the object.

1.7   Future Directions

Although considerable progress has been made in the computational study of early vision, much remains to be done. Many algorithms now exist for modules such as binocular stereo and motion, yet none has the full capability of the human visual system. Many have been designed to work on the artificial stimuli used by psychophysicists, such as random dot stereograms, whereas on more realistic scenes the human visual system may use different strategies.

A second important problem lies in interaction between modules. There are many ways in which information from one module could help the calculations of another. For example, there is probably a complicated interaction between the binocular stereo and motion modules. These questions are now being studied (see, for instance, Bulthoff and Mallot's (1987) psychophysical experiments on the interaction of different depth cues), but only a few results are as yet available.

A third important problem is to relate these theories more directly to neuroscience—for example, to localize the modules in biological vision systems and determine what computations are being performed. Although some progress has been made in the areas of edge detection (Richter and Ullman 1986) and motion processing (Movshon et al. 1985), this is an exceedingly difficult problem in vision research.

Research in computational vision is influenced by attempts to design artificial vision systems. Recent technological advances, such as the development of parallel computers and special-purpose VLSI hardware, suggest that it will soon be possible to develop real-time vision systems that combine different modules. The development of these systems will give a strong stimulus to theoretical research.

Suggestions for Further Reading

This chapter has emphasized an approach to vision developed by the late David Marr and his collaborators, which is described in detail in Marr 1982. Related books on motion include Ullman 1979 and Hildreth 1984, and related books on binocular stereo include Grimson 1981.

Bruce and Green (1985) give a good nonmathematical introduction to vision at an advanced undergraduate level, contrasting Marr's computational theories with other theoretical approaches. In particular, they discuss the "ecological" theories of Gibson (1966), which emphasize the connection between perception and action. Ullman (1980) critiques these theories.

Julesz (1971) gives many fascinating examples of random dot stereograms, and Frisby (1979) discusses a wide range of psychophysical phenomena. Horn (1986) provides an excellent account of vision for robotics, and Ballard and Brown (1982) provide a good survey of computer vision and its relations to the field of artificial intelligence.

Questions

1.1 Hildreth's theory of short-range motion, described in section 1.6, assumes smoothness of the velocity field but does not assume rigidity of the object. For some rigid motion, such as the rotating ellipse, it predicts a nonrigid percept, in agreement with experiment. How would you construct a theory that always gives the correct answer for objects moving rigidly in the image plane? Try this first for parallelograms, then think about the general case (this is much harder).

1.2 The theories of motion measurement and correspondence described in section 1.6 assume that the motion field is computed between two different time frames, ignoring the previous history of the motion (the previous time frames). Think about the following questions, some of which are open problems for current research. How would you modify these theories to allow for the history? How much of the past history would you want to use for this computation? How would you modify the theories if you assume that the motion corresponds to a known object moving rigidly in the image plane?

Some theories use several time frames to make motion measurements. An important class of these theories involves spatiotemporal filters geared to detect frequency activity in the space-time domain (Adelson and Bergen 1985; Watson and Ahumada 1985). Other related theories are based on correlation models that were first used to describe the visual system of the fly and were then extended to human vision (Reichardt 1969; van Santen and Sperling 1985; Little, Bulthoff, and Poggio 1987). A good review of these theories is provided by Hildreth and Koch (1987).

References

Adelson, E. H., and J. Bergen (1985). Spatiotemporal energy models for the perception of motion. *Journal of the Optical Society of America* A2, 284–299.

Ballard, D. H., and C. M. Brown (1982). *Computer vision*. Englewood Cliffs, NJ: Prentice-Hall.

Barrow, H. G., and J. M. Tennenbaum (1981). Computational vision. *Proceedings of the IEEE* 69.5.

Braddick, O. J. (1973). The masking of apparent motion in random-dot patterns. *Vision Research* 13, 355–369.

Braddick, O. J. (1974). A short-range process in apparent motion. *Vision Research* 13, 519–527.

Bruce, V., and P. Green (1985). *Visual perception: Physiology, psychology, and ecology*. Hillsdale, NJ: L. Erlbaum Associates.

Bulthoff, H. H., and H. A. Mallot (1987). Interactions of different modules in depth perception. In *Proceedings of the First International Conference on Computer Vision*. Washington, DC: Computer Society Press of the IEEE.

Collett, T. S. (1985). Extrapolating and interpolating surfaces in depth. *Proceedings of the Royal Society of London* B224, 43–56.

Curtis, S., A. Oppenheim, and J. Lim (1985). Spatial reconstruction from Fourier transform sign information. *IEEE Transactions on Acoustics, Speech and Signal Processing*. ASSP-33, 643–657.

Dawkins, R. (1986). *The blind watchmaker*. Avon, England: Bath Press.

Frisby, J. P. (1979). *Seeing: Mind, brain, and illusion*. Oxford: Oxford University Press.

Gibson, E. J., C. J. Owsley, and J. Johnston (1978). Perception of invariants by five month old infants: Differentiation of two types of motion. *Developmental Psychology* 14, 407–415.

Gibson, J. J. (1966). *The senses considered as perceptual systems*. Boston: Houghton Mifflin.

Grimson, W. E. L. (1981). *From images to surfaces: A computational study of the human early visual system*. Cambridge, MA: MIT Press.

Grzywacz, N. M. (1987). Interactions between Minimal Mapping and Inertia in long-range apparent motion. *Investigative Ophthalmology and Visual Science* 28, 300.

Grzywacz, N. M., E. C. Hildreth, V. K. Inada, and E. H. Adelson (1987). The temporal integration of 3-D structure from motion: A computational and psychophysical study. In W. von Seelen, G. Shaw, and U. M. Leinhos, eds., *Organization of neural networks*. VCH Publishers, Weinhein, FRG.

Held, R. (1987). Visual development in infants. In *The encyclopedia of neuroscience*, vol 2. Boston: Birkhauser.

Hildreth, E. C. (1984). *The measurement of visual motion*. Cambridge, MA: MIT Press.

Hildreth, E. C., and C. Koch (1987). The analysis of visual motion: From computational theory to neuronal mechanism. *Annual Review of Neuroscience* 10, 477–533.

Horn, B. K. P. (1974). Determining lightness from an image. *Computer Graphics and Image Processing* 3, 277–299.

Horn, B. K. P. (1986). *Robot vision*. Cambridge, MA: MIT Press.

Julesz, B. (1971). *Foundations of cyclopean perception*. Chicago: University of Chicago Press.

Julesz, B. (1981). Textons, the elements of texture discrimination and their interactions. *Nature* 290, 91–97.

Land, E. (1964). The retinex. *American Scientist* 52, 247–264.

Little, J., H. Bulthoff, and T. Poggio (1987). Parallel optical flow computation. In L. Baumann, ed., *Proceedings of the SAIC Image Understanding Workshop*. Los Altos, CA: Morgan Kaufmann.

Logan, B. F. (1977). Information in the zero-crossings of bandpass signals. *Bell Systems Technical Journal* 56, 487–510.

Marr, D. (1976). Early processing of visual information. *Philosophical Transactions of the Royal Society of London* B275, 483–524.

Marr, D. (1982). *Vision: A computational investigation into the human representation and processing of visual information.* San Francisco: W. H. Freeman.

Marr, D., and E. C. Hildreth (1980). Theory of edge detection. *Proceedings of the Royal Society of London* B207, 187–217.

Marr, D., and T. Poggio (1979). A computational theory of human stereo vision. *Proceedings of the Royal Society of London* B204, 301–328

Movshon, J. A., E. H. Adelson, M. S. Gizzi, and W. T. Newsome (1985). The analysis of moving visual patterns. In C. Chages, R. Gattis, and C. G. Gross, eds., *Pattern recognition mechanisms*. Rome: Vatican Press.

Pearson, D. E., and J. A. Robinson (1985). Visual communication at very low data rates. *Proceedings of the IEEE* 73.4.

Ramachandran, V. S., and S. M. Anstis (1985). Perceptual organization in multistable apparent motion. *Perception* 14, 135–143.

Reichardt, W. (1969). Motion perception in insects. In W. Reichardt, ed., *Processing of optical data by organisms and machines*. New York: Academic Press.

Richter, J., and S. Ullman (1986). Non-linearities in cortical simple cells and the possible detection of zero crossings. *Biological Cybernetics* 53, 195–202.

Rumelhart, D. E., J. L. McClelland, and the PDP Research Group (1986). *Parallel distributed processing: Explorations in the microstructure of cognition.* Vol. 1: *Foundations.* Cambridge, MA: MIT Press.

Ullman, S. (1979). *The interpretation of visual motion.* Cambridge, MA: MIT Press.

Ullman, S. (1980). Against direct perception. *Behavioral and Brain Sciences* 3, 373–415.

Ullman, S. (1984). Maximizing rigidity: The incremental recovery of 3D structure from rigid and rubbery motion. *Perception* 13, 255–274.

Ullman, S. (1986). Artificial intelligence and the brain: Computational structure of the visual system. *Annual Review of Neuroscience*, 9, 1–26.

Ullman, S., and A. L. Yuille (1987). Rigidity and smoothness of motion. MIT A.I. Memo 989. Artificial Intelligence Laboratory, MIT, Cambridge, MA.

van Santen, J. P. H., and G. Sperling (1985). A temporal covariance model of motion perception. *Journal of the Optical Society of America* A1, 451–473.

Voorhees, H., and T. Poggio (1987). Finding texture boundaries in images. In *Proceedings of the first international conference on computer vision*. Washington, DC: Computer Society Press of the IEEE.

Wallach, H., and D. N. O'Connell (1953). The kinetic depth effect. *Journal of Experimental Psychology* 45, 205–217.

Watson, A. B., and A. J. Ahumada (1985). Model of human visual-motion sensing. *Journal of the Optical Society America* A2, 322–341.

Yuille, A. L., and T. Poggio (1985). Fingerprint theorems for zero-crossings. *Journal of the Optical Society of America* A2, 683–692.

Yuille, A. L., and N. M. Grzywacz (1988). A computational theory for the perception of coherent visual motion. *Nature* 333, 71–74.

Chapter 2

Higher-Level Vision

Irving Biederman

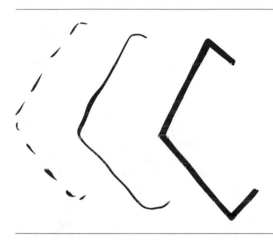

Try this demonstration. Turn on your TV with the sound off. Now change channels with your eyes closed. At each new channel, blink quickly. As the picture appears, you will typically experience little effort and delay (though there is some) in interpreting the image, even though it is one you did not expect and even though you have not previously seen its precise form. You will be able to identify not only the textures, colors, and contours of the scene but also the individual objects and the way in which the objects might be interacting to form a setting or scene or vignette. You will also know where the various entities are in the scene, so that you would be able to point or walk to any one of them should you be transported into the scene itself. Experimental observations confirm these subjective impressions (Intraub 1981; Biederman, Mezzanotte, and Rabinowitz 1982). In a 100-millisecond exposure of a novel scene, people can usually interpret its meaning. However, they cannot attend to every detail; they attend to some aspects of the scene—objects, creatures, ex-

The writing of this chapter was supported by grants 86-0106 and 88-0231 from the Air Force Office of Scientific Research.

pressions, or actions—and not others. In this chapter we will primarily focus on our ability to recognize a pattern in a single glance and our limitations in attending to simultaneous entities in our visual field.

2.1   The Problem of Pattern Recognition

2.1.1   The Nature of Object Recognition

Object recognition is the activation in memory of a representation of a stimulus class—a chair, a giraffe, or a mushroom—from an image projected by an object to the retina. We would have very little to talk about in this chapter if every time an instance of a particular class was viewed it projected the same image to the retina, as occurs, for example, with the digits on a bank check when they are presented for reading by an optical scanner.

But there is a fundamental difference between reading digits on a check and recognizing objects in the real world. The orientation in depth of an object can vary so that any one three-dimensional object can project an infinity of possible images onto a two-dimensional retina, as shown in figure 2.2a. Not only might the object be viewed from a novel orientation, it might be partially occluded behind another surface, or it might be broken into little pieces, as when viewed behind light foliage or drapes, or it might be a novel instance of its class, as for example when we view a new model of a chair. But it is precisely this variation—and the apparent success of our visual system and brain in achieving recognition in the face of it—that makes the problem of pattern recognition so interesting.

Two major problems must be addressed by any complete theory of object recognition. The first is how to represent the information in the image so that it could activate a representation in memory under varied conditions. Here we will focus on the representation of three-dimensional objects, because the problems of stimulus representation have been most extensively studied for such inputs. The second problem is how that stimulus representation is matched against—or activates—a representation in memory. Here we will concentrate on the perception of words.

2.1.2   Representing the Image

Over half a century ago the Gestalt psychologists noted that there is strong agreement among observers concerning the organization of a given pattern. Their observations led to the development of several principles of perception, such as the principle of good continuation, which holds that points that are aligned in a straight line or a smooth curve are interpreted as belonging together, and the law of Prägnanz or good figure, which holds that patterns are seen in such a way that the resulting structure is as simple as possible. The Gestalt demonstrations have become standard fare in most introductory books in psychology and perception.

For decades the Gestalt principles of perceptual organization stood as a curious phenomenon in most treatises on perception, with no explicit link to pattern recognition. Recently there has been considerable success in interpreting these organizational phenomena as special cases of *constraints* imposed by the visual system that (1) allow a solution to the problem of interpreting a three-dimensional world from the two-dimensional image, even when that image is perturbed by noise, and (2) reveal the part structure of an image. These constraints may offer a basis for the construction of a theory of object recognition.

Viewpoint-invariant image properties play a significant role in the task of interpreting a three-dimensional world from a two-dimensional image. Figure 2.1 illustrates several properties of image edges that are extremely unlikely to be a consequence of the particular alignment of eye and object. If the observer changes viewpoint or the edge or edges change orientation, assuming that the same region of the object is still in view, the image will still reflect that property. For example, a straight edge in the image is perceived as being a projection of a straight edge in the three-dimensional world. The visual system ignores the possibility that a (highly unlikely) accidental alignment of eye and a curved edge was projecting the image. Hence, such properties have been termed *nonaccidental* (Lowe 1984). On those rare occasions when an accidental alignment of eye and edge does occur, for example, when a curved edge projects an image that is straight, a slight alteration of viewpoint or object out of the plane will readily reveal that fact.

Figure 2.1 illustrates several nonaccidental properties. In the two-dimensional image, if an edge is straight (collinear) or curved, then it is perceived as a straight or curved edge, respectively. These two constraints imply, of course, the Gestalt principle of good (or smooth) continuation. If two or more two-dimensional image edges terminate at a common point, or are approximately parallel or symmetrical, then the edges projecting those images are similarly interpreted. For reasons that will be apparent when we consider a theory of object recognition, figure 2.1 presents these viewpoint-invariant properties as dichotomous *contrasts*. Given an edge, it can be characterized as straight or curved. For two or more edges, the relation can be described as coterminating or noncoterminating, parallel or nonparallel, symmetrical or asymmetrical. The number of coterminating edges and whether they contain an obtuse angle also does not vary with viewpoint and can serve as a viewpoint-invariant classification of vertex type: L, Y, T, or arrow (or their curved counterparts). In a strict sense, parallelism and symmetry will vary with viewpoint and orientation, as

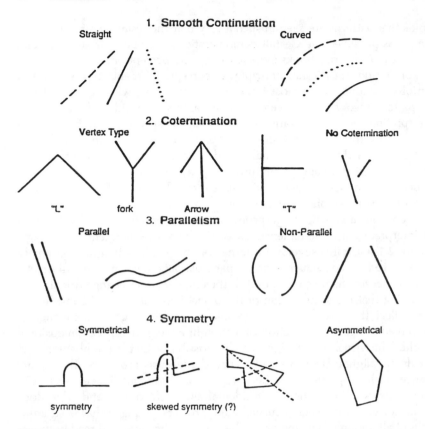

Figure 2.1
Contrasts in four viewpoint-invariant relations. In the case of Parallelism and Symmetry, biases toward parallel and symmetrical percepts when images are not exactly parallel or symmetrical are evidenced. (Adapted by permission of the author from D. Lowe, Perceptual organization and visual recognition, 1984, p. 77, fig. 5.2. Doctoral dissertation, Stanford University.)

occurs, for example, with perspective convergence. But there is a clear bias toward interpreting approximately parallel or symmetrical edges as parallel or symmetrical (Ittelson 1952; King et al. 1976). Within a tolerance range defined by the cues for surface slant, pairs of image edges that *could be* parallel or symmetrical, given uncertainty about the actual orientation of the edges to the eye, are interpreted as parallel or symmetrical (King et al. 1976).

The psychological potency of these viewpoint-invariant properties was demonstrated when Ames and his associates constructed a set of "peephole" perception demonstrations in which subjects viewed three arrangements of wire edges through a peephole, as shown in figure 2.2 (Ittelson 1952). Although all three stimulus arrangements shown in figure 2.2b projected the identical image of a chair, as shown in figure 2.2c, in only one of them (the left-hand one) did the edges actually form a chair. In the middle arrangement the segments all had the same cotermination points as the segments of the chair, except that the surfaces were no longer parallel. In the right-hand arrangement the segments did not even coterminate, yet the perception of this stimulus was indistinguishable from the other two. These results provide strong evidence that the viewpoint-invariant properties shown in figure 2.1 and the biases toward parallelism and symmetry are immediate and compelling and thus could serve as a basis for characterizing image edges for the purposes of recognition.

Complex visual entities almost always invite a decomposition of their elements into simple parts. We readily distinguish the legs, tail, and trunk of an elephant or the shade and the base of a lamp. This decomposition does not depend on familiarity with an object or on differences in surface color or texture, as shown by the fact that it is readily performed on a line drawing. Even nonsense shapes elicit strong agreement among observers concerning their part decomposition.

In general, whenever there are a pair of matched cusps, observers express a strong intuition that the object should be segmented at that region (Connell 1985). This tendency of the visual system to segment complex objects at regions of matched concavities is not an arbitrary bias. Hoffman and Richards (1985) have noted a result from projective geometry—the *transversality* principle—that whenever two shapes are combined, their join is almost always marked by matched concavities, as illustrated in figure 2.3a. Segmenting at such regions provides a basis for appreciating the part structure of objects, as shown for the flashlight in figure 2.3b. The transversality principle also provides much of the basis for the Gestalt principle of good figure. If a shape is segmented at paired cusps, the resulting parts are convex or only singly concave. Such parts appear simple.

(a)

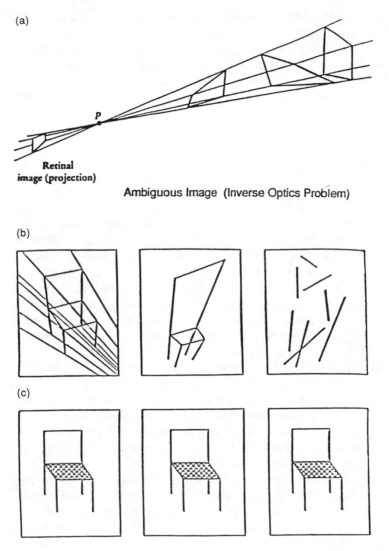

Ambiguous Image (Inverse Optics Problem)

(b)

(c)

Figure 2.2
The Ames peephole perception demonstrations. (a) Illustration of the inverse optics problem: A single image can be produced by an infinity of possible real-world objects. (b) Three stimulus arrangements constructed by the Ames group. The left-hand panel shows the perspective lines from the peephole at the lower right. (c) The percepts from the stimuli in (b). (Adapted by permission of the publisher and author from R. N. Haber and M. Hershenson, *The psychology of visual perception*, 1981, p. 284, fig. 12.5. © 1981 by Holt, Rinehart and Winston.)

(a)   **Concavity 1**

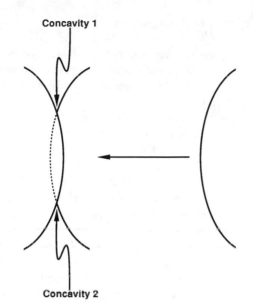

Concavity 2

(b)

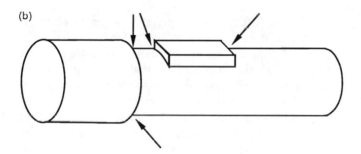

Figure 2.3
An illustration of the transversality principle and how it can be applied to the segmentation of an object's parts.

2.2   RBC: A Theory of Object Recognition

The theory of object recognition known as *recognition-by-components* (RBC) (Biederman 1987, 1988) explains how the edges that have been extracted from an image (as described in chapter 1) could activate an entry-level representation of that object in memory.

Entry level is a term coined by Jolicoeur, Gluck, and Kosslyn (1984) to refer to the initial classification of individual visual entities—for example, a chair, a giraffe, or a mushroom—that share a characteristic shape. Often the term that represents this classification (*chair, giraffe, mushroom*) will be the first that enters the child's vocabulary, and it will be used to a much greater extent than any other term to describe that entity. Entry-level classification is to be distinguished from *subordinate* classification, as for example when a particular subspecies of giraffe is specified. It is also to be distinguished from *superordinate* classification, in which shape descriptions are not specified; *mammal* and *furniture* are terms used at this level. If an entity is not typical for its class, such as penguins and ostriches for the class of birds, then entry-level classification is assumed to be at the individual level; that is, we would first classify the image as a penguin before we determined that it was a bird. Biederman (1988) has estimated that there are approximately 3,000 common entry-level terms in English for familiar concrete objects.

The central assumption of RBC is that a given view of an object is represented as an arrangement of simple primitive volumes, called *geons* (for *geometrical ions*). Five (of the 24) geons are shown in figure 2.4. The relations among the geons are also specified, so that the same geons in different relations will represent different objects (see the cup and pail in figure 2.4). The geons have the desirable properties that they can be distinguished from each other from almost any viewpoint and that they are highly resistant to visual noise. The objects shown in figure 2.4 also illustrate a derivation from the theory: An arrangement of three geons will generally be sufficient to classify any object. We will consider in greater detail the segmenting of the image into regions that will be matched to geons, the description of the image edges in terms of viewpoint-invariant properties, and the geon arrangement that emerges from the parsing and edge processing.

2.2.1   Geons from Viewpoint-Invariant Edge Descriptions

According to RBC, each segmented region of an image is approximated by a geon. Geons are members of a particular set of convex or singly concave volumes that can be modeled as *generalized cones*, a general formalism for representing volumetric shapes (Binford 1971; Brooks 1981). A generalized

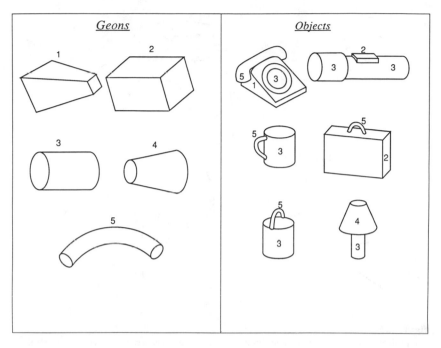

Figure 2.4
(Left) A given view of an object can be represented as an arrangement of simple primitive volumes, or geons, of which five are shown here. (Right) Only two or three geons are required to uniquely specify an object. The relations among the geons matter, as illustrated with the pail and cup.

cone is the volume swept out by a cross section moving along an axis. Marr (1977) showed that the contours generated by any smooth surface could be modeled by a generalized cone with a convex cross section.

The set of geons is so defined that they can be differentiated on the basis of dichotomous or trichotomous contrasts of viewpoint-invariant properties to produce 24 types of geons. The contrasts of the particular set of nonaccidental properties shown in figure 2.4 were emphasized because they may constitute a basis for generating this set of perceptually plausible components. Figure 2.5 illustrates the generation of a subset of the 24 geons from contrasts in the nonaccidental relations of four attributes of generalized cones. Three of the attributes specify characteristics of the cross section: *curvature* (straight versus curved), *size variation* (constant (parallel sides), expanding (nonparallel sides), expanding and contracting (nonparallel sides with a point of maximum convexity)), and *symmetry* (symmetrical versus asymmetrical). One attribute specifies the axis: straight versus curved.

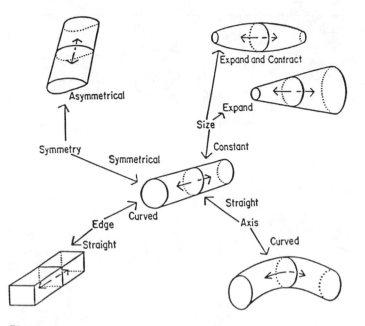

Figure 2.5
An illustration of how variations in three attributes of a cross section (curved versus straight edges; constant versus expanded versus expanded and contracted size; symmetrical versus asymmetrical shape) and one attribute of the shape of the axis (straight versus curved) can generate a set of generalized cones differing in nonaccidental relations. Constant-sized cross sections have parallel sides; expanded or expanded and contracted cross sections have sides that are not parallel. Curved versus straight cross sections and axes are detectable through collinearity or curvature. Shown here are the neighbors of a cylinder. The full family of geons has 24 members. (Adapted by permission of the publisher and author from I. Biederman, Recognition-by-Components: A theory of human image understanding, 1987, *Psychological Review* 94, p. 122, fig. 6. © 1987 by the American Psychological Association.)

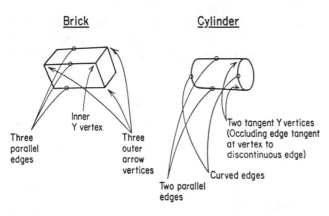

Figure 2.6
Some nonaccidental differences between a brick and a cylinder. (Reprinted by permission of the publisher and author from I. Biederman, Recognition-by-Components: A theory of human image understanding, 1987, *Psychological Review* 94, p. 121, fig. 5. © 1987 by the American Psychological Association.)

When the contrasts in the generating functions are translated into image features, it is apparent that the geons have a larger set of distinctive nonaccidental image features than the four that might be expected from a direct mapping of the contrasts in the generating function. Figure 2.6 shows some of the nonaccidental contrasts distinguishing a brick from a cylinder. The silhouette of a brick contains a series of six vertices, which alternate between Ls and arrows, and an internal Y vertex. By contrast, the vertices of the silhouette of the cylinder alternate between a pair of Ls and a pair of tangent Ys. The internal Y vertex is not present in the cylinder (or any geon with a curved cross section). These differences in image features would be available from a general viewpoint and thus could provide, along with other contrasting image features, a basis for discriminating a brick from a cylinder. The geons are modal types. It is possible that a given region of the image might weakly activate two or more geons if some of the distinguishing image features (vertices and edges) were missing or ambiguous.

Being derived from contrasts in viewpoint-invariant properties, the geons themselves will be invariant under changes in viewpoint. Because the geons are simple (namely, convex or only singly concave), lack sharp concavities, and have redundant image properties, they can be readily restored in the presence of visual noise. Therefore, objects that are represented as an arrangement of geons will possess the same invariance to viewpoint and noise. Since geon activation requires only categorical classification of edge characteristics, processing can be completed quickly and accurately. A representation that would require fine metric specification, such as the degree of curvature or length of a segment, cannot be performed with sufficient speed and accuracy by humans to be the controlling process for object recognition.

2.2.2   Geon Relations and Three-Geon Sufficiency

According to RBC, the capacity to represent the tens of thousands of object images that people can rapidly classify derives from the employment of several viewpoint-invariant relations among geons (for example, TOP-OF, SIDE-CONNECTED, LARGER-THAN). These relations are defined for joined pairs of geons such that the same geons represent different objects if they are in different relations to each other, as with the cup and the pail in figure 2.4. How the relations among the parts of an object are to be described is still an open issue. The current version of RBC specifies 108 possible combinations of six types of relations. Also specified is a categorization of the relative aspect ratio of the geon (axis larger than, smaller than, or equal to the cross section).

With 24 possible geons, the variations in relations and aspect ratio can produce 186,624 possible two-geon objects ($24^2 \times 108 \times 3$). A third geon with its possible relations to another geon yields over 1.4 billion possible three-geon objects.

Although there are only about 3,000 common entry-level object names in English, people are probably familiar with approximately ten times that number of object models in that (1) many objects require a few models for different orientations and (2) some entry-level terms (such as *lamp* and *chair*) have several readily distinguishable object models (Biederman 1988). An estimate of the number of familiar object models would thus be on the order of 30,000. If these familiar models were distributed homogeneously throughout the space of possible object models, then the extraordinary disparity between the number of possible two- or three-geon objects and the number of objects in an individual's object vocabulary—even if the estimate of 30,000 was short by an order of magnitude—means that an arrangement of two or three geons would almost always be sufficient to specify any object.

The theory thus implies a principle of *geon recovery*: If an arrangement of two or three geons can be recovered from the image, objects can be quickly recognized even when they are occluded, rotated in depth, novel, extensively degraded, or lacking customary detail, color, and texture.

2.2.3   Stage Model

Figure 2.7 presents an overall architecture for RBC. An initial edge extraction stage, responsive to differences in surface characteristics, such as sharp

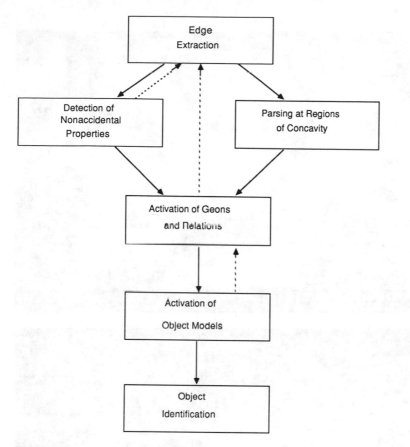

Figure 2.7
RBC's processing stages for object recognition. Possible top-down routes are shown with dashed lines. (Reprinted by permission of the publisher and author from I. Biederman, Recognition-by-Components: A theory of human image understanding, 1987, *Psychological Review* 94, p. 118, fig. 2. © 1987 by the American Psychological Association.)

(a)

(b)

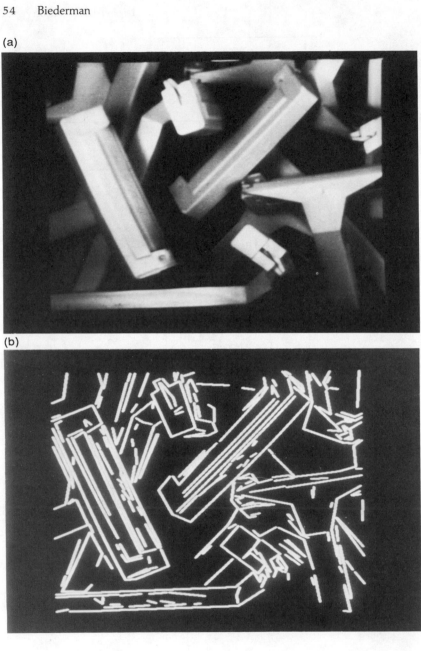

(c)

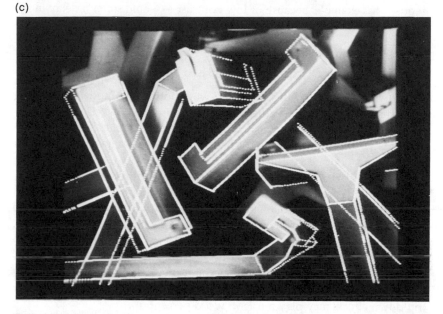

Figure 2.8
Lowe's viewpoint consistency model can find objects at arbitrary orientations and occlusions. (a) The original image of a bin of disposable razors. (b) The straight line segments that SCERPO derived from the image. (c) Final set of successful matches between sets of image segments and five particular viewpoints of the model (shown as bright dotted lines). (Reprinted by permission of the publisher and author from D. Lowe, The viewpoint consistency constraint, 1987, *International Journal of Computer Vision* 1, pp. 66 and 70, figs. 4, 5, and 8. © 1987 by Kluwer Academic Publishers.)

changes in luminance or texture, extracts the edges in the image. The image is then segmented at matched concavities and its edges characterized in terms of their viewpoint-invariant properties. (RBC also specifies additional, albeit weaker, principles for parsing (Biederman 1987). For example, a change in a viewpoint-invariant property, such as the change in parallelism from the base cylinder to the nose cone of a rocket, can also provide a (weaker) basis for parsing.) The geons and their relations are then activated, and this representation in turn activates a like representation in memory. RBC assumes that the activation of the geons and relations occurs in parallel, with no loss in capacity when matching objects with a large number of geons. Partial activation is possible, with the degree of activation assumed to be proportional to the overlap in the geon descriptions of a representation of the image and the representation in memory. Thus, an object missing some of its parts would produce weaker activation of its representation. An image from which it was difficult to determine the geons—for example, because of low contrast—would suffer a delay in the activation of its geons. However, once the geons are activated, the activation of the object models in memory should proceed as with a sharp image.

2.2.4   Top-Down Effects and Model-Based Matching

As shown in figure 2.7, RBC is a one-way, bottom-up model proceeding from image to activation of the representation of the object. Edge extraction is assumed to be accomplished by a module that can proceed independently of the later stages, save for likely effects of the viewpoint-invariant property of smooth curvature.

Does object recognition always proceed as a largely one-way street? Probably not. When edge extraction is difficult, it is likely that top-down effects will be revealed. Such effects could be of two types: (1) they could stem from the viewpoint-invariant properties of cotermination, parallelism, and symmetry or from the geons themselves, and (2) they could stem from object models. The latter route is termed *model-based matching*. Two detailed proposals for such matching have been advanced by Lowe (1987) and by Huttenlocher and Ullman (1987). In section 2.3 we will examine how top-down effects may play a role in word perception.

Lowe's *Spatial Correspondence, Evidential Reasoning, and Perceptual Organization (SCERPO) model* is primarily directed toward determining the orientation and location of objects, even when they are partially occluded by other objects, under conditions where exact object models are available. The model takes as input an image such as the one shown in figure 2.8a, a number of disposable razors in arbitrary orientations. The model detects edges by finding sharp changes in image intensity values as reflected in the zero crossings of a $\nabla^2 G$ convolution across a number of scales, as discussed in chapter 1. The results of this edge detection stage are shown in figure 2.8b. The edges are then grouped according to viewpoint-invariant properties of collinearity, parallelism, and cotermination. A few of these image features are then tentatively matched against a component of the object model in which the orientation of the object is determined that would maximize the fit of those image features. From this initial hypothesis, the location of additional image features (edges) is proposed and their presence in the image evaluated. Figure 2.8c shows the successful final matches for five orientations of the razors. These matches provide segments not detected initially by the zero crossings (figure 2.8b) and discard edges that were initially detected but are not part of the object model, such as the glare edges on the handle of the razor extending horizontally in the lower part of the figure. SCERPO may provide a plausible scheme for characterizing human performance under conditions where the initial extraction of image edges may be uncertain, as when visibility is poor or the orientation of an object is unfamiliar.

Huttenlocher and Ullman's *alignment model* first reorients all the object models that might be possible matches for the image and tests for the fit of the image against the aligned models in memory. The alignment capitalizes on a result that is similar to the structure from motion constraint proposed in theories of low-level vision: namely, that three noncoplanar points are generally sufficient to determine the orientation of any object. In practice, the three points are typically viewpoint invariant in that they are selected at a place where edges coterminate. However, any salient points or even general features would be sufficient for alignment. Although it would appear unlikely that people rotate (align) all possible candidate models in memory prior to matching, the alignment model offers a possible account of those cases where recognition depends on reorientation of a mental model.

2.2.5   Empirical Studies of Object Recognition

A number of experiments have been performed exploring human object recognition in general and various aspects of RBC in particular. In most of these experiments the subject names briefly presented object pictures (where "briefly" is, say, 100 milliseconds). The flash of the picture is followed by a *mask*, an array of meaningless straight and curved line segments, to reduce persistence of the image. Naming reaction times and errors are the primary dependent variables.

1. *Partial objects.* When only two or three geons of a complex object (such as an airplane or elephant) are visible, recognition can be fast and accurate (though, predictably, not as fast as when the complete image is available). This supports the principle of three-geon sufficiency. You can try this for yourself by covering up parts of pictures of common objects. See whether the object remains recognizable to a friend (who did not see the original) if three geons remain in view.

2. *Effect of object complexity.* Complex objects, defined as those such as an airplane or elephant that require six or more geons to appear complete, do not require more time for their recognition than simple objects such as a flashlight or cup (Biederman 1987). This lack of a disadvantage for complex objects is consistent with a model positing parallel activation of the geons rather than a serial trace of the contours of the object. Often a single-geon model is appropriate for several entry-level objects. Other information such as surface color or texture, small details, or context is then required to classify these objects (Biederman and Ju 1988). For example, distinguishing among a peach, a nectarine, and a plum requires that surface color and texture be specified. RBC would predict that identifying such objects would require more time than identifying objects with distinctive geon models.

3. *When does an object become unrecognizable?* Images can be rendered unrecognizable if the contour is deleted so that the geons cannot be

(a)   (b)   (c)

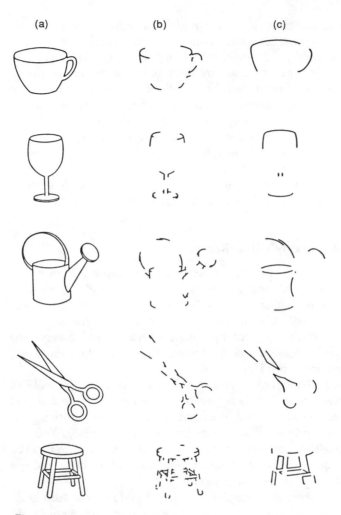

Figure 2.9

Example of five stimulus objects in the experiment on the perception of degraded objects. Column (a) shows the original intact versions. Column (b) shows the recoverable versions. The contours have been deleted in regions where they can be replaced through collinearity or smooth curvature. Column (c) shows the nonrecoverable versions. The contours have been deleted at regions of concavity so that collinearity or smooth curvature of the segments bridges the concavity. In addition, vertices have been altered (for example, from Ys to Ls). (Modified by permission of the publisher and author from I. Biederman, Recognition-by-Components: A theory of human image understanding, 1987, *Psychological Review* 94, p. 135, fig. 16. © 1987 by the American Psychological Association.)

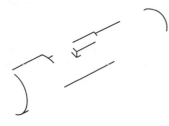

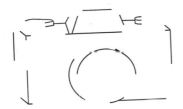

Figure 2.10
Contour-deleted images of two objects

recovered from the image. One technique is to delete the cusps to the point where the remaining contours would bridge the cusp through smooth continuation, as with the handle of the cup in figure 2.9a. Another technique is to alter vertices, as with the stool, and suggest inappropriate ones, as with the watering can. If the same amount of contour is deleted but in regions where the geons can still be activated, as shown in figure 2.9b, objects remain identifiable. Actually, even more contour can be removed from the images in figure 2.9b and they will still remain recognizable. You can test this for yourself by covering up parts of an object (say, the right or left half) and determining whether you or a friend who has not seen the original version can still identify the object.

4. *Features or geons?* According to RBC, an object is represented in terms of its geons, which are activated by image features such as vertices and edges. But if the geons are activated by image features—vertices and edges—why not just represent an object in terms of image features?

To see why this may not work, first identify the recoverable contour-deleted images shown in figure 2.10. Now look at figure 2.11. Do the images in this figure look the same as those you just viewed? Now compare them. You will note that these are actually complementary images, with each member of a pair having alternating vertices and edges. If we were to represent objects in terms of image features, we would need a different representation for each arrangement of occluding contour or for each

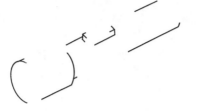

Figure 2.11
The complements to the contour-deleted images of the two objects in figure 2.10. These images contain almost all of the missing edges and vertices of the objects in 2.10, with almost no overlap between the two figures.

slightly altered orientation of the object. There is no doubt that people could code the individual image features, in that they could learn to distinguish the various versions of the complementary images. But the expectation from RBC would be that relying on such coding would slow their identification performance. That is, subjects might more readily identify the complementary version of the camera if they did not attempt to determine whether it contained the particular vertices and segments present in the original version.

5. *Rotation.* Rotation of the object in the plane slows recognition to a much greater extent than rotation in depth (Jolicoeur 1985; Bartram 1974). This result is contrary to what would be expected from the SCERPO and alignment models. According to RBC, rotation in the plane affects the TOP-OF relation, but rotation in depth leaves the geon descriptions themselves largely unaffected. At the heart of RBC is a representation that is invariant with changes of viewpoint in depth. As long as the same geon model can be activated by the image, no loss in recognition latency should be evident. However, mental rotation functions are evident in recognition performance when the TOP-OF relation is violated (Jolicoeur 1985).

6. *An extension to scene perception.* The mystery about the perception of scenes is that the exposure duration an observer requires to have an

(a)

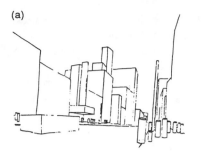

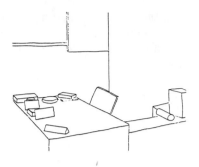

(b)

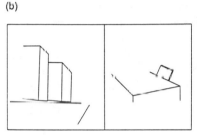

Figure 2.12
(a) Two of Mezzanotte's scenes: "City Street" and "Office." (b) Possible geon clusters for
the scenes in (a).

accurate perception of an integrated real-world scene is not much longer
than what is typically required to perceive individual objects. Recognizing
a visual array as a scene requires not only identifying the various entities
but also semantically specifying the interactions among the objects and
providing an overall semantic specification of the arrangement.

However, the perception of a scene is not necessarily derived from an
initial identification of the individual objects making up that scene
(Biederman 1988). That is, in general we do not first identify a stove,
refrigerator, and coffee cup, in specified physical relations, and then conclude that we are looking at a kitchen.

Some demonstrations and experiments suggest that RBC may provide a
basis for explaining rapid scene recognition. Mezzanotte (described in
Biederman 1988) has shown that a readily interpretable scene can be
constructed from arrangements of single geons that just preserve the overall aspect ratio of the objects, such as those shown in figure 2.12a. In this
kind of scene none of the entities, when shown in isolation, could be

identified as anything other than a simple volumetric body, such as a brick. Most important, such settings could be recognized sufficiently quickly to interfere with the identification of intact objects that were inappropriate to the setting.

It is possible that quick understanding of a scene is mediated by the perception of *geon clusters*. A geon cluster is an arrangement of geons from different objects that preserves the relative size, aspect ratio, and relations of the largest visible geon of each object. In such cases the individual geon will be insufficient to allow identification of the object. However, just as an arrangement of two or three geons almost always allows identification of an object, so an arrangement of two or more geons from different objects may produce a recognizable combination. The cluster acts very much like a large object. Figure 2.12b shows possible geon clusters for the scenes in figure 2.12a. If this account is correct, fast scene perception should only be possible in scenes where such familiar object clusters are present. This account awaits rigorous experimental test, but you may try to gauge it for yourself with the TV "experiment" described in the opening paragraph of this chapter. Are there some scenes that you cannot identify from a single glance? My own experience is that such scenes are those where a familiar geon cluster is not present.

2.3   Activating a Representation: McClelland and Rumelhart's Interactive Activation Model of Word Recognition as an Example of Parallel Distributed Processing

2.3.1   The Interactive Activation Model

The recognition stage of RBC had only been sketched when it was asserted that the representation of the image might "activate" or be "matched against" a like representation in memory. We now turn to one of the few models of image understanding that provides a detailed account of the time course of memorial activation in perceptual recognition: the *interactive activation model* (IAM) of word recognition of McClelland and Rumelhart (1981). This model also provides an account of how information in memory could affect, top-down, the course of perceptual recognition.

Although we have focused in this chapter on object recognition, McClelland and Rumelhart's work on word recognition may have broad applicability to all cases of image understanding. At the very least, humans have only one visual system and it is unlikely that special-purpose mechanisms for reading have developed in the evolutionarily insignificant 5,000 years since the invention of the alphabet. We will consider IAM in some detail because it presaged much current theorizing in cognitive science under the rubrics of *connectionism* or *parallel distributed processing* (Rumelhart and McClelland 1986).

IAM was initially designed to model why the perception of a target letter in a brief, masked presentation of a word was more accurate than when the same letters in the word formed a nonword or even when the individual target letter was presented by itself. This result was found with strict controls for guessing a word (Reicher 1969; Wheeler 1970). For example, following the presentation of a word such as READ, a nonword such as AEDR, or the letter E, the subject might be asked (in the first two cases) whether E or O was in the second letter position or (in the third case) whether the single letter was E or O. Note that either response alternative would produce a common word if inserted in R_AD. Before reading further, you might wish to try your own hand (or mind) at explaining this effect. But you should be warned that it took over a decade of intense research on this problem before a single sufficient account of these results was proposed.

IAM posits three levels of representation arranged in a hierarchy: features, letters, and words. As illustrated in figure 2.13, each level consists of a number of *nodes* at various states of activation for the entities relevant to that level. Each node is connected to a large number of other nodes from

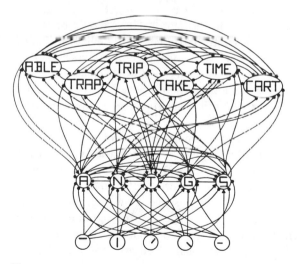

Figure 2.13
The three levels of the interactive activation model for the word superiority effect. (Reprinted by permission of the publisher and author from J. L. McClelland and D. E. Rumelhart, An interactive activation model of context effects in letter perception: Part 1. An account of basic findings, 1981, *Psychological Review* 88, p. 380, fig. 3. © 1981 by the American Psychological Association.)

which it can receive either excitatory inputs (designated by an arrow at the end of the connection in figure 2.13), which raise its activation level, or inhibitory inputs (designated by a small disk in figure 2.13), which lower its activation level. Each node, in turn, transmits its activation as excitatory or inhibitory inputs to other nodes.

The presentation of a letter (actually, the letter's features) causes excitation of the nodes consistent with that letter's features and inhibition of the nodes for those features that are inconsistent with that letter. The nodes whose activity has been increased transmit their excitation by increasing the activation of letter nodes that contain those features and inhibiting letter nodes that do not contain those features. Similarly, the activation of the letter nodes results in excitation of word nodes that contain those letters and inhibition of word nodes that do not contain those letters. At all levels there is strong intralevel inhibition. Each node at a given level inhibits the other nodes at that level. There is also top-down excitation. Activity at the word level can excite or inhibit activity at the letter level.

We can now trace the time course of activation of a given node as a word—WORK, for example—is presented. Assume that the subject successfully detected the first three letters, WOR_, but detected only some of the features of the fourth letter, as indicated in figure 2.14a. Initially there is an increase in the activation level of those letters consistent with the features actually detected (we are only considering the letter nodes corresponding to the fourth position in the word). These would be R and K. These nodes transmit their excitation to the word level. Although WORK can benefit from activation of the K node, there is no word WORR to receive activation from R. As the activation of WORK increases, it starts to excite, top-down, the K node and inhibit the R node. R starts to weaken and the activation level of K grows until it clearly exceeds the activation level of R.

We can now see how IAM handles the major phenomenon of the word superiority effect as well as the advantage of a letter within a word over the letter itself. A nonword would not have a node at the word level. Consequently, there would be less chance for a letter in that string to benefit from top-down activation. It is possible, however, that words sharing letters with the nonword might generate, through their partial activation, some top-down excitation. The individual letter, like a nonword, has less chance to benefit from top-down facilitation from the word level.

2.3.2   General Features of Parallel Distributed Models

Parallel distributed models—the class of models of which IAM was a precursor—have generated much interest in current theorizing in cognitive science, and it is worthwhile to consider some of their general characteristics:

(a)

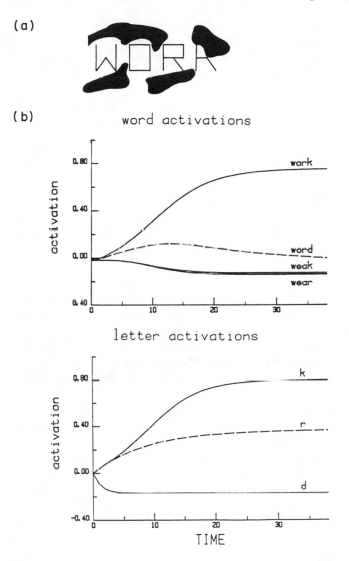

(b)   word activations

letter activations

TIME

Figure 2.14
The interactive activation model's characterization of the activation of the letter K in the fourth position, given that WORK was presented and the features that were extracted were as shown in part (a). (Reprinted by permission of the publisher and author from J. L. McClelland and D. E. Rumelhart, An interactive activation model of context effects in letter perception: Part 1. An account of basic findings, 1981, *Psychological Review* 88, pp. 383 and 384, figs. 5 and 6. © 1981 by the American Psychological Association.)

1. As their name indicates and as illustrated in figure 2.13, these systems are highly parallel. Simultaneous activation is possible for a large number of nodes at a given level and at different levels.

2. The nodes are richly connected. Each node is connected to a large number of other nodes.

3. Partial activation can be transmitted. A node need not exceed a high threshold for it to affect the activation of nodes to which it is connected. It is through this characteristic that IAM was able to handle the advantage of a word over a letter. If the nodes at the word level never became activated until the letters were maximally activated (to the point where they could be identified), then the identification of letters within words could not be superior to the identification of individual letters.

4. There is no explicit appeal to rules or regularities. This point is important and deserves elaboration. In the present context the relevant rules would concern spelling regularities. For example, if we were presented with the word _____I?G, with uncertainty about whether the letter in the position of the question mark was N, R, or M, wouldn't it be reasonable to appeal to our knowledge that many words in English have an -*ing* ending and use that information as a rule to guess that the uncertain letter was N? Not according to McClelland and Rumelhart. They would argue that what appears to be rulelike behavior in perception is merely statistical behavior: the combined effect of our having been exposed to many instances of a given class, in this case the large number of -*ing* words in English.

5. Although a detailed study of connectionism is beyond the scope of this chapter, it should be noted that most current connectionist models do not assign an individual node to represent an individual entity, such as a feature, letter, or word, as in McClelland and Rumelhart's model. Instead, all the nodes at a given level might be used to code all the entities at that level. It is the *pattern* of activation over all the nodes that allows the system to discriminate various inputs. This is accomplished by adjusting the weights by which the nodes activate or inhibit other nodes.

2.4   Visual Attention

Despite our impressive capacities for recognizing an object or scene at a single glance, striking limitations in our abilities for identifying objects at different spatial locations are often evident. These limitations are often encountered, since it is rare that we are faced with only a single entity in our visual field. We often find it necessary to select for attention one from the multitude of objects that may be present in the visual field. The selection is necessary for at least three reasons.

First, on a peripheral level, only the *fovea*—which corresponds to the central 2 degrees of our retina—is capable of resolving fine detail. Even within the 2-degree area there is a marked decline in the capacity to resolve detail from an image at increasing eccentricities from fixation. One aspect of attention, then, consists of moving our eyes in a series of jumps, called *saccades*, from one part of the visual field to another. The locations fixated as we move our eyes around the scene (or page, when we are reading) are decidedly not random. We move our eyes to regions of interest. The maximum rate at which we can make saccades is about three or four per second. Most of the time is spent during the fixation itself; the actual saccade requires only 10 milliseconds.

Second, once our eye is fixated onto a region, we may benefit by shifting attention to another region within the first few hundredths of a second, even without moving our eyes, as demonstrated in an experiment by Sperling (1960). At brief durations after a display of three rows of four random-appearing letters was flashed for a few milliseconds, Sperling sounded a high, middle, or low tone as a cue for the subject to report either the top, middle, or bottom row. Subjects could use the tone to improve their accuracy on the cued row as long as the tone was not delayed beyond 200 milliseconds, at which time the trace (or icon) of the display would have disappeared. During the 200 milliseconds following the flash of the display, the benefit of the tone could not have been produced by eye movements, because the display was no longer present and would only have moved with the eyes if there was some residual retinal activity. Thus, the benefit from cueing a row could only have come from a redirection of attention to the cued row in the icon.

Reeves and Sperling (1986) have shown similar phenomena in a paradigm in which subjects monitored a stream of letters, presented at a high rate (4.6 to 13.4 letters per second) just to the left of a fixation point. When a given target letter occurred, they were to report the next digit (or digits) presented in a stream just to the right of fixation. Reeves and Sperling found that the switch took time, so that often a later letter was reported. As determined by the digit actually reported, the switch often was made by 200 milliseconds.

Third, Treisman and her associates (Treisman and Gelade 1980) have discovered that for a wide range of stimulus attributes, attention must be shifted serially from position to position when we attempt to *conjoin* independent attributes of a single stimulus (for example, color and shape).

In one of Treisman's experiments the subject's task was to hit a key if a predesignated target was present in the display (which it was on half the trials) and another key if it was absent. Two conditions will illustrate the type of display that Treisman used. In the *conjunction* search condition

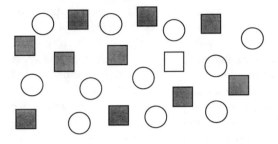

Figure 2.15
An example of a conjunctive search display of the type used by Treisman. The target is a white square (white *and* square, hence a conjunction) and the distractors are white circles and dark squares. Mean reaction times for detecting the target in such displays have been found to increase linearly as a function of the number of distractors.

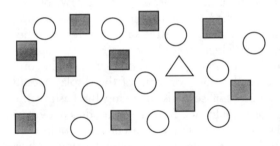

Figure 2.16
An example of a feature search display of the type used by Treisman. The target is a triangle. Mean reaction times for detecting the target in such displays have been found to be independent of the number of distractors.

the target is a white square. See whether you can find it in figure 2.15. You probably had to look carefully to find it among the white circle and dark square distractors. In the *feature* search condition the target is a triangle. Can you find it in figure 2.16? You probably felt that the triangle "popped out." Over trials, Treisman varied the number of items in the display between 1 and 38. In the feature search condition there was no increase in search times as a function of the number of distractors, indicating that all display positions could be examined simultaneously, with no loss in capacity for examining any single position. In the conjunctive condition reaction times increased linearly, suggesting a serial search of the various positions.

Treisman's explanation was that the colors (white versus dark) for the various items activate their locations on a separate "map" for each color. The shapes similarly activate their own maps for the various shape attributes. Treisman argues that we can detect activity on a given map—for example, that there is activity on a map of diagonal edges signaling the presence of a triangle, independent of the number of locations that might possibly contain a triangle. To detect a conjunction, however, we must attend to a particular position on two or more maps. To determine whether a particular square is dark, we must attend to that location on both the map for squares and the map for color. Treisman likens this act to the movement of a narrow flashlight beam that can move through space, illuminating only a single position, on *all* the feature maps, at any one time. The search for a target defined by a conjunction must therefore be performed serially.

Treisman has documented these limitations for a variety of stimulus attributes (for instance, color and shape), and they impose a significant bottleneck on the human's capacity for attending to stimuli distributed across the visual field. It should be noted that not all combinations of stimulus attributes reveal conjunctive limitations (Nakayama and Silverman 1986). For example, given a display with red circles moving up and green circles moving down, a red circle moving down can be detected independent of the number of distractors in the display.

Is the notion of feature maps a farfetched idea physiologically? Not at all. Approximately a dozen regions of the primate visual cortex can be characterized as preserving the spatial relations among stimuli projected onto the retina. These maps have been discovered by presenting stimuli at a given part of the retina and recording the activity from single cortical neurons in a given region of the cortex. The evidence for a map is derived from the finding that adjacent regions of the retina produce activity in adjacent cells in the cortical region. Consistent with Treisman's findings, these maps appear to be specialized for particular attributes—say, a line at a given orientation—although it is common to find cells that appear tuned to several attributes.

Moran and Desimone (1985) have discovered a possible physiological substrate for Sperling's phenomenon of reallocation of spatial attention over a spatial map in the absence of eye movements. Recording from single neurons in the visual cortex (V4), these investigators found a neuron that was sensitive to a particular stimulus, for example, a vertical bar at a particular location on the retina. The monkeys in this experiment were trained to maintain their fixation on a given point (or else they were not rewarded) and to respond by releasing a switch if a second stimulus presented either within or outside of the attended region matched the one that they were attending. When a vertical bar was presented within the attended region, the cell with that receptive field fired. However, when the monkey was not attending to that region, the vertical bar did not produce a response in the neuron, even when it was presented at the identical position on the retina.

2.5   Spatial Processing and Other Visual Activities

In addition to recognition and attention there are other visual activities that might be considered in a chapter entitled "Higher-Level Vision." Other chapters will review imagery, visual development, and oculomotor control.

But much of visual processing entails the employment of space without recognition, as when we navigate in the environment, calculating a course that avoids obstacles and minimizes distances, or when we reach for an object. There is strong evidence that the areas of the brain involved in recognition are anatomically separate from the area involved in spatial processing. Mishkin and his associates (see, for example, Mishkin and Appenzeller 1987) have shown that damage to the monkey's inferior temporal (IT) cortex results in an inability to detect differences among objects but has little effect on its ability to use the knowledge of where an object was located. Damage to the posterior parietal region of the brain has the opposite effect.

The general picture of modularity that emerges from the study of behavioral phenomena in vision is apparent when the brain areas underlying a behavior as fundamental as orientation are explored. Goodale and Milner (1982) have shown that anatomically separate regions of the rodent's brain control orientation toward a goal in central vision and orientation toward stimuli in peripheral vision. Moreover, the brain areas responsible for orientation toward a goal are not the ones that appear to be involved in the avoidance of obstacles.

One of the unsolved problems in vision is how relations among parts— for example, that a cylinder might be CENTERED-BELOW a brick—are derived from the earlier maps of the visual system that preserve retinal space so that we identify the same relation even though it might be on different parts of our retina or at different orientations in depth. It is generally accepted that cells in the visual cortex such as V1, which receive inputs from the retina via the lateral geniculate body, have smaller receptive fields (respond to stimuli over a more circumscribed area of the retina) than cells in later visual regions, such as V2 (which receives inputs from V1), V4, or IT. For V1, individual neurons are tuned to patterns of a given width and orientation (say, vertical) within a 0.5-degree region. Those slightly later, in V2, have receptive fields between 0.5 and 1 degree; those in V4 respond over an area of 1 to 4 degrees; and those in IT that control object recognition have receptive fields as large as 25 degrees. Whether these changes in receptive field size are associated with the human's ability to extract relations and identify objects anywhere on the retina and from arbitrary orientations in depth is yet to be determined.

Suggestions for Further Reading

An excellent treatment of many of the topics discussed in this chapter, and particularly of the interface between lower- and higher-level vision, can be found in chapter 12 of Stillings et al. 1987. Marr 1982 has become a classic in its statement of the issues of vision and its general computational approach to many of the problems of vision. Pinker 1985 provides a broad, critical overview of the more cognitive aspects of vision, including imagery and visual representation. A good general-purpose text on perception, such as Goldstein 1988 or Sekuler and Blake 1985, provides a useful background with which to consider the early constraints on higher-level vision.

Questions

2.1 Consider the features that might be used to recognize the capital letters of the English alphabet. To what extent might they be considered to reflect the workings of a system sensitive to viewpoint-invariant properties of edges?

2.2 Discuss how viewpoint-invariant properties might provide an account of the "good" and "bad" subparts of figure 3.1.

2.3 Discuss RBC as a model analogous to McClelland and Rumelhart's model for word recognition.

2.4 Treisman's experiments reveal striking limitations on the human's ability to attend to conjunctions of stimulus attributes. Discuss why these limitations are not apparent when (1) viewing complex objects that may enjoy a slight advantage in recognition speed compared to simple objects and (2) viewing a scene composed of many objects.

2.5 After reading chapter 4 on visual development, speculate on which aspects of RBC might be present at birth.

References

Bartram, D. (1974). The role of visual and semantic codes in object naming. *Cognitive Psychology* 6, 325–356.

Biederman, I. (1987). Recognition-by-Components: A theory of human image understanding. *Psychological Review* 94, 115–147.

Biederman, I. (1988). Aspects and extensions of a theory of human image understanding. In Z. Pylyshyn, ed., *Computational processes in human vision: An interdisciplinary perspective.* Norwood, NJ: Ablex.

Biederman, I., and G. Ju (1988). Surface vs. edge-based determinants of visual recognition. *Cognitive Psychology* 20, 38–64.

Biederman, I., R. J. Mezzanotte, and J. C. Rabinowitz (1982). Scene perception: Detecting and judging objects undergoing relational violations. *Cognitive Psychology* 14, 143–177.

Binford, T. O. (1971). Visual perception by computer. Paper presented at IEEE Systems Science and Cybernetics Conference, Miami, December.

Brooks, R. A. (1981). Symbolic reasoning among 3-D models and 2-D images. *Artificial Intelligence* 17, 205–244.

Connell, J. H. (1985). Learning shape descriptions: Generating and generalizing models of visual objects. Master's thesis, Department of Electrical Engineering and Computer Science, MIT, Cambridge, MA.

Goldstein, E. B. (1988). *Sensation and perception.* 3rd ed. Belmont, CA: Wadsworth.

Goodale, M. A., and A. D. Milner (1982). Fractioning orientation behavior in rodents. In D. Ingle, M. A. Goodale, and R. Mansfield, eds., *Analysis of visual behavior.* Cambridge, MA: MIT Press.

Hoffman, D. D., and W. Richards (1985). Parts of recognition. *Cognition* 18, 65–96.

Huttenlocher, D. P., and S. Ullman (1987). Object recognition using alignment. In *Proceedings of the first international conference on computer vision*. Washington, DC: Computer Society Press of the IEEE.

Intraub, H. (1981). Identification and naming of briefly glimpsed visual scenes. In D. F. Fisher, R. A. Monty, and J. W. Senders, eds., *Eye movements: Cognition and visual perception*. Hillsdale, NJ: L. Erlbaum Associates.

Ittelson, W. H. (1952). *The Ames demonstrations in perception*. New York: Hafner.

Jolicoeur, P. (1985). The time to name disoriented natural objects. *Memory and Cognition* 13, 289–303.

Jolicoeur, P., M. A. Gluck, and S. M. Kosslyn (1984). Picture and names: Making the connection. *Cognitive Psychology* 16, 243–275.

King, M., G. E. Meyer, J. Tangney, and I. Biederman (1976). Shape constancy and a perceptual bias towards symmetry. *Perception and Psychophysics* 19, 129–136.

Lowe, D. G. (1984). Perceptual organization and visual recognition. Doctoral dissertation, Department of Computer Science, Stanford University, Stanford, CA.

Lowe, D. G. (1987). The viewpoint consistency constraint. *International Journal of Computer Vision* 1, 57–72.

McClelland, J. L., and D. E. Rumelhart (1981). An interactive activation model of context effects in letter perception: Part 1. An account of basic findings. *Psychological Review* 88, 375–407.

Marr, D. (1977). Analysis of occluding contour. *Proceedings of the Royal Society of London* B197, 441–475.

Marr, D. (1982). *Vision: A computational investigation into the human representation and processing of visual information*. San Francisco: W. H. Freeman.

Mishkin, M., and T. Appenzeller (1987). The anatomy of memory. *Scientific American* 256, 80–89.

Moran, J., and R. Desimone (1985). Selective attention gates visual processing in the extrastriate cortex. *Science* 229, 782–784.

Nakayama, K., and G. H. Silverman (1986). Serial and parallel processing of visual feature conjunctions. *Nature* 320, 264–265.

Pinker, S. (1985). Visual cognition. An introduction. In S. Pinker, ed., *Visual cognition*. Cambridge, MA: MIT Press.

Reeves, A., and G. Sperling (1986). Attention gating in short-term visual memory. *Psychological Review* 93, 180–206.

Reicher, G. M. (1969). Perceptual recognition as a function of meaningfulness of the stimulus material. *Journal of Experimental Psychology* 81, 275–280.

Rumelhart, D. E., J. L. McClelland, and the PDP Research Group (1986). *Parallel distributed processing: Explorations in the microstructure of cognition*. Vol. 1: *Foundations*. Cambridge, MA: MIT Press.

Sekuler, R., and R. Blake (1985). *Perception*. New York: Knopf.

Sperling, G. (1960). The information available in brief visual presentations. *Psychological Monographs* 74 (11, Whole No. 498).

Stillings, N. A., M. H. Feinstein, J. L. Garfield, E. L. Rissland, D. A. Rosenbaum, S. E. Weisler, and L. Baker-Ward (1987). Vision. In *Cognitive Science: An Introduction*. Cambridge, MA: MIT Press.

Treisman, A., and G. Gelade (1980). A feature integration theory of attention. *Cognitive Psychology* 12, 97–136.

Wheeler, D. D. (1970). Processes in word recognition. *Cognitive Psychology* 1, 59–85.

Chapter 3

Mental Imagery

Stephen Michael Kosslyn

What seems to happen when you try to decide which is higher off the ground, the tip of a racehorse's tail or its rear knees? Or when you think about how a new arrangement of furniture would look in your living room? Many people report that in performing these tasks, they "see" with their "mind's eye" the horse's tail and the furniture. Visual mental imagery is "seeing" in the absence of the appropriate immediate sensory input; imagery is a "perception" of remembered information, not new input. But if all one is doing is "mentally perceiving" what has already been perceived, what is the use of imagery? And in what way does it make sense to talk about "seeing," "hearing," and the like without actually perceiving? Indeed, the very idea of mental images is fraught with puzzles and possible paradoxes. What, exactly, is being "perceived"? Surely images cannot be actual pictures in the brain; there is no light in there, and who or what would look at the pictures, even if they were there? And, given that there are no hands in the brain, how do we "move things around" in images?

At first glance (and even at second glance!) these are knotty problems indeed. In this chapter we will explore the recent attempts to answer these and related questions. Because most research has focused on visual imagery, we will concentrate on that type of imagery here, although many people report experiencing imagery in all sensory modalities ("hearing" with the "mind's ear," "smelling" with the "mind's nose," and so on).

3.1   Purposes and Problems

It is helpful to begin by considering the purposes of imagery. Once we have a sense of what imagery is used for, we can ask about the nature of the "problems" that must be solved by a system (including a brain) to accomplish these purposes.

3.1.1   What Is Imagery For?

All characterizations of imagery rest on its resemblance to perception. One way to consider the purposes of imagery is to explore the parallels between imagery and perception in the same modality. For example, we use vision for two kinds of purposes: in recognition, to identify objects and their parts, and in spatial processing, to track moving objects and to navigate as we move through space. Similarly, one purpose of imagery is to "recognize" properties of imaged objects, which allows us to retrieve information from memory. For example, consider how you answer the following questions: What shape are a beagle's ears? Which is darker green, a Christmas tree or a frozen pea? Which is bigger, a tennis ball or a 100-watt light bulb? Most people claim that they visualize the objects and "look" at them in order to answer these questions. In these cases we apparently call on some of the machinery used in recognition to classify parts or properties that previously were noticed (and stored in memory) but were not explicitly labeled or categorized at the time.

Imagery is used to retrieve information from memory in a variety of circumstances, but primarily when three conditions are met: (1) the information to be remembered is a subtle visual property; (2) the property has not been explicitly considered previously (and hence labeled); and (3) the property cannot easily be deduced from other stored information (for example, from information about the general category to which the object belongs). To get a feel for these principles, try the following experiment on a friend (and "watch" what happens as you think about it as well). Ask your friend to describe the shape of Snoopy's ears. After she answers, ask her again. And then again (begging patience!). After about the third time, your friend will probably report no longer using imagery; at this point she will simply remember the answer (say, "rounded"). The change was in condition (2); the property became categorized, and hence imagery was not needed (see Kosslyn and Jolicoeur 1980). Can you think of ways of testing the other two conditions?

A second purpose of imagery parallels our perceptual navigation and tracking abilities: imagery is a way of anticipating what will happen if one's body or physical objects move in a particular way. For example, we can image a container and "see" whether there is room for it on the top shelf in the refrigerator; or we can mentally project an object's trajectory, "seeing" where it will land. In short, imagery is used when we reason about the appearance of an object when it is transformed, especially when we want to know about subtle spatial relations.

These two uses of imagery constitute the basis for a whole host of uses. Kosslyn et al. (in press) asked people to keep a diary in which they recorded the kinds of images they formed and the purposes of each image. As we would expect from the previous discussion, some respondents reported using imagery in memory retrieval and problem solving. For example, one subject reported that she visualized what she wore the day before when getting dressed in the morning. Surprisingly, however, the most often reported imagery was in the service of "free association," for no specific purpose. In addition, people used imagery to help produce descriptions, to help understand descriptions, as part of "mental practice" (one subject visualized a "mental scenario" of what he would say when asking a professor about a grade change), and to induce emotional or motivational states (one subject imaged what she would look like thinner to help her stay on her diet). These reports are consistent with Shepard and Cooper's (1982) descriptions of cases in which scientists used "imaged models" as aids to reasoning and Paivio's (1971) evidence that memory can be improved if one visualizes the material and then encodes the images into memory.

3.1.2 Problems To Be Solved

If we were going to program a computer to mimic human imagery, the system would have to be able to solve (at least) four kinds of problems. First, it would have to be able to *generate* images. That is, images come to mind only when we are faced with a specific situation. We store in long-term memory the information necessary to form images, but some process or processes must use that information to create the image per se. Second, once we have an image, we must be able to interpret the shapes in the image. To "see" that Snoopy has rounded ears, we must be able to to *inspect* the object in the image, classifying it in a new way. Third, in many imagery tasks we must be able to *retain* the image over time. Unless the property is very salient and immediately obvious, careful "inspection" may be necessary; a process or processes must be available for hanging onto the image as long as necessary. Finally, in many situations we want to *transform* the object in an image in some way. A wide variety of such transformations is possible, and there must be some means of carrying them out.

3.2   The Human Processing System

A fair amount is now known about how the brain solves these problems. Let us consider each in turn.

3.2.1   Image Generation

The fact that images must be generated does not imply that there is a single mechanism that generates images, nor does it imply that there is a mechanism that is dedicated to generating images. That is, several mechanisms working together could generate images, and these mechanisms may have other roles as well. By analogy, a car can slow down if one simply takes one's foot off the gas, which does not use a separate "slowing down" system. Similarly, it now appears that at least two—and probably more—subsystems are used in image generation.

One subsystem seems to be used to build up images on the basis of distinct parts that are activated individually. Reed (1974) showed subjects patterns such as those in figure 3.1, then showed them parts of patterns and asked whether any of the previous patterns had contained the parts. Subjects were more successful with "good" parts than with "bad" ones (in the Gestalt sense). Presumably, the pattern was initially broken down perceptually into units, which later were used to generate the image. If the probed part corresponded to one of the parts that were encoded initially, well and good; if not, it was difficult to make the comparison.

Consistent with this idea, the time needed to form images increases with each additional part to be included. Indeed, the time needed to form images changes when the number of parts is varied in a host of ways, including simply asking people to construe a pattern in one way or another. For

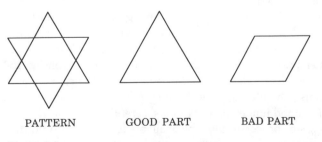

PATTERN   GOOD PART   BAD PART

Figure 3.1
Examples of types of stimuli used by Reed. Some parts are more difficult to see in a pattern than others, both in perception and in imagery.

example, a Star of David can be seen as relatively few overlapping figures (two triangles) or as relatively many adjacent figures (a hexagon with six small triangles). If subjects "see" it the latter way, they require much more time later to form an image of the pattern (for a brief review, see Kosslyn 1983).

A second subsystem (or subsystems) apparently is used in order to position the parts in the image. This idea is consistent with the observation that the brain processes location information separately from shape information (Ungerleider and Mishkin 1982; Mishkin and Ungerleider 1982). If the two types of information are entered into memory separately, it is reasonable that separate subsystems use each type of information when the system is running in the other direction—forming an image rather than encoding one. Many researchers (for example, Pylyshyn 1973) had noticed that parts could be imaged in the wrong location, which is consistent with the idea that shape and location are processed by separate mechanisms even in imagery. Indeed, the simple fact that people can arrange imaged objects according to a description suggests that the locations are processed separately from the shapes. For example, can you image George Washington floating above a horse? Or George Bush riding on an elephant?

Some findings that support this view were reported by Farah et al. (1985) and Kosslyn et al. (1985). They tested patients who, for medical reasons, had had their corpus callosum—the major connection between the two hemispheres of the brain—surgically severed. Thus, in these people the left and right halves of the brain no longer communicate effectively. These researchers found that the left hemisphere could perform imagery tasks that required putting parts together. For example, one patient was asked whether animals such as cats and apes have ears that protrude above the top of the skull. This task requires imaging the ears in the correct relationship to the head. The left hemisphere could also perform tasks that required forming a global image and assessing overall shape. For example, the patient was asked whether an animal such as a hog is larger (as seen from the side) than a goat. This task does not require putting parts together in a high-resolution image; the general shape will do. In contrast, the right hemisphere could only effectively perform the latter kind of imagery task; it could form images but had great difficulty performing tasks that require putting parts together. Thus, there is evidence for a distinction between the two subsystems: one that activates individual stored perceptual units operates in both hemispheres, but one that juxtaposes parts operates effectively only in the left hemisphere. Such a dissociation would not occur if the mechanisms were not distinct. Consistent with the idea that the left hemisphere is critically involved in generating multipart images of the sort described here, Farah (1984) found that virtually all patients who could not generate images had a lesion in the (posterior) left cerebral hemisphere.

3.2.2 Image Inspection

Given the apparent parallels between the uses of imagery and those of like-modality perception, it is not surprising that imagery apparently shares some of the same processing mechanisms used in recognition, navigation, and tracking. In fact, objects seem to be "inspected" in imagery just as they are in actual perception: once a representation is formed, it apparently is treated the same way regardless of whether it arose from the senses or from memory.

There are numerous sources of evidence that imagery shares processing mechanisms with like-modality perception (for an excellent review, see Finke and Shepard 1986). One is the finding that imagery selectively interferes with like-modality perception. For example, Segal and Fusella (1970) asked subjects to hold an image while trying to detect a faint auditory or visual stimulus. They found that holding a visual image (say, of a flower) impairs visual perception more than auditory perception, but holding an auditory image (say, the sound of a telephone ringing) has the reverse effect. Thus, they found *modality-specific* interference, which suggests that imagery and like-modality perception share common mechanisms that are not used in other-modality processing (see also Farah 1985).

Indeed, the process of "looking" at objects in images shares many properties of actual perception. As another example, image a honeybee at a very small size, and then try to decide what color its head is. Many people report having to "zoom in" in order to "see" the head, which is not necessary if the object is imaged at a larger size (Kosslyn 1983). And in fact, more time is required to "see" parts of objects when they are imaged at smaller sizes.

Neuropsychological data also support the idea that image inspection is accomplished by the same mechanisms used in perceptual recognition. For example, patients who have suffered damage to the right parietal lobe sometimes show "unilateral visual neglect": they ignore objects to their left side (the right side of the brain receives input from the left side, and vice versa). Bisiach and Luzzatti (1978) asked such patients to image a scene that was very familiar prior to the stroke that caused their brain damage. In one experiment subjects were to image standing on one side of a plaza and were to report what they could "see." These patients were very familiar with the plaza prior to the stroke and had no difficulty forming the image. However, they described only buildings to their right, ignoring buildings to their left (just as they would do in perception). Bisiach and Luzzatti then asked the patients to image standing at the opposite side of the plaza, looking toward where they had previously stood, and again to report what they could "see." They again mentioned only buildings to their right, which led them to name the buildings they had previously ignored and ignore those they had previously mentioned!

Levine, Warach, and Farah (1985) present additional evidence that perceptual recognition mechanisms are also used in imagery. They found patients who had lost the ability to perceive either shape or location and tested their ability to image the same properties. As expected, patients who could not recognize faces perceptually also could not interpret faces in imagery (for instance, when asked whether George Washington had a beard); similarly, patients who could not register locations perceptually could not do so in imagery (for instance, when asked to describe how to get from one place to another).

3.2.3   Image Retention

Ask a friend to participate in the following informal experiment. His job is to listen to a set of directions and to form an image of a 1-inch line segment for each direction, connecting it to the end of the previously imaged segment. If you read "North," your friend should image a vertical 1-inch line; if you then read "West," he should connect the right end of a horizontal line to the top of the first line, and so on. Ask your friend to image the path described by the following directions: North, Northeast, North, West, South, West, West, South, East, Northeast, West, Southwest, East. Ask him to report back the series. If he is a normal human, you will find that he will not recall all of them. In addition, you will find that he recalls nonrandom combinations of segments. For example, he is apt to recall "North, West, South," because it forms a simple visual pattern, whereas he may not recall "West, West," because people may forget the length of the line, only remembering that there is a line in that direction.

This simple experiment illustrates the most important aspects of what we know about image retention. First, we can retain relatively little information in an image at once (see also Weber and Harnish 1974). Second, the critical measure is the number of "chunks," the number of "perceptual units" that are present. That is, we can remember roughly as many squares as individual, unorganized line segments: what is important is the number of groups of units.

If images do indeed occur in visual cortex, the limited capacity of imagery makes sense. In vision, we do not want sensory input to stick around; if it did, we would get blurring whenever we shift our eyes to a new stimulus. What is a virtue in vision—the fast fade rate, as it were—is a drawback in imagery. When we form an image, it fades rapidly and effort is required to keep it in place. Many people report that holding an image is a little like a juggling act: each part is refreshed while other parts are fading. Presumably, the total amount that can be kept in mind at once depends on the speed with which the parts are refreshed and the speed with which they fade.

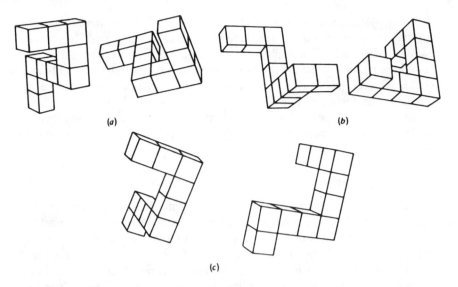

(a)   (b)

(c)

Figure 3.2
Examples of stimuli used by Shepard and Metzler (1971). The time to decide whether the figures are identical increases with the amount of mental rotation necessary to align them. (Reprinted by permission of the publisher and author from R. N. Shepard and J. Metzler, Mental rotation of three-dimensional objects, 1971, *Science* 171, 701–703. © 1971 by the AAAS.)

3.2.4   Image Transformation

Examine the pairs of stimuli in figure 3.2. Are the members of each pair identical, regardless of their individual orientations? If you had measured the time you required to make each judgment, you would have found that the time increases as the disparity in orientation between the members of a pair increases (Shepard and Metzler 1971). We can "mentally rotate" imaged objects, and the time increases linearly with increasing amounts of rotation (Shepard and Cooper 1982). If you think about it, this finding is remarkable: mental images are not actual objects that must obey the laws of physics. That is, real objects must pass through intermediate points along the trajectory as they change orientation, but objects in images need not obey the laws of physics; they are not real, rigid entities. At least one part of our transformation mechanism seems to be built to mimic perceptual processes. Shepard and Cooper (1982) argue that this makes good sense from an evolutionary point of view, given that one of the purposes of imagery is to mimic what would happen in actual physical situations.

In addition to being rotated, imaged objects can be expanded or reduced in size. For example, consider the stimuli in figure 3.3. Are they the same or

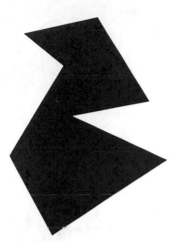

Figure 3.3
Examples of types of stimuli used by Bundesen and Larsen. The time to decide whether the forms are identical increases with the degree of size scaling necessary to align them.

different? Again, the time to decide increases linearly with the disparity in sizes (Bundesen and Larsen 1975). Furthermore, it is possible to perform such esoteric transformations as mentally folding cubes. Shepard and Feng (1972) asked subjects to view stimuli like those illustrated in figure 3.4 and to decide whether the arrows would meet (the shaded side is the base). The time to decide increased linearly with the number of sides that had to be shifted in the image to fold the cube.

At least one of the processes used in image transformations is more effective in the right hemisphere of the brain (Ratcliff 1979). Researchers have found that subjects with damage to the right parietal lobe have difficulty with mental rotation tasks and other image transformation tasks such as cube folding. Consistent with these findings, the isolated right hemisphere of a split-brain patient has been found to be better than the isolated left hemisphere at performing spatial-manipulation tasks. However, other studies have provided evidence that the left hemisphere also plays a role in image transformations, such as rotation (for a discussion, see Kosslyn 1987).

3.3   Individual Differences

The scientific study of imagery has always been intimately bound to the study of individual differences in imagery. Indeed, Sir Francis Galton, who is credited as one of the founders of the scientific study of individual

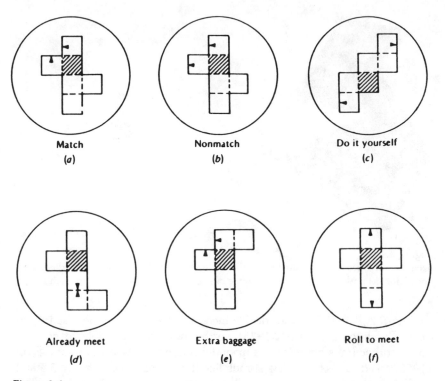

Match   Nonmatch   Do it yourself
(a)   (b)   (c)

Already meet   Extra baggage   Roll to meet
(d)   (e)   (f)

Figure 3.4
Examples of the unfolded cubes used by Shepard and Feng (1972). The time to decide
whether the arrows will meet when the cube is folded (using the shaded square as the base)
increases with the number of sides that must be mentally moved. (Reprinted by permission of the publisher and author from R. N. Shepard and C. Feng, A chronometric study of
mental paper folding, 1972, *Cognitive Psychology 3*, 228–243.)

differences in intelligence and personality, was one of the first to study imagery. In 1883 Galton asked people to image their breakfast table and report what was present that morning. To his surprise, his initial queries often met with blank stares at the mention of imagery; his subjects professed not to know what he was talking about. As it turned out, his initial inquiries were to his friends, who tended to be professional men; as he broadened his sampling, he found that about 12 percent of the people queried reported not having the experience of mental imagery. In a more recent study, however, only about 3 percent of the respondents reported not experiencing visual imagery. What makes this result particularly puzzling is that the more recent respondents were members of Mensa, a society for people who score high on IQ tests, who presumably were similar to the professional people who made up Galton's nonimaging 12 percent (McKellar 1965). Even small differences in the wording of the two questionnaires may have led the subjects to think about the situation differently.

In addition to the apparent unreliability of simple introspective reports, there is a deeper reason for the disparity in the two studies. Imagery ability is not all-or-none; a given person is not generally good or bad at imagery. Consider the following study: a wide range of people were given 13 different imagery tasks, including ones that required rotation, retention, generation, and so on, in different combinations (Kosslyn et al. 1984). If imagery ability is a single trait, then those who did well on one task should have done well on the others. This did not occur. Rather, there was a wide range of correlations in the performance of the tasks. Indeed, for some pairs of tasks, doing well on one implied doing poorly on the other! These results make sense if different aspects of imagery are accomplished by using separate subsystems, which are invoked in different combinations depending on the task. A person who is poor at some process such as rotation (because one or more necessary subsystems are ineffective) will be poor at all tasks that require it. Thus, the precise nature of the task is an important variable in assessing imagery ability, and different tasks will not necessarily produce similar results.

This discovery is consistent with what we know about how imagery is carried out in the brain. As noted above, the generation of multipart images apparently involves left-hemisphere processes, and image rotation and inspection involve right-hemisphere processes (probably in addition to left-hemisphere ones). In general, imagery is not carried out by a single "center," or even one cerebral hemisphere (Erlichman and Barrett 1983; Farah 1984; Kosslyn 1987). Rather, imagery appears to depend on mechanisms located in various parts of the brain, and the combination of mechanisms that will be recruited depends on the task.

3.4   What Is a Mental Image?

We have been discussing mental images rather blithely, relying heavily on introspection and intuition. Not surprisingly, much effort has been expended in recent years to understand what a mental image *is*. Mental images are fleeting, ethereal entities; how should we conceptualize them in a way that explains not only how they can represent information about the world but also how "mental" images relate to the physical brain itself? This issue has plagued theorists at least since the time of Plato, who in his *Theaetetus* likened images to patterns etched on a block of wax (individual differences in imagery ability were explained by differences in the hardness and purity of the wax).

The brain is an organ of the body, and like other organs of the body it can be described at numerous distinct levels of analysis. We can divide these levels into two general classes, the physical and the functional. For example, stomachs can be described either in terms of cell types, enzymes, and so on, or in terms of their role in digestion. Similarly, brains can be described in terms of their physical composition—cells, connections, neuro-transmitters, and so on—or in terms of their functions (see chapter 1 for a more detailed treatment of the idea of "levels of analysis"). And the primary function of brains is to store and process information. A "mental representation" is a description at the functional level of analysis of how the brain stores information.

The debate about the nature of "mental imagery representations" entered a new stage in the early 1970s. No one denies that people experience "seeing with the mind's eye," but there is controversy over what this experience reveals about how the brain actually stores the relevant infor-mation. Two means of representation have been proposed for mental images, one that confers a special status on images and one that treats them as no different in kind from the representations of linguistic meaning.

The two alternatives are called *depictive* and *propositional* representation. These are different *formats*, different types of codes. Every type of code is distinguished in part by a specific *syntax*. The syntax is characterized by (1) the elementary, or "primitive," symbols and (2) a set of rules for combining the symbols. Symbols usually belong to different "form classes" ("noun," "verb," "determiner," and so on), and the rules of combination are defined in terms of these classes—which allows them to generalize over an infinite number of distinct symbols.

A format is also defined in part by the *semantics* of a code. The semantics is determined by how meaning is conveyed by individual symbols and combinations of symbols. For example, the symbol "A" can be interpreted as a part of speech if read as a word, or as a configuration of birds in flight (as seen from above) if interpreted as a picture. The same marks are used in both formats, but what differs is how they are interpreted as conveying meaning. The rules of semantics assign a meaning (or sometimes more than one, if the symbol is ambiguous) to a specific symbol.

In contrast, the *content* of a representation is the specific information conveyed. The same content can be conveyed in numerous different formats. For example, the information in this sentence could be conveyed by speaking it aloud (where the symbols are composed of sound waves), by writing it down in Morse code (where the symbols are dots and dashes), and so on. Palmer (1978) offers a more elaborate treatment of these distinctions, but this overview is sufficient for present purposes.

In order to see how the results from experiments can distinguish between the use of propositional and depictive representations, we will need to go into more detail in characterizing these representational types.

3.4.1   Propositional Representations

Consider a *propositional representation* of a simple scene, containing a ball sitting on a box. We can write the representation using the notation "ON (BALL, BOX)." This kind of notation is close to the way propositions are represented in computers and also serves to make it clear that we are not talking about sentences in a natural language (like English). A propositional format can be characterized as follows:

The syntax: (1) The symbols belong to a variety of form classes, corresponding to relations (e.g., on), entities (e.g., ball, box), properties (e.g., red, new), and logical relations (e.g., if, not, some). (2) The rules of symbol combination require that all propositional representations have at least one relation ("BALL, BOX" does not assert anything). (3) Specific relations have specific requirements concerning the number and types of symbols that must be used (ON(BOX) is unacceptable because ON relates one object to another, and hence at least two symbols must be used).

The semantics: (1) The meaning of individual symbols is arbitrarily assigned, requiring the existence of a lexicon (as is true for words in natural languages, whose meanings must be looked up in a dictionary). (2) A propositional representation is defined to be unambiguous, unlike words or sentences in natural languages. A different propositional symbol is used for each of the senses of ambiguous words. (3) A propositional representation is abstract. That is, (a) it can refer to nonpicturable entities, such as "sentimentality," (b) it can refer to classes of objects, not simply individual ones (such as boxes in general), and (c) it is not tied to any specific modality (a propositional representation can store information seen, communicated via language, felt, and so on). (4) Some theorists add another characteristic to the semantics of propositions: they are either true or false (see, for example, Anderson and Bower 1973). However, this seems to me to be, not a property of the representation per se, but a relation between the representation and a specific state of the world (see Palmer 1978).

3.4.2   Depictive Representations

Now make a drawing of the same scene, of a ball on a box. The drawing is an example of a *depictive representation*. Depictive representations differ from propositional ones on almost every count. There is no explicit symbol that stands for the relation ("on" is not represented separately, but only emerges from the juxtaposition of the symbols standing for the ball and the box). The rules of combination are not defined over form classes (indeed, the rules are very lax; any dot can be placed in any relationship to any other dot—as surrealist painters have delighted in demonstrating to us). The semantics are not arbitrarily assigned to depictions, and depictions are inherently ambiguous, because depictions are interpreted as resembling an object (and a picture can be seen as resembling more than one object). Depictions are not abstract: they cannot directly refer to nonpicturable concepts; they represent individual instances (not classes); and they are visual.

Thus, depictions are not propositions. But what are they? We can characterize depictive representations as follows:

The syntax: (1) The symbols belong to two form classes: points and empty space. (2) The points can be arranged so tightly as to produce continuous variations or so sparsely as to be distinct (like the dots in a comic strip). (3) The rules for combining symbols require only that points be placed in spatial relation to one another.

The semantics: (1) The association between a representation and what it stands for is not arbitrary; rather, depictions "resemble" the represented object or objects. That is, (a) each part of the representation must correspond to a visible part of the object or objects, and (b) the represented "distances" among the parts of the representation must mirror the distances among the corresponding parts of the actual object (as they appear from a particular point of view). Thus, a pattern in an array in a computer can be a depiction because the points can correspond to points on the surface of an object with the corresponding distances on the object being preserved by the number of cells (filled or empty) between the points in the array. Similarly, there need be no actual picture in the brain to have a depiction: all that is needed is a "functional space" in which distance can be defined vis-à-vis how information is interpreted. (For a more detailed treatment of the idea of a functional space, see Kosslyn 1983.)

However, although all that is required in order to have a depiction is a functional space, there may actually *be* physical depictive representations in the brain: we know that visual cortex contains numerous "maps" in which the pattern striking the retina is physically laid out across cortex; some of these maps may be involved in imagery, in which case there could literally be a "picture in the head." Notice, however, that there need be nobody in there looking at such pictures: just as in vision proper, the neural connections to other areas serve to pass the information along for additional processing, eventually leading to the accessing of relevant stored information (and hence interpretation; see chapters 1 and 2).

3.5   The Imagery Debate

The modern debate about mental imagery has gone through two distinct phases. The first began in 1973, with the publication of Pylyshyn's paper "What the Mind's Eye Tells the Mind's Brain: A Critique of Mental Imagery" and Anderson and Bower's book *Human Associative Memory*. Pylyshyn's critique of mental imagery focused on arguments that the very idea of imagery was paradoxical (Who looks at the images?) or muddled (In what ways are images like pictures? Why can't you see the number of stripes on an imaged tiger?). The thrust of the critique of imagery was that a depictive representation does not occur in the brain when we experience mental images; instead, propositional representations are used for all forms of cognition—including imagery. The depictive features of images that are evident to introspection were thus taken to be "epiphenomenal": these features have nothing to do with the representation used to perform the task, just as the lights flashing on the outside of a mainframe computer have nothing to do with carrying out the internal processing (the lights could be removed and it would keep working just as well).

Let us now consider one example of the sort of data gathered to address this issue, and see how these sorts of data led to elaboration of the propositional arguments, which in turn led to more experimentation, which in turn led to the second phase of the debate.

3.5.1   Scanning Visual Mental Images

By their very nature, depictions embody space (recall that "distance" is an intrinsic part of the representation). Thus, if depictive representations underlie the experience of "having an image," then the spatial nature of the representation should affect how images are processed. On the other hand, if the underlying representation is propositional, we have no reason to expect distance to affect processing times (given that the description of an object's appearance would be stored in a list or network of some kind, just as in language).

Different Mechanisms? The First Phase of the Debate

In this section we will consider a series of experiments that were carried out largely by my colleagues and me; these experiments represent a kind of "case study," illustrating how one can make abstract ideas concrete and how one can grasp a conceptual issue by the horns, so to speak.

We reasoned that one way to discover whether image representations embody space is to see whether it takes more time to shift attention greater distances across an imaged object. If subjects take more time to scan a long distance across an imaged object than to scan a short distance, we would have evidence that distance was indeed embodied in the representation of the object.

The first experiment began by asking subjects to memorize a set of drawings (Kosslyn 1973). Half of these drawings were vertical and half were horizontal, as illustrated in figure 3.5. After the subjects had memorized the drawings, they closed their eyes, heard the name of one (say, "speed-boat"), and visualized it. Once it was imaged, the subjects were asked to mentally focus ("stare" with the "mind's eye") at one end of the object in the image. Then the name of a possible component of the object (say, "motor") was presented on tape. On half the trials the name labeled part of the drawing, and on the other half it did not. The subjects were asked to "look for" the named component on the image object.

An important aspect of this experiment was that the probed parts were either at one end or the other of a drawing or in the middle. The subjects were told that we were interested in how long it took to "see" a feature on an imaged object (the word *scan* was never mentioned in the instructions), and they pressed the "true" button only after "seeing" the named com-

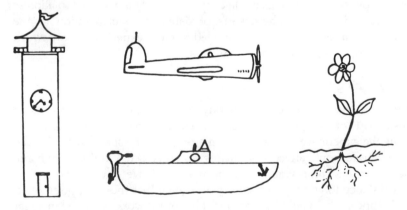

Figure 3.5
Examples of the drawings used by Kosslyn (1973) to study image scanning.

ponent and the "false" button only after "looking" but failing to find it. We reasoned that if image representations depict information, then it ought to take more time to locate the representations of parts located farther from the point of focus. And in fact this is exactly what occurred.

At first glance, the results from this experiment seemed to show that depictive representations are used in imagery. But it soon became clear that a propositional explanation could easily be formulated. Bobrow (personal communication) suggested that the visual appearance of an object is stored in a propositional structure like that illustrated in figure 3.6. This representation is a series of linked hierarchies of propositions, with each hierarchy describing a part of the object. Note that we could rewrite the propositions illustrated here as BOTTOM-OF(PROPELLER,MOTOR), REAR-OF (MOTOR,REAR DECK), and so on. That is, each link is a relation that combines the symbols at the connected nodes into a proposition.

According to Bobrow's theory, people automatically (and unconsciously) construct these sorts of propositional descriptions when asked to memorize the appearance of drawings. When the subjects were asked to focus on one end of the drawing, they would then activate one part of the representation (for instance, for speedboat, the node for motor). When subsequently asked about a part, they then searched the network for its name. The more links they had to traverse through the network before locating the name, the more time it took to respond. For example, for speedboat it took more time to find "anchor" than "porthole" after having been focused on the motor because four links had to be traversed from motor to anchor but only three from motor to porthole. Thus, the effect of "distance" on scanning time may have nothing to do with distance being embodied in an underlying

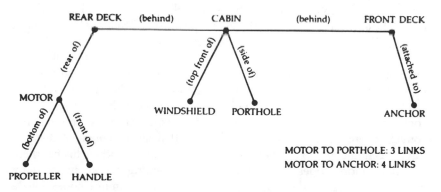

Figure 3.6
A propositional representation of the drawing of a speedboat illustrated in figure 3.5. The greater the distance between two parts on the drawing, the larger the number of links between them in the network.

depictive representation but may instead simply reflect the organization of a propositional network (see also Lea 1975). The conscious experience of scanning a pictorial mental image may somehow be produced by processing this network, and the depictive aspects of images open to introspection may simply be epiphenomenal.

It should now be clear why it was necessary to go into so much detail in characterizing the differences between the types of representations: we need a reasonably precise characterization of the two representations if we are to perform experiments to discriminate between them. According to our characterization, although propositional structures can be formulated to capture the spatial arrangement of the drawings, they are not depictions. Recall that in depictions, in contrast to this sort of propositional representation, the shape of empty space is represented as clearly as the shape of filled space and there is no explicit representation of relations (such as REAR-OF).

The next experiment was designed to eliminate the problem with the first one. In this experiment we independently varied the distance scanned across and the number of items scanned over. The results of this experiment were straightforward: both distance and amount of material scanned over affected the reaction times. Time increased linearly with increasing distance scanned over, even when the amount of material scanned over was kept constant (for details, see Kosslyn, Ball, and Reiser 1978), as expected if images depict.

The notion of depiction leads us to expect that image representations embody distance in at least two dimensions. To test this idea, we asked subjects to memorize the map illustrated in figure 3.7. On this map were seven objects, which could be related by twos to form 21 pairs. The subjects learned to draw the locations of each of the seven objects on the map. These objects were positioned in such a way that the members of each of the 21 pairs were a different distance apart.

As is evident in figure 3.8, time to scan the image increased linearly with increasing distance scanned across. This result is exactly as predicted by the idea that image representations depict information. But it is possible to create a propositional counterexplanation even here. Now the network contains "dummy nodes" that mark off distance. That is, these nodes convey no information other than the fact that an increment of distance (say, 5 centimeters) exists between one object and another; hence, there would be more nodes between nodes representing parts separated by greater distances on the map. By putting enough dummy nodes into a network, the propositional theory developed for the original results can be extended to these results as well.

To attempt to rule out this propositional counterexplanation, we conducted a control experiment, which involved a variation on the map-

Figure 3.7
A map that was memorized and later imaged and scanned. The seven objects were placed in such a way that the members of each of the 21 pairs were a different distance apart.

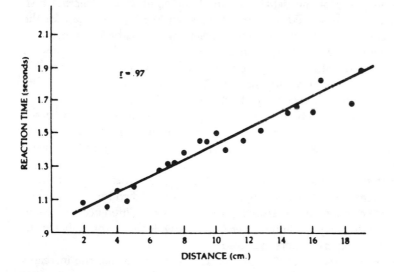

Figure 3.8
The time to scan between pairs of objects on an image of the map illustrated in figure 3.7.

scanning task. In this experiment subjects again imaged the map and focused their attention on a particular point, but now they were told simply to decide as quickly as possible whether the probe named an object on the map. If the propositional theory is correct, we reasoned, then we should find effects of distance here too; after all, we asked the subjects to form the image (which corresponds to accessing the appropriate network). However, there were absolutely no effects of the distance from the focus to target objects on response times.

In other experiments we varied the size of the imaged objects being scanned, asking subjects to adjust the size of an object in the image after they memorized it. Not only did time increase with the distance scanned, but more time was required to scan across larger images. The finding of effects of size on scanning time allows us to eliminate yet another non-depictive explanation for the effects of distance on response times. One could argue that the closer two parts are on an object or drawing, the more likely it is that they will be grouped into a single perceptual "chunk" and stored as a single unit, and hence the easier it will later be to look up two parts in succession. Because the size of the image was not manipulated until after the actual drawing was removed, this explanation cannot account for the effects of size on scanning time.

Demand Characteristics? The Second Phase of the Debate

The second phase of the debate began about eight years after the first, when Pylyshyn elaborated his views (Pylyshyn 1981). This phase of the debate focused on the data collected earlier. Whereas the proponents of depictive representation claimed that the data reflected the processing of depictive representations, the propositionalists now focused on possible methodological problems with the experiments. Two such problems were raised: "experimenter expectancy effects" and "task demands."

Intons-Peterson (1983) performed an experiment in which she compared scanning images to scanning physically present displays. Half of the experimenters were told that the image scanning should be faster and half were told that the perceptual scanning should be faster. She found that the experimenters' expectations influenced the results: when experimenters expected faster perceptual scanning, the subjects produced this result; when they expected faster image scanning, there was no difference in overall times. Thus, the experimenters were somehow leading the subjects to respond as the experimenters expected.

Jolicoeur and Kosslyn (1985) decided to test the idea that the increases in times with increasing distance scanned reflect the subjects' responding to experimenter expectancy effects. We performed a series of experiments using Intons-Peterson's methodology. For example, we told one experimenter that we expected a U-shaped function, with the most time being required to scan the shortest and longest distances. The reason for this prediction, we explained, was that the four closest objects "group" into a single chunk—because of the Gestalt laws of similarity and proximity—and so they are "cluttered" together, making it difficult to scan among them. And the longest distances require more time than the medium ones because more scanning is involved.

The results from this experiment were identical to those found previously: times increased linearly with increasing distance. In additional experiments Jolicoeur and Kosslyn varied experimenter expectancy in different ways, none of which affected scan times. Indeed, these experimenters failed to replicate Intons-Peterson's original finding. What could be going on here? Many details of such experiments can differ from laboratory to laboratory (for instance, making sure subjects always keep their fingers on the response buttons), and these details could be critical for obtaining experimenter expectancy effects. The important point is that, whatever caused the experimenter expectancy effect in Intons-Peterson's study, it was not present in the procedures used in the initial studies of image scanning. Thus, these results cannot be explained away as simply reflecting how well subjects can satisfy the expectations of the experimenter.

Taking an alternative tack, Pylyshyn (1981) claimed that the very instruction to scan an image induces subjects to pretend to scan an actual object—which leads them to take more time to respond when they think they would have taken more time to scan across a visible object. The way the subjects estimate how long to wait (unconsciously) would involve propositional processing of some sort.

This potential concern was ruled out by image-scanning experiments that eliminated all references to imagery in the instructions. Finke and Pinker (1982, 1983; see also Pinker, Choate, and Finke 1984) showed subjects a set of random dots on a card, removed the card, and presented an arrow. The question was, if the arrow were superimposed over the card containing the dots, would it point directly at a dot? Subjects reported using imagery to perform this task, and Finke and Pinker found that the response times increased linearly with increasing distance from the arrow to a dot. Furthermore, the rate of increase in time with distance was almost identical to what we had found in our earlier experiments. Because no imagery instructions were used, let alone mention of scanning an image, a task-demands explanation seems highly implausible.

Goldston, Hinrichs, and Richman (1985) actually went so far as to tell the subjects the predictions, which is never done in typical psychological experiments. Even when subjects were told that the experimenter expected longer times with shorter distances, they still displayed increased times with distance scanned. Telling subjects different predictions did affect the degree of the increase with distance, but this result is not surprising: given the purposes of imagery, one had better be able to control imaged events! What is impressive is that even when subjects were, if anything, trying for the opposite result, they still took longer to scan across longer distances.

Finally, Denis and Carfantan (1985) described the basic scanning experiment to naive subjects and asked them to predict the outcome. Although these subjects were good at predicting many of the effects of imagery (for example, that it will help one to memorize information), they were very poor at predicting the results of scanning experiments and the like. If subjects are using knowledge about perception and physics to "fake" the data in the experiments, it is puzzling that they evince no such knowledge in this situation.

3.5.2   Conclusions from the Scanning Experiments

The simplest account for all of the results of the scanning experiments taken together is that image representations depict information, and more time is required to shift attention longer distances across an imaged object. Although alternative explanations are possible for each of the individual results, different alternative explanations will be necessary to explain the different effects (such as the effects of size scale or of distance and number of intervening items on scan times). In contrast, the depictive imagery theory is general to all of the results and is simpler. These experiments illustrate how behavioral data can be collected to distinguish among alternative theories of mental representation. Such research is cumulative: once we establish that scanning reflects processing the representation, scanning can then be used to study additional issues. For example, Pinker (1980) and others have used scanning to study how images represent information in three dimensions.

We have briefly glimpsed the promise that theories of information processing hold for understanding how mental functions are actually embodied in the brain itself. The insight that imagery is not a single entity was critical in beginning to understand how it is carried out in the brain (Farah 1984); before investigators had some idea of the component processes, it was not known what kinds of functions should be carried out in a single location.

The study of mental imagery is interesting in part as a bridge between perception and mental activity. As such, it is the cognitive faculty "closest to the neurology" because so much is now known about the neural mechanisms of perception. Given its long history, it seems fitting that the study of imagery may end up providing one of the first case studies in how the brain creates the mind.

Suggestions for Further Reading

Although the experimental study of mental imagery has developed in a number of different directions, the most vigorous research in the field has recently focused on two of them. One line of work centers on exploring the relationship between imagery and like-modality perception. Perhaps the best overview of this work is by Finke and Shepard (1986), who point out numerous and varied examples of experiments that demonstrate the existence of common mechanisms in imagery and perception. In addition, Shepard and Cooper (1982) review the evidence that transformations of objects in images are in many ways analogues of corresponding transformations of the actual objects. A particularly intriguing contribution to this line of inquiry is provided by Farah (1988), who reviews previously overlooked evidence for the visual nature of visual mental imagery. This evidence, which springs from neuropsychology, concerns the common neural systems used in imagery and like-modality perception.

The other line of work focuses on questions about the nature of the processing system used in imagery. This research has become increasingly neuropsychological, on the one hand, and computational, on the other. Farah (1984) offers a neuropsychological analysis of imagery into separate processes, as does Kosslyn (1987). Both authors attempt to decompose imagery into underlying processing components. Pinker (1985) reviews much of the work focusing on the computational approach, some of which grows out of research in artificial intelligence.

Finally, Morris and Hampson (1983) explore the role of consciousness in imagery (and vice versa), a topic not reviewed in this chapter, and Paivio's (1971) now-classic book plumbs the uses of imagery in learning and memory. The *Journal of Mental Imagery* publishes a very wide range of material on imagery (from case reports of the use of imagery in psychotherapy to experimental studies of individual differences in imaging ability), and provides good illustrations of the different approaches to studying imagery and applying research on imagery.

These sources provide references to a very large literature, all of which serves to integrate the study of imagery into the study of cognition more generally.

Questions

3.1 Generate an account for each of the following results based on both a descriptive and a depictive representation:
   a. Subjects take more time to inspect objects that are imaged at small sizes than ones that are imaged at large sizes. (Example: Objects are represented as lists of descriptions of properties. When asked to form an image at a small size, subjects recall fewer properties of the object and thus are more likely to have to dig into memory when subsequently asked about a particular property.)
   b. Subjects can name a picture more quickly if they form an image of the object in advance, but this effect is most pronounced if the picture is of exactly the same object (same size, orientation, and so on) as the one being imaged.
   c. Subjects require more time to rotate objects greater amounts.
3.2 How could you discover whether experimenter expectancy effects were due to ESP?
3.3 Imagery has been thought to be both a "primitive" form of thought and a very advanced form of thought. What arguments can you offer for each of these extreme positions?
3.4 Captain DeWitt is interested in hiring only good imagers to navigate his yacht. Thus, he gives them the DeWitt Imagery Test (DIT). This test requires people to rate how vividly they can form images of common objects. What is wrong with the test?

3.5 The Minister of Education of a wealthy foreign country is interested in raising the IQ of his population. Thus, he hits on the idea of training everyone to use imagery more in their thinking. Is this a good idea?

References

Anderson, J. R., and G. H. Bower (1973). *Human associative memory*. New York: V. H. Winston.

Bisiach, E., and C. Luzzatti (1978). Unilateral neglect of representational space. *Cortex* 14, 129–133.

Bundesen, C., and A. Larsen (1975). Visual transformation of size. *Journal of Experimental Psychology: Human Perception and Performance* 1, 214–220.

Denis, M., and M. Carfantan (1985). People's knowledge about images. *Cognition* 20, 49–60.

Erlichman, H., and J. Barrett (1983). Right hemisphere specialization for mental imagery: A review of the evidence. *Brain and Cognition* 2, 55–76.

Farah, M. J. (1984). The neurological basis of mental imagery: A componential analysis. *Cognition* 18, 245–272.

Farah, M. J. (1985). Psychophysical evidence for a shared representational medium for mental images and percepts. *Journal of Experimental Psychology: General* 114, 91–103.

Farah, M. J. (1988). Is visual imagery really visual? Overlooked evidence from neuro-psychology. *Psychological Review* 95, 307–317.

Farah, M. J., M. S. Gazzaniga, J. D. Holtzman, and S. M. Kosslyn (1985). A left hemisphere basis for visual imagery? *Neuropsychologia* 23, 115–118.

Finke, R. A., and S. Pinker (1982). Spontaneous imagery scanning in mental extrapolation. *Journal of Experimental Psychology: Human Learning and Memory* 8, 142–147.

Finke, R. A., and S. Pinker (1983). Directional scanning of remembered visual patterns. *Journal of Experimental Psychology: Learning, Memory, and Cognition* 9, 398–410.

Finke, R. A., and R. N. Shepard (1986). Visual functions of mental imagery. In K. R. Boff, L. Kaufman, and J. P. Thomas, eds., *Handbook of perception and human performance*. New York: Wiley.

Galton, F. (1883). *Inquiries into human faculty and its development*. London: Macmillan.

Goldston, D. B., J. V. Hinrichs, and C. L. Richman (1985). Subjects' expectations, individual variability, and the scanning of mental images. *Memory and Cognition* 13, 365–370.

Intons-Peterson, M. J. (1983). Imagery paradigms: How vulnerable are they to experimenters' expectations? *Journal of Experimental Psychology: Human Perception and Performance* 9, 394–412.

Jolicoeur, P., and S. M. Kosslyn (1985). Is time to scan visual images due to demand characteristics? *Memory and Cognition* 13, 320–332.

Kosslyn, S. M. (1973). Scanning visual images: Some structural implications. *Perception and Psychophysics* 14, 90–94.

Kosslyn, S. M. (1983). *Ghosts in the mind's machine*. New York: Norton.

Kosslyn, S. M. (1987). Seeing and imagining in the cerebral hemispheres: A computational approach. *Psychological Review* 94, 148–175.

Kosslyn, S. M., T. M. Ball, and B. J. Reiser (1978). Visual images preserve metric spatial information: Evidence from studies of image scanning. *Journal of Experimental Psychology: Human Perception and Performance* 4, 47–60.

Kosslyn, S. M., J. Brunn, K. R. Cave, and R. W. Wallach (1984). Individual differences in mental imagery ability: A computational analysis. *Cognition* 18, 195–243.

Kosslyn, S. M., J. D. Holtzman, M. J. Farah, and M. S. Gazzaniga (1985). A computational analysis of mental image generation: Evidence from functional dissociations in split-brain patients. *Journal of Experimental Psychology: General* 114, 311–341.

Kosslyn, S. M., and P. Jolicoeur (1980). A theory-based approach to the study of individual differences in mental imagery. In R. E. Snow, P. A. Federico, and W. E. Montague, eds., *Aptitude, learning, and instruction: Cognitive processes analyses of aptitude,* vol. 1. Hillsdale, NJ: L. Erlbaum Associates.

Kosslyn, S. M., C. Segar, J. D. Pani, and L. A. Hillger (in press). What is imagery for? *Journal of Mental Imagery.*

Lea, G. (1975). Chronometric analysis of the method of loci. *Journal of Experimental Psychology: Human Perception and Performance* 2, 95–104.

Levine, D. N., J. Warach, and M. J. Farah (1985). Two visual systems in mental imagery: Dissociation of "what" and "where" in imagery disorders due to bilateral posterior cerebral lesions. *Neurology* 35, 1010–1018.

McKellar, P. (1965). The investigation of mental images. In S. A. Barnett and A. McLaren, eds., *Penguin science survey.* Harmondsworth, England: Penguin Books.

Mishkin, M., and L. G. Ungerleider (1982). Contribution of striate inputs to the visuospatial functions of parieto-preoccipital cortex in monkeys. *Behavioural Brain Research* 6, 57–77.

Morris, P. E., and P. J. Hampson (1983). *Imagery and consciousness.* New York: Academic Press.

Paivio, A. (1971). *Imagery and verbal processes.* New York: Holt, Rinehart and Winston.

Palmer, S. E. (1978). Fundamental aspects of cognitive representation. In E. Rosch and B. Lloyd, eds., *Cognition and categorization.* Hillsdale, NJ: L. Erlbaum Associates.

Pinker, S. (1980). Mental imagery and the third dimension. *Journal of Experimental Psychology: General* 109, 354–371.

Pinker, S. (1985). Visual cognition. An introduction. In S. Pinker, ed., *Visual cognition.* Cambridge, MA: MIT Press.

Pinker, S., P. A. Choate, and R. A. Finke (1984). Mental extrapolation in patterns constructed from memory. *Memory and Cognition* 12, 207–218.

Pylyshyn, Z. W. (1973). What the mind's eye tells the mind's brain: A critique of mental imagery. *Psychological Bulletin* 80, 1–24.

Pylyshyn, Z. W. (1981). The imagery debate: Analogue media versus tacit knowledge. *Psychological Review* 87, 16–45.

Ratcliff, G. (1979). Spatial thought, mental rotation and the right cerebral hemisphere. *Neuropsychologia* 17, 49–54.

Reed, S. K. (1974). Structural descriptions and the limitations of visual images. *Memory and Cognition* 2, 329–336.

Segal, S. J., and V. Fusella (1970). Influence of imaged pictures and sounds on detection of visual and auditory signals. *Journal of Experimental Psychology* 83, 458–464.

Shepard, R. N., and L. A. Cooper (1982). *Mental images and their transformations.* Cambridge, MA: MIT Press.

Shepard, R. N., and C. Feng (1972). A chronometric study of mental paper folding. *Cognitive Psychology* 3, 228–243.

Shepard, R. N., and J. Metzler (1971). Mental rotation of three-dimensional objects. *Science* 171, 701–703.

Ungerleider, L. G., and M. Mishkin (1982). Two cortical visual systems. In D. J. Ingle, M. A. Goodale, and R. J. W. Mansfield, eds., *Analysis of visual behavior.* Cambridge, MA: MIT Press.

Weber, R. J., and R. Harnish (1974). Visual imagery for words: The Hebb Test. *Journal of Experimental Psychology* 102, 409–414.

Chapter 4

Origins of Visual Knowledge

Elizabeth S. Spelke

A new enterprise has emerged over the last thirty years: the experimental study of visual perception and visual processes in human infants. This enterprise, made possible by the development of some simple techniques, has been fruitful in a number of ways. First, it has led to a greater appreciation of young infants and their abilities. Infants, we now know, have considerable capacity to make sense of the world. Second, it has given pediatricians, and those engaged in medical research, ways of assessing problems in the development of individual infants and insights into the potentially harmful effects of early sensory abnormalities. Third, it has helped neurobiologists and psychobiologists to chart relationships between visual experience and its physical basis, through studies of how perception changes with the development of the nervous system. Fourth, it has begun to reveal something about human beings as adults: our visual processes, visual experience, and visual knowledge.

The present chapter focuses on this fourth set of insights, for it is here that the study of early visual development joins the enterprise of cognitive science. As philosophers and psychologists have long hoped, studies of the origins of visual knowledge are beginning to suggest which aspects of visual experience are intrinsic to humans, deriving from biologically given capacities, and which aspects depend on the particularities of our encounters with light-reflecting surfaces and objects. In addition, these studies are beginning to suggest how our mature capacities are structured. Since our earliest developing perceptual capacities give rise to the first experiences through which we learn, the things we learn will bear their imprint. Initial visual capacities will therefore tend to remain central to our experience of the visual world. Moreover, those initial capacities will set boundaries on what we are capable of learning, limiting the states of the world that we are able to perceive or understand. Studies of infancy therefore promise to shed light on the nature and the limits of the cognitive functioning of adults.

4.1   Problems for a Developing Visual System

There are two basic problems that the newborn infant's visual system must solve. First, that system must be able to learn, improving its operation in response to the experience it receives. The need for a learning capacity is clear when one considers the perceptual accomplishments of adults. We as adults perceive three-dimensional arrangements of familiar and meaningful objects from highly limited arrays of visual information, such as static two-dimensional images of cluttered environments. Our ability to do this testifies, in part, to the knowledge we have acquired about the characteristic shapes, sizes, and arrangements of familiar objects. Moreover, adults adapt to new visual experiences: we adjust to unfamiliar optical devices (new glasses, a microscope) and acquire new visual skills (distinguishing species of birds, identifying types of baseball pitches). These adjustments also testify to the influence of experience on visual perception.

The need for a learning capacity is equally clear when one considers the physical growth of the visual system in infancy and childhood. Over the course of development each eye increases in size, the two eyes move farther apart, and neurons in the visual system undergo numerous changes of state, position, and connectivity. Perceivers must adjust to these changes, in order to avoid growth-related distortions of perception. For example, changes in the distance between the two eyes affect important sources of information for depth. Depth perception would become systematically distorted, with development, if perceivers could not adapt to these changes.

If perceivers are to learn from visual experience, however, their immature visual systems must deliver experience in usable form: they must detect some of the order that inheres in visual encounters with the surrounding world. This requirement places a different, seemingly contradictory demand upon the visual system. The system must include mechanisms, themselves unlearned, that order visual experience in ways that permit learning. The existence of perceptual learning thus raises two questions: what are the innate mechanisms by which humans first experience the visual world, and how are these mechanisms modified by the experiences they deliver?

In the rest of this chapter we will consider these questions and outline what appear to be some answers to them. We will on two aspects of visual development: first on the development of perception of the surface layout, particularly perception of surface arrangements in depth, and then on the development of object perception, particularly perception of objects as unitary, bounded, and persisting physical bodies.

4.2   Perception of the Surface Layout

4.2.1   The Problem of Surface Perception

For many centuries philosophers, physiologists, and psychologists have pondered the capacity of humans to perceive visible layouts of surfaces. Fundamentally, the puzzle of surface perception derives from the geometry of the surface layout in relation to the geometry of the arrays of light it reflects to the eyes. The layout itself is a three-dimensional array of surfaces. Each surface has a particular size, shape, and curvature, is encountered at a particular orientation, distance, and direction, and undergoes a particular pattern of motion or change. In contrast, visual information about the layout is contained in two two-dimensional arrays of light, one reflected to the retina of each eye, that preserve none of these properties in a straight forward way. Surface distance, orientation, and curvature are obviously lost when a three-dimensional layout is reflected onto a two-dimensional surface (see figure 2.2). Surface size and shape are also lost, because the size and shape of a surface's image are affected by the surface's distance and orientation. Even surface direction and motion are lost, because changes in the position of a surface's image occur constantly as the observer scans the layout by moving her eyes, head, or body.

As adults, we perceive a stable layout of three-dimensional surfaces, not two changing arrangements of two-dimensional forms. Our perception corresponds, at least approximately, to the true spatial properties of surfaces: things that look far away usually are far away. We perceive depth relations in the layout by detecting a variety of relationships within the patterns of light at the eyes. Two of these relationships are particularly important. First, there are systematic optical motions that occur as a perceiver moves through a rigid environment (Gibson 1966; Longuet-Higgins and Prazdny 1980) or as rigid objects move in front of him (Wallach and O'Connell 1953; Ullman 1979). The extent and the direction of the motion of any point in the image depend, in part, on the distance from the observer of its source in the layout. Human adults can perceive the three-dimensional relationships among surfaces by analyzing these two-dimensional patterns of optical motion. Second, there are systematic differences between the two images that a layout projects to the two eyes. For any given point in the layout, the magnitude of the difference in the location of its images depends, in part, on its distance from the observer. This relationship is the basis of *stereopsis*: human adults perceive depth by detecting these binocular differences, or "disparities."

4.2.2   Nativism and Empiricism

How does depth perception develop? This question has been at the heart of theories of visual perception for at least 300 years, since the French philosopher and mathematician René Descartes (1638) and the Anglican philosopher and theologian George Berkeley (1709) propounded sharply contrasting views of the development of visual knowledge. Although kinetic and stereoscopic depth perception were not recognized at that time, Descartes and Berkeley offered accounts of the development of depth perception that continue, in some ways, to animate theories of visual development. Much of their discussion focused on a different source of information for depth: the degree of convergence of the two eyes as they are directed to a single object.

Descartes noted that geometric principles govern the relationship between the convergence of the eyes and the distance of an object. When the two eyes are directed to the same object, the distance of the object and the distance between the eyes determine the eyes' angles of regard (figure 4.1). Thus, Descartes reasoned, a perceiver could compute object distance "by a sort of natural geometry" (1638, VI). Given a certain interocular distance and two angles of convergence, the distance of the object that is converged upon can be inferred. According to Descartes, knowledge of geometry originates in humankind's divinely given reason (Descartes 1637). Principles of geometry, grasped by humans innately and tacitly, allow us to infer the three-dimensional sources of two-dimensional stimulations.

In contrast, Berkeley denied that geometric computations enter into the apprehension of space: "I appeal to anyone's experience whether upon sight of an *object*, he computes its distance by the bigness of the *angle* made by the meeting of the two *optic axes*? . . . In vain shall all the mathematicians in the world tell me that I perceive certain lines and angles . . . so long as I myself am conscious of no such thing" (1709, XII). Instead, Berkeley proposed, space perception results from learned associations between sensations: in this case associations between the muscular sensations produced by turning the eyes inward to direct them at an object and the muscular

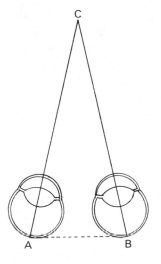

Figure 4.1
Schematic drawing (after Descartes, 1638, VI) illustrates the distance information provided by convergence. Given the distance between the centers of the two retinas (AB) and the eyes' angles of regard ($\angle$CAB and $\angle$CBA), the distance of the fixated object C can be computed.

sensations that accompany other behaviors directed at the object such as reaching or locomoting toward it. In general, humans learn to see a three-dimensional world by associating the sensations evoked by looking at objects with the sensations that accompany object-directed actions. Because these sensations tend to occur together, perceivers can learn to relate them directly, without recourse to reasoning.

The debate between *nativists* such as Descartes, who root perceptual abilities in inborn capacities, and *empiricists* such as Berkeley, who root perceptual capacities in a history of learning, has undergone many changes since the seventeenth century. At the heart of the nativist-empiricist debate, however, are enduring questions: What is the initial basis of visual depth perception, and how does depth perception change with experience? Would the layout of the world look different if perceivers had to cope with different surface-to-image relationships? What aspects of the capacity to perceive depth are most central to us as humans and most protected from the vagaries of experience?

4.2.3   The Modifiability of Surface Perception in Adults

Experiments addressed to these questions began in the nineteenth century with the work of the great physicist, physiologist, and psychologist Hermann von Helmholtz (1866). Helmholtz did not attempt to study surface perception in human infants. Rather, he sought to uncover the origins of space perception by studying its modifiability in adults. If space perception can be modified by altering the visual information that an adult receives, Helmholtz suggested, it is simplest and most reasonable to assume that space perception depends initially on learning. Any process of learning that can be observed with adults might be presumed to be present and functional at earlier ages, when it would be most useful for shaping children's perception in response to their experience.

Helmholtz noted that perception of the positions of objects could be modified by wearing spectacles of various kinds. If one looks at objects through prism spectacles that displace the objects' images to the left, for example, one initially makes errors in reaching for the objects, reaching too far to the left. These errors decrease with time, however, and they eventually disappear. Helmholtz concluded that visual perception of space can be modified in adults. Like Berkeley, he proposed that vision is modified as perceivers act on the world by reaching or moving around, observing the systematic effects of their actions on visible objects.

Helmholtz's observation is familiar to anyone who has had to adjust to new glasses or other optical devices, and it has been reproduced in hundreds of laboratory experiments. These experiments have not always supported the Berkeley/Helmholtz view of perceptual adaptability, however. They challenge that view in three principal ways.

First, experiments show that when perceivers adapt to a conflict between vision and action by learning to reach for an optically displaced target or learning to walk in an optically distorted world, the changes that occur most often are not changes in visual perception. Instead, changes occur in the perceivers' tactile sense of the positions of their limbs and body (Harris 1980) or in the systems that coordinate visual perception with active movement (Held 1965).

Consider, for example, this experiment by Harris (1963).[1] An observer wears prism spectacles that displace everything she sees to the right. She is allowed to adapt to the distortion by pointing to and reaching for visible objects, but only with her right hand. After a short period of practice, her pointing has greatly improved: she has adapted to the discrepancy between vision and reaching, as in the experiment described by Helmholtz. But which perceptual system has undergone the adaptation: vision or touch? Harris addressed this question by asking the adapted subject to point to the objects with her untrained *left* hand. If the period of practice had produced a visual change, pointing should have been as accurate with the left as with the right hand. In fact, however, the accuracy of pointing with the two hands differed greatly. Subjects made the same errors with the untrained

---

1. The description of this experiment (and later ones) has been simplified in certain respects.

hand that they had made at the start of the session. Clearly, this adaptation experience did not bring about a change in vision. Harris suggested instead that the experience of reaching with the right hand led to a change in perception of the hand's felt position. Visual perception appears to be more resistant to change than tactile perception in this situation, contrary to Helmholtz's view.

A second challenge to the Berkeley/Helmholtz theory comes from studies of adaptation to purely visual conflicts. True changes in visual perception appear to occur most readily when two sources of visual information are brought into conflict with each other. Wallach (1976) has extensively investigated the effects of such visual conflicts. In one set of experiments (see Wallach 1976, chap. 10) he introduced a conflict between the two sources of visual depth information mentioned earlier: kinetic information and stereoscopic information. A stationary observer was allowed to watch an object that rotated in front of him so as to provide kinetic information for its three-dimensional shape. The observer looked at the object through an optical device that increased the differences between the two eyes' views of the objects: these increased disparities made the object appear thicker than it actually was. Wallach thus produced a conflict between two sources of information for the three-dimensional shape of the object.

As in Harris's experiment, adaptation occurred in this situation, reducing the perceptual conflict. Subsequent testing revealed that the adaptation experience had produced a change in stereoscopic depth perception but no change in kinetic depth perception. Based on this and other experiments, Wallach has suggested that kinetic depth perception is not modifiable. Instead, it serves as a basis for modifying other sources of depth information. The existence of an unmodifiable capacity to perceive depth would seem to support aspects of a nativist view of space perception.

Wallach's study also provides evidence that vision can be modified in the absence of any conflict with touch. Wallach's observers experienced a change in stereoscopic depth perception, even though they watched a rotating object without moving their heads, arms, or bodies, and thus without encountering any discrepancy between vision and action. Actions such as reaching and locomotion play no essential role in processes of visual adaptation.

Research on perceptual adaptation challenges the Berkeley/Helmholtz view in a third way. It appears that perceivers cannot adjust to all perceptual modifications with equal ease. Instead, there are limits, or *constraints*, on the kinds of conflicts between two sources of spatial information that humans easily learn to resolve. An experiment by Bedford (1989) makes this point most clearly. Like Helmholtz and Harris, Bedford introduced a discrepancy between the seen and the felt positions of objects. She went

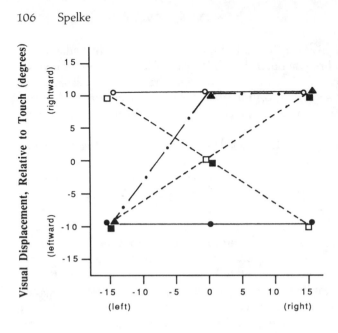

Figure 4.2
Some visual rearrangements studied by Bedford (1989): a uniform leftward displacement (filled circles), a uniform rightward displacement (open circles), a uniform expansion (filled squares), a uniform contraction (open squares), and a nonlinear change (triangles). Subjects experienced shifts of 10 degrees left or right at 2 or 3 locations: 15 degrees left, center, and 15 degrees right. (Figure adapted from Bedford 1989.)

beyond her predecessors, however, in investigating discrepancies of three kinds: (1) a uniform leftward or rightward displacement of the visual field, relative to touch, (2) a uniform expansion or contraction of the visual field, relative to touch, and (3) a change in which different parts of the visual field were displaced in different directions, relative to touch (figure 4.2). Subjects adapted to the first two changes but not to the third. Instead, they coped with the third change by rescaling and shifting the visual-tactile relation to minimize (but not eliminate) the conflict. Bedford suggested that human adults adapt most readily to *linear* changes in the relation between vision and touch: lateral shifts and/or changes of scale.

Bedford's experiment seems to point to a deficiency in our capacity to adjust to changes in the perceptual world. Bedford showed, however, that this limitation has a positive side. In principle, any linear change in the relation between two systems for perceiving spatial direction can be specified uniquely by information about the discrepancy at just two spatial locations: two points define a line. Bedford showed that people can take advantage of this constraint. After exposure to a visual-tactile discrepancy at two spatial positions, her subjects showed a change in pointing to all directions between those positions. Indeed, the change was as large for positions that were never experienced during the adaptation period as for the positions on which the subjects were trained. Intrinsic constraints appear to limit our adaptability as perceivers, but they also enable us to adapt quickly, on the basis of a small number of encounters with the seen and felt world.

In summary, visual perception is difficult to modify. Some visual systems, such as the system for computing depth from motion, may never be modified when they are brought into conflict with other systems. Some visual systems may be modifiable, but only when they are placed in conflict with another visual system, not when they are placed in conflict with touch. Finally, visual and tactile systems may only be modifiable in a restricted set of ways. Taken together, these findings reveal considerable limits on the adaptability of mature visual capacities to perceive space. With logic similar to that of Helmholtz, we might speculate that these limits derive from innate properties of the human visual system. This speculation can only be tested, however, through studies of human infants.

4.2.4   Depth Perception in Infancy

Experimental studies of the origins of surface perception began some thirty years ago, with investigations that focused on infants' visually guided, spatially appropriate behavior. In studies by Gibson and Walk (1960) young animals of various species were tested on the "visual cliff." The infant stood on a narrow central board facing two horizontal surfaces, one a short distance below it and the other much farther away. (The surfaces were actually covered with Plexiglas just below the centerboard, both to protect the infant and to ensure that only visual information specified the drop-off on the more distant side.) Gibson and Walk observed whether the infant animal avoided the visually specified drop-off. Such avoidance would suggest that it perceived the surfaces' relative distances, at least approximately.

Gibson and Walk found evidence of cliff avoidance in nearly every terrestrial animal they tested. Avoidance was observed as early as an animal could be tested—that is, as soon as it became capable of independent locomotion. In species that can see and walk at birth, such as goats, cliff avoidance was observed at 1 day of age. In species that begin to see and to locomote by sight at later ages, such as rats, cliff avoidance could not be tested at birth. When rats were tested at 4 weeks of age, however, cliff avoidance was observed. Moreover, cliff avoidance in rats was shown to be independent of experience: dark-reared rats, tested on first exposure to light at 3 months, consistently avoided the visual cliff. Depth perception appears to develop without visual experience in many species.

Gibson and Walk's studies of human infants were limited by the fact that humans do not begin to locomote independently until about 7 months of age. Although human infants avoided the cliff at that time, the earlier development of this ability remains a subject of dispute (for discussion, see Gibson and Spelke 1983). Accordingly, some investigators have turned to observations of other spatially appropriate behaviors for insights into the earlier development of space perception in humans.

Between 4 and 5 months human infants begin to reach effectively for visible objects. At that time reaching is adapted to an object's direction, distance, and pattern of motion: infants reach farther for a more distant object, and they reach ahead of a moving object so as to intercept it. These observations indicate that infants perceive an object's position and motion appropriately by 5 months of age (von Hofsten 1986). Three-month-old infants engage in a different spatially appropriate behavior: they react defensively to an approaching object by blinking or withdrawing their heads (Yonas and Granrud 1984). These reactions suggest that the changing distance of an approaching object is perceived by 3 months of age. Unfortunately, neither object-directed arm movements nor defensive reactions provide clear evidence concerning surface perception at younger ages (von Hofsten 1982; Yonas and Granrud 1984).

Although these studies leave the newborn human infant's capacities in some doubt, they provide evidence that infants' actions are spatially appropriate as soon as they emerge. A capacity to perceive depth appears to arise early and spontaneously in humans, as in other animals. This capacity evidently does not depend on learning about surfaces by reaching for them or locomoting around them, as Berkeley and Helmholtz proposed. Depth perception precedes the development of these actions and it may help to guide their development.

Studies of reaching, of behavior on the visual cliff, and of defensive reactions to approaching objects have been used to investigate the emergence of sensitivity to different kinds of visual depth information. In these studies infants are presented with selected kinds of depth information and their locomotion, reaching, or defensive reactions are observed in order to discover the stimulus conditions under which they can act in a spatially appropriate way. The studies suggest that motion provides the first effective information for depth. The kinetic patterns that accompany the motions of the infant or the motions of an object specify depth relations to human infants by 3 months of age, and perhaps earlier (Yonas and Granrud 1984). For a variety of other species, motion appears to specify depth innately. For example, motion serves as effective information for depth in dark-reared rats and for newborn animals with functioning visual and locomotor systems (Gibson and Walk 1960). These converging findings of human and animal studies suggest that kinetic depth perception becomes functional on the basis of little or no visual experience.[2]

In contrast, human infants do not begin to perceive depth from stereo-scopic information until about 4 months of age (for a review, see Banks and Salapatek 1983). The development of stereopsis has been shown to depend on cortical maturation in monkeys, and it is probably maturationally de-pendent in humans as well (Held 1985). It is also affected by visual experience: human and monkey infants with abnormal binocular experience (caused, for example, by muscular abnormalities preventing the infant from directing the two eyes to the same object) fail to develop normal binocular-ity (for discussion, see Mitchell 1988). Visual experience would seem to be necessary for the development of binocular depth perception because the distance between the two eyes increases with age, changing the relation-ship between binocular disparity and object distance.

What are the mechanisms by which binocular experience leads to the development of stereopsis in humans? Although this question has not been answered fully, the findings of some recent experiments support two sug-gestions. First, as noted, stereopsis develops in the 4th month of life. Since infants of 4 months can neither reach for objects nor locomote around them, the development of stereopsis does not appear to depend on active movement or object manipulation. Rather, infants may learn to perceive depth from binocular disparity by correlating disparity information with the already functional kinetic information for depth. That is, infants may use kinetic information to perceive a three-dimensional surface layout, and then they may assign to disparity values in the binocular representation of that layout the depth values specified by motion. Second, stereopsis has been found to develop quite rapidly in individual infants (Held 1985). The speed of this development suggests that the learning mechanism exploits con-straints on the possible mappings between binocular disparity and object distance. Infants may learn to perceive stereoscopic depth by detecting rela-tionships between binocular disparity and kinetic depth at a restricted set of locations, mapping the entire field on the basis of a limited set of inputs.

4.2.5   Overview

In summary, research on infants of a variety of species, including humans, suggests that the visual capacity to perceive depth forms part of our innate

2. Kinetic depth perception does require some modification during development, because of the growth of the infant's eyes and because of growth-related movements of individual neurons in the retina (see Aslin 1988; Banks 1988). Banks has shown, however, that kinetic depth perception can be recalibrated internally, through the detection and elimination of inconsistencies in the kinetic patterns produced by a functioning, but poorly calibrated, system (Banks 1988). Other depth information need not enter the calibration process.

endowment. Kinetic depth perception appears to develop in the absence of any specific visual experience. Although stereoscopic depth perception is affected by experience, the effects of experience appear to be limited by the infant's maturational state and perhaps by constraints on the binocular arrangements to which infants can accommodate. These findings are contrary to the empiricist theories of Berkeley and Helmholtz; they lend some support to nativist theories such as that of Descartes.

The findings of developmental experiments with infants converge in interesting ways with the findings of adaptation experiments with adults. Kinetic information, the least modifiable depth information for adults, is also the first effective depth information for infants. Binocular disparity, which undergoes adaptation in adults when it is placed in conflict with kinetic information for depth, may develop in infants through a process that builds on the already effective kinetic information. Visual learning occurs rapidly both for adults and for infants, suggesting that constraints on the modifiability of systems for perceiving depth operate both in adulthood and in infancy. These findings suggest that the mechanisms of adaptation observed with adults are also the mechanisms of perceptual learning, just as Helmholtz proposed. These mechanisms may operate throughout life, allowing humans to develop and adjust their visual capacities on the basis of visual experience.

4.3   Object Perception

4.3.1   Problems of Perceiving Objects

The capacity to perceive objects is as intriguing as the capacity to perceive surfaces, and it raises new issues and problems. As adults, we perceive the surrounding world as a layout of persisting physical bodies. Perception of objects is usually immediate, effortless, and accurate. Object perception is a puzzling achievement, however, because visual information for objects is both incomplete and potentially misleading. Objects come to us in a continuous surface array in which they sit upon and beside each other. Objects also are partly hidden: the back of every opaque object is hidden by its front, and the front surfaces of most objects are partly hidden behind other objects (figure 4.3). Finally, the images of objects continually enter and leave the visual field as we shift fixation and as objects move in relation to one another. Despite these complexities, we perceive objects as bounded bodies that are distinct from one another, as complete bodies that continue where they are hidden, and as persisting bodies that exist whether they are in or out of view.

Figure 4.3
A typical visual environment (child's birthday party). Cups, plates, napkins, and chairs are recognizable, although each is partly occluded. Cups and plates are also seen as distinct, even when their images are adjacent.

4.3.2   Theories of Object Perception and Its Development

Like those who study surface perception, students of object perception have attempted to shed light on these abilities, in part, by turning to development. Two theories have dominated discussion. According to one thesis, again from the empiricist tradition, newborn perceivers experience just the momentarily visible surfaces in a scene. As children move around surfaces and manipulate them, they learn how different views of an object are related (Helmholtz 1866) and how object unity and boundaries can be predicted from certain properties of visible surfaces such as their proximity, their similarity in texture and color, and the alignment of their edges (Brunswik and Kamiya 1953). This learning eventually allows children to infer complete and bounded objects from partial visual information.

The principal rival to empiricist theory has come from Gestalt psychology, an early twentieth-century movement that attempted to explain perception in terms of the intrinsic organizational properties of complex physical systems (see Koffka 1935; Köhler 1947). Because of its nature as a physical system, the brain was thought to tend toward a state of equilibrium. This physical tendency was thought to have a psycholgical counterpart: perceivers tend to confer the simplest, most regular, and most balanced organization on their experience. Thus, perceivers group together surfaces so as to form units that are maximally homogeneous in color and texture and maximally smooth and regular in shape (Wertheimer 1923; Koffka 1935). The tendency toward simplicity allows perceivers to apprehend the boundaries, the unity, and the persistence of most objects, because physical objects tend to be relatively homogeneous in substance and regular in form. Since the tendency toward simplicity follows from innate properties of the nervous system, learning was thought to play no essential role in the development of object perception.

Like theories of surface perception, these theories changed over the years as more was learned about perception, its physical basis, and its computational structure. The core of the debate between empiricist and Gestalt theories has remained alive, however, and it has stimulated research both on the modifiability of object perception in adults and on the development of object perception in infancy.

4.3.3   The Modifiability of Object Perception in Adults

Like Helmholtz, the Gestalt psychologists attempted to test their theory by studying the effects of experience on a mature perceiver's apprehension of objects. Their experiments appeared to show, however, that experience has little or no effect on object perception. In the most famous learning experiments (Gottschaldt 1926) subjects were repeatedly shown a complex figure, and then they were shown a simple figure that had been embedded within it (figure 4.4a). They were asked if the simple figure looked familiar. Even after viewing the complex figure on hundreds of occasions, the subjects failed to recognize the simpler figure within it. What they learned from their encounters with the complex visual display appeared to depend on their organization of that display.

In a later demonstration (Michotte, Thinès, and Crabbé 1964) Michotte showed subjects a triangle with an irregular center, and then he covered its irregular regions by a finger (see figure 4.4b). Asked what they saw when the figure was covered, Michotte's subjects reported a complete, regular triangle, despite what they had apparently learned about the display. Michotte concluded that intrinsic organizing tendencies are impervious to explicit knowledge or instruction. Demonstrations by Wertheimer (1923; figure 4.4c) and by Kanizsa (1979) support the same conclusion.

These experiments have been thoroughly criticized. Just because learning cannot be demonstrated in one laboratory session with adults, it is argued, one cannot conclude that learning does not occur in infancy. Adults might learn to perceive objects differently if they were given more time in which to learn. Moreover, even if learning never occurred for adults, such

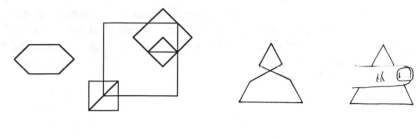

(a)   (b)

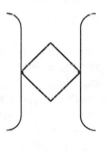

(c)

Figure 4.4
Some noneffects of knowledge or experience on perceptual organization: (a) after hundreds of exposures to a complex figure (right), subjects fail to recognize a simpler figure embedded with it (left) (after Gottschaldt 1926); (b) after viewing an irregular triangle, subjects still perceive a simple, complete figure when the irregular region is occluded, contrary to what they know is there (after Michotte, Thinès, and Crabbé 1964); (c) a single abstract figure is perceived, despite the presence of the familiar embedded letters "M" and "W" (after Wertheimer 1923).

learning might occur earlier in life. For example, most adults never learn to speak a second language without a detectable foreign accent. Accents are not innate, however; they are acquired by speakers as children. Demonstrations of a lack of plasticity in adults do not imply a lack of plasticity during development.

Nevertheless, a different lesson may be drawn from the Gestalt experiments: what one learns from a given experience depends on how one organizes that experience. This lesson comes originally from the work of the philosopher Immanuel Kant (1781). It was expounded forcefully by Köhler (1947) in a classic critique of the empiricist theory of object perception. Suppose, Köhler reasoned, that object perception is learned. How does this learning take place? An empiricist would reply that children learn to perceive objects by encountering them repeatedly, observing each object under various circumstances. For example, a child might learn to perceive a violin by encountering the violin on a table, in its case, in the hands of a violinist, and so forth. At different times the violin would appear at different distances and orientations and under different conditions of illumination. Eventually, each of these encounters would become associated with the others and with experiences such as hearing a violin sonata, touching the violin's strings, and hearing the word *violin*. Perception of the violin would emerge from this network of associations.

To proponents of such a theory, Köhler posed this question: How does the child determine which of his sensory experiences should be associated together to form the perceptual experience of a violin? What tells the child, for example, that the sight of a violin on a table should be linked to the sight of a violin in the hands of a violinst and not to the sight of a lamp on a table? In order to associate the violin's appearances with one another, one needs to perceive, somehow, that all those appearances are appearances of the same object—the violin. But that perceptual ability is just what the empiricists were attempting to explain by learning. The empiricist explanation seems to turn in a circle, presupposing the very ability that it seeks to explain: how one perceives a bounded, unitary, and constant violin from changing and varying arrays of light.

Köhler's argument suggests that what one learns from experience will depend on how one organizes that experience, and the demonstrations by Gottschaldt, Michotte, and Wertheimer appear to underline the point. Can this point be reconciled with the possibility that perceptual organization itself is subject to learning? I think it can, if the organization of surfaces into objects, like the perception of surfaces in depth, normally depends on multiple and redundant sources of information. If perceivers begin with a small set of mechanisms for detecting this organization, sufficient for recognizing objects under certain conditions, then they could learn to perceive objects by other means. But how do infants perceive objects initially, and how do they extend their initial abilities by learning? Developmental research can best address this question.

4.3.4   Object Perception in Infancy

Research on object perception in infancy began with studies of perception of partly occluded objects (Kellman and Spelke 1983). These studies used an experimental method, developed by Fantz (1961), that assesses infants' preferential looking at familiar and novel displays. When young infants are presented repeatedly with the same visual display, they tend to look at it less and less. If the infants are then presented with the original display and with a new display, they tend to look longer at the new display. This preference indicates that infants discriminate the two displays and detect the novelty of the second display. Fantz's method—often called the *habituation/dishabituation method*—has since been used to study a variety of perceptual capacities in infancy, including the capacity to perceive the complete shape of an object that is partly hidden.

Four-month-old infants were presented with an object whose top and bottom were visible but whose center was occluded by a nearer object (figure 4.5). They saw this display repeatedly until their visual interest declined, and then they were shown a complete object, which corresponded to the display adults report seeing behind the occluder, and two object fragments, which corresponded to the visible surfaces of the partly hidden object. Infants were expected to look longer at whichever display appeared more novel to them. If they experienced the display as a mosaic of visible surface fragments, they should have looked longer at the complete object; if they organized the occlusion display into a single continuous unit, they should have looked longer at the fragmented object.

Like adults, infants were found to perceive a center-occluded object as a complete and continuous unit if the visible areas of the object moved in unison. Motion in depth was as effective as vertical or lateral motion—further evidence for depth perception in infancy. Unlike adults, however, infants did not perceive the completeness of a center-occluded, stationary object of a simple shape. Familiarization with such an object was followed by increased looking both at the complete and at the fragmented displays, with no preference between those displays. It appeared that the infants' perception of the stationary displays was indeterminate, as is an adult's perception of a stationary, center-occluded object with irregular coloring and form.

These studies provided evidence that motion specifies object unity to infants but that static configurational properties do not. Similar conclusions were suggested by investigations of young infants' perception of object boundaries. Three- to five-month-old infants were presented with displays

Center-Occluded Object

Complete Object   **Fragmented Object**

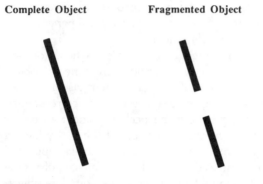

Figure 4.5
Habituation display (top) and test displays (bottom) for an experiment on infants' perception of partly occluded objects (after Kellman and Spelke 1983).

of two objects, arranged so that their images overlapped at the infants' eyes. Perception of the objects' boundaries was tested in various ways, including preferential looking methods (for details, see Spelke 1985). All the studies provided evidence that infants perceived object boundaries by detecting the spatial arrangements of surfaces: two objects were perceived as distinct units if they were separated in depth. Infants also perceived object boundaries by detecting the relative motions of surfaces: two objects were perceived as distinct if they moved independently, even if they touched throughout their motion. Infants did *not* perceive object boundaries, however, by analyzing the static, configurational properties of surfaces: two adjacent, motionless objects were not perceived as distinct, even if they differed in color, texture, and shape. Unlike adults, young infants perceived neither the unity nor the boundaries of objects by analyzing the static, configurational properties of visual arrays.

Experiments by Schmidt (1985) have focused on the development of sensitivity to static configurational information for object unity. Children are sensitive to the properties of figural simplicity and color/texture similarity by 2 years of age. Sensitivity to these properties appears to emerge gradually; the development of gestalt perception is a slow process. For example, 7-month-old infants perceive a stationary, center-occluded object as a single, continuous unit if the object is three-dimensional and its visible surfaces are coplanar, with collinear edges and homogeneous coloring. If these same relationships indicate that two partly occluded surfaces lie on distinct objects, however, 7-month-old infants' perception of the occlusion display is indeterminate, in contrast to the perceptions of adults. These findings suggest that gestalt organization by the principles of good continuation and similarity (see figures 2.14 and 3.1) is not a unitary phenomenon.

We have considered infants' perception of objects as unitary and bounded. What about their perception of objects as persisting over a succession of sporadic encounters? Experimenters have recently begun to investigate this ability, by means of the same preferential looking method. In one study 4-month-old infants were habituated to events in which one or two objects moved in and out of view behind one or two occluders (for details, see Spelke 1988). For different groups of subjects, the identity or distinctness of the object(s) was specified by the apparent continuity of the path of object motion, the apparent discontinuity of the path of object motion, the apparently constant speed of object motion, or the apparently irregular speed of object motion. Figure 4.6 depicts the displays for the first and second conditions. Perception of object identity or distinctness was assessed by presenting the infants, after habituation, with fully visible events involving one or two objects (figure 4.6). Patterns of looking at these test events provided evidence that the infants perceived object identity by analyzing the spatiotemporal continuity of motion, as do adults: when object motion was discontinuous, infants perceived two objects, each moving continuously through part of the scene. In contrast to adults, infants did not perceive object identity or distinctness by analyzing the apparent constancy or change of an object's speed of motion. The development of this last ability has not been investigated.

In summary, humans have some early-developing abilities to perceive the unity, the boundaries, and the identity of objects in visual scenes. These abilities are present before the onset of visually directed reaching or independent locomotion. Capacities to apprehend objects appear to emerge without benefit of trial-and-error motor learning.

Unlike adults, young infants fail to apprehend objects by analyzing the static configurational properties or the velocity relations of surfaces so as to form units that are maximally simple and homogeneous or that move in

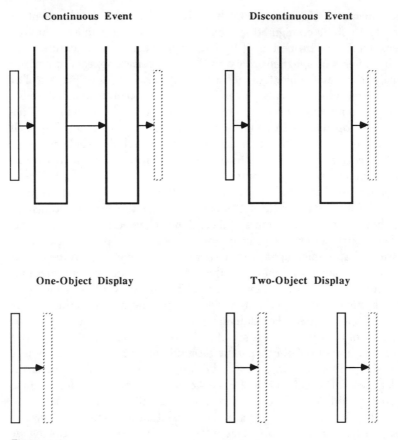

Figure 4.6
Habituation displays (top) and test displays (bottom) for an experiment on infants' apprehension of the identity of objects that leave and return to the field of view. An object's
initial and final positions are indicated, respectively, by solid and dotted lines (after Spelke
1988).

maximally regular ways. Some of the latter abilities have been shown to emerge quite early in development, however, before infants can locomote around objects or communicate with others about them. Capacities to perceive objects thus appear to be extended spontaneously over the course of early development.

Experiments on infants' perception of objects cast doubt on the two theories with which we began. Contrary to empiricist theory, infants can perceive the unity and boundaries of certain objects before they can reach for objects or locomote around them. Contrary to Gestalt theory, however, infants fail to perceive objects by organizing arrays of surfaces into units with the most regular shapes, colors, and textures. This failure is especially striking, because experiments provide evidence that infants do detect these configurational properties (for discussion, see Spelke 1988). Infants detect the static configurational properties of a visual scene, but they do not appear to use these properties when they divide the scene into objects. Young infants divide surfaces into objects only by analyzing the three-dimensional arrangements and motions of surfaces.

On the positive side, young infants appear to apprehend objects by analyzing the arrangements and the motions of surfaces so as to form units that are *cohesive* (the units are spatially connected and move as wholes), *bounded* (the units are spatially distinct from one another and move independently), and *spatiotemporally continuous* (the units exist continuously and move on connected paths). What kind of mechanism could accomplish this?

Two sets of experiments provide evidence that the mechanism of object perception is quite central. The first studies, by Kellman (see especially Kellman, Gleitman, and Spelke 1987), investigated the conditions under which infants perceive object unity from surface motion. In particular, the experiments investigated whether infants perceive the unity of an object by analyzing the two-dimensional displacements of its images in a relatively low-level representation (such as Marr's primal sketch) or by analyzing the three-dimensional displacements of its surfaces in a higher-level representation (such as Marr's $2\frac{1}{2}$-D sketch).

Infants were presented with a center-occluded object under four conditions of motion (figure 4.7). In the first condition both the infant and the object were stationary. In the second condition the infant was stationary and the object moved laterally, producing both image and surface displacements. In the third condition the infant was moved in an arc around the stationary object; the motion of the infant produced nearly the same two-dimensional displacement of the object's images as the object motion in the second condition, without any true displacement of the object's surfaces. In the fourth condition the infant again was moved in an arc but the object moved so as to cancel any two-dimensional displacement of the object's images. Infants were found to perceive the unity of the object in

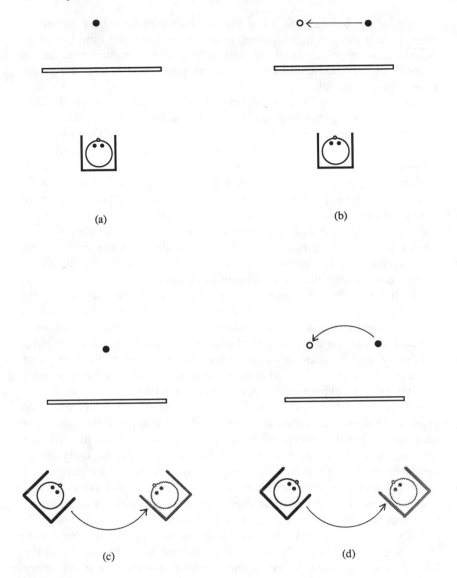

(a)

(b)

(c)

(d)

Figure 4.7
Habituation displays for experiments on the effects of motion on object perception, seen from above (after Kellman and Spelke 1983 and Kellman, Gleitman, and Spelke 1987). The displays present (a) neither image motion nor object motion, (b) both image motion and object motion, (c) image motion but no object motion, and (d) object motion but no image motion.

the second and fourth conditions, in which the object moved, but not in the first or third condition, in which it did not. Two-dimensional image displacements were neither necessary (fourth condition) nor sufficient (third condition) for perception of object unity. It appears, therefore, that mechanisms for perceiving objects take as input representations of the three-dimensional layout as it is perceived, rather than operating on more primitive, two-dimensional image representations. Representations of objects are constructed after, and on the basis of, representations of three-dimensional surface arrangements and motions.

The second series of studies, by Streri and Spelke (1988, in press), investigated object perception in the tactile mode. In particular, the experiments investigated whether infants perceive the unity and boundaries of objects under the same conditions when they feel objects as when they see them. Four-month-old infants held two spatially separated rings, one in each hand, under a cloth that blocked their view of the rings and of the space between them (figure 4.8). In different conditions the rings either could be moved rigidly together or could be moved independently, and they either shared a common substance, texture, and shape or differed on these dimensions. Perception of the connectedness or separateness of the rings was tested by means of a habituation-of-holding-time method similar to that used with visual displays (for details, see Streri and Spelke 1988).

The infants were found to perceive the two rings as a single unit that extended between their hands if the rings could only be moved rigidly together; they perceived the rings as two distinct objects separated by a gap if the rings could be moved independently. Perception was unaffected by the static configurational properties of the ring displays. These findings indicate that 4-month-old infants perceive object unity and boundaries under the same conditions in the visual and tactile modes. That finding, in turn, suggests that the mechanisms of object perception are amodal. Humans may not be endowed with visual and tactile mechanisms for perceiving objects; we may perceive objects by means of a single set of mechanisms, located more centrally in the brain, that operate on representations of surfaces derived from either sensory modality.

All these findings suggest that perceiving objects may be more akin to *thinking* about the physical world than to *sensing* the immediate environment (Spelke 1988). That suggestion, in turn, echoes suggestions from philosophers and historians of science that theories of the world determine the objects one takes to inhabit the world (Quine 1960; Kuhn 1962; Jacob 1970). Just as scientists may be led by their conceptions of biological activities and processes to divide living beings into organs, cells, and molecules, so infants may divide perceived surfaces into objects in accord with implicit conceptions that physical bodies move as wholes, separately from one another, on connected paths.

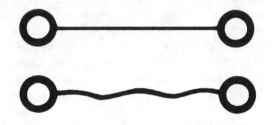

Figure 4.8
Habituation displays for an experiment on infants' perception of object boundaries through active touch (Streri and Spelke 1988).

4.3.5   Overview

Before human infants can reach for objects to manipulate them, they can already perceive objects as bounded, as complete, and as persisting over occlusion, under certain conditions. As Köhler proposed, mechanisms for organizing the world into objects may be present and functional before infants learn about particular objects and their properties, and they may serve as a foundation for such learning.

Nevertheless, young infants do not appear to experience the same arrangements of objects that adults do. When they face a stationary array such as that in figure 4.3, they do not segment that array into objects by analyzing relationships such as edge and surface continuity, or color and texture similarity, in accord with a tendency to maximize figural goodness. The development of this tendency is not understood, but it appears to be a long and gradual process. Gestalt organizational phenomena may not depend, at any age, on general rules or wholistic processes but rather on a wealth of slowly accumulated knowledge about objects and their properties. If that is the case, then there are aspects of object perception in infancy that lend some support to empiricist conceptions of perceptual learning.

Research on the mechanisms of object perception in infancy suggests that those mechanisms are relatively central in two respects: they take as input a representation of the surface layout as it is perceived, rather than operating directly on more primitive sensory representations, and they are amodal, operating on representations derived from different perceptual systems. Object perception may depend on the same mechanisms for adults, despite the rapidity and the apparent "impenetrability" of the processes by which we as adults apprehend the things around us. Here is a case in which studies of infancy may shed light on mature cognitive processes: they may reveal processes that operate throughout life but that are hard to discern in adulthood beneath the layers of skills and knowledge that adults have acquired.

There is a second way in which studies of infants may shed light on the perceptual knowledge of adults. The properties that infants appear to find in the things around them—cohesion, bounds, and spatiotemporal continuity—are among the properties that are most central to our mature intuitive conceptions of physical bodies. Adults conceive quite easily of physical bodies with poor Gestalt properties: bodies that are irregular in shape (rocks), heterogeneous in substance (vacuum cleaners), and subject to complex patterns of motion (flags). We do not readily consider something as a physical body, however, if it lacks cohesion (a pile of leaves), bounds (a drop of water in a pool), or continuity (a row of flashing lights). The latter entities may be collections of objects or parts of objects, but they are not unitary and independent objects for us.

These observations suggest that the infant's first mechanisms for apprehending objects remain central to human perception and thought. As in the case of depth perception, early-developing capacities to apprehend objects may remain powerful capacities for adults. These capacities may be enriched but not fundamentally changed by the wealth of further abilities whose acquisition they support. Studies of infancy may help to reveal what these core capacities are.

Suggestions for Further Reading

The best place to start on the nativist-empiricist debate is to plunge into the writings of some of its original protagonists, especially Descartes (1637, 1638), Berkeley (1709), J. S. Mill (1865), Hering (1864), and Helmholtz (1866, especially chapter 26). Herrnstein and Boring (1965) collect key excerpts from these sources, and Hochberg (1959) offers a summary and discussion of the work of these writers and others. Kitcher (forthcoming) provides an excellent discussion of Kant's (1781) philosophy as it pertains to issues in cognitive science. On Gestalt psychology, Koffka (1935) provides an introduction, and Hochberg (1974) provides a retrospective overview and critique. The Gestalt experiments of Gottschaldt and others have been translated, in abridged form, by Ellis (1939).

Those who wish to explore the voluminous literature on adaptation to rearrangements of visual space may choose from a number of guides. Rock (1966) provides a review and discussion that is still illuminating, especially if complemented by the updating of Welch (1974). To delve more deeply into this literature, and into the controversies it has engendered, readers may turn to papers by Held (1965), Harris (1980), Wallach (1976, chapter 10), and Bedford (1989).

Banks and Salapatek (1983) give a good general introduction to the sensory capacities of infants and a brief discussion of perception of space and form. Gibson and Spelke (1983) provide an introductory discussion of infants' perception of surfaces, objects, and events. For more detailed discussions of surface perception in infancy, see the papers by Held (1985), Yonas and Granrud (1984), and Banks (1988). Spelke provides methodological (1985) and theoretical (1988) reviews of research on object perception in infancy.

There are few studies of the origins and development of surface and object perception in nonhuman animals. This lack is especially regrettable, since animal research is indispensable to the study of the neural basis of perception, and it provides a variety of means to address the nativist-empiricist controversy (through studies of newborn, precocial animals, for example, and through controlled-rearing experiments). Binocular functions relevant to stereopsis have been studied quite extensively in animals (for a review, see Mitchell 1988). Capacities for motion-based depth perception and for object perception, in contrast, have received less attention. If this chapter stimulates any beginning investigator to study when and how infant rats, cats, or monkeys begin to perceive depth from motion or to segment the continuous visible layout into units, it will have served its prupose.

Questions

4.1 In the case of adaptation to visual rearrangements of space, there seems to be a relation between the size of the set of rearrangements perceivers can adjust to and the amount of experience that is needed to make each adjustment: the more limited the changes are that a perceiver can adapt to, the less experience the adaptation requires. Why might this be true? Should it be true for all cases of visual learning? All cases of learning?

4.2 Design an experiment to test whether human infants can adapt to prism spectacles that change the visible directions of objects. Would you expect infants to adapt to this change?

4.3 Human infants have been found to begin using the Gestalt relation of good continuation as information for object continuity over occlusion between 5 and 7 months of age. How might one study the relative contributions of maturation and of learning to this developmental change?

4.4 Do inexperienced animals perceive the continuous existence of an object that moves fully out of view? Design an experiment to address this question, with the species and method of your choice.

References

Aslin, R. N. (1988). Anatomical constraints on oculomotor development: Implications for infant perception. In A. Yonas, ed., *Perceptual development in infancy. The Minnesota Symposia on Child Psychology, Vol. 20.* Hillsdale, NJ: L. Erlbaum Associates.

Banks, M. S. (1988). Visual recalibration and the development of contrast and optical flow perception. In A. Yonas, ed., *Perceptual development in infancy. The Minnesota Symposia on Child Psychology, Vol. 20.* Hillsdale, NJ: L. Erlbaum Associates.

Banks, M. S., and P. Salapatek (1983). Infant visual perception. In M. M. Haith and J. Campos, eds., *Infancy and biological development.* Vol. 2 of P. Mussen, ed., *Handbook of child psychology.* New York: Wiley.

Bedford, F. (1989). Constraints on learning new mappings between perceptual dimensions. *Journal of Experimental Psychology: Human Perception and Performance* 15, 232–248.

Berkeley, G. (1709). *Essay toward a new theory of vision.* Dublin.

Brunswik, E., and J. Kamiya (1953). Ecological cue-validity of "proximity" and of other Gestalt factors. *The American Journal of Psychology* 66, 20–32.

Descartes, R. (1637). *Discourse on method.* Leiden: Maire. (Numerous translations are available.)

Descartes, R. (1638). *The optics.* Leiden: Maire. (Several translations are available.)

Ellis, W. D. (1939). *A source book of Gestalt psychology.* New York: Harcourt, Brace.

Fantz, R. L. (1961). The origin of form perception. *Scientific American* 204, 66–72.

Gibson, E. J., and E. S. Spelke (1983). The development of perception. In J. H. Flavell and E. Markman, eds., *Cognitive development.* Vol. 3 of P. Mussen, ed., *Handbook of child psychology.* New York: Wiley.

Gibson, E. J., and R. D. Walk (1960). The "visual cliff." *Scientific American* 202, 64–71.

Gibson, J. J. (1966). *The senses considered as perceptual systems.* Boston: Houghton Mifflin.

Gottschaldt, K. (1926). On the influence of experience on the recognition of figures. *Psychologische Forschungen* 8, 261–317. (Edited and translated in Ellis 1939.)

Harris, C. S. (1963). Adaptation to displaced vision: Visual, motor, or proprioceptive change? *Science* 140, 812–813.

Harris, C. S. (1980). Insight or out of sight? Two examples of perceptual plasticity in the human adult. In C. S. Harris, ed., *Visual coding and adaptability.* Hillsdale, NJ: L. Erlbaum Associates.

Held, R. M. (1965). Plasticity in sensory-motor systems. *Scientific American* 213, 84–94.

Held, R. M. (1985). Binocular vision: Behavioral and neuronal development. In J. Mehler and R. Fox, eds., *Neonate cognition.* Hillsdale, NJ: L. Erlbaum Associates.

Helmholtz, H. von (1866). *Treatise on physiological optics, Vol. III.* (Translated by J. P. C. Southall, Optical Society of America, 1925.)

Hering, G. (1864). *On the theory of spatial organization of the eye*. Leipzig: Engelmann. (A selection is translated in Herrnstein and Boring 1965.)

Herrnstein, R. J., and E. G. Boring, eds. (1965). *A source book in the history of psychology*. Cambridge, MA: Harvard University Press.

Hochberg, J. E. (1959). Nativism and empiricism in perception. In L. Postman, ed., *Psychology in the making*. New York: Knopf.

Hochberg, J. E. (1974). Organization and the Gestalt tradition. In E. C. Carterette and M. P. Friedman, eds., *Handbook of perception*. Vol. 1: *Historical and philosophical roots of perception*. New York: Academic Press.

Hofsten, C. von (1982). Eye-hand coordination in newborns. *Developmental Psychology* 18, 450–461.

Hofsten, C. von (1986). Early spatial perception taken in reference to manual action. *Acta Psychologica* 63, 323–335.

Jacob, F. (1970). *The logic of life*. Paris: Gallimard. (Translated by B. E. Spillman. New York: Pantheon, 1972.)

Kanizsa, G. (1979). *Organization in vision*. New York: Praeger.

Kant, I. (1781). Critique of pure reason. Tr. N. Kemp Smith. London: Macmillan (1929).

Kellman, P. J., H. Gleitman, and E. S. Spelke (1987). Object and observer motion in the perception of objects by infants. *Journal of Experimental Psychology: Human Perception and Performance* 13, 586–593.

Kellman, P. J., and E. S. Spelke (1983). Perception of partly occluded objects in infancy. *Cognitive Psychology* 15, 483–524.

Kitcher, P. (forthcoming). Kant's transcendental psychology. Oxford: Oxford University Press.

Koffka, K. (1935). *Principles of Gestalt psychology*. New York: Harcourt, Brace.

Köhler, W. (1947). *Gestalt psychology*. London: Liveright.

Kuhn, T. S. (1962). *The structure of scientific revolutions*. Chicago: University of Chicago Press.

Longuet-Higgins, H. C., and K. Prazdny (1980). The interpretation of a moving retinal image. *Proceedings of the Royal Society of London* B208, 385–397.

Michotte, A., R. Thinès, and G. Crabbé (1964). *The amodal completion of perceptual structures*. Louvain, Belgium: Publications Universitaires de Louvain.

Mill, J. S. (1865). *An examination of Sir William Hamilton's philosophy*. London.

Mitchell, D. E. (1988). The recovery from early monocular visual deprivation in kittens. In A. Yonas, ed., *Perceptual development in infancy. The Minnesota Symposia on Child Psychology, Vol. 20*. Hillsdale, NJ: L. Erlbaum Associates.

Quine, W. V. O. (1960). *Word and object*. Cambridge, MA: MIT Press.

Rock, I. (1966). *The nature of perceptual adaptation*. New York: Basic Books.

Schmidt, H. (1985). Gestalt perception in early childhood. Doctoral dissertation, Department of Psychology, University of Pennsylvania, Philadelphia, PA.

Spelke, E. S. (1985). Preferential looking methods as tools for the study of cognition in infancy. In G. Gottlieb and N. Krasnegor, eds., *Measurement of audition and vision in the first year of postnatal life*. Norwood, NJ: Ablex.

Spelke, E. S. (1988). Where perceiving ends and thinking begins: The apprehension of objects in infancy. In A. Yonas, ed., *Perceptual development in infancy. The Minnesota Symposia on Child Psychology, Vol. 20*. Hillsdale, NJ: L. Erlbaum Associates.

Streri, A., and E. S. Spelke (1988). Haptic perception of objects in infancy. *Cognitive Psychology* 20, 1–23.

Streri, A., and E. S. Spelke (in press). Effects of motion and figural goodness on haptic object perception in infancy. *Child Development*.

Ullman, S. (1979). *The interpretation of visual motion*. Cambridge, MA: MIT Press.

Wallach, H. (1976). *On perception*. New York: Quadrangle.

Wallach, H., and D. N. O'Connell (1953). The kinetic depth effect. *Journal of Experimental Psychology* 45, 205–217.

Welch, R. B. (1974). Research on adaptation to rearranged vision: 1966–1974. *Perception 3,* 367–392.

Wertheimer, M. (1923). Principles of perceptual organization. *Psychologische Forschungen* 4, 301–350. (Edited and translated by M. Wertheimer in D. C. Beardslee and M. Wertheimer, eds., *Readings in perception*. Princeton, NJ: Van Nostrand, 1958.)

Yonas, A., and C. E. Granrud (1984). The development of sensitivity to kinetic, binocular, and pictorial depth information in human infants. In D. Ingle, D. Lee, and M. Jeannerod, eds., *Brain mechanisms and spatial vision*. Amsterdam: Nijhoff.

Chapter 5

Seeing, Believing, and Knowing

Fred Dretske

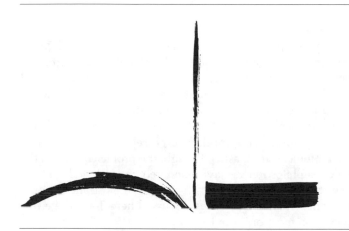

Epistemology is a branch of philosophy devoted to the study of knowledge and topics—such as truth, memory, perception—relating to knowledge. Epistemology is a philosopher's version of cognitive studies.

Truth is an important part of this study because a central conception of knowledge is knowledge *of the truth*. Though you can know that something isn't so—that, say, the cat *isn't* under the sofa—you can't know something —that the cat *is* under the sofa—that isn't so. To know the whereabouts of the cat requires one to be in possession of the truth about the cat's location. This being so, the idea of truth, as a necessary condition for knowledge, has figured prominently in philosophical discussions of cognition.

Memory and perception also occupy a prominent place in epistemology. Much of our knowledge (some would say *all* of our knowledge) is acquired

This chapter was prepared while I was a Fellow at the Center for Advanced Study in the Behavioral Sciences, Stanford, California. I am grateful for the financial support of the Center, the National Endowment for the Humanities grant FC-20060-85, and the Andrew W. Mellon Foundation.

by perceptual means: we come to know where the cat is by seeing it on the sofa. We might also hear, smell, and feel the cat. These are some of the ways we have of finding out, ways of coming to know, the content and character of our world. The general term for such ways of finding out, ways of coming to know, is *perception*. *Memory* is the name we give to the ways we have for retaining (through time) the acquired knowledge. Powerful mechanisms for acquiring knowledge (keen eyesight, for example) are of little value to animals that cannot remember, if even for a few seconds, anything they learn. A large storage capacity, on the other hand, is wasted on systems with no way of getting information to be stored.

As earlier chapters reveal, there has been a dramatic increase in our scientific understanding of *how* we know some of the things we know. Nevertheless, despite this progress, certain classical philosophical problems, problems concerning the nature, scope, and limits of visual cognition, remain unanswered—or, better, remain without answers that command widespread assent. As we learn more about the way things actually work, these problems tend to be expressed in somewhat different ways. In the past forty years, for instance, computer terminology, a terminology that is embodied in information-processing models of perception and cognition, has become popular. Nomenclature aside, though, the problems are still the old problems, the ones philosophers have pondered and debated for centuries. John Locke, the famous seventeenth-century philosopher, would have little trouble understanding the issues discussed here. Indeed, he had well-developed views on most of these topics.

Although some find it frustrating, this continuing lack of agreement about the right answers to certain puzzling questions—the so-called philosophical questions—is not unexpected. Problems tend to be classified *as* philosophical when they elude established methods, including scientific methods, of solution. But this is no reason to belittle the problems or to despair of their eventual solution. Solutions may lie in finding better methods. This chapter is an attempt to survey some of the more intractable of these problems, to indicate options for dealing with them, and to introduce, when it seems useful, appropriate distinctions and clarifications.

5.1   Seeing Objects and Seeing Facts

When cognitive scientists speak of visual perception, it seems reasonable to suppose that they are referring to something that we normally describe using the verb *to see*. Seeing the cat on the sofa is to visually perceive the cat on the sofa.

To avoid misunderstanding, though, one should ask, at the very beginning, whether visual perception (or seeing) is to be reserved for objects, facts, or something else. After all, we normally speak of seeing objects (like cats and sofas), the properties of objects (the color of a cat, the size of the sofa), events (the cat's jumping onto the sofa), states of affairs (the cat's being on the sofa), and facts (*that* the cat is on the sofa). If these are all to be counted as instances of visual perception, as they appear to be in ordinary language, then care must be taken in a scientific study of visual perception to specify *what* is being perceived: an object, a property, an event, a state of affairs, or a fact. For it is not at all clear that the *same* processes and mechanisms are, or need be, involved in the perception of these different things. Quite the contrary.

Consider, for example, a small child glancing at the sofa and mistaking a sleeping cat for an old sweater. Does the child see an object? Yes, of course. Besides the sofa there is an object, the black cat on the sofa, that the child mistakenly believes to be a black sweater. Though the child does not recognize the cat (*as* a cat), she must, in some sense, see the cat in order to mistake it for a sweater. Nevertheless, though the child sees a black cat on the sofa, sees an object fitting this description, she does not realize that this is a correct description of what she sees. She thereby fails to see the corresponding fact: *that* there is a black cat on the sofa. She sees an object (the black cat on the sofa) but not the fact (that there is a black cat on the sofa) corresponding to it. Shall we say, then, that the child *perceives* the black cat on the sofa? The answer to this question will obviously depend on whether one is thinking of objects (black cats) or facts (that they are black cats).

We can, of course, merely stipulate that visual perception is a way of seeing objects that involves, in some essential way, a knowledge of the object. So when a child—or, indeed, any other kind of animal (an unsuspecting mouse, for instance)—sees a cat on the sofa without realizing what it is, without learning or coming to know that it is a cat, then this way of seeing the cat will not count as *perceiving* the cat. To perceive a cat is, according to this way of using words, to come to know, by visual means, by the use of one's eyes, that it is a cat. Perception is restricted to seeing facts—to seeing that a cat is a cat.

We are free to use words as we please. There is nothing to prevent our restricting visual perception to visual cognition, to a coming-to-know-by-visual-means. It would seem that this particular restriction is, in fact, rather widespread in cognitive psychology. Interested, as they are, in what subjects learn in their perceptual encounters with objects, cognitive psychologists tend to focus on a subject's recognition or identification of objects, ways of seeing (hearing, smelling) things that require some knowledge of what is seen (heard, smelled). So, for instance, recognizing a geometric figure *as* a triangle requires the subject to realize, to come to know, upon seeing it, that it *is* a triangle. If he, upon seeing it, doesn't know what kind of figure it is, doesn't at least distinguish it from other sorts of figures, then he doesn't *recognize* it—not, at least, *as* a triangle. Recognizing triangles is a way of seeing a fact—the fact, namely, that they are triangles.

We are indeed free to use words as we please. But this proposed restriction of visual perception to the perception of facts, to recognition, to a way of seeing things that requires a knowledge of the thing seen, has unfortunate consequences. For we now have no natural way of describing the child who mistakes the cat for a sweater. Since the child does not know it is a cat, she does not, on this way of using words, *perceive* the cat. What, then, is the relation that exists between the child and the cat? The child is not blind. Light rays, reflected from the cat, are entering the child's eyes and, in some perfectly normal way, causing within her a visual experience that would be quite different if the cat were not there. This being so, it seems most natural to say, from a commonsense standpoint, that the child sees the cat but does not realize that this is what she sees. If, because of the way we have decided to use the word *perception*, this does not count as perceiving the cat, it must surely count as *seeing* the cat. Using the word *perception* in this restricted way, then, would not let us count, as visual perception, a person's seeing a cat in perfectly normal circumstances.

It seems preferable, therefore, to distinguish between seeing objects and seeing facts, not (as above) by artificially reserving the word *perception* for one way of seeing, the way of seeing that requires knowledge of the thing seen (that is, seeing facts), but rather by distinguishing two forms of perception, two ways of seeing. We are then free to speak of seeing a black cat without necessarily realizing (knowing or believing) that it is a black cat (or, indeed, an animal at all) as, say, *sense perception* (of a black cat), and another, recognitional, way of seeing the cat as, say, *cognitive perception* (that it is a black cat). This brings our use of the term *visual perception* (including as it now does both cognitive and sense perception) into closer harmony with the ordinary verb *to see* and at the same time allows us to preserve the important distinction between seeing a cat on the sofa and seeing what it is that is on the sofa.

Given this way of using words, we are then free to describe the efforts of cognitive scientists as investigating the processes underlying these forms of perception, examining their differences and commonalities. Perhaps it will turn out, for instance, that processes described as early vision are merely the processes involved in sense perception, the seeing of objects, and later vision comprises whatever additional conceptual or cognitive processes are essential to the perception of facts (cognitive perception) relating to these objects. Perhaps, also, debates about whether perceptual processes are top-down or bottom-up, about the inferential or constructive character of perceptual processes, about whether these processes are massively parallel or sequential, and about their modularity are all debates that can be given sharper focus by distinguishing between the *kind* of perception the debate is a debate about. Discussions or perceptual learning and development will also benefit by a close observance of the difference between cognitive and sensory forms of perception.

For these reasons we will adopt in this chapter the device of speaking of sensory and cognitive perception. The first is a way of seeing (or perceiving) cats (or triangles) that does not require (though it may in fact be accompanied by) knowledge that it is a cat (or a triangle) that is seen. This is what we have been calling *object perception. Cognitive perception* of a cat (or triangle) will be reserved for that way of seeing the cat (triangle) that necessarily involves a coming to know, a cognition (in fact, a recognition), that it is a cat (a triangle). If one, as we ordinarily describe things, sees a cat (a triangle) and recognizes it only as an animal (a figure) of some sort, fails (for whatever reason) to know or realize that it is a cat (a triangle), then one has sensory, but not cognitive, perception of a cat (triangle). Cognitively one perceives only an animal (figure) of some (unspecified) sort. I leave open the question (but see question 5.1) of whether it is possible to have sensory perception of an object without *any* cognitive perception of it— whether, for instance, one might see a cat without recognizing it as anything whatsoever (not even as an animal of some sort).[1]

5.2 Perceptual Objects

Many, perhaps most, of our cognitive perceptions, the facts we come to know by visual means, are mediated in some way. Our visual knowledge of A depends on, and derives from, our visual knowledge of B. We see that we need gas (come to know, by visual means, that we need gas) by seeing that our fuel gauge registers "empty." We see one fact (that our gas tank is nearly empty) by seeing another fact (that our gauge registers "empty"). We see *by the newspapers* that there has been a tragic plane crash, *by the*

---

1. The topic of *seeing as*—at one time a fashionable topic in the philosophy of perception— is a hybrid form of perception, a way of seeing that goes beyond sensory perception (requiring a fairly specific cognitive or judgmental attitude or tendency on the part of the perceiver) but falling short of full cognitive perception (knowledge not being required). One sees a stick as a snake. The stick obviously does not have to *be* a snake for one to see it as a snake. Hence, this cannot be cognitive perception, at least not cognitive perception of a snake (for this would require one to recognize it as a snake, something one cannot do of something, like a stick, that is not a snake). Nonetheless, one sees (sensory perception) the stick and takes or judges it to be a snake. The knowledge required of cognitive perception (knowing that the X is an X) is replaced by some variant of belief: one believes, or is inclined to believe, or would believe if one did not know better, of the object (it may or may not be an X) that it is an X.

tracks that the animal went this way, *by her frown* that she is displeased, and *by the thermometer* that the patient has a fever.

Given this dependence of some visually known facts on other visually known facts, the question naturally arises whether some facts are basic in the sense of being known directly and without this kind of dependence on other visually known facts. If my knowledge of the plane crash derives, or is somehow inferred, from my knowledge of what is printed in the newspapers, if my knowledge of what other people are thinking and feeling is somehow inferred from what I can see of their observable behavior and expression, are the latter pieces of knowledge themselves derived from some more fundamental, even more basic, kind of knowledge—possibly a knowledge of how the light (reflected from a newspaper page or a person's face) is structured, how this light is affecting my eyes, or how my brain is reacting to all these external events? Might it turn out, as some philosophers have argued, that all our knowledge of external, objective, facts—that there was a plane crash, that the newspaper reports a plane crash, that Susan is displeased, that she is frowning—derive, ultimately, from our knowledge of subjective facts, facts about the current state of our own mind (how things look)?

This is a question about cognitive perception, about the structure of our knowledge. Are there some facts we know that are fundamental—*foundational*, as philosophers like to put it—in the sense that all other things we know are derived from them? Is our knowledge of the way the world *is* derived from, and ultimately dependent upon, our knowledge of the way the world *appears*?

The answer to this question depends on the answer to a somewhat different question, a question about sense perception. What objects do we see? Do we see cats, sofas, newspapers, and people? If not, then it would seem that our knowledge of these things (the fact, for instance, that the newspapers say there was a plane crash and the fact that Susan is frowning) must derive from our factual knowledge about other things (whatever objects we do see). My knowledge of the plane crash derives from my knowledge of the newspapers because I did not *see* the plane crash. I see only the newspaper. Hence, whatever facts I learn about the plane crash, including the fact that there was a plane crash, must derive from facts I learn about the newspaper.

What facts we see, and which of these facts are fundamental, therefore depends on what objects we see. If you don't see the gas tank, then your visual knowledge of the gas tank, that it still contains gas, must derive from your visual knowledge about whatever objects you do see—in this case, typically, facts about your fuel gauge. You see that you have some gas left *by* seeing what your gauge registers, and this dependence among cognitive perceptions (your knowledge of the gauge being primary) derives from a fact about sensory perception, from the fact, namely, that you see the gauge but not the tank.

Even when we speak of perceiving one object *by, through,* or *in* perceiving another—in the way we speak, for instance, of seeing the game *on* TV or seeing someone *in* a movie (or photograph)—our knowledge of the game or person will be secondary relative to our knowledge of the electronic or photographic image. Insofar as we regard the image appearing on our television or movie screen as the primary, or real, *object* of perception, we regard facts about these images as cognitively primary. Facts about the people and events being represented are secondary. For instance, we learn (see) that a player kicked a field goal by observing the behavior of the electronically produced images of the player, the ball, and the goalposts appearing on our television screen.

Hence, a question about the structure of cognitive perception—whether in fact there is a fundamental level of visual knowledge, and if so, whether this is knowledge of objective or subjective facts—awaits the answer to a prior question: What is the structure of sense perception? What objects do we see? The answer to this question will constrain, if not determine, the answer to the questions about cognitive perception. If we do not see physical objects, if we are (in sense perception) always aware of mental images (representations) of external objects (as some philosophers and psychologists seem to believe), then our knowledge of objective reality (if, indeed, we have such knowledge) will necessarily be derivative from and secondary to our knowledge of our own mental states.

Discussions of these issues are often clouded by failure to appreciate the difference between cognitive perception and sense perception. It is sometimes argued, for instance, that we do not perceive ordinary physical objects because, for whatever reason (the reason is usually skeptical in character), we do not know, or cannot be absolutely certain, that there *are* physical objects. For all we know, all experience, even the experience we take to be *of* a real external world, may be illusory. It could all be a dream. This argument, though it has a distinguished history, is a fairly obvious conflation of cognitive perception and sense perception. One does not have to know, let alone know for certain (whatever that might mean), that there are physical objects in order to see (sense perception) physical objects. Such knowledge is only required for cognitive perception. Just as the child described above saw a cat on the sofa without knowing what it was, it may turn out that we see ordinary physical objects (including cats and sofas) every moment of our waking life without ever being able to know (if the philosophical skeptic is right) that this is what we are seeing. Questions about what objects we see are quite different from questions about what facts we know.

Failure to keep the distinction between sense and cognitive perception clearly in mind also tempts students into mistakenly supposing that if our knowledge of physical objects is somehow derivative from the way they *appear* to us, from the way they *look*, then what we really perceive when (as we ordinarily say) we see a cat is an internal mental image of the cat. We see (as it were) the *look* or *appearance* of the cat. Such an inference would be fallacious because even if our cognitive perceptions rest on subjective foundations (on the way things look to us), our sense perceptions need not rest on similar foundations. We may know that there are physical objects by the way they appear to us (so that cognitive perception has, in this sense, a subjective basis), but our sense perception of objects is itself direct and unmediated. In other words, we may come to know (see) it is a cat (a fact) by the way it appears, but what we see (the object) is the cat itself, not its appearance.

Aside from these possible confusions, though, there are a variety of positions that have been, and continue to be, taken on the nature of both cognitive and sense perception—on what facts and objects are most immediately and directly seen. Though these theories, in both their classical and their modern form, are often hard to classify because of their failure to be clear about whether it is cognitive perception or sense perception they are talking about, they can be roughly characterized as follows.

Direct (Naive) Realism (sometimes said to be the view of the person-on-the-street) holds (1) that there is a real physical world, objects and facts whose existence is independent of our perception of them (this makes the view a form of physical *realism*) and (2) that under normal conditions we are, in a direct and unmediated way, perceptually aware of these objects and facts (hence, *direct* and therefore, according to its detractors, *naive* realism). In other words, what we are directly aware of in sense perception is, unlike a headache or an afterimage, something physical that continues to exist when we are no longer aware of it.

Representative Realism (also called the *Causal Theory of Perception*) shares with Direct Realism (and common sense) the first of these two doctrines. It disagrees, though, about the second. According to Representative Realism, our perception of physical objects is indirect, mediated by a more direct apprehension of something mental, some internal representation (hence the name *representative* realism) of external physical reality. These mental representations have been given various names: sensations, ideas, impressions, percepts, sense-data, experiences, and so on. But the idea is almost always the same. Just as we see what is happening on the playing field *by* seeing what is happening on our television screen (so that our knowledge of the game, when viewed on television, is indirect), so knowledge of even the most obvious physical fact—the fact, say, that there is a table (or, indeed, a television set) in front of us—is itself indirect. We see that there is a table in front of us *by* seeing, or somehow being aware of, its internal, mental representation. When we are watching a game on television, then, our knowledge of the actual game is *doubly* indirect: we know about a game occurring 1,000 miles away by knowing what is happening on a television screen a few feet away, and we come to know what is happening a few feet away by becoming aware of what is happening (presumably *no* distance away) in our own minds. In the last analysis, then, all our knowledge of objective (physical) fact rests on a knowledge of subjective (mental) fact because the only objects perceived (directly) are mental objects—the way things appear.

Going beyond these forms of realism are various forms of *idealism* (sometimes called *phenomenalism*), theories that deny an objective physical reality altogether. Everything that exists depends for its existence (like a headache or an afterimage) on someone's awareness of it; hence, everything is in the nature of a mental entity like an idea (hence, *idea*lism). Since these extreme views have few, if any, serious advocates within the philosophical (not to mention cognitive science) community today, we will leave them without further comment.

As indicated earlier, one might be a Direct Realist on sense perception but an Indirect Realist on cognitive perception. The objects we see are physical objects, but we know about them via their effect on us (the way they appear to us) in sense perception. The problem with this mixed position is the problem of saying just how one might come to know how objects look—which, according to some theorists, is a knowledge of how, in sense perception, we internally represent them—without thereby becoming aware of, and hence perceiving, the internal representations themselves (thereby becoming an Indirect Realist on sense perception also). To put it crudely, how can one *know* how things look without perceiving, or somehow being aware of, their look?

The debate between Direct and Indirect Realists becomes very technical at this point. Indirect Realists maintain that we are directly aware of mental objects—images—in hallucinations and dreams. Aside from the *cause* of the experience, though, there is no reason to distinguish between these illusory experiences and our ordinary veridical perception of (physical) objects. In both cases we are directly aware of the internal mental representation. When we speak, as we commonly do, of seeing an ordinary object (like a cat), we are, if we speak truly, being caused to experience some catlike image by a real cat (a real cat that we do not directly perceive). When we hallucinate or dream of a cat, there is no such external cause— hence, we speak of these experiences as illusory. In all cases, though, it is the image that we directly experience. Only the cause of the experience is different. Direct Realists try to counter this, and related, arguments by insisting that although sensory perception of real objects requires the having (and thereby the existence) of internal representations, and though such representations in fact determine the way these objects look or appear to us, there is no reason to suppose we perceive these representations themselves. We perceive a cat by (internally) representing a cat, not by perceiving an internal representation of a cat.

5.3   Perceptual Processes

The debate about the objects of perception is related to a debate (not always clearly distinguished from it) about the kind of processes underlying perception. Do perceptual processes, those culminating in our seeing something, exhibit the qualities of reason and intelligence? Do they, despite being unconscious, have an inferential or computational character, moving from premise to conclusion (deductive reasoning), or from data to explanatory hypothesis (inductive reasoning), in something like the way human agents consciously solve problems? When I see a cat on the sofa, or that there is a cat on the sofa, does my visual system do something similar to what clever detectives do when they infer, on the basis of certain clues and signs, that a certain state of affairs not directly apprehended *must be* the case?

We can, of course, metaphorically describe the operations of anything, even the simplest machine, in thoughtlike, semicognitive terms. We are especially fond of doing this with computers. We say they know, that they remember, recognize, infer, and conclude. If one counts arithmetical operations as forms of computation, even dime store calculators perform (or are *described* as performing) impressive feats of reasoning—multiplying, taking square roots, and calculating percentages in fractions of a second. We even speak of such comparatively humble devices as thermostats and electric eyes in quasi-perceptual terms—as, for example, "sensing" a drop in room temperature or the approach of a person and responding by turning the furnace on or opening a door. The question, then, is not whether we *can* speak this way, not even whether it is sometimes useful to talk this way (to adopt what Dennett (1987) calls the *intentional stance*), but whether this is anything more than a metaphorical crutch—a figure of speech that conceals or masks our ignorance about underlying causal processes and mechanisms. Do visual systems ever literally solve problems, infer that something is so, formulate (on the basis of sensory input) hypotheses about the distant source of stimulation in the way that rational agents do this at the conscious level?

Hermann von Helmholtz, the great nineteenth-century physiologist, thought so, and many investigators today (see, for example, Gregory 1974a, 1978; Rock 1977, 1983; Ullman 1980) are inclined to agree. At least they view the processing of visual information as a form of problem solving and hence as a form of reasoning that, though unconscious, exhibits enough of the essential properties of fully rational thought and judgment to make it, in a fairly literal sense, an instance of problem solving itself. The light reaching the receptors (sometimes called the *proximal stimulus*) carries information—fragmentary and impoverished (and thereby ambiguous) information to be sure, but information nonetheless—about distant situations (the *distal stimuli*). The visual system's function is to take these data and to construct, as best it can, a reasonable conjecture (hypothesis, judgment) about the distal source of this stimulation. It begins with premises describing receptor activity, data concerning the distribution and intensity of energy reaching the receptor surface, and is charged with the task of arriving at useful conclusions about the distal source of this stimulation. The conclusion it reaches (for instance, it must be a cat out there causing this pattern of retinal activity) constitutes the subject's perception of a cat. If the visual system reaches a different conclusion—that, for instance, it is probably an old black sweater—the subject sees an old black sweater instead of a fluffy black cat. If the perceptual system can't make up its mind, or keeps changing its mind (it's a cat; no, on second thought, it's probably a sweater; no, that can't be right, it's probably a cat), the subject sees first a cat, then a sweater, then a cat again. Though such flip-flopping seldom occurs when we are looking at real cats (because, in normal circumstances, light from real cats is generally richer in information—hence, less ambiguous—about the kind of object that has structured the light), it sometimes happens with specially constructed figures viewed under restricted (say, monocular) conditions—Necker cubes, for instance. Since so much emphasis is placed on the visual system's efforts at constructing a reasonable interpretation or hypothesis (about the distal stimulus) from information reaching the receptor surfaces, this approach to perceptual processing is often described as a *Constructivist* or *Computational* approach to visual perception.

Since Constructivists regard sensory stimulation, even in the best of viewing conditions, as inherently ambiguous (there are always a variety of distal arrangements that could have produced that pattern of proximal stimulation), they view perceptual processing as primarily a matter of *adding* information to the stimulus (or *supplementing* the information available in the stimulus) to reach a perceptual outcome: seeing a cat. Since the proximal stimulation does not unequivocally specify the distant object as a cat, and since we nonetheless (under optimal viewing conditions) see a cat (the visual system reaches this conclusion), the perceptual system must exploit some other source of information to reach this judgment—adding or supplementing (via some inductive inference) the information contained in the stimulus.

There has been a vigorous challenge to this (more or less) orthodox position in the last forty years. Gibson, in a series of influential books (1950, 1966, 1979) and articles (1960, 1972) has argued that the stimulus, *properly understood*, contains all the information needed to specify the distal state of affairs. If the proximal stimulus is understood, not as a static distribution of energy occurring on the receptor surfaces *at a time*, but as the total dynamic pattern of stimulation reaching a mobile observer *over time*, there is no need for inference, reasoning, and problem solving. There is sufficient information in the stimulus (thus broadly conceived) to specify (unambiguously determine) the character of the distal object. Why reason about what is out there when the stimulus tells you what is out there? Why suppose, as Constructivists do, that perceptual systems are smart detectives when all they really have to be (given reliable informants—that is, information-rich stimuli) is good listeners, good extractors of the information in the signals reaching the receptors? Since this approach tends to eliminate all intervening cognitive (indeed, all intervening psychological) mechanisms from the processes resulting in our perception of objects, it is often referred to as a *Direct Theory* of perceptual processing.

Relevant to the question of whether perceptual systems are more like good detectives doing their best with ambiguous data (Constructivism) or more like good listeners faithfully registering stimulus information (Direct Theory) is what Fodor (1983) describes as the *modularity* of information-processing systems. A system is (comparatively) modular when it is (comparatively) insulated from information available to other parts of the total system. If I am told (and thereby know) that it is a cat on the sofa, for instance, does this, *can* this, affect my visual perception of the cat? If not, my visual system exhibits modularity with respect to this kind of information (information available to the central processor from auditory sources). If this collateral information is capable of affecting what I see, then the visual system (understood as that subsystem responsible for my seeing what I see) is not modular in relation to this kind of information.

If the visual system is modular, its operation (and therefore presumably what the subject perceives) is unaffected by what other information may be available to other parts of the system (or what the subject may know as a result of information received from these other parts). Modular systems are therefore described as *stimulus-driven* (the processing is bottom-up rather than top-down): it is the stimulus itself (information at the bottom, as it were), not the system's (possibly variable) hypotheses about that stimulus (information available at the top) that guides the processing of incoming signals and thereby determines what the subject perceives. Modular systems are therefore most naturally thought of in the second of the two ways described above—as good extractors of preexistent information, information that is already in the stimuli, not as good detectives or problem solvers about the best interpretation of informationally ambiguous stimuli. There is no point in supposing that a process of reasoning is occurring in modular systems when the process, being modular, is not allowed to use information (other than what is in the stimulus itself) to generate perceptual conclusions. Modular systems are not intelligent. They don't have to be. They have no problems to solve. They just do what the stimulus tells them to do.

It is by no means obvious that these two approaches to the analysis of perceptual processes are incompatible. It may turn out, for example, that although the stimulus, properly understood, *is* rich in information about distal objects, rich enough (let us suppose) to unambiguously determine what distal objects produced it, it nonetheless requires inferential (reason-like) processes to decode the signal, to extract this information from the stimulus. Fingerprints, being unique to their bearers, may unambiguously determine or specify (in an information-theoretic sense) who held the gun. It nevertheless takes a good deal of problem solving, after one has discovered the incriminating prints, to figure out who held the gun. One has to know which people go with which prints, and this may take memory, inference, and prior learning (the sort of cognitive work that organizations like the FBI invest into the creation of a fingerprint file). As Ullman (1980, 380–381) puts it, the role of processing may not be to create information, but to extract it, integrate it, make it explicit and usable.

There are, then, a variety of ways of expressing questions about the nature of those processes underlying our perception of the world. But these questions should not be confused, as they often are, with questions about the objects of perception, the questions discussed in section 5.2. Gibson's views have been described (by both Gibson and others) as a theory of *direct* perception. This can be misleading. It certainly is confusing. The sense (if any) in which this theory is direct is much different from the sense in which Direct Realism is direct. Direct Realism is a theory about the *objects* of perception, about *what* we see. The kind of direct realism we are now talking about, the kind associated with Gibson's work, is a theory about the processes underlying perception, about *how* we see what we see. One can be a Direct Realist about the objects of perception, holding that we directly apprehend physical objects (not sensations or mental intermediaries), and be a Constructivist about the processes underlying our (direct) perception of these objects. One can suppose that intelligence, some kind of thought-like process, is involved in the construction of internal representations without supposing that one thereby sees (or in any way perceives) the representations so constructed. One can, in other words, be a Direct Realist about the objects of perception and an Indirect Realist, a Constructivist, about the processes underlying this direct relationship.

Once again, though, controversy about the intelligence, or lack of it, of perceptual processes is often muddled by failure to be clear about exactly which processes are in question. It should be obvious that cognitive perception—our perception of facts, our seeing *that* (and hence coming to know that) there is a cat on the sofa—is the result of a process that is strongly influenced by higher-level cognitive factors. Cognitive perception is clearly not modular. A subject who does not already know what a cat is, or does not already know what they look like—a small child or an inexperienced animal, say—will be unable to *see* (recognize) *what* is on the sofa, unable to *see that* there is a cat there (to be carefully distinguished from an ability to see the cat there). For cognitive perception of the cat on the sofa, in contrast to sense perception of the cat, requires not only the appropriate concepts (for *cat* and *sofa*) but some intelligence in the application of these concepts to the objects being perceived (the cat and the sofa). The upshot of cognitive perception is some *known fact* (say, that there is a cat on the sofa) and such facts are not learned without the cooperation of the entire cognitive system. By changing a subject's cognitive set—changing what the subject knows or believes about the way things look, for instance—one easily changes what the subject learns, comes to know, hence perceives in a cognitive way, about the objects it sees (in a sensory way). Some form of Constructivism or Computationalism is therefore inevitable for seeing *facts*.

The real question is, or should be, whether that part of the visual system given over to *sense perception*, to seeing objects (like cats and sofas), is also intelligent. Does *it* exhibit some (any? all?) of the marks of reasoned judgment? Is *it* modular?

The answer to this question will depend on just what one takes to be involved in the perception of objects, in seeing, say, a cat on the sofa or a person in the room. If the upshot or outcome of cognitive perception is some known fact—that there is a cat on the sofa or a person in the room—what is the upshot or culmination of sense perception? When, at exactly what stage in the processing of incoming information, do we see the cat on the sofa and the person in the room? If recognizing the object *as* a cat or *as* a person is not necessary to the sensory perception of these objects (as it is to their cognitive perception), what is necessary? Since we can see a cat at a distance, in bad lighting, or in unusual conditions (circumstances in which it does not even look like a cat), we cannot suppose, following Gibson, that to see a cat is to have information in the stimulus that specifies the cat *as* a cat. For in such cases there may be no information in the stimulus about what it is we see. That does not prevent our seeing it.

It is true, but unilluminating, to be told that the sensory perception of an object occurs when the visual system constructs a sensory representation of the object. What we want to know is what kind of representation a sensory representation is. If cognitive perception of a cat occurs when the system constructs a cognitive representation of the cat, an internal judgment or belief that it is a cat (some kind of internal description of the cat *as a cat*), what is a sensory representation of the cat, the kind of internal representation whose occurrence constitutes a sensory perception of the cat? Is it something like what philosophers and psychologists used to call a *sensation*? Or is it more like what they (or some of them) now call a *percept*? Or, to use even more fashionable jargon, is it more like what Marr (1982) and his associates call a $2\frac{1}{2}$-*D sketch*?

Until these questions are answered, we can expect little progress on questions about the nature of perception itself. How can we tell whether sensory perception is best thought of in terms of a clever detective or a good listener if we cannot say, in any clear way, what final product, what kind of internal representation, this kind of perception is supposed to produce?

5.4 Perceptual Change

Do we learn to see things? Does prolonged experience of the world change what we perceive or the way we perceive it? Do people with radically different languages, radically different ways of describing their surroundings, see their surroundings differently? Do completely different world views—what Kuhn (1962), for instance, calls *incommensurable scientific theories*—generate differences in what people can observe and, hence, in the data on which their theoretical differences rest?

Such questions have fascinated philosophers and psychologists, linguists and anthropologists, for centuries. The answers to these questions are not easy. Nevertheless, some things seem reasonably clear—if not the final answers themselves, then at least the sorts of considerations that must inform the search for final answers.

The first point, a point that has been made repeatedly in this chapter, is that before rushing in with answers to any of these questions, one should first be very clear about the question. What kind of perception is the question a question about?

As a case in point, the question about whether we learn to see things has a reasonably straightforward answer if it is a question about cognitive perception, about the facts we come to know by visual means. The first time (as a very small child presumably) I saw a maple tree I probably didn't know what kind of tree it was. Having no experience or knowledge of maple trees, being ignorant of what maple trees looked like (or, indeed, of what maple trees were), I didn't recognize what I saw *as* a maple tree. I didn't see what kind of tree it was. Now, however, I am quite expert in this kind of identification. I can look at maples, at least the more common varieties, and quickly recognize them as maples. I can see, by their general shape, their bark and leaf structure, *what kind of tree* they are, that they are maple trees. There has been a change, therefore, in my ability to cognitively perceive objects around me, a change that came about by experience, learning, and (in this case) diligent study and practice. Learning of this kind is a pervasive and familiar phenomenon.

But if the question about perceptual learning is a question about sensory perception, about the objects we see, about whether we learn to see maple trees themselves (and not just the fact that they are maple trees), the answer appears to be quite different. I did not learn to see maple trees. I could do that when I was a very young child—before I learned to recognize them. What I learned is how to identify the things I saw, things I therefore saw before I learned to identify them. Sensory perception of objects normally comes before the cognitive perception of these same objects. If it did not, there would be no way to learn what objects look like. How can you learn what objects look like if you cannot see them? Humans do not see things at the moment of birth, of course. Certain physiological changes must first occur before we can, for instance, focus on objects and coherently process information contained in light. But these maturational processes are not to be classified as *learning* in any ordinary sense. We no more learn to see solid objects than we learn to digest solid food.

This is not to say that some changes in our perception, our sensory perception, of objects may not occur after prolonged experience. Perhaps objects start looking different after they become familiar or after we know certain things about them. Does a familiar face—the face of a loved one, say—look different after it has become familiar from the way it looked the first time you saw it? Do coins look larger to poor children than they do to rich children? Do lines in an optical illusion that look to be of different lengths start looking the same after you learn (by measuring them) that they are the same length? These questions are questions about the way things look, about the character of our visual experience, about something we earlier dubbed (without really knowing or explaining what it was) the *sensory representation* of objects. They are not questions about the way we cognitively represent objects, about our perceptual beliefs or judgments. Changes and differences in cognitive representations are an obvious and familiar fact of life. That such changes exist is not worth arguing about (though the changes themselves are certainly worth studying). Changes, if any, in our sensory representations are not so obvious. Quite the contrary. To document such changes one has to be very clear about what sensory representations are and what constitutes a change in them. To answer questions about whether we learn to see in this sense, then, requires a clear, at least a much better, understanding of the nature of sensory representation, of what kind of internal response to an external object constitutes our seeing the object.

Similar remarks can be made about various forms of perceptual *relativity*. Is perception relative? Well, cognitive perception is certainly relative to many things—everything, in fact, capable of influencing what one comes to believe. If not having a word for X or a theory about X means I cannot come to have certain beliefs about X, then not having a word (or a theory) for X will prevent me from cognitively perceiving X. Without an appropriate language for talking about oxygen, without some knowledge (however crude) of chemical theory, I can hardly be expected to see *when* oxidation is occurring (see *that* it is occurring) even when it happens under my nose. I just will not recognize it—certainly not *as* oxidation. So the cognitive perception of oxidation is relative to those factors—factors like possession of the right concepts and knowledge of the appropriate scientific theories—that are essential to a knowledge that oxidation is occurring. For the same reason, people who have badly mistaken astronomical views will not be able to see what others see when a lunar eclipse occurs—that the moon is moving into the earth's shadow. They will not see that a lunar eclipse is occurring because, with mistaken views about what is happening (they think the gods are showing displeasure by extinguishing the moon), they will not learn what everyone else learns when they see the same thing: that the earth is casting a shadow on the moon.

But though cognitive perception is obviously relative in this way, there is no reason to think—in fact, there is a lot of reason *not* to think—that sensory perception is similarly relative. Though the astronomically ignorant may not see that an eclipse is occurring, they certainly see *the eclipse* (= the earth's shadow moving across the face of the moon). That, in fact, is what frightens them. And though the chemically ignorant can hardly be expected to see that oxidation is occurring, they can, given normal eyesight, witness the oxidation, the blazing fire, as well as everyone else.

To say that perception is relative to a certain factor is to say that our perception of things depends on that factor. Change that factor (enough) and we change what is perceived or, possibly, whether anything at all is perceived. To suggest, then, that sense perception is *not* relative to a variety of factors affecting our perception of facts is a way of suggesting that sense perception is comparatively modular. It is *not* sensitive to the cognitive influences (a subject's language, conceptual scheme, or scientific world view) that determine one's perception of facts. The issue of perceptual relativity, and more generally of perceptual change and learning, then, is merely another way of approaching questions raised in earlier sections of this chapter about perceptual processes in general. It seems, therefore, that the answers to a variety of questions, both philosophical (raised in this chapter) and scientific (addressed in earlier chapters), depends on a deeper understanding of perceptual processes and the different outcomes, sensory versus cognitive, that they support. Achieving deeper understanding of this sort will require the combined efforts of investigators from many fields.

Suggestions for Further Reading

For more detailed treatments of the distinction between the perception of objects and the perception of facts, and for a defense of the idea that sense perception does not require cognitive perception, that seeing is not (or at least not necessarily) believing, see Dretske 1969, 1978, 1981, Sibley 1971, and Warnock 1955. For opposing viewpoints (defending the idea that all perception involves, if not knowledge, then a kind of judgment or belief), read Armstrong 1961, Hamlyn 1957, Heil 1983, and Pitcher 1971.

For discussion of the issues surrounding the controversy between Direct (Naive) and Representative Realists about the objects of perception (whether we directly see physical objects or some mental surrogate), see Dretske 1969, 1981, Goldman 1977, Sanford 1976, and Chisholm 1957 for direct theories and Jackson 1977, Ayer 1956, 1962, and Price 1932 for indirect theories. A (by now) classic article on causal theories of perception is Grice 1961.

Concerning the question of whether perceptual processes are constructive or not, an exchange that brings out most of the issues can be found in Ullman 1980, an article in the Constructivist vein, and the comments on it (many of which defend a direct theory). For vigorous exposition and defense of Constructivism, see Gregory 1974a,b, 1978, Rock 1977, 1983, and Fodor and Pylyshyn 1981. Works generally supportive of a direct theory of perceptual processing (and therefore sympathetic to many of Gibson's ideas) include Turvey 1977, Mace 1977, Michaels and Carello 1981, and many of the contributions to Shaw and Bransford 1977 and Macleod and Pick 1974. For further discussion, including evaluations of the empirical status of these two approaches, see Hayes-Roth 1977, Johansson, von Hofsten, and Jansson 1980, and Epstein 1973.

For perceptual learning, change, and development, consult the references in chapter 4. For perceptual relativity, see Churchland 1979, 1988, chapter 5 of Dretske 1969, Hanson 1958, Kuhn 1962, Brown 1987, and Shapere 1982.

Questions

5.1 Is sensory perception possible without cognitive perception? Can one see an object—like a cat—without thereby coming to know *something* (not necessarily that it is a cat) about it? If not, does this mean that some kind of conceptual ability (whatever is needed to know) is necessary for vision—the ability to see things?

   Do animals see the same things we do? Do they have beliefs? If so, do they have the same kind of beliefs we have? Does every animal with eyes (and therefore, presumably, vision—the ability to see things) have thoughts?

5.2 Is it possible to see facts while seeing no objects—to have cognitive perception without sense perception? What is the best way to describe what happens when one detects a change in overall illumination (that the lights went out, say) with one's eyes closed? Is this a case of seeing a fact (that the lights went out) without seeing an object?

5.3 Is seeing an event (the cat's jumping on the sofa) and a state of affairs (the cat's being on the sofa) more like seeing objects (the cat on the sofa) or more like seeing facts (that the cat is on the sofa)? What is required to see the properties of objects—say, the size or color of a cat? Does one see the color of a black cat when one sees another (different) object of the same color (say, a black ball)?

5.4 Are objects and facts seen in dreams and hallucinations? Or does one merely dream (or hallucinate) that one is seeing an object or a fact? (Is this difference, the difference between seeing an object in one's dream and dreaming one sees an object, a *real* difference?) Are these colored things (of which one is aware in dreams and hallucinations) in the mind? Are there round red things *in the brain* when one dreams of something red and round?

5.5 If a star explodes and disappears when the light from it is still on its way to earth, does one nonetheless still see the star when the light reaches the earth many years later? If so, does this mean that one can see things that do not exist (any longer)? If not, what (if anything) does one see when the light from the star enters one's eyes and gives rise to an "experience" of a twinkling spot of light?

5.6 Are experts in a given field—auto mechanics (on cars), cooks (on food), and tailors (on fabrics), for instance—able to see things that the nonexpert, the layperson, cannot see? How is one to interpret auto mechanics' claims that they can *hear* things that laypeople can't hear—that, for example, a car's valves need adjusting or that it needs a tune-up? What kind of perception is this?

References

Armstrong, D, M. (1961). *Perception and the physical world.* London: Routledge and Kegan Paul.

Ayer, A. J. (1956). *The problems of knowledge.* London: Penguin Books.

Ayer, A. J. (1962). *The foundations of empirical knowledge.* London. Macmillan.

Brown, H. (1987). *Observation and objectivity.* Oxford. Oxford University Press.

Chisholm, R. (1957). *Perceiving: A philosophical study.* Ithaca, NY: Cornell University Press.

Churchland, P. (1979). *Scientific realism and the plasticity of mind.* Cambridge: Cambridge University Press.

Churchland, P. (1988). Perceptual plasticity and theoretical neutrality: A reply to Jerry Fodor. *Philosophy of Science* 55, 167–187.

Dennett, D. (1987). *The intentional stance.* Cambridge, MA: MIT Press.

Dretske, F. (1969). *Seeing and knowing.* Chicago: University of Chicago Press

Dretske, F. (1978). The role of the percept in visual cognition. In C. Wade Savage, ed., *Perception and cognition.* (Minnesota Studies in the Philosophy of Science 9.) Minneapolis, MN: University of Minnesota Press.

Dretske, F. (1981). *Knowledge and the flow of information.* Cambridge, MA: MIT Press.

Epstein, W. (1973). The process of "taking-into-account" in visual perception. *Perception* 2, 267–285.

Fodor, J. (1983). *The modularity of mind.* Cambridge, MA: MIT Press.

Fodor, J., and Z. Pylyshyn (1981). How direct is visual perception?: Some reflections on Gibson's "ecological approach." *Cognition* 9, 139–196.

Gibson, J. J. (1950). *The perception of the visual world.* Boston: Houghton Mifflin.

Gibson, J. J. (1960). The concept of the stimulus in psychology. *American Psychologist* 15, 694–703.

Gibson, J. J. (1966). *The senses considered as perceptual systems.* Boston: Houghton Mifflin.

Gibson, J. J. (1972). A theory of direct visual perception. In J. R. Royce and W. W. Rozeboom, eds., *The psychology of knowing.* New York: Gordon and Breach.

Gibson, J. J. (1979). *The ecological approach to visual perception.* Boston: Houghton Mifflin.

Goldman, A. (1977). Perceptual objects. *Synthese* 35, 257–284.

Gregory, R. (1974a). Choosing a paradigm for perception. In E. C. Carterette and M. P. Friedman, eds., *Handbook of perception.* Vol. 1: *Historical and philosophical roots of perception.* New York: Academic Press.

Gregory, R. (1974b). Perceptions as hypotheses. In S. C. Brown, ed., *Philosophy of psychology*. London: Macmillan.

Gregory, R. (1978). *Eye and brain: The psychology of seeing*. 3rd ed. New York: McGraw-Hill.

Grice, P. (1961) The causal theory of perception. *Proceedings of the Aristotelian Society, Supplementary Volume 35*.

Hamlyn, D. W. (1957). *The psychology of perception*. London: Routledge and Kegan Paul.

Hanson, N. R. (1958). *Patterns of discovery*. London: Cambridge University Press.

Hayes-Roth, F. (1977). Critique of Turvey's "Contrasting orientations to the theory of visual information processing." *Psychological Review* 84, 531–535.

Heil, J. (1983). *Perception and cognition*. Berkeley, CA: University of California Press.

Jackson, F. (1977). *Perception*. Cambridge: Cambridge University Press.

Johansson, G., C. von Hofsten, and G. Jansson (1980). Event perception. *Annual Review of Psychology* 31, 27–63.

Kuhn, T. S. (1962). *The structure of scientific revolutions*. Chicago: University of Chicago Press.

Mace, W. M. (1977). James Gibson's strategy for perceiving: Ask not what's in your head, but what your head is inside of. In Shaw and Bransford 1977.

Macleod, R. B., and H. L. Pick, Jr. eds. (1974). *Perception: Essays in honor of James J. Gibson*. Ithaca, NY: Cornell University Press.

Marr, D. (1982). *Vision: A computational investigation into the human representation and processing of visual information*. San Francisco: W. H. Freeman.

Michaels, C. F., and C. Carello (1981). *Direct perception*. Englewood Cliffs, NJ: Prentice-Hall.

Pitcher, G. (1971). *A theory of perception*. Princeton, NJ: Princeton University Press.

Price, H. H. (1932). *Perception*. London: Methuen.

Rock, I. (1977). In defense of unconscious inference. In W. Epstein, ed., *Stability and constancy in visual perception*. New York: Wiley.

Rock, I. (1983). *The logic of perception*. Cambridge, MA: MIT Press.

Sanford, D. (1976). The primary objects of perception. *Mind* 85, 189–208.

Shapere, D. (1982). The concept of observation in science and philosophy. *Philosophy of Science* 49, 485–525.

Shaw, R., and J. Bransford, eds. (1977). *Perceiving, acting and knowing*. Hillsdale, NJ: L. Erlbaum Associates.

Sibley, F. N. (1971). Analyzing seeing. In F. N. Sibley, ed., *Perception*. London: Methuen.

Turvey, M. T. (1977). Contrasting orientations to the theory of visual information processing. *Psychological Review* 84, 67–88.

Ullman, S. (1980). Against direct perception. *Behavioral and Brain Sciences* 3, 373–415.

Warnock, J. (1955). Seeing. *Aristotelian Society Proceedings* 55.

Action

Action: Introduction

John M. Hollerbach

Actions such as walking, speaking, looking around a room, or grasping a pencil are so automatic and easy for us that we may be tempted to understimate the information-processing complexity of human movement (also referred to as motor control). Yet underlying even seemingly simple tasks like flexing our elbows is a highly complex neural and biomechanical apparatus whose functioning we are just beginning to understand.

The six chapters of "Action" provide just a sampling of the research that has been done on the control of human movement, and even then confined to just two aspects: the control and sequencing of arm and hand movements, and the control of eye movements. Nevertheless, arm and eye movements are two of the better-understood motor competences, and they provide a good introduction to general issues of motor control.

Understanding motor control requires an understanding of many topics: properties of neural circuitry, sensory receptors, and muscle; the mechanics of movement, including kinematics and dynamics; control theory; and movement planning, including the planning of sequences. Chapter 1 provides a brief introduction to these topics, and later chapters build and rely upon this background. Chapters 2 and 5 deal primarily with planning issues, and chapters 3 and 4 primarily with control. Chapter 2 examines what the planning variables and coordination strategy are for arm movement. Chapter 3 considers how arm movement may be controlled. Chapter 4 considers the control of eye movement, which has special features that distinguish it from arm movement. Chapter 5 deals with motor sequences in typewriting. Chapter 6 reflects on the philosophy of action.

Insofar as possible, verbal descriptions are given of technical concepts. Yet there is a limit to the use of language to describe motor control, and the use of mathematics is inevitable. A basic knowledge of geometry, trigonometry, algebra, and physics is assumed. For those with a more advanced mathematical background, including calculus and differential equations, more technical details are provided and set off with rules. It is not necessary for those without this background to understand the ruled-off material in order to read the chapters, however.

Chapter 1

Fundamentals of Motor Behavior

John M. Hollerbach

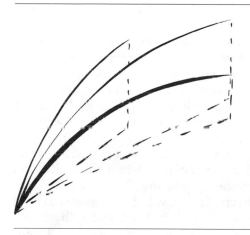

In this introductory chapter on the control of movement, we will begin by drawing a distinction between planning and control for movement. We will consider the mechanics of motion in both its geometrical aspect (kinematics) and its force aspect (dynamics). We will define trajectory planning in terms of a set of coordinates and a coordination strategy. We will examine trajectory control in terms of two basic alternatives: feedforward control versus feedback control. We will look at elementary control concepts in the context of feedback control, and then see how intrinsic muscle properties may facilitate this type of control. Finally, we will consider the role of motor programs in providing an organizing structure for motor sequences or chains of movement.

This research was supported by NIH grant AM26710. I would also like to acknowledge support from an NSF Presidential Young Investigator Award. This chapter was produced using facilities of the MIT Artificial Intelligence Laboratory, partially supported by DARPA contract N00014-85-K-0124.

1.1 Planning versus Control

To begin this introduction to movement, it will prove useful to separate planning from control. Generally speaking, planning processes generate the movement goals or intents, and control processes are responsible for realizing the planning goals.

When we reach for a cup full of coffee and carry it to the mouth for drinking, planning enters in several ways. First we visually define the target, the location of the cup and its shape. From the cup shape, we determine how the hand should enclose the cup to grasp it stably. Then we plan a coordination strategy for moving the arm from its current position to the cup, and from the grasp location to the mouth.

This is just the sketch of a plan, and details and exceptions must be taken into account. For example, in addition to grasping the cup stably, the hand must grasp it in a configuration that will allow us to tilt and drink from it. Holding the cup from the top is no good in this situation; grasping it by the handle might be our best choice, if indeed it has a handle. In moving the arm and hand to the cup, we must be sure nothing is in the way that we could bump into. If there is, we will have to fashion a trajectory around this obstacle. Once we grasp the cup, we should move it carefully to avoid spilling. We should keep it level during transport, which means the hand orientation must be strictly controlled. (Note that this requirement was absent in initially reaching for the cup.) Spilling will also be minimized if we move the cup smoothly, preferably in a straight line and with smooth acceleration and deceleration. If the cup is not well insulated and there is no handle, we will want to make this movement rather quickly to avoid being burned. If grasping a cup while walking past a counter, we must take into account the velocity of the whole body with respect to the cup.

All of this seems obvious and easy, and we don't hesitate in grabbing a cup for drinking. Yet imagine that you were faced with the task of programming a robot arm on a computer to pick up a cup. You would have to take into account every tedious detail and possibility. Robotics researchers are continually faced with just this kind of task in trying to make manipulators more capable, and they have contributed to our understanding of human motor control by pointing out serious difficulties that might otherwise be glossed over or even not recognized. The fact that we can pick up a coffee cup so easily is a reflection, not of the triviality of the task, but of the enormous sophistication of our motor control systems and their learning abilities.

It is up to the control processes to ensure that every aspect of the movement plan is carried out. The hand has to grasp the cup with enough but not excessive force to hold it without slipping. To accomplish this, we have to estimate how much the cup weighs and how slippery the surface is, a task that humans do quite precisely (Johansson and Westling 1984). If the arm has not brought the hand to an appropriate position for grasping, we make use of the tactile sensing in our fingers to adjust the hand position.

In moving the arm to the cup or to the mouth, the joints must be coordinated so that the hand position and orientation are as planned. Thus, to hold the cup level, the wrist and shoulder joints must be coordinated. Appropriate muscle forces must be generated to move the arm in the desired manner.

If a motion goes awry, it can be the fault either of the planning or of the control processes. For example, if the liquid spills during transport, it is probably because we were not able to control the cup's orientation or acceleration sufficiently well. On the other hand, if the planning processes determine that just the index finger through the handle of a heavy cup is an appropriate grasp shape, then there may be nothing the control processes can do to hold the cup steady because just one finger is too weak to grasp the handle. In this case it is the plan that is flawed, even though it appears that the control has failed.

In the next two sections we will look at some of the planning and control issues that will be dealt with in more detail in the following chapters.

1.2   Kinematics

Kinematics is concerned with the geometry of the external world, the geometry of a limb, and the transformations between them. To describe either geometry, a sufficient number of variables must be chosen. In this section we will look at how the positions of objects in space can be described, how arm position can be described, and what kinematic transformations hold between arms and objects.

1.2.1   Locating Objects in Space

Location is a set of variables that completely specifies where an object is in space. In our normal three-dimensional world an object location is specified by six variables, three for *position* and three for *orientation*. For position, one possibility is to choose the *Cartesian coordinates* (x, y, z) of a reference point, such as the center of a cup or a point on the cup handle (figure 1.1). For orientation, another common choice is the *roll, pitch,* and *yaw* angles. (Imagine you are flying a plane. If you climb or dive, you are changing the pitch angle. If you turn left or right, you are changing the yaw angle. If you rotate about the long axis of the plane, you are changing the roll angle.)

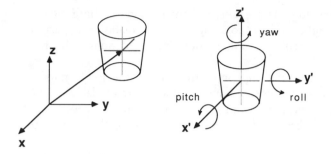

Figure 1.1
Six variables are required to locate an object in space. For this cup, a reference point has been chosen in the cup center, and the Cartesian coordinates (x, y, z) of the reference point measure its position with respect to a global coordinate system. If coordinate axes (x', y', z') are placed at the reference point that are intrinsic to the cup, then the orientation of the cup's coordinate system with respect to the global coordinates can be described by roll, pitch, and yaw angles.

The hand itself can be considered an object in space and hence requires six variables to be located. As in the example of the cup in figure 1.1, three variables are required to locate the position of a reference point on the hand, and three variables are required to describe the orientation of the hand with respect to a reference coordinate system. The goal in grasping can then be restated as matching the position and orientation of the hand to the position and orientation of an object.

1.2.2   Describing Arm Configuration

Limbs of the body such as arms and legs are made of segments connected together at joints. For example, the arm is composed of an upper arm segment connected to the torso by the shoulder joint, a forearm segment connected to the upper arm by the elbow joint, and a hand segment connected to the forearm by a wrist joint. In addition, there are a number of finger segments connected to the hand. What is the best way to describe the geometry of a limb, given that the relative position of two neighboring segments is constrained by a joint?

Consider the elbow joint, which is a *hinge joint* that rotates the forearm about a fixed axis relative to the upper arm like a door swinging about its hinges. For the case of the door, one possibility for describing its geometry is to consider that the door is a three-dimensional object and hence requires six variables to describe its location. However, the door is not free to move in six directions relative to the wall, because its movement is constrained by the hinges. In fact, the door can only rotate about a vertical axis defined by the hinges (let's call this the yaw motion). It cannot translate horizon-

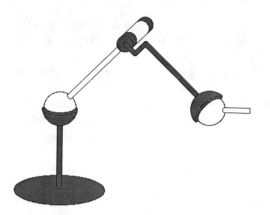

Figure 1.2
Kinematics of the human arm include a spherical shoulder joint, a rotary or hinged elbow
joint, and a spherical wrist joint.

tally or vertically, and it cannot rotate in the roll or pitch directions. In
reality, only one variable is required to describe where the door is relative
to the wall at any point in time: the yaw angle about the hinges. Consequently, the door is said to have one *degree of freedom*: when it moves, it
is free to do so in only one direction.

Since the elbow joint is geometrically equivalent to the door's hinge
joint, it is also only necessary to use the elbow joint angle to locate the
forearm relative to the upper arm. Thus, the elbow joint is a one degree-of-
freedom joint.

Another major kind of joint connecting limb segments is the *spherical
joint*, like the shoulder joint, the wrist joint, and the eyeball. Unlike a hinge
joint, a spherical joint requires three variables to describe the relative
location of the attached limb segments. Think of a ball joint in a socket,
such as the eyeball. The position of the center of the eyeball cannot be
changed relative to the socket, but the orientation of the eyeball can be
arbitrarily changed. Since three variables are required to describe orientation, the eyeball is a three degree-of-freedom joint. For the shoulder joint,
if we think of the upper arm as an airplane, then we can change the pitch,
yaw, and roll of the upper arm. Similarly, the wrist is a spherical joint with
three degrees of freedom (though we cannot achieve all roll, pitch, and yaw
angles with the wrist because of joint limits imposed by bones and tendons).

Considering all joints and limb segments, then, the human arm consists
of a three degree-of-freedom shoulder joint, a one degree-of-freedom elbow joint, and a three degree-of-freedom wrist joint (figure 1.2). (Here we
do not count shrugging movements of the shoulder or intrinsic movements
of the fingers.) In total, the human arm has seven degrees of freedom.

Therefore, only seven variables are required to describe its geometry in the most parsimonious way. The set of joint angles that completely specify the geometry of the arm is called its *configuration*.

The net result of motion of all of the arm joints is to change the position and orientation of the hand in space. The structure of these joints is such as to allow the hand to assume any position and orientation, within constraints imposed by joint angle limits and the outer workspace boundary (points of maximum reach). The hand therefore has the ability to execute six degree-of-freedom motion.

Let us now reexamine the task of grasping. In the terminology we have been using, an object in space has six degrees of freedom. Since the structure of the human arm also allows the hand to have six degrees of freedom, it is possible for the hand to match the position and orientation of any object within its reach.

In turn, we can conceive that the goal of the arm control system is to chase the disembodied moving hand. The wrist, elbow, and shoulder angles must be changed to match the position and orientation of this hand. One advantage of thinking of arm movement this way is that the hand operations can be planned without worrying about the arm. The hand can then be viewed as an ideal effector that can attach to objects and generate positions and forces. Since the hand can rigidly grasp objects, in turn we could just plan the movements of objects in space in a manner suited to a task. Of course, the arm control system imposes constraints on this process and must be sufficiently sophisticated to realize it.

If the arm has seven degrees of freedom, what happened to the extra degree of freedom considering that the hand has six degrees of freedom? The arm's extra degree of freedom is manifested as an internal motion of the limb segments that does not move the hand. If you fix your hand position by grasping something rigid and immobile such as the edge of a table, you will still find it possible to swing the elbow about a line joining the shoulder joint to the wrist joint. This situation is called a *kinematic redundancy*, because the arm has one degree of freedom in excess of that required for general positioning. During this internal motion, the wrist and shoulder joint angles are changing in a fixed relationship, and the elbow joint does not vary. Therefore, specifying the hand location is not adequate to specify the joint angles of the arm, because many joint angles can yield exactly the same hand location. Possible advantages of redundant human arm kinematics include obstacle avoidance and joint limit avoidance, by using the arm's internal motion for finding a better configuration.

In robotics, general-purpose manipulators in fact have just six degrees of freedom. Many of these manipulators have a geometry similar to that of the human arm, except that the shoulder is a two degree-of-freedom joint (yaw and pitch angles) rather than a three degree-of-freedom spherical joint. More generally, in order to grasp an object in space, an arm must have at least as many independent degrees of freedom as the object. For objects in three-dimensional space, if our arms did not have at least six degrees of freedom, then either we could not move our arms to the object or we could not orient our hands properly to grasp it.

1.2.3   Inverse Kinematics

In order to attach the arm to the hand or to grasp an object with the hand, the *inverse kinematics* transformation must be solved: given the position and orientation of the hand or of an object in space, find the joint angles that locate the arm or hand at that point. The *direct kinematics* transformation goes in the other direction: given the joint angles, find the hand location. The adjectives *inverse* and *direct* refer to the direction between the more intrinsic variables (joint angles) and the more extrinsic variables (hand position), a direct transformation going from intrinsic to extrinsic variables and an inverse transformation the other way.

In general, inverse kinematics is conceptually much more difficult than direct kinematics. Calculating the hand position given the joint angles is always straightforward, but the inverse is not. In fact, from a mathematical standpoint the inverse kinematic transformation is only computationally efficient if the mechanical linkage is structured in one of a few ways. One such structure is the presence of a spherical joint, usually at the wrist, which allows separation of positioning from orienting. Most robot manipulators are designed with spherical wrists. It is probably no accident that humans have spherical wrist joints as well. As noted earlier, the human arm actually is redundant because it has seven degrees of freedom. It has been argued that the particular kinematic arrangement of spherical wrist, hinged elbow, and spherical shoulder joint is optimal in terms of the advantages of such redundancies.

The nonlinear mapping between joint angles and external coordinates is a crucial aspect of movement. The difficulty of dealing with this nonlinear mapping has far-reaching implications both for planning and for control, and much of the discussion in this chapter and those that follow concerns various ways of coming to grips with it.

1.2.4   Planar Two-Link Manipulator

Although the discussion to this point has taken into account the full kinematic complexity of the human arm, the studies in chapters 2 and 3 use a reduced model of the arm confined to a plane (figure 1.3). In this plane the shoulder joint is confined to rotate in the same direction as the elbow joint; hence, the shoulder joint has only one degree of freedom with respect to this plane. The wrist joint is considered to be frozen, so that the hand is

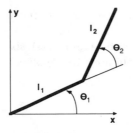

Figure 1.3
A reduced model of the human arm, where the shoulder joint has a single degree of freedom measured by angle θ_1 and the elbow joint has the degree of freedom measured by θ_2. The lengths of the two links are l_1 and l_2, and the endpoint is located by the Cartesian coordinate (x, y).

lumped in with the forearm. Therefore, only the shoulder joint θ_1 and the elbow joint θ_2 are capable of movement. Located in the distal end of the forearm is a reference point with Cartesian position (x, y). (*Distal* refers to the end of a limb that is farthest from the body, and *proximal* to the end closest to the body.) The term *endpoint coordinates* is often used to refer to the Cartesian coordinates of the distal end of the forearm.

This reduced arm configuration, known as a *planar two-link manipulator*, has been extensively studied in motor control and in robotics. Reasons for studying just this reduced arm movement include ease of experimentation and analysis. Nevertheless, even two-joint arm movement is sufficiently rich to develop and illuminate many issues in movement planning and control. Corresponding to the two degree-of-freedom planar arm movement, objects in a plane will be considered to have two translational degrees of freedom.

Although the eyeball is a spherical joint, for purposes of modeling and experimentation in chapter 4, once again the degrees of freedom of the system are restricted to a horizontal plane. The eyeball is then a one degree-of-freedom joint with respect to this plane. Notice that in either the one or the three degree-of-freedom case, kinematics is a trival issue, since the joint and task variables are the same.

1.3   Trajectory Planning

Trajectory planning is the time evolution of kinematic variables. Thus, a trajectory has both spatial and temporal aspects: the spatial aspect is the sequence of locations of an arm or object from start to goal (a *path*), and the temporal aspect is the time dependence along a path. We will refer to the planning variables as *coordinates* and to the form of the trajectory as the *coordination strategy*.

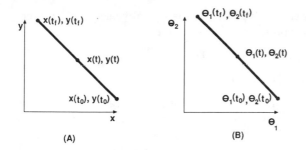

Figure 1.4
Straight-line paths in terms of endpoint Cartesian coordinates (a) and joint angles (b).

Abstractly, any set of kinematic variables can serve as a trajectory plan. One common set is the Cartesian coordinates of the hand, which for the planar two-link manipulator are the tip coordinates (x, y). In addition, it is necessary to define a coordination strategy, which defines a path and a time dependence along the path. The simplest path is a straight line in these Cartesian coordinates (figure 1.4a):

$$\frac{y(t) - y(t_0)}{x(t) - x(t_0)} = \frac{y(t_f) - y(t_0)}{x(t_f) - x(t_0)}. \tag{1}$$

Here the Cartesian variables $(x(t), y(t))$ have been expressed as a function of time t. The initial point at time t_0 is given by $(x(t_0), y(t_0))$ and the final point at time t_f by $(x(t_f), y(t_f))$.

The straight-line form (1) does not explicitly indicate how time evolves during the trajectory. This dependency is made clear in the interpolation form, by introducing a common time function $f(t)$ that parameterizes each variable:

$$x(t) = (x(t_f) - x(t_0))f(t) + x(t_0)$$
$$y(t) = (y(t_f) - y(t_0))f(t) + y(t_0). \tag{2}$$

The time function starts and stops appropriately ($f(t_0) = 0$ and $f(t_f) = 1$). A simple example of a time function is a constant velocity from start to finish ($f(t) = (t - t_0)/(t_f - t_0)$). It is important that exactly the same time function $f(t)$ be used for each variable; otherwise, a straight line would not result (see question 1.1).

Another possibility for a trajectory plan is the use of joint angles. Similar to the use of Cartesian coordinates, we could choose a straight line in terms of joint angles as the path (figure 1.4b):

$$\frac{\theta_1(t) - \theta_1(t_0)}{\theta_2(t) - \theta_2(t_0)} = \frac{\theta_1(t_f) - \theta_1(t_0)}{\theta_2(t_f) - \theta_2(t_0)}. \tag{3}$$

Again, the time dependence along the path is best revealed by the interpolation form, which in robotics is called *joint interpolation*:

$$\theta_1(t) = (\theta_1(t_f) - \theta_1(t_0))f(t) + \theta_1(t_0)$$
$$\theta_2(t) = (\theta_2(t_f) - \theta_2(t_0))f(t) + \theta_2(t_0).$$

(4)

If the trajectory plan is formed in terms of endpoint variables, then it is necessary for the motor processes to solve the inverse kinematics problem to find the joint angles that correspond to the sequence of endpoint positions. On the other hand, if the trajectory plan is formed in terms of joint angles, then an inverse kinematics transformation is obviously not required (we already have the joint angles). This is an advantage for joint angle planning, but the disadvantage is the loss of endpoint control along the trajectory. Chapter 2 goes into more detail on the pros and cons of joint angle versus endpoint variable planning.

To undertake the study of trajectory planning in human motor systems, the first step therefore is to infer the set of planning variables. The second step is to infer how the planning variables coevolve—in other words, to infer the coordination strategy. Chapter 2 explores in detail whether arm movement planning is done in terms of endpoint coordinates or joint coordinates and whether interpolation is the coordination strategy—problems of considerable depth that are not easy to answer.

Eye movements present a slightly different picture of trajectory planning. In fast-phase movements the eyes are servoed on position error (see chapter 4). The shape of the velocity profile is similar to that for the hand, except that the eye profile is slightly asymmetrical, with the velocity peak occurring somewhat earlier. In slow-phase movements the eye is tracking a slowly moving target. In this case the eye trajectory is primarily determined by the outside target.

1.4   Dynamics

In order to make the limbs move, torques must be exerted about the joints by the muscles. *Dynamics* is the relation between joint torques and joint position, velocities, and accelerations. When the problem is to find the joint torques corresponding to the desired time sequence of joint angles derived from a trajectory planner, the transformation is referred to as *inverse dynamics*. When the problem is to find the joint motion corresponding to a known sequence of input torques, the transformation is referred to as *direct dynamics*; direct dynamics is the process required to simulate or predict movement. Here again, the adjectives *direct* and *inverse* refer to the direction of transformation between the more intrinsic variables (in this case joint torque) and extrinsic variables (in this case joint angles).

Under the hypothesis that the motor control system is attempting to generate movement according to a plan, it must come to grips with inverse dynamics. In section 1.5 we will consider how the motor control system might do this; for the moment we will continue to examine inverse dynamics and why it is a difficult problem in controlling limb movement.

The inverse dynamic equations for the two-link planar manipulator of figure 1.3 are presented below, under the assumptions that the center of gravity of each link lies midway on the line joining the two ends of the link and that gravity g points downward (Brady et al. 1982). The symbols in this equation are τ_i for joint torque, m_i for link mass, and I_i for link rotary inertia about the center of gravity.

$$\tau_1 = \ddot{\theta}_1 \left(I_1 + I_2 + m_2 l_1 l_2 \cos \theta_2 + \frac{m_1 l_1^2 + m_2 l_2^2}{4} + m_2 l_1^2 \right)$$

$$+ \ddot{\theta}_2 \left(I_2 + \frac{m_2 l_1 l_2}{2} \cos \theta_2 + \frac{m_2 l_2^2}{4} \right)$$

$$- \dot{\theta}_2^2 \frac{m_2 l_1 l_2}{2} \sin \theta_2 - \dot{\theta}_1 \dot{\theta}_2 m_2 l_1 l_2 \sin \theta_2$$

$$+ g \left(\frac{m_2 l_2}{2} \cos(\theta_1 + \theta_2) + l_1 \left(\frac{m_1}{2} + m_2 \right) \cos \theta_1 \right)$$

$$\tau_2 = \ddot{\theta}_1 \left(I_2 + \frac{m_2 l_1 l_2}{2} \cos \theta_2 + \frac{m_2 l_2^2}{4} \right) + \ddot{\theta}_2 \left(I_2 + \frac{m_2 l_2^2}{4} \right)$$

$$+ \dot{\theta}_1^2 \frac{m_2 l_1 l_2}{2} \sin \theta_2 + g \frac{m_2 l_2}{2} \cos(\theta_1 + \theta_2)$$

Gravity torques: Terms preceded by the symbol g are the gravity torques at the two joints.
Inertial torques: For joint 1 the torque due to its own acceleration $\ddot{\theta}_1$, and for joint 2 the torque from $\ddot{\theta}_2$.
Reaction torques: For joint 1 the torque due to acceleration $\ddot{\theta}_2$ of joint 2, and for joint 2 the torque from $\ddot{\theta}_1$.
Centripetal torques: For joint 1 the term with $\dot{\theta}_2^2$ due to joint 2 motion, and for joint 2 the term with $\dot{\theta}_1^2$ due to joint 1 motion.
Coriolis torque: For joint 1 the term with $\dot{\theta}_1 \dot{\theta}_2$. There is no Coriolis torque at the elbow.

Dynamics is difficult because of the presence of complex interaction forces among moving joint segments, including gravity torques, inertial torques, reaction torques, centripetal torques, and Coriolis torques. Let us begin with *gravity torques*. If you make your arm straight and hold it horizontally in front of you, then gravity is exerting the maximum torque about the shoulder. The center of gravity of the outstretched arm is roughly at the elbow joint, and the force of gravity exerts a torque about the shoulder through the lever from the shoulder to the center of gravity. If you now bend your elbow 90 degrees, then the center of gravity of the arm moves closer to the shoulder and the gravity torque about the shoulder is less because the moment arm is smaller. (A moment arm is the lever through which a force is exerted on a point of rotation. The longer the lever, the less force is required to exert a given torque.) Finally, if you make your arm straight and hold it vertically, then gravity exerts no torque about the shoulder because the moment arm is zero. Thus, the gravity torques at joints depend on the configuration of the arm.

Inertial torques are torques due to acceleration of bodies. The familiar Newton's second law, $f = ma$, says that to accelerate a mass m linearly with acceleration a takes a linear force f. Euler's equation is the corresponding relation for rotation, $\tau = I\ddot{\theta}$, which says that to rotate a body with inertia I about a fixed point with angular acceleration $\ddot{\theta}$ requires a torque τ.[1] For the two-link planar manipulator, the inertia at the shoulder joint has the additional complexity of depending on the elbow angle.

Acceleration at one joint also creates *reaction torques* at all the other joints. Suppose you place a pencil flat on a frictionless glass surface and push on one end of the pencil with your finger. The pencil will rotate about its center of gravity corresponding to the acceleration of the end being pushed. It is the same with your arm. Picture your forearm as the pencil and the upper arm as the finger, which pushes against the forearm at the elbow joint like the finger pushed the pencil. Thus, moving your upper arm will cause your elbow to rotate. Analogously, moving your elbow will cause your shoulder to rotate. If you suddenly flex your elbow, your shoulder will accelerate as well due to the presence of these reaction torques.

Another intersegment interaction torque is due to *centripetal acceleration*. If you whirl a ball tied to a string in a circle above your head, then there is a centripetal acceleration directed along the string that keeps the ball in a circular orbit rather than flying off into space. Analogously, the forearm whirls in an orbit about the shoulder joint, attached to it by the upper arm.

---

1. This Euler's equation is a reduced version of the three-dimensional law that is somewhat more complex due to a six-dimensional inertia matrix and the presence of gyroscopic torques, but we will use the planar version because it corresponds to the reduced kinematics of the studies in this chapter and those to follow.

Thus, a centripetal torque must exist at the elbow joint. Similarly, there is also a centripetal torque about the shoulder due to elbow rotation.

The most exotic and computationally most complex of the interaction torques is the *Coriolis torque*, due to the interaction of rotating coordinate systems. An example of Coriolis forces is provided by weather patterns. The rotation of the earth creates prevailing westerly winds due to drag on the atmosphere. At the same time there is a flow of warm to cold air from the equator to the north pole. The interaction of the two air flows creates counterclockwise vortical forces in the northern hemisphere, which explains why the clouds circle counterclockwise.

For arm movement, the interacting rotating coordinate systems are shoulder joint rotation and elbow joint rotation, and the result is a Coriolis torque at the shoulder (there is no Coriolis torque at the elbow). It is hard to give a more intuitive feel for Coriolis torques, but one way is to compare the effects of these torques on the shoulder joint for different trajectories. Consider first a straight-line trajectory that intersects the shoulder (figure 1.5a) for the two-link planar manipulator. For this special movement, the Coriolis torque exactly cancels the centripetal torque (see question 1.3), so that the shoulder torque does not depend on joint velocity terms. Consider next a vertical straight-line trajectory, and a point on this trajectory where the endpoint is closest to the shoulder (figure 1.5b). The Coriolis torque is zero at this point (see question 1.4). If the movement proceeds upward past this point, then the Coriolis torque begins generating a counterclockwise torque at the shoulder (a positive torque according to the normal convention) that increases the higher up the movement goes. Since the shoulder joint needs to move counterclockwise as the endpoint moves upward, the Coriolis torque is therefore assisting the required movement of the shoulder joint.

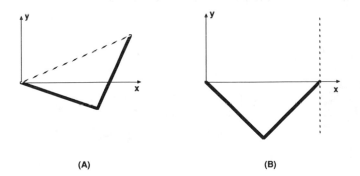

(A)   (B)

Figure 1.5
(a) Straight-line movement through the shoulder joint. (b) A vertical straight-line motion.

1.4.1   Force Distribution

Muscle produces linear forces, and these linear forces generate joint torque by pulling on a lever or moment arm at the joint. In general, there are many muscles acting about each joint, with different sizes and with differing moment arms. Acting about the elbow joint, for example, are the biceps and brachialis for flexion, and the triceps for extension. Moreover, the action of many muscles spans more than one joint. For example, one portion of the biceps spans the shoulder joint as well as the elbow joint. Such two-joint muscles will generate torque at both joints.

As a consequence of this complex anatomy, there are more muscles at the shoulder and elbow joints than are required to produce torque in one or another direction. Various explanations have been suggested for this redundant musculature, but in any case there is a consequent problem of distributing a net joint torque about the muscles acting at that joint. This is referred to as the *force distribution problem*. The force distribution problem can be considered a special case of the inverse dynamics problem, where again the transformation is in the direction of the external dynamic variable (joint torque) to the more internal dynamic variable (muscle force).

One complicating aspect of force distribution is that a muscle-pulling lever usually depends on the joint angle. For the human shoulder joint, most muscles follow a straight path from their origin on the torso to the insertion on the humerus bone of the upper arm (figure 1.6a). By simple trigonometry, it is easy to see that changing the shoulder joint angle changes how effectively the muscle generates torque. For the human eyeball, by contrast, the insertion wraps around a sphere, so that the radius r of the sphere defines a constant pulling lever for all eye positions (figure 1.6b).

Why there are two-joint muscles, and why there is redundant musculature around most joints, are matters of current debate. One possibility is

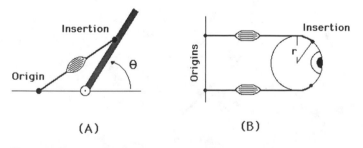

(A)   (B)

Figure 1.6
(a) A linear muscle trajectory from origin to insertion causes the effective moment arm to vary with joint angle. (b) For muscle insertion around a spherical joint such as the eyeball, the moment arm is constant for any joint position.

the control of stiffness about a joint. In holding an elbow posture or moving the elbow slowly, for example, usually muscles on both sides of the elbow joint are active (the muscles causing joint motion in the desired direction are called *agonists*, the muscles opposing or stopping joint motion are called *antagonists*). When agonists and antagonists are both active at the same time, they are said to be in a state of *coactivation* or *cocontraction*.[2] Coactivation increases joint stiffness and allows perturbations to the limb to be handled more effectively.

1.4.2   Muscle Activation

Once a force has been assigned to a particular muscle, that muscle must be activated appropriately by the motor neurons in the spinal cord.

Muscle is composed of both fast and slow fibers, grouped into *motor units* (the muscle fibers activated by a single motor neuron). It is highly complex in terms of the properties of length, velocity, and activation. Nevertheless, as we will see in preliminary fashion in section 1.5.6 and in more detail in chapter 3, muscle can be approximated by damped springs, and certain control advantages accrue from utilizing springlike properties.

The neural circuitry for movement is extensive and complex. The functioning of this circuitry is not well understood in the context of arm movements, and we will not consider it in any depth (though in section 1.5.5 we will examine the activation and feedback loop between muscle and spinal cord).

In the context of eye movements, however, we are far more advanced in tying control strategies to actual neural centers. In fact, eye movement control is one of the best examples we have of tying behavior to neurons, and the discussion in chapter 4 will therefore be of particular interest.

1.5   Control

The task of the control processes is to generate the required joint torques corresponding to the joint motion. There are essentially two ways to control motion: feedforward control and feedback control. In *feedforward control* a prediction is made about the correct joint torques based on a model of the system or on a motor memory derived from learning. In *feedback control* joint torque is based on an error signal between the actual and intended motion. In this section we will first consider feedforward control and then look at difficulties in implementing this control that

---

2. For fast motions, coactivation gives way to alternating activation, where first the agonist turns on and the antagonist turns off to accelerate the joint, and then the antagonist turns on and the agonist turns off to decelerate the joint.

require feedback control. We will focus especially on one particular type of feedback control, linear feedback control, in order to provide background for the ideas in chapters 3 and 4. In particular, we will see how the utilization of muscle properties may realize a feedback controller.

1.5.1   Feedforward Control

Let us assume that we are given a desired trajectory expressed as a time sequence of joint angles $\theta_d(t)$ and that our task is to generate the joint torques that cause the arm to follow this desired trajectory as closely as possible. How can this be done?

In discussing the dynamics of arm motion, we have already defined direct dynamics as the joint motion $\theta(t)$ that results when a time sequence of joint torques $\tau(t)$ is applied. We denote the functional relation between the two by

$$\theta(t) = R(\tau(t)).$$

The function R is also referred to as the *plant dynamics*. What we are actually interested in is to invert this function (denoted R^{-1}) to find what joint torques are required to follow the desired trajectory:

$$\tau(t) = R^{-1}(\theta_d(t)).$$

Solving this inverse dynamics problem would seem to solve the problem of control, but serious difficulties arise in implementing this solution.

1. *We may not have a good dynamic model of the plant or arm.* This may result either because the plant is too complex to model or because we cannot identify parameters of the model accurately. (For instance, what is the inertia of each limb segment?) We can express this mathematically by calling R the true plant dynamics and $\hat{R}$ our estimated model of the plant. Thus, the inverse dynamics solution that we can actually compute is

$$\tau(t) = \hat{R}^{-1}(\theta_d(t)),$$

where $\hat{R}^{-1}$ is the inverse of the estimated model. Applying this torque to the true plant dynamics, we find that

$$\theta(t) = R(\hat{R}^{-1}(\theta_d(t))), \tag{5}$$

where $\theta(t)$ is the actual arm trajectory produced. Now if our model of the plant is accurate, then $R = \hat{R}$, and $R\hat{R}^{-1}$ will cancel out, leaving $\theta(t) = \theta_d(t)$. Thus, the actual and desired trajectories will be the same, which is what we wanted. If our model of the plant is not accurate, then the actual trajectory $\theta(t)$ will differ from the desired trajectory $\theta_d(t)$. How they differ is then described mathematically as follows from equation (5),

$$e(t) = \theta_d(t) - \theta(t) = \theta_d(t) - R(\hat{R}^{-1}(\theta_d(t))),$$

where $e(t)$ is the trajectory error. The worse the model, the more the actual trajectory will deviate from the desired trajectory.

2. *The initial conditions of the movement may differ from the original plan.* For example, suppose you wish to move your arm between two fixed points in space according to some trajectory $\theta_d(t)$. Let $\tau(t)$ be the predicted joint torques based on our plant model. Suppose now that at the beginning of the movement your arm was not actually at the starting point you had planned (for example, because of neglect). Then applying this time sequence $\tau(t)$ of joint torques to the wrong initial arm position will not cause the trajectory to be followed successfully, even if the original plant model was exact.

3. *Unmodeled perturbations may exist that deflect the movement from its intended path.* The arm may brush against a surface during a motion, throwing it off. A heavy coat may encumber arm motion. Making a motion in the presence of a strong wind is also more difficult. Another kind of perturbation is due to such effects as fatigue: when we are tired, it takes more effort to make the same motion that we otherwise make easily.

4. *The inverse dynamics may be too complex for the central nervous system to compute quickly for purposes of control, even if a sufficiently accurate dynamics model could be formulated.* In robotics, because of the existence of fast computers, it is relatively straightforward to evaluate the inverse dynamics equations for the control of fast arm motion (Craig 1986). Though this is a good idea for robotics and computer control, it has been argued that limitations on the numerical computing ability of the nervous system preclude the possibility of explicit dynamics computation (Loeb 1983).

Instead of evaluating a complex set of equations, another possibility in feedforward control is learning a torque profile through repetition. If the same movement is repeated over and over again, it is possible to convert trajectory errors to corrective torques over the original torque profile. It has been shown that this scheme will eventually converge to a torque profile that executes the movement exactly, without error. The convergence is guaranteed and made stable if a sufficiently accurate model of the system exists to convert trajectory errors to corrective torques (An, Atkeson, and Hollerbach 1988).

One disadvantage of torque learning is that the torque profile is good only for the movement learned and does not generalize to other movements. To produce another movement, it is necessary to repeat the other movement over and over again also. Thus, torque learning is similar to the concept of a *motor tape*, which is formed by learning and is played out from start to finish, but is good for that particular movement only. It is not out of the question that this kind of learning is utilized in human movement, and it has a sort of intuitive ring about it from our experiences with specificity of training and the like.

From a computational standpoint, though, torque learning leads to a memory saturation because there must be a motor tape for every distinct movement and there is no sharing of information between tapes to reduce what needs to be memorized. Moreover, torque learning does not obviate the need for a good dynamics model of the limb, since otherwise trajectory errors cannot properly be transformed to corrective torques. The need for a good dynamics model is a general property of feedforward control strategies, and there is a debate in the biological motor control community about whether the biological controller can form such a model given its complex biomechanical structure—namely, the mass, location of the center of gravity, and moments of inertia of each limb; the muscle geometry; and the nonlinear muscle dynamics.

1.5.2   Linear Feedback Control

Given these four problems with the use of feedforward control alone, it can be argued that the control of arm motion cannot be based solely on a prediction of the joint torques from a dynamic model. There must be some knowledge of the *state* of the arm, which is defined as its actual position and velocity at every instance of time. The arm's state is then denoted by $(\theta(t), \dot{\theta}(t))$, where $\dot{\theta}(t)$ is the joint velocity.

When the state of the arm differs from the desired state based on the planned trajectory, then some additional corrective action is required to move the arm back onto the intended path. The most general form of control combines the actual state, the desired state, and a dynamics model to predict the joint torques:

$$\tau(t) = f(\theta(t), \dot{\theta}(t), \theta_d(t), \dot{\theta}_d(t), \hat{R}).$$

Many proposals have been made in the robot control literature about the form this function f takes. We will explore just one of them: *linear feedback control*.

Linear feedback control derives corrective torques as a linear function of the errors in state, and it does not incorporate a dynamic model of the arm. Particularly because of its simplicity in eliminating the need for a dynamic model, linear feedback control is a commonly proposed control strategy in both robotics and motor control. We will look at several common forms of this type of control.

In feedback control the required joint torques are generated in response to a trajectory error. Consider a single-joint elbow movement (figure 1.7), with joint angle θ. The torque τ at the elbow joint is generated proportionally to the joint position error. Thus,

$$\tau(t) = K_p(\theta_d(t) - \theta(t)), \tag{6}$$

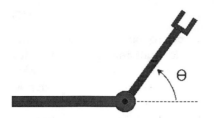

Figure 1.7
A single-joint elbow movement.

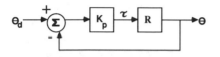

Figure 1.8
Block diagram of linear feedback controller working on a system R.

where the constant of proportionality K_p is the *position feedback gain*. The gain magnitude determines how forcefully the controller corrects for an error. The larger this constant, the larger the torque to overcome the error. If the gain is low, then the feedback will not be effective in correcting the error. Choices of gain are limited by the strengths of the actuators and by stability of motion.

In a robot the feedback control law (6) would be implemented by having a joint angle sensor that tells what the actual robot elbow angle θ is. The computer would know what the desired joint angle θ_d is, based on some trajectory plan, and would output a torque to the elbow motor based on the feedback law (6).

If a perturbation to movement causes the joint error to increase, the amount of corrective torque is increased as well by the feedback law (6). A key point about feedback control is that the complex dynamic interactions discussed in section 1.4 are considered as perturbations to be rejected by feedback. These perturbations will introduce joint position errors, which the feedback law (6) counteracts. To understand how feedback can compensate for movement dynamics, we will look at some elementary principles of control theory that will also be required in the discussions of chapter 4 on eye movements.

Consider the block diagram of figure 1.8. It consists of the system to be controlled R and the feedback loop around it. On the left is an input θ_d of the desired joint angle. The feedback loop subtracts the actual from the desired position and multiplies the result by the feedback gain K_p. The complete equation including the system dynamics would then be

$$\theta(t) = R(K_p(\theta_d(t) - \theta(t))). \tag{7}$$

Next let us consider how the ratio of output to input, θ/θ_d, varies as the feedback gain K_p increases. Ideally, we would want this ratio to be 1 for perfect tracking. Notice the functional composition of equation (7), where the output of the control law $\tau = K_p(\theta_d - \theta)$ is the input to the function R. Because R is usually a complicated nonlinear function, it is not a simple matter to rework the equation in its present form to derive the input/output ratio. If the dynamics is a linear system, then it is possible to proceed relatively straightforwardly. Since we are currently dealing just with elbow joint motion, the assumption of linearity is not too bad. Hence, the following development assumes that R is linear, primarily to keep the mathematics simple but also because the main ideas about feedback control can be developed with this assumption.[3]

Since R is assumed linear, it is possible to replace the functional composition by a functional multiplication by the use of Laplace transforms.[4] The input/output ratio is then found to be

$$\frac{\theta(s)}{\theta_d(s)} = \frac{K_p R(s)}{1 + K_p R(s)}, \tag{8}$$

where the Laplace variable s substitutes for the time t. This ratio of the output to input, represented by the expression on the right of equation (8), is referred to as the *system transfer function*. The most important point to note about this equation is that a high position feedback gain K_p effectively cancels the system dynamics R, and the feedback errors can be made arbitrarily small by increasing the feedback gain K_p.

By definition, the Laplace transform $f(s)$ of a function $f(t)$, where t is the time dependence, is defined as

$$f(s) = \int_0^\infty e^{-st} f(t)\, dt.$$

A very useful property is the Laplace transform of the functional convolution $f(g(t))$, where f and g are linear functions, which turns out to be $f(s)g(s)$. Taking the Laplace transform of equation (7),

3. The nonlinear case for R can be handled analogously but requires the use of operator theory, which is beyond the scope of the present discussion (see Zames 1960).

4. Information on Laplace transforms can be found in books on differential equations such as Rainville 1964.

$$\theta(s) = R(s)K_p(\theta_d(s) - \theta(s)),$$

where $\theta(s)$ and $\theta_d(s)$ are the Laplace transforms of the input and output and $R(s)$ is the Laplace transform of the system dynamics, we can solve for the input/output ratio:

$$\frac{\theta(s)}{\theta_d(s)} = \frac{K_p R(s)}{1 + K_p R(s)}.$$

As K_p is made larger, the denominator $1 + K_p R(s)$ becomes approximately $K_p R(s)$, and the input/output ratio becomes approximately 1.

Some details remain to be attended to because equation (6) by itself is not adequate. The first is to provide some *damping* to movement. Equation (6) is identical to the equation for a spring, where K_p can be interpreted as a spring constant or stiffness and θ_d can be interpreted as the rest length of the spring. A spring with a mass on it will oscillate indefinitely unless some way is found of taking energy out of it, such as friction or damping. Similarly, the controller defined by equation (6) is prone to oscillation at the endpoint. (In fact, this may be one source of physiological tremor.) To cause the oscillation to die out rapidly, a damping term is usually added to this law, namely,

$$\tau(t) = K_p(\theta_d(t) - \theta(t)) - K_v\dot{\theta}(t), \tag{9}$$

where $\dot{\theta}$ is the joint velocity and K_v is the viscosity or damping coefficient. The viscous damping $K_v\dot{\theta}$ creates a greater drag the faster the movement is. The feedback control law (9) is extremely common in engineering control systems and is referred to as *PD (proportional derivative) control*. The feedback law (6) is referred to simply as *P control*.

Another detail that requires attention is *steady-state offset*. Suppose gravity acts on the elbow joint, producing a torque g. At rest or steady state, the joint velocity $\dot{\theta}$ is zero, so the system equation is

$$K_p(\theta_d(t) - \theta(t)) = g(t).$$

Thus, there will be a steady-state error $\theta_d - \theta = g/K_p$ at the end of movement, but reducing this error to zero by increasing K_p to infinity is not a viable option. To overcome this problem, a common solution is to add integral control as follows,

$$\tau(t) = K_p(\theta_d(t) - \theta(t)) + K_v\dot{\theta}(t) + K_i \int_{t_0}^{t} (\theta_d(t) - \theta(t))\, dt, \tag{10}$$

where K_i is the integral gain. This control law is commonly referred to as

PID (proportional, integral, derivative) control. The integral term increases the torque more and more until the error is finally zero.[5]

Equation (10) can be analyzed in the steady state by Laplace transforms:

$$K_p(\theta_d(s) - \theta(s)) - sK_v\theta(s) + \frac{K_i}{s}(\theta_d(s) - \theta(s)) = g(s).$$

Multiplying across by s and taking the limit $s = 0$ in the steady state, it is easy to verify that $\theta_d(s) - \theta(s) = 0$; that is, the steady-state error has been eliminated (see question 1.5).

For any of these forms of linear feedback control, there are practical limits to how high the position gain K_p can be made because of limits in the amount of torque a motor or muscle can produce and because of the potential for instability. Linear feedback control will be most effective when the perturbations are not too large. If dynamics is treated as a perturbation, then ultimately the controllability of fast movements is limited, because these perturbations increase as the square of movement speed (see question 1.6).

1.5.3　Feedback plus Feedforward Control

We have now considered two basic forms of control, feedforward and feedback, and discussed advantages and disadvantages of using each alone. If the dynamic model is accurate, then feedforward control has the potential for also generating the most accurate motions. If the model is inaccurate or if disturbances arise from errors in the initial state or from unexpected perturbations, then feedforward control alone is inadequate.

The advantage of feedback control is that disturbances to motion can be overcome: the actual state of the arm is *fed back* to the controller, compared to the desired state, and used to generate a corrective action. Moreover, the form of this control law is simple, and a model of the system dynamics is not needed. Thus, feedback control would seem to fix many of the problems with feedforward control. On the other hand, the use of feedback control alone has its own set of problems. Generally speaking, the larger the error in state, the larger the corrective torque generated by feedback control. Thus, feedback control is error driven, so that there must by

---

5. Integration can be thought of as summing the position error over time, from a past reference time t_0 to the current time t.

definition be an error for this control to be active. Moreover, there are limitations on the magnitudes of the feedback gains, due to stability and actuator saturation considerations. Hence, a desired trajectory cannot be followed without significant error with feedback control alone.

Since both feedforward control and feedback control have advantages and disadvantages, the best form of control may combine the two. Feedback control could be used in conjunction with feedforward control to handle disturbances. In turn, feedforward control could reduce the errors that feedback control needs to correct, by eliminating as far as possible the plant dynamics as a source of perturbations. The combination of the two has been strongly advocated in robotics (An, Atkeson, and Hollerbach 1988). Whether this is an option for the biological motor controller is a subject of current debate, again having to do with whether the central nervous system could either form an adequate dynamic model or compute it quickly enough. In section 1.5.5 we will examine the possibility that the biological motor control system may use feedback control alone.

1.5.4   Task-Level Feedback

In the previous section the feedback laws were cast in terms of joint angles and joint errors. In the most general form, the feedback law relating trajectory errors to corrective torques can instead be cast in terms of endpoint variables. After all, in controlling hand position, errors are most sensibly corrected in terms of hand coordinates rather than in terms of joint coordinates, given the complex relation between joint errors and endpoint positions.

It is interesting that studies of reflexes in humans indicate that corrections often occur, not in muscles, joints, or even limbs to which a perturbation is applied, but in remote sites that are appropriate for the motor tasks. Abbs and Gracco (1983) studied both speech movements and two-fingered oppositional grasping. In speech, when a perturbation was applied to the lower lip, the upper lip compensated to maintain the mouth opening size and speech goals. That the compensation did not happen in the part that was perturbed, the lower lip, indicates that the reflex action was oriented toward the task goals. Similarly, when a perturbation was applied to one finger in a pinching task, the other finger compensated. This separation of the response from the point of sensing is a necessary capability for achieving sophisticated control and argues against narrow reflexology.

1.5.5   Active Feedback Control via Stretch Reflexes

Is active feedback control a viable biological option? To answer this question, we begin by looking at the neural and sensory apparatus involved in

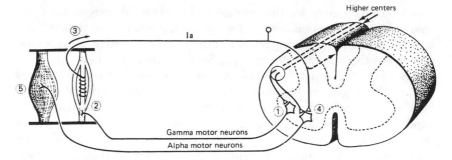

Figure 1.9
Activation of alpha motor neurons via the gamma loop. The gamma motor neuron is activated by input from higher centers (1), producing shortening of the spindle (2), which gives rise to an increase in Ia fiber discharge (3), which in turn increases the alpha motor neuron output (4), thereby producing contraction of the extrafusal muscle (5). (Reprinted by permission of the publisher from E. R. Kandel and J. H. Schwartz, eds., *Principles of neural science*, 1981, fig. 26–5. © 1981 by Elsevier Science Publishing Co., Inc.)

muscle control (figure 1.9). The regular muscle fibers in a muscle responsible for producing force are called *extrafusal fibers*. Parallel to the extrafusal fibers are the *intrafusal fibers*, also called *muscle spindles*, which serve to measure muscle length and motion. Extrafusal fibers are innervated by *alpha motor neurons* in the spinal cord; intrafusal fibers are separately innervated by *gamma motor neurons*. There are sensory endings on the muscle spindles that send feedback about the length and motion of the spindles to the spinal cord over the *Ia afferent fibers*.[6] The muscle spindles, joint receptors, and Golgi tendon organs are called *proprioceptors*, because they give information about the mechanical state of the limb.[7]

The gamma motor neurons cause the muscle spindles to contract to a length that serves as a reference for the extrafusal fibers, and a muscle spindle outputs a signal that reflects the difference in length between it and the neighboring extrafusal fibers. If a muscle is suddenly stretched, the muscle spindles are stretched and increase their output to the spinal cord. This feedback to the spinal cord may lead to an increased firing of the motor neurons that increases the muscle force to overcome the perturbation. This process is referred to as the *stretch reflex*. The stretch reflex usually has two components: a fast response at 25 milliseconds, and a slow

6. Afferent fibers are sensory input fibers that originate from biological sensors and go to the spinal cord neurons. Efferent fibers are motor output fibers that originate from motor neurons in the spinal cord and go to muscle fibers.

7. Golgi tendon organs measure tendon tension. Joint receptors reside in the joint capsules and give some information about joint angle.

response at 100 milliseconds. The fast response is due to monosynaptic connections in the spinal cord from the Ia afferent fibers directly into the alpha motor neurons. The slow response involves many more intermediate neurons, perhaps up to the cortex itself, before the alpha motor neurons are stimulated.

It thus appears that the neural machinery is in place for possible active feedback control, and indeed a strategy similar to active feedback control was hypothesized in the past for the control of human arm movements. In this *gamma drive hypothesis*, the gamma motor neurons set a reference length, and the muscle spindles generate a signal back to the spinal cord that is proportional to the difference in length between the muscle spindle and the regular muscle fiber. The spinal cord then generates a feedback torque similar to equation (6). The gamma system is thus driving the alpha motor neurons.

The gamma drive hypothesis is now discounted, because it was found that the gamma motor neurons are activated at the same time as the alpha motor neurons—not before, as the gamma drive hypothesis would have required. A more serious problem with a scheme that relies on active feedback is the existence of transmission delays in the nerves connecting muscle to the spinal cord and processing delays by the neural centers involved in movement. Although the monosynaptic stretch reflex is only 25 milliseconds, it has been shown that this fast feedback loop has too low a gain for effective load compensation (Bizzi, Morasso, and Polit 1978). The longer latency reflex of about 100 milliseconds does effectively compensate for the load. However, this processing delay of 100 milliseconds in the active feedback loop is too long and prevents a simple feedback loop like equation (6) from serving as the arm control strategy. For moderately fast arm movements, by the time a corrective response can take effect, the limb will have reached a new state for which the response is inappropriate.

Although delays can be compensated for if higher-order derivatives of the error are known, it has been argued that it is unlikely that the nervous system could accurately compute these derivatives (Arbib and Amari 1985). For example, it would be necessary to compute higher-order derivatives of the error—not only of velocity error, but also of acceleration error and even higher error derivatives. The sensory feedback in the human limb is quite unlikely to be accurate enough to derive these higher error derivatives, aside from any processing limitations.

For these reasons, it has been argued that control for fast to moderately fast arm movements must be open-loop. An *open-loop controller* outputs a control torque without using feedback; a *closed-loop controller* does use feedback. For an open-loop controller, feedback may indeed be present during the movement but is not used to generate instantaneous control torques. For the biological system, feedback is more likely to play a role in

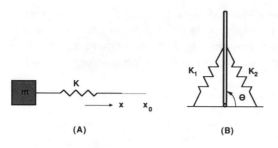

Figure 1.10
(a) A linear spring with spring constant K is attached on the left to a mass m. Initially the free right end is at rest at position x. When the right end is suddenly moved to position x_0, a new rest length is defined. (b) Coactivation of springs around a joint produces springlike joint behavior.

parameter tuning, adaptation of subsequent movements, or correcting for major disturbances that would require reprogramming.

1.5.6   Passive Feedback Control via Muscle Properties

Although *active* feedback control does not appear to be a viable option for arm movements, *passive* feedback control may well be (see chapter 3). To introduce this notion, suppose muscle is approximated as a tuneable spring. In figure 1.10a, a linear spring is depicted with one end attached to a load mass. Suppose we can grab the other end of the spring and pull it. If the spring and mass are initially at rest with the free spring end at position x, and we suddenly stretch the end of the spring to a position x_0, then the force f that the spring generates on the mass m is

$$f = K(x_0 - x),$$

where K is the spring constant or stiffness. The spring constant indicates how stiff the spring is. After a period of oscillation, the mass will finally come to rest when $x_0 = x$ and no more force acts on it. The length x_0 is variously called the *equilibrium position*, the *rest length*, or the *zero reference length*. It has been hypothesized that muscle is like a tuneable spring in that neural activation changes both the spring constant and the rest length (see chapter 3). In general, the more a muscle is activated, the stiffer it gets. So far it has not been shown that the rest length for a single muscle can be controlled independently of the stiffness.

Now consider the opposing pairs of agonist and antagonist muscles around a joint. By coactivation of this musculature, the springlike muscle properties are transferred to the joint (figure 1.10b). We can then speak of joint stiffness K_θ and zero reference angle θ_0. If the joint is perturbed from this reference angle, the resulting elbow torque τ will be

$$\tau = K_\theta(\theta_0 - \theta). \tag{11}$$

Because of coactivation, it is now possible to control the joint stiffness K_θ separately from the joint equilibrium point θ_0 (see question 1.7). This is because for an isolated spring or muscle, there is only one input and hence only one output that can be controlled. With several muscles around a joint that can be controlled separately, there are several inputs and hence several output variables that can be controlled.

Equation (11) is identical to equation (6), which was derived for an active feedback loop. If the active feedback mechanism of figure 1.8 and the passive mechanism of figure 1.10b were placed in black boxes, we could not tell which system was being used to generate input and output angles. From a functional standpoint, there is no difference between the two systems, even though the underlying implementation is different.

An advantage for passive feedback is that because it is mechanically derived from muscle properties, it acts instantaneously to resist perturbations and hence overcomes the basic speed limitations of active feedback. In addition, muscle has intrinsic viscosity, so that damping of endpoint oscillations as in equation (9) is automatically provided. A trajectory can be fashioned by changing the equilibrium point θ_0 from start to goal. This *reference trajectory hypothesis* of movement control is treated in detail in chapter 3. A restatement of this hypothesis in more standard control terminology is that arm movements are controlled by linear PD control, where the feedback source is passive.

1.6   Motor Programs and Sequences

In sections 1.2–1.5 we have primarily considered the control of single, isolated movements. Of course, many motions we make are actually chains of movements. When picking up a cup, we don't move our arm to the cup, stop, close our hand, and then move the cup. Instead, we tend to blend these movements together so that they overlap. Other common examples of chains of motion are speech, handwriting, and typing.

How are such motions chained together, and is there a sense in which one element of the motion influences others? The concept of *motor program*, discussed in chapter 5, has been put forth to explain these influences. As we have seen, each individual motion has its own plan. A motor program can be considered a plan for a sequence of individual motions that influence each other. There may also be higher-level plans that combine a number of motor programs, but unlike the individual motions that make up the motor program, the elements of these higher-level plans are relatively independent. Thus, the question asked in chapter 5 is, How can we identify the motor programs and their elements in a motion sequence? For example, when we type a word, phrase, or sentence, what combination of keystrokes defines a motor program?

Suggestions for Further Reading

Much of the theory of movement planning, mechanics, and control is being pursued most vigorously in robotics. Mechanics forms the backbone for analyzing movement, and a good source book on mechanics is Symon 1971. A very good introductory text to robotics is Craig 1986. More advanced texts are Paul 1981, Brady et al. 1982, and An, Atkeson, and Hollerbach 1988. As an introduction to locomotion, a good book from a robotics perspective is Raibert 1986. There are many introductory texts on linear control theory, such as Melsa and Schultz 1969.

Basic texts in motor control include Kandel and Schwartz 1985 on motor physiology and McMahon 1984 on muscle and locomotion. Evarts, Wise, and Bousfield 1985 surveys current topics in motor physiology and control, and Gallistel 1980 offers a perspective on historical concepts in motor control. Motor programs and motor learning are discussed in Schmidt 1982.

A general discussion relating robotics and artificial intelligence research to biological research may be found in Hildreth and Hollerbach 1987, and a discussion of the levels of planning in movement control in Saltzman 1979.

Questions

1.1 Show that the interpolation form (equation (2)) is the same as the straight-line form (equation (1)).

1.2 Verify that the time form $f(t) = (t - t_0)/(t_f - t_0)$ results in a constant velocity, given equation (2).

1.3 For the movement of figure 1.5a, assume that the link lengths are of equal unit length ($l_1 = l_2 = 1$). Show that the Coriolis torque exactly cancels the centripetal torque at the shoulder.

1.4 For the movement of figure 1.5b, again assume equal link lengths. When the endpoint is closest to the shoulder along the vertical line trajectory, show that the Coriolis torque at the shoulder is zero.

1.5 Derive the Laplace transform of equation (9), and verify that $\theta_d(s) - \theta(s) = 0$ in the steady state.

1.6 Consider Euler's equation $\tau = I\ddot{\theta}$. Suppose that $\theta(t)$ defines a trajectory as a function of the time t. Now suppose that the movement is sped up by a factor c; that is, the new trajectory is $\theta(ct)$. Show that the torque scales by c^2.

1.7 Consider a system analogous to but simpler than the coactivated joint of figure 1.10b, depicted in figure 1.11a. Two springs act in parallel on a mass m, whose position is x. Suppose that K_1 and K_2 are the two spring stiffnesses and that x_1 and x_2 are the positions of the free ends. Assume that the rest lengths of the springs are zero. Show that the stiffness of the mass is $K_1 + K_2$.

1.8 Suppose that each spring is tuneable, modeled by the length-tension diagram of figure 1.11b. Changing the activation u_i of each spring changes both the rest length x_i and the spring constant K_i. Each length-tension curve intersects at the same point $-T_0$ on the tension axis T_i when the spring length x is zero. Show that the stiffness of the mass can be controlled separately from the mass's equilibrium point.

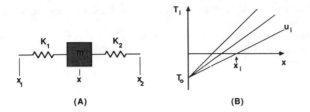

Figure 1.11
(a) Parallel connection of two springs to a mass m. (b) Hypothetical length-tension diagrams for tuneable springs.

References

Abbs, J. H., and V. L. Gracco (1983). Sensorimotor actions in the control of multi-movement speech gestures. *Trends in Neurosciences* 6, 391–395.

An, C. H., C. G. Atkeson, and J. M. Hollerbach (1988). *Model-based control of a robot manipulator.* Cambridge, MA: MIT Press.

Arbib, M. A., and S. -I. Amari (1985). Sensori-motor transformations in the brain (with a critique of the tensor theory of cerebellum). *Journal of Theoretical Biology* 112, 123–155.

Bizzi, E., P. Dev, P. Morasso, and A. Polit (1978). Effect of load disturbances during centrally initiated movements. *Journal of Neurophysiology* 41, 542–556.

Brady, J. M., J. M. Hollerbach, T. L. Johnson, T. Lozano-Perez, and M. T. Mason, eds. (1982). *Robot motion: Planning and control.* Cambridge, MA: MIT Press.

Craig, J. J. (1986). *Introduction to robotics: Mechanics and control.* Reading, MA: Addison-Wesley.

Evarts, E. V., S. P. Wise, and D. Bousfield (1985). *The motor system in neurobiology.* Amsterdam: Elsevier.

Gallistel, C. R. (1980). *The organization of action: A new synthesis.* Hillsdale, NJ: L. Erlbaum Associates.

Hildreth, E. C., and J. M. Hollerbach (1987). Artificial intelligence: Computational approach to vision and motor control. In F. Plum, ed., *Handbook of physiology, section 1: The nervous system, vol. 5: Higher functions of the brain, part 2.* Bethesda, MD: American Physiological Society.

Johansson, R. S., and G. Westling (1984). Roles of glabrous skin receptors and sensorimotor memory in automatic control of precision grip when lifting rougher or more slippery objects. *Experimental Brain Research* 56, 550–564.

Kandel, E. R., and J. H. Schwartz, eds. (1985). *Principles of neural science.* New York: Elsevier.

Loeb, G. E. (1983). Finding common ground between robotics and physiology. *Trends in Neurosciences* 6, 203–204.

McMahon, T. A. (1984). *Muscles, reflexes, and locomotion.* Princeton, NJ: Princeton University Press.

Melsa, J. L., and D. G. Schultz (1969). *Linear control systems.* New York: McGraw-Hill.

Paul, R. P. (1981). *Robot manipulators: Mathematics, programming, and control.* Cambridge, MA: MIT Press.

Raibert, M. H. (1986). *Legged robots that balance.* Cambridge, MA: MIT Press.

Rainville, E. D. (1964). *Elementary differential equations.* New York: Macmillan.

Saltzman, E. (1979). Levels of sensorimotor representation. *Journal of Mathematical Psychology* 20, 91–163.

Schmidt, R. A. (1982). *Motor control and learning: A behavioral emphasis*. Champaign, IL: Human Kinetics Publishers.

Symon, K. R. (1971). *Mechanics*. Reading, MA: Addison-Wesley.

Zames, G. (1960). Nonlinear operators for system analysis. Doctoral dissertation, Department of Electrical Engineering, MIT, Cambridge, MA.

Chapter 2

Planning of Arm Movements

John M. Hollerbach

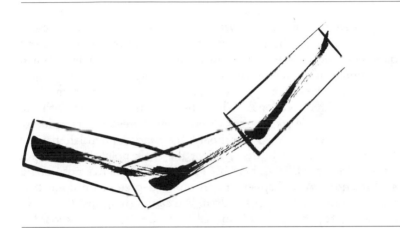

Arm movements are something we do without thinking, but with considerable skill. Yet in accomplishing the many tasks we are capable of, the human motor control system must lay out a plan for movement. What is the nature of this plan, and how may we discover it experimentally? In this chapter we will consider the constraints on arm movement and what they imply for planning, and we will examine various possibilities for planning and some experiments that have been conducted to decide among them.

2.1 Task Constraints

Movement of an arm is not just a matter of freely generating trajectories. It is constrained both by task demands such as accurate throwing and by physical contact with external surfaces. The geometry of the external world

This research was supported by NIH grant AM26710. I would also like to acknowledge support from an NSF Presidential Young Investigator Award. This chapter was produced using facilities of the MIT Artificial Intelligence Laboratory, partially supported by DARPA contract N00014-85-K-0124.

constrains how movement may take place, by defining a set of natural coordinates in terms of which movement is most easily planned. In the example of picking up a cup, an external coordinate system can be defined that reflects the direction of gravity. A coordinate system internal to the cup then measures how the cup is oriented relative to gravity to avoid spilling. This internal coordinate system also defines the cup position and orientation, to be matched by an approach direction and a grasp.

Motion can also be constrained by physical contact with an environmental surface. Writing on a blackboard requires that movement take place only parallel to the board and not into or away from the board. The board sets up a natural coordinate system defining these allowable movement directions plus another direction in which force can be generated. We can screw in a lightbulb in practically any position and orientation—above our head, to the side, when we're upside down—matching our movements and force application to the external coordinates of the light socket.

Objects in three-dimensional space have six degrees of freedom, three translational and three rotational. When the hand is in contact with the environment, the normal six degrees of positioning freedom are reduced. For example, when writing on a blackboard, the hand can translate parallel to the board and it can rotate freely about the chalk point, but it cannot move through the board. Thus, blackboard writing allows five positioning degrees of freedom. What happens to the sixth degree of freedom? It is converted into a force degree of freedom. We can push against the blackboard and generate some level of normal force, and if the blackboard is sturdy, it will push back on the hand with an equal and opposite force.

More generally, it is a law of mechanics that the number of positioning freedoms and the number of force freedoms always add up to six. If you cannot move in a particular direction, it is because the contact conditions prevent the movement and only allow you to push in that direction. If you cannot push against the environment in a particular direction, you are then free to move in that direction. The partitioning between position and force freedoms depends on the geometry of the task. For example, at the other extreme from blackboard writing, the task of opening a door allows one positioning degree of freedom (the swinging of the door about its hinges) and five force degrees of freedom (assuming the door handle does not rotate). It is an obvious but important point to remember that appropriate muscular contractions are required to generate both the position freedoms and the force freedoms. Put another way, when a constrained motion is taking place, a description of how the hand generates positions does not give a full account of how the motor control system is controlling the motion, because the force freedoms have not been observed or taken into account.

Suppose that the blackboard is tilted at a different angle than you expected, or that the surface is irregular. How can you still write and maintain contact with the surface, given that your plan of the environment is somewhat incorrect? This is a fundamental problem in motion control, known as the problem of *force control* or *compliant motion control*.[1] Any solution must be robust with respect to modeling errors of the environment: the hand must move along the blackboard even when it is unexpectedly tilted, or the hand must comply to irregularities in the writing surface.

Therefore, a trajectory plan must have a strategy not just for the positioning degrees of freedom, but for the force degrees of freedom as well. The environment signals that the trajectory plan is wrong by pushing with more or less force than expected against the hand. In blackboard writing, for example, if there is less force than expected, it is because the hand is moving away from the board, and it is then necessary to correct the writing movement by pushing harder against the board. If there is more force than expected, then the hand is partly trying to move through the board, and it should be pulled away from the board somewhat.

In this chapter we will concentrate on *position control*, where the hand is not in contact with the environment, rather than on trajectory control in its most general form, namely, compliant motion control. This focus is primarily due to the state of research in motor control, since position control has been much more thoroughly investigated and is much better understood than compliant motion control. Nevertheless, keep in mind that we are dealing with just part of the trajectory planning problem, which is substantially more complicated than simply generating free motions.

2.2   Levels of Movement Planning

Given external geometric constraints on movement, a basic issue is the level at which human arm movement is planned. There are three conceptual levels for movement planning: planning in endpoint coordinates, planning in joint angle coordinates, and planning in muscle coordinates. Each of these planning levels has had proponents and supporting experimental evidence. In this section we will consider how these planning levels are related and what the implications are for planning at a particular level.

In robotics these levels form a hierarchy (figure 2.1). In examining this hierarchy, we can draw a basic distinction between kinematic levels and kinetic levels. *Kinematic* levels reflect geometry, *kinetic* levels reflect forces. Endpoint variables and joint angle variables are kinematic variables, since

---

1. Strictly speaking, compliant motion control is a subset of force control, since it refers to viscoelastic behavior during contact.

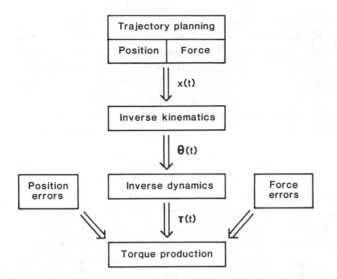

Figure 2.1
A modular planning and control structure for robot arm movement. A trajectory is planned in endpoint coordinates, synthesizing a hybrid force-position strategy. The endpoint trajectory $x(t)$ is transformed into a joint trajectory $\theta(t)$ by solving the inverse kinematics. The feedforward torques $\tau(t)$ are then found by solving the inverse dynamics and are corrected by feedback for force and position errors.

they describe the positions of objects in space or the configurations of the arm. Joint torques and muscle activations represent kinetic variables, since they involve inertial forces and force production.

It would almost seem teleologically imperative that the motor control system have an ability to plan in endpoint coordinates. The tasks of writing on a board, picking up and moving a cup, and screwing in a lightbulb that were given as examples of external constraints would seem to demand this ability. Planning in endpoint coordinates allows the external constraints to be most easily captured. The alternative of planning in more intrinsic coordinates presents the difficulty of predicting the consequences of movement, given the complex transformations between the various levels.

If movements are planned in endpoint coordinates, then an inverse kinematics transformation is implied to produce a corresponding joint angle time profile. The control processes then need to realize this joint trajectory plan by producing the appropriate joint torques and muscle activations (figure 2.1).

Other investigators have proposed that trajectories are planned in terms of joint angle coordinates. An advantage of joint angle planning is that an inverse kinematics transformation is not required (except for the end-

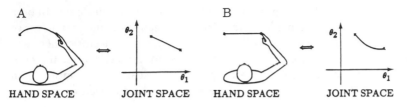

Figure 2.2
Different planning variables and their resultant trajectories for planar two-joint arm move-ment. (a) A straight line in joint coordinates generates a complex curved endpoint trajec-tory. (b) A straight line in Cartesian coordinates requires a relatively complex elbow and shoulder joint movement.

points). Although planning in more intrinsic coordinates such as joint coordinates offers greater ease in organizing movement, this possibility is only viable if simplifying strategies can be found that exhibit near-general, or at least adequate, behavior. Ordinarily one would expect that simple trajectories at one level yield complex trajectories at another level; for example, a straight line in hand coordinates yields a complex joint angle trajectory, whereas a straight line in joint coordinates yields a complex endpoint trajectory (figure 2.2).

Conceptually speaking, once a joint angle plan has been formed, it needs to be converted into a time sequence of joint torques $\tau(t)$ by solving the inverse dynamics problem and by feedback correction of errors based on position and force (figure 2.1). The joint torque is transformed into muscle activations in biological motor control by solving the force distribution problem, as mentioned in chapter 1.

Still other investigators have proposed that trajectories are planned in terms of muscle coordinates. One clear advantage for this type of planning is that the inverse dynamics and force distribution computations are easier to manage. On the other hand, such planning is particularly difficult to reconcile with geometric constraints imposed by the environment. Muscle force and joint torque are only indirectly related to joint position (the relation is described by direct dynamics), and it is not a trivial matter to predict where the limb will be at a particular instant in time.

Put another way, there is a conservation of complexity in movement planning. A so-called simplifying strategy at one level makes the computa-tions or predictions at the other levels more difficult. With intrinsic plan-ning coordinates, it must be explained how external constraints can be matched without yielding a controller more complicated than one operating at a higher level and performing the necessary transformations on lower levels.

Note that endpoint planning and inverse kinematics must be present at the endpoints of a motion, whatever the planning strategy: otherwise, we could not achieve a target in space. The main issue we are dealing with here is the course of the intermediate trajectory between start and goal. Most of the studies of arm coordination have dealt with free trajectories between predefined targets. Since there are constraints on motion only at the endpoints, and none during the trajectory, it is not clear that the motor plan has to specify endpoint variables in these intermediate trajectory regions.

2.3   Deducing Planning Variables from External Observations

The rest of this chapter is devoted to experimental evidence for one or the other of the planning levels: endpoint coordinates, joint angle coordinates, or muscle coordinates. First, some prefatory remarks regarding research strategy.

Teleological and computational arguments may provide some intuition about how movements are planned, but they are not proofs. The way the motor control system works may in reality be far different from these preconceptions. In the final analysis, experimental evidence must be found to support a particular viewpoint. How does one go about obtaining experimental evidence for planning variables?

There are two basic ways of approaching this question experimentally: through *invasive* studies and *external* or *noninvasive* studies. Invasive studies involve actually recording from or modifying the neural tissue in the spinal cord, brain stem, or cortical areas. These studies must of course be performed on animals. Many difficulties arise in performing these experiments and interpreting the results. Though such studies have brought about some progress in understanding arm movements, the experimental difficulties and the incomplete state of our current knowledge about the motor control system have restricted the benefits to be gained from them. The situation is different for eye movement control, where the theories and experimental techniques are more compatible (see chapter 4).

Noninvasive studies involve external observations of movement. To infer planning variables, as in this chapter, the kinematic features of movement are recorded and models are applied to characterize these features. To study control strategies, as in chapter 3, perturbations are applied and the responses are recorded to infer how the mechanical properties of joints and muscle are being modulated.

Bernstein (1967), a Russian scientist who was in advance of the research community when he did his work forty years ago, provided an intellectual basis for inferring planning variables through a *principle of equal simplicity*:

> If we are concerned with any given system, the structure of which is unknown to us but whose operation we may observe under a variety of conditions, then by a comparison of the changes *in the variable S*

(speed, accuracy, variation, etc.) encountered as a function of each of the variables in the conditions, we may come to determinate conclusions as to the structure of the system which are unattainable by direct means. (p. 52)

Bernstein's principle of equal simplicity is essentially an argument based on Occam's razor: the simplest description of movement reflects how the movement is generated. In the context of arm trajectories, an application of this principle led Bernstein to make the following statement:

If the spatial shape of a trajectory is invariant irrespective of the muscle scheme or the joint scheme, then the motor plan must be closely related to the topology of the trajectory and considerably removed from joints and muscles. (p. 55)

Our research strategy should therefore search for invariances in the kinematic data across a variety of experimental conditions. These conditions may involve movements to different targets, movements at different speeds, and movements with different hand-held weights or loads. If a set of planning variables and coordination strategy provides an invariant description of movement across all of these conditions, then we have evidence that the motor control system actually uses these variables internally to plan movement.

2.4   Kinematic versus Kinetic Planning

The first experimental test we will discuss decides between kinematic and kinetic planning variables. If the speed of movement between two fixed targets is changed or if the weight held by the hand is changed, then the underlying movement dynamics are significantly modified. If kinematic regularities can be found despite the changing movement dynamics, then kinetic planning variables would not be supported: any regular kinetic planning strategy would not give rise to kinematic invariances because of the complicated dynamic equations mentioned in chapter 1. Another experimental test involves movement to different targets, which also drastically changes the movement dynamics. If the kinematic form of movement is similar for different target pairs, again kinetic variables will not be supported.

One aspect of a trajectory is its path. Atkeson and Hollerbach (1985) investigated point-to-point arm movements in a sagittal plane (a vertical plane running from the shoulder forward). Arm kinematics were measured with a motion-tracking system, which yields three-dimensional positions of markers attached to a limb every few milliseconds during a motion. Markers

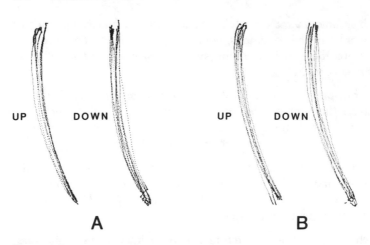

Figure 2.3
Path invariance across speed and load. (a) Slow, medium, and fast movements in both directions. (b) Medium speed movement with no weights, 2-pound weights, and 4-pound weights held by the hand.

were placed on the hand to measure the endpoint location, and on the upper arm and forearm to measure joint angles.

Figure 2.3 shows the trace of the wrist motion between two fixed targets that are roughly aligned vertically. In figure 2.3a three movements in each direction are shown under varying speeds: slow (around 1200 milliseconds), medium (around 800 milliseconds), and fast (around 400 milliseconds). In figure 2.3b three medium-speed movements in each direction are shown for conditions of unloaded motion, 2-pound hand-held weights, and 4-pound weights. In all cases the path that the hand follows is not much affected: it is the same regardless of movement speed or load.

The other aspect of a trajectory is the time dependence along its path. This is most conveniently expressed by the tangential velocity, which is the speed along the path.[2] Figure 2.4 compares the tangential velocity profiles for different movement conditions. Again, for different speeds and loads, the tangential velocity profiles after normalization are virtually identical (see question 2.1). Furthermore, even when different targets are reached or comparisions are made across subjects, the shape constancy remains. Thus, the tangential velocity profile shape is a strong invariance: even though many profiles are conceptually possible, subjects across the various experimental conditions produced only one shape.[3]

2. Mathematically, the tangential velocity v of the endpoint (x, y) is given by $v^2 = \dot{x}^2 + \dot{y}^2$.
3. The same invariances seem to hold for eye movements.

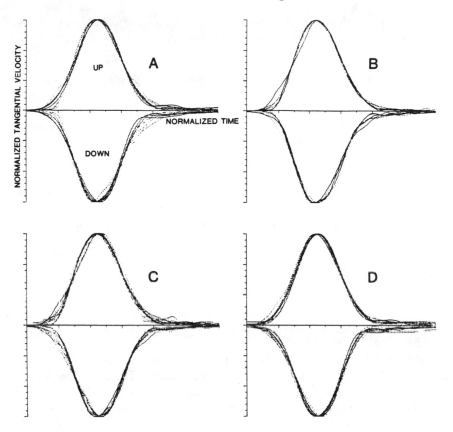

Figure 2.4
Tangential velocity profiles normalized for speed and distance and aligned at their peaks.
(a) Different speeds. (b) Different loads. (c) Different targets. (d) Different subjects.

Taken together, the path invariance and tangential velocity profile invariance support kinematic variables for planning.

2.5   Kinematic Variables and Coordination Strategies

In this section we will examine two forms of kinematic variables, joint angle versus Cartesian endpoint variables, as possible planning variables.

To distinguish joint angle planning from endpoint planning, it is necessary to characterize the trajectories that can be generated from either set of planning variables. Then quantitative features are extracted from the experimental trajectories and are compared to quantitative features of synthetic trajectories predicted from a model. These quantitative features can include degree of straightness, curvature along the path, or tangential velocity profile overlap.

Let us first look at the two kinematic planning variables and their interrelationships.

2.5.1   Kinematics

We will represent the human arm as a two-link planar manipulator (figure 2.5a). For this two-joint arm, θ_1 represents the shoulder angle and θ_2 represents the elbow angle. No motion of the wrist is assumed, and the length of the hand is included in the forearm length. The upper arm length l_1 is assumed equal to the forearm plus hand length l_2, which is a good approximation for the human forearm plus hand relative to the upper arm (Hollerbach and Flash 1982). For convenience, both lengths are set to 1. The endpoint position is given either by the Cartesian coordinates x, y or

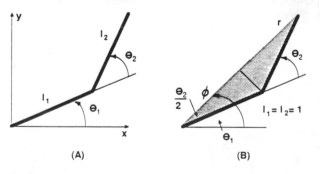

Figure 2.5
(a) A planar two-link arm, with endpoint position described by the Cartesian coordinates x, y. θ_1 and θ_2 are the joint angles, and l_1 and l_2 are the link lengths. (b) The case of equal length links, with $l_1 = l_2 = 1$. The endpoint position is now described by the polar coordinates (r, ϕ).

by polar coordinates r, ϕ. The kinematic planning variables that will be contrasted are the endpoint Cartesian coordinates x, y and the joint coordinates θ_1, θ_2.

To decide whether a given trajectory has been executed under one or the other set of coordinates, a description of the trajectory must be given in terms of each set of coordinates. Direct kinematics derives the endpoint Cartesian coordinates from the joint angles. From figure 2.5a:

$$x = l_1 \cos \theta_1 + l_2 \cos(\theta_1 + \theta_2)$$
$$y = l_1 \sin \theta_1 + l_2 \sin(\theta_1 + \theta_2). \tag{1}$$

Inverse kinematics derives the joint angles from the endpoint position and is more computationally complex than direct kinematics. It can be shown that

$$\cos(\theta_2/2) = \sqrt{x^2 + y^2}/2$$
$$\theta_1 = \tan^{-1}(y/x) - \theta_2/2. \tag{2}$$

From figure 2.5b, since the link lengths are assumed equal ($l_1 = l_2 = 1$), an isosceles triangle is formed with the radial line r to the endpoint. From the half-angle formula, each of the two equal interior angles is half the exterior angle θ_2.

$$\cos(\theta_2/2) = r/2 = \sqrt{x^2 + y^2}/2,$$

where the perpendicular from the elbow bisects the radial line of length $r = \sqrt{x^2 + y^2}$ from shoulder to endpoint. The shoulder angle θ_1 is simply the difference between the polar angle $\phi = \tan^{-1}(y/x)$ and the interior angle $\theta_2/2$:

$$\theta_1 = \tan^{-1}(y/x) - \theta_2/2.$$

The time parameter (t) has been left out for convenience.

In examining the kinematics, the transcendental functions relating joint angles to endpoint positions would lead one to expect complex curves in one set of coordinates corresponding to simple curves or straight lines in the other set of coordinates.

2.5.2   Coordination Strategy

Given a set of kinematic planning variables, a trajectory is formed when a coordination strategy is specified. If there were no restriction on the coordination strategy, then any trajectory could be generated and there would be no hope of inferring anything from the trajectory shapes. This is because any set of planning variables at any level could generate a given trajectory if there were no limitations on how these planning variables are used.

Coordination only becomes interesting when it is limited, and trajectories only tell us something about planning when they are stereotyped. Let us make the hypothesis that the human motor control system is not capable of executing all possible trajectories, unlike a robot control system, but possesses restrictions that are manifested as regularities or invariances in arm trajectories. The hope is that these regularities reveal something about the planning structure, because only certain planning variables and a certain coordination strategy could have given rise to them. The stereotypical paths and tangential velocity profiles of figures 2.3 and 2.4 indicate that the human motor control system may indeed be limited in how it can plan arm movements.

How do we characterize the coordination of a stereotypical movement? Given a set of planning variables, we must hypothesize different coordination strategies and quantify the fit between the predicted trajectories and the experimental trajectories. If a coordination strategy provides a good fit across many experimental conditions, we are justified in assuming that this coordination strategy is the one used by the human motor control system.

We have already seen one example of a coordination strategy in chapter 1, namely, a straight-line path. We looked at two forms for a straight-line path: a straight-line form where the time dependence is implicit (equation (1) for Cartesian coordinates and equation (3) for joint coordinates), and an interpolation form where the time dependence is explicit (equations (2) and (4)). One interesting aspect of a straight-line coordination strategy is that the path is unaffected by the choice of time function $f(t)$ (see question 1.1).

It will prove useful to rewrite equations (1) and (3) of chapter 1 in a more traditional straight-line form. For Cartesian coordinates,

$$y(t) = mx(t) + b, \tag{3}$$

where $m = (y(t_f) - y(t_0))/(x(t_f) - x(t_0))$ and $b = y(t_0) - mx(t_0)$. For joint coordinates,

$$\theta_1(t) = K\theta_2(t) + \phi_0, \tag{4}$$

where $K = (\theta_1(t_f) - \theta_1(t_0))/(\theta_2(t_f) - \theta_2(t_0))$ and $\phi_0 = \theta_1(t_0) - K\theta_2(t_0)$.

To be sure, other coordination strategies than linear interpolation could have been proposed, and we must bear in mind that our limited set of a priori possibilities may not span the actual one. As we will see in a later section, there is a strategy called staggered joint interpolation that is sometimes very difficult to distinguish from Cartesian coordinate planning.

2.6   Predicted Trajectories

Our next step is to find the trajectories predicted from a coordination strategy (linear interpolation) and two different sets of planning variables (joint angle planning and endpoint variable planning), which we will later compare against experimentally measured trajectories. We will then be in a position to ask whether joint angle planning is readily distinguished from endpoint variable planning under linear interpolation by external observation, or whether there are any difficulties in discriminating between them.

2.6.1   Trajectories under Joint Interpolation

We will begin by characterizing the trajectories generated under linear joint interpolation, since this is the easiest case. When the link lengths for the two-link planar manipulator are the same, endpoint trajectories arising from straight lines in joint space can be succinctly expressed using polar coordinates (figure 2.5b):

$$\phi - \theta_1 + \theta_2/2$$
$$r = 2\cos(\theta_2/2).$$

Given the straight line in joint coordinates (equation (4)) and substituting above,

$$r = 2\cos\left(\frac{\phi - \phi_0}{2K + 1}\right).$$

This class of polar coordinate curves is known as an *N-leaved rose* (Burlington 1942), presumably because each complete curve looks like a rose petal, whose thickness is determined by some slope N. When the link lengths are substantially different, such a simple expression does not arise.

Figure 2.6 illustrates some straight-line joint paths (a) and the corresponding endpoint Cartesian paths (b). The straight-line joint paths chosen here all pass through the origin, corresponding to both angles at 0 degrees when the arm is perfectly straight and horizontal, and are numbered from 1 to 13. The endpoint Cartesian paths corresponding to them are also numbered from 1 to 13. Arrows in both diagrams indicate the direction of travel in each. The endpoint Cartesian curves are symmetrical, although only half of each curve has been presented because of elbow joint limits.

As we can see from figure 2.6b, N-leaved roses tend to be strongly curved, especially for movements that are not primarily radial movements through the shoulder. Hence, joint interpolation generally yields trajectories readily distinguishable from straight-line hand paths. There is one important special case where the two planning strategies can be confused:

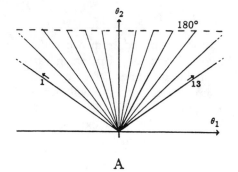

A

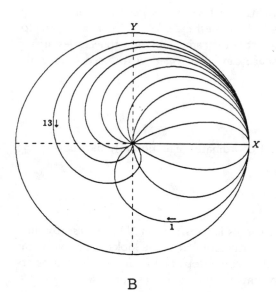

B

Figure 2.6
(a) A sampling of the straight lines in joint space from the origin. (b) The corresponding endpoint trajectories.

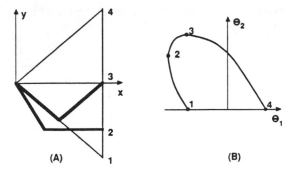

Figure 2.7
(a) A vertical straight-line motion with extremal points 1 and 4 and joint reversal points 2 and 3 for the shoulder and elbow, respectively. (b) Corresponding joint angle plot, with joint angles identified for endpoints 1 and 4.

any Cartesian straight line through the shoulder. Then $y/x = m$ and $b = 0$ from equation (3), and from equation (2)

$$\theta_1 = \tan^{-1} m - \theta_2/2. \tag{5}$$

In terms of joint variables θ_1 and θ_2 the trajectory is also straight. This is the only circumstance in which endpoint Cartesian variables and joint variables simultaneously result in a straight line. In figure 2.6 this would correspond to trajectory 4 (a rose petal of zero width in (b)).

2.6.2   Trajectories under Endpoint Interpolation

The exact relationship between endpoint Cartesian coordinates and joint angles is highly specific to the workspace region occupied by the straight line. To analyze this relationship, it proves useful to focus on joint reversal points. Figure 2.7a shows a hypothetical vertical straight-line motion. Points 1 and 4 correspond to maximum reach, when the elbow joint is straight out. When the forearm is perpendicular to the straight line, the shoulder joint reverses direction; that is to say, the shoulder angular velocity $\dot\theta_1$ changes sign. This corresponds to point 2: both an upward and a downward motion from this point cause the shoulder joint to rotate counterclockwise. When the endpoint is closest to the shoulder, the elbow joint reverses direction. This point 3 can also be characterized as the normal intersection from the shoulder to the straight line. Motion either upward or downward from point 3 causes clockwise rotation at the elbow joint.

Figure 2.7b shows the joint angle plot, where the specific joint angles are identified corresponding to the four endpoints of figure 2.7a. In general, the joint angle profile is curved. The extent of curvature depends on the portion of the curve traversed, as determined by the exact start and stop points chosen along the straight line.

1. When the start and stop points do not cross a joint reversal point, the joint curves are a bit simpler. This comprises motion within target pairs 1–2, 2–3, and 3–4.

2. A motion crosses exactly one joint reversal point when, for the case of shoulder reversal, one target is between 1 and 2 and the other target is between 2 and 3, and for the case of elbow reversal, when one target is between 2 and 3 and the other target is between 3 and 4. These single-joint reversal trajectories will be somewhat more complex than the former trajectories.

3. For long enough motions, both joints can reverse: one target is between 1 and 2 and the other between 3 and 4. These motions will yield the most complex joint angle plots.

This analysis covers all straight-line motions. First, if the straight line is at a different inclination, the coordinate system can be rotated so that the line will appear vertical. This would merely correspond in figure 2.7b to the joint angle plot translating along the θ_1 axis, corresponding to different initial shoulder angles. Second, if the straight line is at a different normal distance from the shoulder, the topology of the joint reversal points remains the same.

In examining figure 2.7b, it appears that the joint angle plot between point 4 and the θ_2 axis is nearly straight. Although the exact relationship is not linear, one can easily imagine with imperfect experimental data that a Cartesian straight-line trajectory would appear to have been coordinated instead by joint interpolation. This comment illustrates that one of the difficulties in the general strategy of this chapter is extracting metric features from imprecise or noisy experimental data, since no human-produced movement is likely to be perfectly straight. When do we consider a line straight? When are the deviations significant enough that we consider a line not to be straight? In reality, we can only speak of degrees of straightness, and we must keep in mind that there may be coordination strategies that yield approximately straight lines within a reasonable statistical measure. (It will turn out that staggered joint interpolation is such a strategy.) The departure from linearity may be small but significant, and not detectable within experimental error.

At point 4 the elbow angle is zero; that is, given our joint angle convention (figure 2.5), it is straight. The endpoint is then at the extreme of reach. If the elbow is kept straight and the shoulder angle is varied, the endpoint traces out a circle. This circle, beyond which the arm cannot reach, is called the *workspace boundary*. We can then rephrase the observation of the previous paragraph by saying that when a straight-line motion approaches the workspace boundary, it will appear that the joint angle plot is straight as well.

It turns out that all trajectories that approach the workspace boundary share this feature. Because of a peculiar property of kinematics, when a motion approaches the workspace boundary, it will always appear to have been coordinated by joint interpolation, whether or not this is the case. This boundary artifact has misled some researchers in the past. Thus, if we wish to investigate whether the planning coordinates are endpoint variables or joint angles, we must be careful not to place our targets at the extremes of reach.

To see that motions toward the workspace boundary appear to support joint angle planning, whether or not this is the case, we begin by noting that joint interpolation is equivalent to a constant ratio of elbow joint velocity to shoulder joint velocity (see question 2.5). Thus, we can demonstrate the boundary artifact by showing that any trajectory nearing the boundary approaches a constant joint rate ratio. To solve for the joint velocity ratio for a trajectory approaching the workspace boundary, the endpoint Cartesian velocities are related to joint velocities by differentiating equation (1):

$$\dot{x} = -\dot{\theta}_1 l_1 \sin \theta_1 - (\dot{\theta}_1 + \dot{\theta}_2) l_2 \sin(\theta_1 + \theta_2)$$
$$\dot{y} = \dot{\theta}_1 l_1 \cos \theta_1 + (\dot{\theta}_1 + \dot{\theta}_2) l_2 \cos(\theta_1 + \theta_2).$$

Conversely, the joint velocities can be found in terms of the endpoint Cartesian velocities by solving the equations above:

$$\dot{\theta}_1 = \frac{\dot{x} l_2 \cos(\theta_1 + \theta_2) + \dot{y} l_2 \sin(\theta_1 + \theta_2)}{l_2 l_2 \sin \theta_2}$$

$$\dot{\theta}_2 = -\frac{\dot{x}(l_1 \cos \theta_1 + l_2 \cos(\theta_1 + \theta_2)) + \dot{y}(l_1 \sin \theta_1 + l_2 \sin(\theta_1 + \theta_2))}{l_1 l_2 \sin \theta_2}.$$

At the edge of the workspace the elbow becomes straight; that is, $\theta_2 = 0$. Taking the limit of the joint rate ratio at the workspace boundary,

$$\lim_{\theta_2 \to 0} \frac{\dot{\theta}_2}{\dot{\theta}_1} = -\frac{l_1 + l_2}{l_2}.$$

Surprisingly, the joint rate ratio is a constant, dependent only on the link lengths. The constancy holds for any point on the workspace boundary and for any trajectory that approaches the boundary.

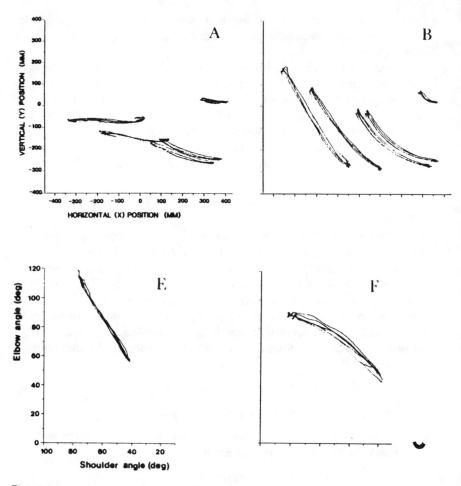

Figure 2.8
Endpoint trajectories ((a)–(d)) and corresponding joint angle plots ((e)–(h)) for four different movements in a sagittal plane.

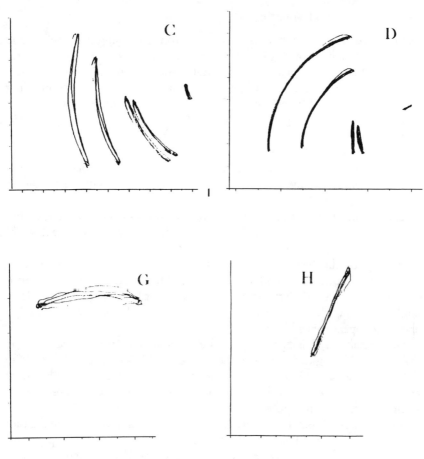

2.6.3   Experimental Trajectories

Having found the trajectories predicted from joint angle planning and endpoint variable planning, let us compare them with experimental recordings of actual trajectories in the sagittal plane. In figure 2.8a–d four different movements of the hand are shown, along with the corresponding joint angle plots in figure 2.8e–h. These movements were measured in the same way as those depicted in figure 2.3. Trajectory 2.8a represents a horizontal movement, where the left end of the path is farthest from the subject. Trajectory 2.8c represents a vertical movement. Trajectory 2.8b represents an upward and outward diagonal motion. Trajectory 2.8d represents an upward and inward diagonal movement, ending above the subject's head.

These data show that the predicted trajectories do not provide a consistent explanation of the actual trajectories. Some trajectories are straight and others are curved when the variables plotted are either endpoint Cartesian coordinates or joint angles. For the endpoint Cartesian coordinates, trajectories 2.8a and 2.8b are straight, whereas trajectory 2.8c is moderately curved and trajectory 2.8d is strongly curved. For the joint angle plots, trajectories 2.8e and 2.8h are straight, whereas trajectories 2.8f and 2.8g appear curved.

Superficially, it thus appears that the coordination strategy depends on the workspace region in which the movement is executed. Rather than accept this unpalatable explanation, let us entertain the notion that joint angle planning is in effect. Trajectories 2.8a/e and 2.8d/h are already straight lines in joint space. A reexamination of trajectory 2.8a/e shows that it is a straight line nearly through the shoulder, and the joint angle plot of trajectory 2.8e verifies the simultaneous straight line in joint space (see equation (5)). Thus, this trajectory can be interpreted as evidence for joint interpolation just as well as for endpoint interpolation. Trajectory 2.8c/g moves between vertical endpoints. In the experimental situation targets happened to be placed so that the beginning and final elbow joint angles were the same, and joint angle plot 2.8g shows that the subject chose to move only the shoulder joint. Trivially then, this is an example of joint interpolation, and the endpoint naturally follows a circular arc caused by swinging the whole arm through the shoulder.

Thus, only trajectory 2.8b/f is left unexplained by joint interpolation, since its joint angle plot 2.8f is clearly curved. In the next section we will look at a slight generalization of joint interpolation that explains trajectory 2.8b/f and unifies all results.

2.7 Staggered Joint Interpolation

In joint interpolation both joints execute the same time profile. Suppose instead that the onset of one joint is staggered relative to the onset of the other by a time offset δ and that its time profile $f(t)$ is scaled uniformly by a factor c. The new time profile is $f(ct + \delta)$, yielding from equation (3) of chapter 1

$$\theta_1(t) = (\theta_1(t_f) - \theta_1(t_0)) f(t) + \theta_1(t_0)$$

$$\theta_2(t) = (\theta_2(t_f) - \theta_2(t_0)) f(ct + \delta) + \theta_2(t_0).$$

(6)

The difference from the interpolation form is that one joint can start or stop before the other joint, although both joints have the same time profile shape $f(t)$. The time-scaling factor c uniformly compresses or expands the time profile shape to compensate for the time delay, so that joint 2 can end at the same time as joint 1 if its start is different, or joint 2 can start at the same time as joint 1 if its finish is different. Given that one of these two conditions holds, this strategy has only one free variable δ, since the other can be determined by $c = 1 - \delta/(t_f - t_0)$ (see question 2.7).

To proceed with this discussion, it is helpful to recast equation (6) in terms of joint velocities. By differentiating this equation,

$$\dot{\theta}_1(t) = \Delta\theta_1 \dot{f}(t)$$

$$\dot{\theta}_2(t) = \Delta\theta_2 c \dot{f}(ct + \delta),$$

where $\Delta\theta_i = \theta_i(t_f) - \theta_i(t_0)$ is the total displacement joint i moves through and $\dot{f}$ is the derivative of the time profile. Figure 2.9 compares hypothetical velocity profiles for the two joints under joint interpolation (a) and staggered joint interpolation (b). These profile shapes, which are similar to

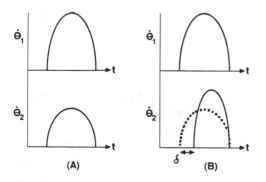

(A)   (B)

Figure 2.9
(a) Under joint interpolation, joint time profiles have the same shape. (b) Under staggered joint interpolation, the joint 2 time profile has been delayed and scaled.

those in figure 2.4, have been characterized as minimizing the jerk of the motion (Hogan 1984).[4] In figure 2.9a the velocity profiles have exactly the same shape, starting and stopping together. In figure 2.9b the elbow profile starts a time δ after the shoulder profile but ends at the same time. In order for the ends to be the same, the magnitude of the velocity profile must be scaled by a factor c. By changing whether δ is positive or negative, one or the other joint can be made to start or end first.

The motion of trajectory 2.8b/f can be simulated by computer, and staggered joint interpolation can be shown to provide an explanation for it. Figure 2.10a—b simulates this upward and outward diagonal movement. The solid line in figure 2.10a represents a perfect straight line in Cartesian coordinates, and the solid line in figure 2.10b the inverse kinematic joint angle solution. The outer dotted line in figure 2.10a represents the endpoint trajectory resulting from simple joint interpolation; this corresponds in figure 2.10b to the dotted straight-line joint path. The remaining dotted lines are staggered joint interpolations with increasing relative joint offset. Finally an offset value is found that generates a trajectory nearly indistinguishable from the Cartesian straight-line paths. It is hard to see in the figure because the overlap is so good. Thus, all trajectories in figure 2.8 can be explained in terms of joint variable planning, when the coordination strategy is generalized to staggered interpolation.

2.7.1 Limitations of Staggered Joint Interpolation

Since staggered joint interpolation made trajectory 2.8b straight, couldn't this strategy be used to make trajectories 2.8c and 2.8d straight as well? The answer is no, as we can see from the respective simulations of these trajectories in figures 2.10c and 2.10e.

Trajectory 2.8c/g represents motion between vertical targets. These vertical targets span the elbow joint reversal point 3 for the theoretical straight-line motion of figure 2.7. For the subject to have made a perfectly straight line, a substantial amount of elbow joint reversal would have been required, as in the simulation in figure 2.10d. For the upward and inward diagonal movement shown in figure 2.10e, reversal is required in both joints (figure 2.10f).

By definition, interpolation does not allow a reversal in any variable. Thus, staggered joint interpolation is incapable of approximating a Cartesian straight line whenever a substantial amount of joint reversal is required. This means that whenever point 2 or 3 of the prototype straight line in figure 2.7a is spanned by targets, a curved line should result because

---

4. *Jerk* is the time derivative of acceleration, and *mimimum jerk* refers to the jerk integrated across the whole trajectory.

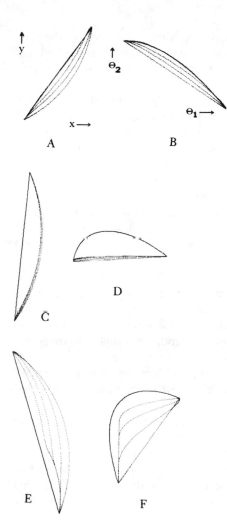

Figure 2.10
(a)–(b) Simulation of trajectory 2.8b/f. (c)–(d) Simulation of trajectory 2.8c/g. (e)–(f) Simulation of trajectory 2.8d/h.

staggered joint interpolation breaks down. Movements within the joint reversal zones—namely, between points 1 and 2, 2 and 3, and 3 and 4 of figure 2.7a—do not require joint reversal and hence can be made fairly straight by staggered joint interpolation.

Even though a Cartesian straight line does not result, staggered joint interpolation can sometimes make trajectories straighter than they might be otherwise. Though trajectory 2.10e requires a reversal in both elbow and shoulder joint movement to produce a straight line (figure 2.10f), increasing the delay in relative joint onset produces a series of curves that eventually makes the joint-interpolated path straighter. The dotted straight line in joint space 2.10f corresponds to the substantially curved outer dotted line in figure 2.10e. As the shoulder motion is increasingly offset from the elbow motion, curves intermediate in straightness are generated. From figure 2.10f we can see that the best strategy would be an almost complete decoupling in the joint movements to approximate the theoretical joint angle plotted as a solid line. The elbow should move alone, generating a straight vertical line, and then the shoulder should move alone, generating a straight horizontal line. Apparently such a strategy was occasionally used in some of the experimental movements reported by Hollerbach, Moore, and Atkeson (1986). For endpoints similar to trajectory 2.8d for a different subject, figure 2.11 shows a large degree of decoupling between elbow and shoulder joints. This subject therefore was able to make this motion much straighter than the subject whose motion is represented as trajectory 2.8d.

On the other hand, staggering has no effect on the trajectories in figure 2.10c. The beginning and final elbow joint angles are nearly the same, and there is hardly any elbow joint displacement during joint interpolation. Hence, introducing an offset in the elbow joint motion has almost no effect on the trajectory, as seen by the clustering of the dotted lines. Staggered joint interpolation cannot make the vertical movement of trajectory 2.8c straighter because the elbow joint is not moving, and substantial elbow joint reversal is required to achieve a perfect Cartesian straight line.

2.7.2   Planning Considerations

Our hypothesis, therefore, is that the motor control system plans in terms of joint angles rather than in terms of endpoint coordinates. Of course, we are talking here about the intermediate trajectory points, since endpoint planning must take place at the beginning and end of the motion to the visual targets. An advantage of staggered joint interpolation is that an inverse kinematics transformation is not required during the trajectory, making this strategy computationally simpler than endpoint planning. The disadvantage is some loss of endpoint control, resulting in curved motions.

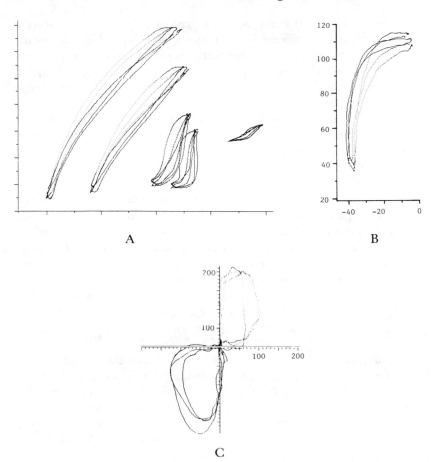

A   B   C

Figure 2.11
(a) An inward and upward diagonal movement for a different subject. (b) The joint angle
plot. (c) The joint velocity plot.

We may speculate that the planning goal of subjects is to execute a straight-line Cartesian motion but that this goal is limited by the restrictions of joint interpolation. (1) When joint reversal is not required, subjects achieve a very good approximation to a straight line through staggered joint interpolation. This is the best case for this strategy, because a linear endpoint trajectory is achieved without solving inverse kinematics. (2) When joint reversal would be required to realize a straight line, joint interpolation breaks down and a curved motion results. (3) Even for trajectories requiring joint reversal to achieve a Cartesian straight line, these trajectories can be made straighter by decoupling the joints through staggered joint interpolation. In keeping with our definition of joint interpolation, subjects in the experiments of Atkeson and Hollerbach (1985) almost never reversed a joint motion, either in the shoulder or in the elbow joint.

How does the subject know which joints to stagger and by how much? At present we can only speculate about this issue. Presumably knowledge of the staggering delay δ is built up with experience, with learning perhaps based on feedback from vision or environmental contact constraints. When indexed by the endpoints, this parameter can then be simply retrieved from motor memory. As with the issue of motor tapes discussed in chapter 1, a potential problem of memory saturation exists, since a delay must be remembered for every possible pair of endpoints. Further examination of this coordination strategy may indicate, however, that the memory saturation is not as bad as it might seem. As indicated in figure 2.7, all straight lines can be stylized as vertical lines at varying distances from the shoulder. Moreover, the topology of the joint reversal points does not change with the distance of the straight line from the shoulder. It may therefore be possible to come up with simple rules that generalize to all straight-line motions, based on only one prototypical trajectory.

The experiments presented in this chapter have dealt with unconstrained motion; that is, the hand was not touching any surface during motion. How can staggered joint interpolation be reconciled with constrained motion? Recall, for instance, the example of writing on a blackboard. If you stand directly in front of the blackboard and make a vertical motion, staggered joint interpolation would predict that your hand attempts to make a curved motion that drives your hand through the blackboard, violating this environmental constraint. We may speculate that the natural compliance of the arm accommodates staggered joint interpolation to the geometry of the external world. We would predict that the force of the hand against the blackboard increases the more the hand wants to move into the blackboard. Preliminary experimental evidence confirms this prediction.

Joint interpolation could be generalized further by adding more adjustable parameters, which would conceivably result in a better ability to achieve approximate endpoint goals. Nevertheless, we must be wary of engaging in mere curve fitting. It is a matter of judgment whether the added reduction of the data justifies the additional parameters, since the more parameters one adds to a mathematical model, the easier it is to fit diverse data. In the extreme, an overly parameterized joint-based planning strategy would not be clearly distinguishable from or less complicated than an endpoint-based planning strategy. In the present case staggered joint interpolation requires just one additional variable, since the time scaling is dependent on the delay. The data reduction is an underlying explanation for both straight and curved movements and the identification of just one planning strategy used anywhere in the workspace.

Suggestions for Further Reading

Though Bernstein's (1967) pioneering book is now out of print, an interesting edition has been brought out by Whiting (1984). Each of Bernstein's original chapters is accompanied by two discussions by modern motor control researchers, who examine its relevance and importance to current research.

The study of the coordination of arm movements can be further pursued in several journal articles. The scaling of arm movements is discussed in Atkeson and Hollerbach 1985 and in Hollerbach and Flash 1982. Issues of endpoint versus joint angle planning as presented in this chapter can be pursued by reading Hollerbach and Atkeson 1987 and Hollerbach, Moore, and Atkeson 1986. Discussion supporting endpoint planning can be found in Morasso 1981, Abend, Bizzi, and Morasso 1982, and Viviani and Terzuolo 1982 and discussion supporting joint angle planning can be found in Soechting and Lacquaniti 1981 and Kaminski and Gentile 1986. The resolution of redundant arm configurations is considered in Cruse and Brüwer 1987. Three-dimensional arm movements have also been studied, and planning strategies have been proposed for the observed trajectories; see Morasso 1983 and Soechting, Lacquaniti, and Terzuolo 1986.

Certainly some of the most complex trajectories we produce are in handwriting. There are several theories of how handwriting shapes are produced. For a sampling of such theories, see Hollerbach 1981, Edelman and Flash 1987, and Morasso and Mussa-Ivaldi 1982. Another communication medium via motor control is signing by the deaf. For a study of signing trajectories, see Loomis et al. 1983.

An approach totally different from explicit kinematic planning is optimization. It may seem intuitive that we minimize energy, time, or effort when we make a movement, and it is possible to set up an optimization problem that derives the trajectories implicitly. Examples include minimum jerk motions (Hogan 1984; Flash and Hogan 1985) and minimum effort motions (Nelson 1983; Hasan 1986). A paper offering very good insight into the optimization approach is Stein, Oguztoreli, and Capaday 1986. An entertaining roundtable discussion of the variables that the motor control system might use in control is reported in Stein 1982.

Questions

2.1 Suppose that all paths are Cartesian straight lines. Consider two different paths with lengths d_1 and d_2 and movement durations of T_1 and T_2, respectively. Let $v_1(t)$ and $v_2(t)$ be the corresponding tangential velocity profiles. In order to compare the tangential velocity profile shapes, it is necessary to normalize the movements for distance and duration, as in figure 2.4. How would you modify $v_2(t)$ in order to normalize it with respect to $v_1(t)$?

2.2 Suppose the link lengths in figure 2.5 are unequal ($l_1 \neq l_2$). Rederive the inverse kinematic equations as in figure 2.2.

2.3 Suppose the elbow angle is described by the absolute elbow angle $\phi = \theta_1 + \theta_2$. Show that joint interpolation in terms of θ_1 and ϕ also yields an N-leaved rose.

2.4 Again consider a joint angle description in terms of the absolute elbow angle ϕ and the shoulder angle θ_1. For a vertical straight-line motion as in figure 2.7, find the new joint reversal points.

2.5 Suppose the joint rate ratio $\dot{\theta}_1/\dot{\theta}_2$ is constant. Show that the trajectories are the same as straight lines in joint space.

2.6 One feature of linear interpolation is that the time function does not change the path (see section 1.3). Is this true of staggered joint interpolation?

2.7 If staggering in relative joint onset can occur at only the beginning or the end of a motion, but not both, show that $c = 1 - \delta/(t_f - t_0)$.

References

Abend, W., E. Bizzi, and P. Morasso (1982). Human arm trajectory formation. *Brain* 105, 331–348.

Atkeson, C. G., and J. M. Hollerbach (1985). Kinematic features of unrestrained vertical arm movements. *Journal of Neuroscience* 5, 2318–2330.

Bernstein, N. (1967). *The coordination and regulation of movements.* Oxford: Pergamon Press.

Burlington, R. S. (1942). *Handbook of mathematical tables and formulas.* Sandusky, OH: Handbook Publ. Inc.

Cruse, H., and M. Brüwer (1987). The human arm as a redundant manipulator: The control of path and joint angles. *Biological Cybernetics* 57, 137–144.

Edelman, S., and T. Flash (1987). A model of handwriting. *Biological Cybernetics* 57, 25–36.

Flash, T., and N. Hogan (1985). The coordination of arm movements: An experimentally confirmed mathematical model. *Journal of Neuroscience* 5, 1688–1703.

Hasan, Z. (1986). Optimized movement trajectories and joint stiffness in unperturbed, inertially loaded movements. *Biological Cybernetics* 53, 373–382.

Hogan, N. (1984). An organizing principle for a class of voluntary movements. *Journal of Neuroscience* 4, 2745–2754.

Hollerbach, J. M. (1981). An oscillation theory of handwriting. *Biological Cybernetics* 39, 139–156.

Hollerbach, J. M., and C. G. Atkeson (1987). Deducing planning variables from experimental arm trajectories: Pitfalls and possibilities. *Biological Cybernetics* 56, 279–292.

Hollerbach, J. M., and T. Flash (1982). Dynamic interactions between limb segments during planar arm movement. *Biological Cybernetics* 44, 67–77.

Hollerbach, J. M., S. P. Moore, and C. G. Atkeson (1986). Workspace effect in arm movement kinematics derived by joint interpolation. In G. Gantchev, B. Dimitrov, and P. Gatev, eds., *Motor control.* New York: Plenum.

Kaminski, T., and A. M. Gentile (1986). Joint control strategies and hand trajectories in multijoint pointing movements. *Journal of Motor Behavior* 18, 261–278.

Loomis, J., H. Poizner, U. Bellugi, A. Blakemore, and J. Hollerbach (1983). Computer graphic modeling of American Sign Language. *Computer Graphics* 17, 105–114.

Morasso, P. (1981). Spatial control of arm movements. *Experimental Brain Research* 42, 223–227.

Morasso, P. (1983). Three dimensional arm trajectories. *Biological Cybernetics* 48, 187–194.

Morasso, P., and F. A. Mussa-Ivaldi (1982). Trajectory formation and handwriting: A computational model. *Biological Cybernetics* 45, 131–142.

Nelson, W. (1983). Physical principle for economies of skilled movements. *Biological Cybernetics* 46, 135–147.

Soechting, J. F., and F. Lacquaniti (1981). Invariant characteristics of a pointing movement in man. *Journal of Neuroscience* 1, 710–720.

Soechting, J. F., F. Lacquaniti, and C. A. Terzuolo (1986). Coordination of arm movements in three-dimensional space: Sensorimotor mapping during drawing movement. *Neuroscience* 17, 295–311.

Stein, R. B. (1982). What muscle variable(s) does the nervous system control in limb movements? *Behavioral and Brain Sciences* 5, 535–577.

Stein, R. B., M. N. Oguztoreli, and C. Capaday (1986). What is optimized in muscular movements? In N. L. Jones, N. McCartney, and A. J. McComas, eds., *Human muscle power*. Champaign, IL: Human Kinetics Publishers.

Viviani, P., and C. Terzuolo (1982). Trajectory determines movement dynamics. *Neuroscience* 7, 431–437.

Whiting, H. T. A., ed. (1984). *Human motor actions: Bernstein reassessed*. Amsterdam: North Holland.

Chapter 3

Muscle Properties and the Control of Arm Movement

E. Bizzi and F. A. Mussa-Ivaldi

In this chapter we will focus on the control of arm movements and, in particular, on the way in which the central nervous system (CNS) proceeds from the planning of trajectories to their execution by creating appropriate patterns of joint torques and neural commands.

The investigations described here indicate that the brain can take advantage of the biological design of the arm in order to simplify some of the computational tasks described in chapter 1.

3.1 The Formation of Arm Trajectories

The first step in planning an arm trajectory is to develop a CNS representation of the position of both the target and the initial posture of the hand. This initial step is contingent upon transforming the retinal image of the target into head-centered and ultimately body-centered coordinates.

This work was supported by NIH grants NS09343 and AR26710, ONR grant N00014/88/K/0372, and a grant from the Sloan Foundation.

According to recent studies by Andersen, Essick, and Siegel (1987), this transformation occurs in the parietal areas of the cerebral cortex (figure 3.1). Visual processing in retinotopic coordinates takes place in the occipital lobe. Visual information then flows from the occipital to the parietal lobe, where it combines with signals representing eye position in the orbit. The combination of visual and eye-position signals gives rise to head- and perhaps body-centered representations of the target.

In order to plan the arm trajectory, the CNS must also represent the initial arm configuration. If the hand's initial position is detected visually, then the process is identical to the one utilized for locating the target. However, if the arm's configuration is perceived through a combination of joint, muscle, and tendon receptors, then a complex and poorly understood set of transformations must occur; the position of the hand must be derived from activities related to muscle length and joint angle. We do not know how the CNS accomplishes this complex readout.

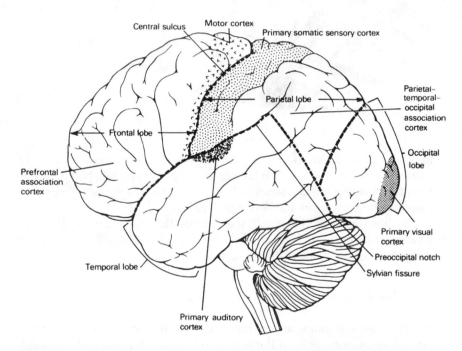

Figure 3.1
The major divisions of the human cerebral cortex. A lateral view of the hemisphere. (Reprinted by permission of the publisher from J. P. Kelley, Principles of the functional and anatomical organization of the nervous system. In E. R. Kandel and J. H. Schwartz, eds., *Principles of neural science*, 2nd ed., 1985, p. 214, fig. 19.3. © 1985 by Elsevier Science Publishing Co., Inc.)

Once the initial position and the final target are represented in the same coordinate frame, the CNS must solve the problem of representing the trajectory, by planning the path and the velocity of the hand in space. There is some evidence that this representation may be formed in the posterior parietal cortex and the medial regions of the frontal lobe.

Results obtained by Georgopoulos et al. (1982, 1983) based on recording single neurons from the parietal cortex of monkeys, indicate a correlation between neural activity and the direction of the arm's movement. These experiments consisted of recording activity from individual cortical cells as the monkey executed movements from a fixed location to a set of targets placed around the starting point. The results indicated that the curves relating the frequency of discharge of a cell to the direction of movement were characterized by a single maximum, corresponding to the "preferred direction" of the cell. The average direction of a cell ensemble (defined as the weighted sum of all the preferred directions with the weights given by the cell activities) was found to be in good agreement with the direction of hand movements.

It is tempting to speculate that the signals from the motor cortex may represent the physiological substrate of trajectory planning in spatial coordinates. However, the viability of an alternative hypothesis has been demonstrated—namely, that Georgopoulos's results can also be interpreted as evidence that cortical cells encode muscle activations instead of the direction of hand movements (Mussa-Ivaldi 1988).

Another difficult challenge for motor neurophysiologists is to understand the transformation from trajectory representation into the appropriate joint motion and joint torques. In the past, physiologists did not specifically address this question. The signals from "motor" areas were assumed to activate the segmental spinal cord apparatus and generate the desired movement. Very little attention was paid to the complex problem of deriving joint motions and joint torques and compensating for dynamic interactions. In contrast, these issues have been central concerns for investigators in the field of robotics, who have proposed two distinct but not mutually exclusive approaches for transforming the planned trajectory into the appropriate joint motions and torques—namely, the feedforward and feedback control approaches described in chapter 1.

In this chapter we will discuss how the transformation from planning to joint motion and forces is handled in the context of biological systems. We will also present a neurobiological view of torque generation based on exploiting muscle mechanical and geometrical properties.

3.2   Role of Muscle Mechanical Properties

First we will consider how the CNS exploits the elastic behavior of muscles. This issue deserves special emphasis because it is very likely that the features displayed by the neural controller have evolved as a result of the need not only to control but also to take advantage of the mechanical properties of the musculoskeletal apparatus.

A case for this approach has been made by Feldman (1974a,b), who investigated the springlike properties of the human arm. Muscles do indeed behave like tuneable springs in the sense that the force they generate is a function of length and level of neural activation (Rack and Westbury 1974).

The force-length relationship in individual muscle fibers was studied by Gordon, Huxley, and Julian (1966), who related the development of tension at different muscle lengths to the degree of overlap between actin and myosin filaments (figure 3.2).[1] According to the sliding-filaments theory of muscle contraction (Huxley 1963, 1969), the process of generating force is caused, within the muscles, by the physical interaction between myosin and actin filaments. This interaction leads to the formation of cross-bridges. The increase in muscle stiffness, observed as the motorneuronal drive to the muscle increases, is considered a direct consequence of the generation of new cross-bridges.

In addition, muscles are arranged about the joints in an agonist-antagonist configuration. If we attribute springlike properties to muscles, then a limb's posture is maintained when the forces exerted by the agonist and antagonist muscle groups are equal and opposite. This fact implies that when an external force is applied, the limb is displaced by an amount that varies with both the external force and the stiffness of the muscles. When the external force is removed, the limb should return to its original position. Experimental studies of arm movements in monkeys have shown that a forearm posture is indeed an equilibrium point between opposing springlike forces (Bizzi, Polit, and Morasso 1976).

The observation that posture is obtained from the equilibrium between the length-tension properties of opposing muscles led to the hypothesis, first proposed by Feldman (1966), that movements result from a shift of the equilibrium point. The studies by Bizzi, Polit, and Morasso (1976), Kelso (1977), Kelso and Holt (1980), and Bizzi et al. (1984) provided the experimental evidence to support this hypothesis. In particular, Bizzi et al. (1984) demonstrated that the transition from one arm posture to another is achieved by adjusting the relative intensity of neural signals directed to each of the opposing muscles. According to this result, a single-joint arm

1. In the structural organization of vertebrate striated muscles, sarcomeres are the units that are repeated longitudinally along the fibrils. These units consist primarily of comblike arrays of overlapping actin and myosin arrays (see figure 3.2).

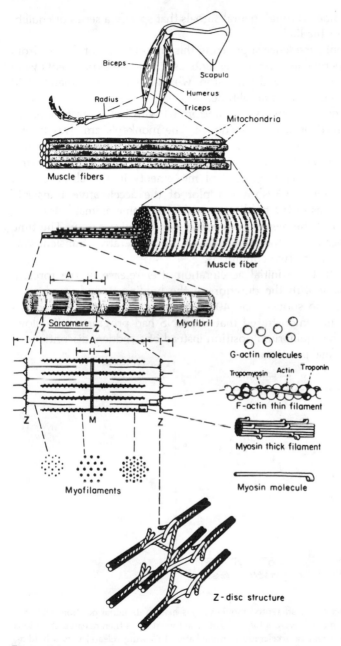

Figure 3.2
Organization of striated muscle structure, showing the nomenclature applied to the bands and the proteins that make up the thick and thin filaments. (Reprinted by permission of the publisher and author from T. A. McMahon, *Muscles, reflexes, and locomotion*, 1984, p. 56, fig. 3.2. © 1984 by Thomas A. McMahon. Published by Princeton University Press.)

trajectory is obtained through neural signals that specify a series of equilibrium positions for the limb.

The experimental evidence supporting this important point derives from three sets of experiments. The movements used in these experiments were single-joint elbow flexion and extension, which lasted approximately 700 milliseconds for a 60-degree amplitude.

The first set of experiments was performed with both intact monkeys and those deprived of sensory feedback. The monkey's arm was briefly held in its initial position after a target light that indicated final position had been presented. It was found that movements to the target after the arm was released were faster than control movements in the absence of a holding action. Figure 3.3 shows a plot of the accelerative transients against the durations of the holding period in the same animal before and after interruption of the nerves conveying sensory information. The time course of the increase in the amplitude of the accelerative transient was virtually identical in the two conditions.

It was found that the initial acceleration after release of the forearm increased gradually with the duration of the holding period, reaching a steady-state value no sooner than 400 milliseconds after muscles' activation. These results demonstrated that the CNS had programmed a slow, gradual shift of the equilibrium position instead of a sudden, discontinuous transition to the final position.

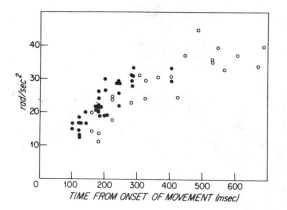

Figure 3.3
The forearm of intact and deafferented monkeys was held in its initial position while the animal attempted to move toward a target light. The forearm was then released at various times. This figure is a plot of acceleration (immediately following release) versus holding time. The abscissa shows time in milliseconds; the ordinate shows radians per second squared. Solid circles: intact animal; open circles: deafferented animal. (Reprinted by permission from E. Bizzi, N. Accornero, W. Chapple, and N. Hogan, Posture control and trajectory formation during arm movement, 1984, *Journal of Neuroscience* 4, 2738–2744.)

The same conclusions are supported by a second set of experiments (Bizzi et al. 1984) based on forcing the forearm to a target position through an assisting torque pulse applied at the beginning of a visually triggered forearm movement. The goal of this experiment was to move the limb ahead of the equilibrium position with an externally imposed displacement in the direction of the target. It was found that the forearm, after being forced by the assisting pulse to the target position, returned to a point between the initial and the final position before moving to the endpoint. This outcome results from the fact that a restoring force is generated by the elastic muscle properties. If muscles merely generated force or if the elastic properties were negligible, this return motion of the limb would not have been observed. Since the same response to the torque pulse was also observed in monkeys deprived of sensory feedback (Bizzi et al. 1984), it was inferred that proprioceptive reflexes are not essential to the generation of restoring forces. Taken together, these results suggest that alpha motor-neuronal activity specifies a series of equilibrium positions throughout the movement.

In the third set of experiments the arm was not only driven to the target location but also held there for a variable amount of time (1 to 3 seconds), after which a target light at the new position was activated (figure 3.4). A cover prevented the animal from seeing its arm. After the reaction time to the presentation of the light, the monkey activated its muscles (flexors in the case of figure 3.4) to reach the target position. At this point, usually shortly after the onset of muscle activity, the servo that held the arm was deactivated. The arm then returned to a point inter-mediate between the initial and the target positions before moving back to the target position. Note that, during the return movement that required extension, evident flexor activity was present. The amplitude of the return movement was a function of the duration of the holding action. If enough time elapsed between activation of the target light and deactivation of the servo, the arm remained in the target position upon release.

These observations provide further support for the view that motor-neuronal activity specifies a series of equilibrium positions throughout the movement. If the muscles merely generated force during the transient phase of a movement, the pronounced return motion of the limb during flexor muscle activity would not be observed (figure 3.4). This series of equilibrium positions has been termed the *virtual trajectory* (Hogan 1984).

3.3   Implications of the Virtual Trajectory

The idea of a moving equilibrium point is a direct consequence of two known facts: (1) that a limb is at static equilibrium when all the torques

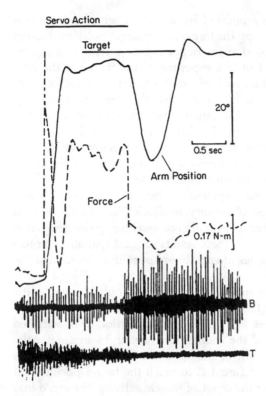

Figure 3.4
Forearm movements of deafferented monkeys with a holding action in the final position. While the target light remained off, the servo moved the arm to the target position. Then the target light was activated, and the servo was turned off. The arm returned to a position intermediate between the initial and target positions before moving back to the target position. Similar results were obtained in many trials with two monkeys. The upper bar indicates duration of servo action. The lower bar indicates onset of the target light. The solid trace shows arm position; the dashed trace shows torque. B: flexor (biceps); T: extensor (triceps). (Reprinted by permission from E. Bizzi, N. Accornero, W. Chapple, and N. Hogan, Posture control and trajectory formation during arm movement, 1984, *Journal of Neuroscience* 4, 2738–2744.)

generated by opposing muscles cancel out, and (2) that the neural input to each muscle has the effect of selecting a length-tension curve. It follows that at all times the neural activities directed to all the muscles acting on a limb can be "translated" into the corresponding equilibrium angle, which is given by the balance of the elastic torques.

During the execution of a movement, these equilibria or virtual positions act as "centers of attraction." The difference between actual and virtual position generates an elastic force directed toward a virtual position. The end course of the movement is determined by the interaction of this elastic force with limb inertia and viscosity. However, if the neural inputs were suddenly frozen, the limb would ultimately come to rest in the virtual position encoded by the current values of the inputs.

With respect to the mathematical significance of the virtual trajectory, note that muscles are activated by firing rates of a large population of motor neurons and that their firing rates are difficult to interpret in terms of their consequences on motor behavior. In contrast, the virtual position of a limb, such as the forearm, is a single number (a joint angle). The virtual position's physical significance as an attractive point is well understood. Hence, the virtual trajectory provides reduction of dimensionality (the mapping of many numbers into a single one or a few) together with a physical interpretation.

The virtual trajectory can be defined only with a nonzero joint stiffness. This is a consequence of the fact that the equilibrium condition

$$\text{Torque} = F(\text{joint angle, muscle inputs}) = 0$$

provides a unique relation from muscle inputs to joint equilibrium-angle only when the derivative of the function, F, with respect to the joint angle (that is, the joint stiffness) is not zero. If instead this derivative were zero, then the joint torque would not depend upon the joint angle, and the muscles would be ideal force generators. If muscles had properties of force generators with negligible stiffness, then the torques necessary to produce a desired motion would be computed explicitly by the CNS. In contrast, the fact that muscles have significant elastic properties led to the notion that limb movement is obtained by shifting the equilibrium position (that is, the virtual position) defined by the elastic actuators. According to this view, the CNS does not explicitly compute torques at the joints.

Let us look at a specific example that illustrates the notion of the virtual trajectory as a map that transforms a set of neural inputs into a kinematic variable. In this very simple situation (figure 3.5) a single limb is operated by a pair of muscles, a flexor, F, and an extensor, E, each of which is

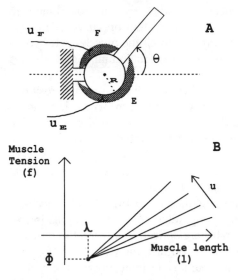

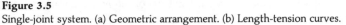

Figure 3.5
Single-joint system. (a) Geometric arrangement. (b) Length-tension curves.

controlled by a single input, u. We will consider the map from the two inputs, u_F and u_E, to the equilibrium angle, θ_0. For simplicity, let us assume that the two muscles are wrapped on a single pulley of radius R. Then their lengths are linearly related to the joint angle:

$$l_F = R(\pi - \theta)$$
$$l_E = R(\pi + \theta).$$

Accordingly, the net joint torque also is linearly related to the forces developed by the two muscles, f_F and f_E:

$$T = R(f_E - f_F).$$

Here we adopt the convention that a positive force corresponds to the muscle being pulled.

The two muscles are characterized by linear length-tension curves:

$$f = k(u)(l - l_0(u)).$$

In this expression both the stiffness, k, and the rest-length, l_0, are regulated by the control output, u. Let us assume that the stiffness depends linearly on the control input,

$$k = \alpha u,$$

and that the curves intersect at a point (λ, ϕ) on the length-tension plane with $\phi < 0$. The latter condition ensures that increasing the input, u, causes the muscle rest-length (at which $f = 0$) to decrease; that is, the unloaded muscle shortens. Then the rest-length is

$$l_0 = \lambda + \phi/k(u).$$

For the sake of simplicity, we also assume that the constants, λ, ϕ, and α, are identical in both muscles.

With these hypotheses the equilibrium condition becomes

$$T = R(f_E - f_F) = R[(k_E + k_F)R\theta + (k_E - k_F)R\pi + k_F l_{0F} - k_E l_{0E}]$$

$$= 0.$$

This expression can be solved for θ so that a map from the two muscle inputs to the joint angles is defined. However, this map is possible if and only if $k_E + k_F \neq 0$—that is, if the net joint stiffness, $R^2(k_E + k_F)$, is not zero. Then the equilibrium angle is

$$\theta_{equil} = \frac{k_F - k_E}{k_F + k_E}\left(\pi - \frac{\lambda}{R}\right) - \frac{u_F - u_E}{u_F + u_E}\left(\pi - \frac{\lambda}{R}\right),$$

The virtual trajectories relate to the concepts of feedforward and feedback control. For movements at moderate or low speed, the CNS can directly express the desired trajectory as a sequence of equilibrium positions. In fact, at low speeds and accelerations, viscous and inertial torques are modest and can be regarded as "perturbing torques" that make the arm deviate from the virtual trajectory by an acceptable amount.

This control scheme is analogous to the position feedback strategy described in section 1.5.2. However, it must be stressed that the elastic forces generated by a virtual trajectory are obtained from muscle properties and need not be derived from position signals fed back to the controller. Biological feedback is indeed characterized by transmission delays of the order of 30 milliseconds. A position servo relying on feedback with such large delays would be prone to instabilities (Stein and Oguztoreli 1976) and would be ineffective in compensating for disturbances at frequencies above 2 hertz (Hogan et al. 1987). In contrast, elastic muscle properties provide the equivalent of an ideal position feedback with zero delay and variable gain.

As the speed of movement increases, limb inertia and viscosity are expected to cause larger deviations from the virtual trajectory. These deviations may cease to be acceptable, and they can be prevented by increasing the stiffness and by modifying the virtual trajectory itself. The increase in stiffness would be analogous to the increase of feedback gain described in section 1.5.2. The latter solution is effectively equivalent to the feedforward control scheme described in section 1.5.1.; here, however, instead of explicitly computing a joint torque, the virtual path is changed according to the dynamics of the controlled system. Therefore, the virtual trajectory provides a unique framework for combining feedback and feedforward control schemes without postulating separate computational mechanisms.

Deviations from the intended trajectory may also result from external perturbations. In this case compensatory changes depend upon proprioceptive reflexes, which provide a way to increase stiffness via spinal cord connectivity and also signal to planning centers for reprogramming.

Traditionally, in motor control, behaviors like maintaining posture, generating movements, and generating forces have been considered separate endeavors requiring different control schemes. In contrast, we have seen here that these apparently diverse behaviors share a common information-processing scheme. We have also seen that this unification is contingent upon the mechanical properties of the musculoskeletal system as well as the characterization of the proprioceptive system.

3.4   Reflex Control of Muscles

How effectively do primates compensate when their movements are met by unexpected load disturbances? Recent experimental evidence has revealed that a number of processes are called into action by the sudden application of a load opposing a centrally initiated movement. Basically, load disturbances are initially resisted by two mechanisms: (1) the purely elastic action of the activated muscle tissue and (2) the reflex action. Both mechanisms generate a force opposing the increased load, but the relative contribution of the reflex and mechanical actions may depend on the state of muscular activity and the magnitude of load disturbance.

Although it is well known that the elasticity of an activated muscle resists loads, the resistance generated by the reflex response to a change in the load depends on a number of factors. Among these , perhaps the most relevant is the existence of alpha-gamma coactivation during centrally programmed movements. This coactivation has been observed by many investigators in a number of systems (Granit, Holmgren, and Merton 1955; Vallbo 1970, 1973).

In particular, the experiments by Severin, Orlovsky, and Shik (1967) have shown that during locomotion reflex activity from muscle spindle receptors is greater from the shortening agonist muscle than it is from the lengthening antagonists. Results such as these indicate that gamma impulses are sent to the muscle spindles just prior to or during extrafusal contraction, which results in intrafusal muscle contraction. As a result, there is an increase of reflex activity. It has been suggested that through this coactivation of alpha and gamma elements, a mobile part of the body is servo-assisted so as to adjust force output to compensate for changes in load (Mattews 1972; see also section 1.5.5).

However, to properly evaluate the complexities underlying load compensation, it is important to consider some of the interacting processes that occur at spinal and supraspinal levels following the application of a load. With respect to these processes, it is relevant that alpha motor neurons receive not only facilitation from muscle spindle afferents but also an inhibitory input from Golgi tendon organs. In addition, afferent proprioceptive impulses reach subcortical and cortical areas (Brooks et al. 1976; Conrad et al. 1974; Evarts 1973), generating impulses that play back on the spinal cord apparatus, via corticospinal pathways. These long-loop reflexes may be influenced by preexisting sets of instructions (Evarts and Tanji 1976). These few examples suggest an exceedingly complex situation characterized by parallel processing along various spinal and supraspinal pathways.

Recent experimental evidence has provided some answers concerning the contributions made by the reflex and mechanical mechanisms to the increased force produced by muscles when loads are unexpectedly applied during centrally programmed movements.

The question of evaluating the increment of the reflex and mechanical torque generated by an animal was approached by comparing head movements before and after surgical interruption of the sensory pathways. These pathways enter the spinal cord via the dorsal roots (see figure 1.9). The results indicate that the compensatory torque of reflex origin, stimulated by the application of an opposing force, was from 10 to 30 percent of the torque required for perfect compensation. However, the larger fraction of the observed compensation was due to the mechanical (inertial, viscous, and elastic) properties of the neck musculature. Further, the combined action of reflex and mechanical processes never completely compensated for the disturbance (Bizzi et al. 1978).

These results are in agreement with those of Vallbo (1973) in normal human subjects, of Grillner (1972) in cats, and of Allum (1975) on postural resetting. The conclusion derived from the experiments is that reflex load compensation is rather modest.

Given the widespread spinal and supraspinal distribution of afferent proprioceptive signals, it is entirely possible that short latency but modest load compensation represents the first line of defense against an opposing load before the intervention of longer-latency cortical modifications. (See also section 1.5.5.)

Here we will see that the length-dependent component of neural feedback is equivalent to an additional muscle-stiffness term. We will refer to the simplified single-joint system described in the previous math box. However, here we will adopt a more general definition of the muscle's length-tension curves: at steady state the tension developed by each muscle is a function of its length, l, and of its neural input, u. Then for a flexor, F, and an extensor, E, we have

$$f_F = f_F(l_F, u_F)$$

$$f_E = f_E(l_E, u_E).$$

The derivatives of these functions with respect to the muscle length and the neural input define the intrinsic stiffness ($k = \partial f/\partial l$) and the "input sensitivity" ($\sigma = \partial f/\partial u$) of the muscle. Hence, with two muscles, we have the four coefficients k_F, k_E, σ_F, σ_E.

Each of the neural inputs can be expressed as the combination of a central component, u_C, and a reflex component, u_R. For the sake of simplicity, we will assume a simple additive rule, and we will consider only length-dependent reflexes; we will ignore velocity and force-dependent reflexes (see question 3.1) as well as the interactions between central and reflex mechanisms provided by the coactivation of alpha and gamma motor neurons. (For a more detailed discussion, see Nichols and Houk 1976.) Then for the two neural inputs we have

$$u_F = u_{FC} + u_{FR}(l_F, l_E)$$

$$u_E = u_{EC} + u_{ER}(l_E, l_F).$$

The reflex gains are the derivative of the neural inputs with respect to the muscle lengths. Hence, we have four gain coefficients: $g_{FF} = \partial u_F/\partial l_F$, $g_{FE} = \partial u_F/\partial l_E$, $g_{EF} = \partial u_E/\partial l_F$, $g_{EE} = \partial u_E/\partial l_E$. Note that each muscle has a direct feedback gain, associated with the change in length of the muscle itself. Furthermore, there is a coupling feedback gain, associated with the antagonist's length change.

If the length of the two muscles is forced to change by two small amounts, dl_F and dl_E, then the flexor's tension will change as

$$df_F = \frac{df_F}{dl_F} dl_F + \frac{df_F}{dl_E} dl_E.$$

Using the chain rule, this expression becomes

$$df_F = \left(\frac{\partial f_F}{\partial l_F} + \frac{\partial f_F}{\partial u_F}\frac{\partial u_F}{\partial l_F}\right)dl_F + \frac{\partial f_F}{\partial u_F}\frac{\partial u_F}{\partial l_E}dl_E$$

$$= (k_F + k'_{FF})dl_F + k'_{FE}dl_E, \tag{1}$$

with $k'_{FF} = \sigma_F g_{FF}$ and $k'_{FE} = \sigma_F g_{FE}$.

A similar expression is obtained for the extensor's tension. The terms k'_{FF} and k'_{FE} are derived from a combination of reflex gains and input sensitivity coefficients. They have the same dimensions as the intrinsic stiffness, k (force divided by length), and the same physical meaning. However, there are differences due to the fact that the k' derive from information-processing mechanisms. In particular, a difference between reflex and intrinsic stiffness is due to the delay of neural transmission, τ. This delay should be taken into account during movement. Then equation (1) must be corrected to relate to a change in force at time t and to the change in length at t (intrinsic stiffness) and at $t - \tau$ (reflex stiffness):

$$df_F(t) = k_F dl_F(t) + k'_{FF}dl_F(t - \tau) + k'_{FE}dl_E(t - \tau).$$

3.5   Multijoint Posture and Movement

In the previous two sections we have considered the muscle's elastic behavior, the execution of single-joint movement, and the central and reflex activities leading to the control of muscle stiffness. One of the main lessons to be derived from single-joint experiments is that movement is nothing more than a series of sequentially implemented postures. To use the terminology of this chapter, movement derives from shifting the equilibrium point between agonist and antagonist length-tension curves. Though it is easy to understand these experimental results in the context of single-joint motion, it is the multijoint case that poses the most difficult challenge for this theory.

Multijoint studies involve approaching qualitatively different aspects of motor control. For example, single-joint studies have demonstrated that the CNS achieves a stable posture of the forearm by selecting appropriate length-tension curves of the elbow muscles so that, at the desired elbow angle, the torque generated by the flexors is equal and opposite to the torque generated by the extensors. As a small external perturbation displaces the limb $\delta\theta$ degrees from its equilibrium location, the elastic muscle properties generate a restoring torque δT. The ratio of this torque to the imposed displacement is a single number expressing the stiffness of the elbow. (See section 1.5.6.) By contrast, in a multijoint situation, if a displacement is externally imposed on the hand, rather than on a single articulation, the amount of stretch experienced by the muscles depends not only upon the amplitude of the perturbation but also upon the direction of the forces. Then a single number is no longer sufficient to describe the force-displacement relation.

To deal with this more complex situation, a new experimental approach to the study of posture and movement was developed (Mussa-Ivaldi, Hogan, and Bizzi 1985). This approach was based on measuring the net springlike behavior of the multijoint arm by displacing the hand in several directions (figure 3.6). As the hand came to rest at the end of each displacement, the force, $\mathbf{F} = (F_x, F_y)$, exerted by the subject on the handle was measured. Since the hand was stationary, this force had no viscous or inertial components and could only be due to muscle length-tension properties (including reflex components).

With a small displacement of the hand, $\delta \mathbf{r} = (\delta x, \delta y)$, it is legitimate to assume a linear relation of the form

$$F_x = K_{xx}\,\delta x + K_{xy}\,\delta y$$
$$F_y = K_{yx}\,\delta x + K_{yy}\,\delta y. \tag{2}$$

Then, by measuring forces and displacements in different directions, it is possible to estimate the K coefficients from a linear regression applied independently to both expressions in (2). These coefficients can be represented by a single entity: a table, or matrix, expressing the multidimensional stiffness of the hand:

$$\mathbf{K} = \begin{bmatrix} K_{xx} & K_{xy} \\ K_{yx} & K_{yy} \end{bmatrix}.$$

With this notation, equation (2) assumes a more compact form, $\mathbf{F} = \mathbf{K}\delta\mathbf{r}$, which is analogous to the equation describing the behavior of a one-dimensional system such as a single joint. However, in the multijoint situation the stiffness matrix is a more complex entity than the single-joint stiffness and provides new insights into multijoint posture.

Extending the notion of springlike behavior to the two-joint arm described in section 1.2.4 requires that for any setting of the control inputs, two conditions are satisfied. First, the force, $\mathbf{F} = (F_x, F_y)$, measured at the hand after imposing a displacement, must be a function of the hand position, $\mathbf{r} = (x, y)$. In other words, each setting of the muscle inputs must define a vector field, $\mathbf{F} = \mathbf{F}(\mathbf{r})$. Second, the mechanical work in this field must be integrable. In other words, when the hand is displaced, the potential energy stored by the arm must be defined as a function of the new position in the workspace but not of the path used to reach it.

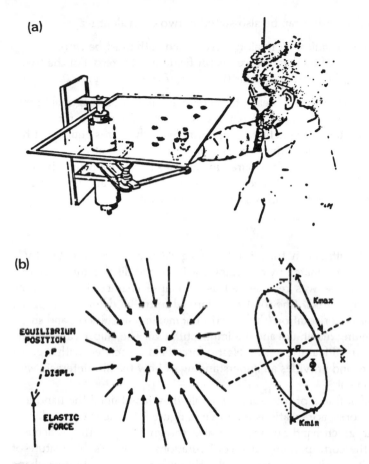

Figure 3.6
(a) Experimental setup for measuring the net springlike behavior of the multijoint arm: sketch of the apparatus in a typical experimental situation. (b) Stiffness representation. Left: When the hand is displaced from its equilibrium position, an elastic restoring force is observed that in general is not collinear with the displacement vector. Center: Several displacements of variable amplitude and direction are plotted together with the restoring forces computed from a measured hand stiffness. Right: The trajectory of the force vectors obtained by means of the previous procedure is an ellipse with the major and minor axes indicated by K_{max} and K_{min}, respectively. The angle, Φ, between the major axis and the fixed x-axis is the stiffness orientation. The shape is given by the ratio, K_{max}/K_{min}, and the size, or magnitude, is the area enclosed by the ellipse. (Modified by permission from F. A. Mussa-Ivaldi, N. Hogan, and E. Bizzi, Neural, mechanical, and geometric factors subserving arm posture in humans, 1985, *Journal of Neuroscience* 5, 2732–2743.)

The latter condition can be also stated in two equivalent ways:

1. The mechanical work along any closed path must be zero.
2. The curl of the hand-force vector field must be zero. For the two-joint arm, the condition is $\text{curl}(\mathbf{F}) = (\partial F_y / \partial x) - (\partial F_x / \partial y) = 0$.

In the last expression it is easy to recognize the two off-diagonal terms of the stiffness matrix, $K_{yx} = \partial F_y / \partial x$ and $K_{x,y} = \partial F_x / \partial y$. Hence, for the planar two-joint arm, the definition of springlike behavior is equivalent to requiring that the hand stiffness be symmetrical, that is, that $K_{x,y} = K_{y,x}$. The stiffness matrices measured in several subjects by Mussa-Ivaldi, Hogan, and Bizzi (1985) satisfied this condition, demonstrating that the multijoint posture of the arm is a springlike behavior.

The hand stiffness in the vicinity of equilibrium is represented by a matrix that was estimated by analyzing the force and displacement vectors. The hand stiffness was represented as an ellipse characterized by three parameters: magnitude (the total area derived from the determinant of the stiffness matrix), orientation (the direction of maximum stiffness), and shape (the ratio among maximum and minimum stiffness). The ellipse captures the main geometrical features of the elastic-force field associated with a given hand posture and provides an understanding of how the arm interacts with the environment.

The hand stiffness of four subjects while they maintained the hand in a number of workspace locations is shown in figure 3.7. The stiffness ellipses measured at given hand postures are also shown, along with a schematic display of the corresponding arm configurations. A remarkable feature of these data is the similarity across subjects with respect to stiffness shape and orientation. By contrast, the stiffness magnitude varies considerably. This graphic representation provides a "gestalt" and affords a qualitative understanding of the way in which the hand may interact with external forces that could change its posture.

Describing hand posture as an "oriented stiffness ellipse" helps us to determine which elements of motor behavior require accurate coordination of neural signals and which result from the arm's biomechanical design. To address this issue, Mussa-Ivaldi, Hogan, and Bizzi (1987) measured the postural stiffness in four different conditions: with no load and with a 10-newton force applied 0, 45, and 90 degrees. These forces were applied in order to elicit different patterns of contraction in different sets of muscles and thus to test how variations in neural input affect the parameters of postural stiffness measured at a given location.

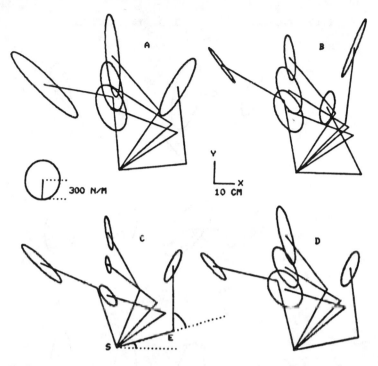

Figure 3.7
Stiffness ellipses obtained from four subjects during the postural task. Each ellipse has been derived by regression on about 60 force and displacement vectors. The upper arm and the forearm are indicated schematically by two line segments, and the ellipses are placed on the hand. The calibration for the stiffness is provided by the circle to the left, which represents an isotropic hand stiffness of 300 newtons per meter. (Reprinted by permission from F. A. Mussa-Invaldi, N. Hogan, and E. Bizzi, Neural, mechanical, and geometric factors subserving arm posture in humans, 1985, *Journal of Neuroscience* 5, 2732–2743.)

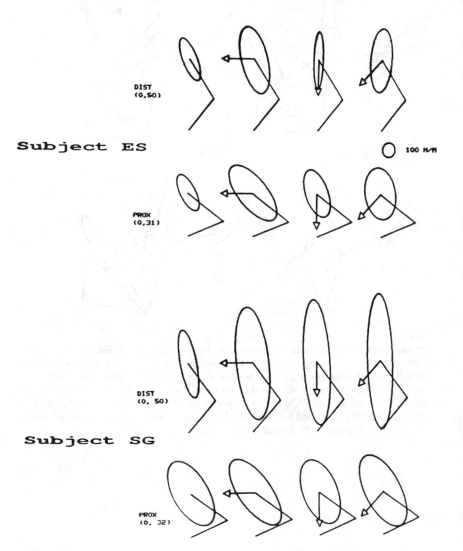

Figure 3.8
Postural stiffness without and with loads. The arrows indicate the directions of the 10-newton load.

This procedure generated a surprising result (figure 3.8): there were large changes in stiffness amplitude, but only small changes in orientation and shape. The result means that the parameters of orientation and shape depend predominantly upon musculoskeletal geometrical properties of the arm.

It was found that one way to affect the stiffness shape and orientation is to change the configuration of the arm while the hand remains in a given position. This finding suggests that an effective strategy for modifying all parameters of the postural stiffness may be to combine variations of neural input to the muscles with variation of configuration of the "extra" or redundant degrees of freedom of the limb. (See also section 1.2.2.) Changes in configuration also have a relevant effect on other components of motor impedance. Indeed, changing arm configuration is the only way the CNS can change the endpoint inertia of the limb (Hogan 1985). From this point of view, it can be seen that the configuration of the limb should be regarded as one of the "commanding inputs" available to the CNS for controlling posture. Redundancy of the musculoskeletal system is usually regarded as a problem to be overcome by the CNS in coordinating limb movements (Bernstein 1967); instead, the results reported here show that redundancy may also offer alternative ways to control postural dynamics.

The springlike behavior of the two-joint arm can be described in either hand or joint coordinates. In the first case a displacement (dx, dy) applied to the hand induces a steady-state force whose components are

$$F_x = K_{xx} dx + K_{xy} dy$$

$$F_y = K_{yx} dx + K_{yy} dy.$$

The four coefficients, K_{xx}, K_{xy}, K_{yx}, and K_{yy}, are the elements of the hand-stiffness matrix, $\mathbf{K}$. In joint coordinates the same displacement is expressed as a vector of angular displacements $(d\theta_S, d\theta_E)$ of the shoulder and the elbow, respectively. This angular displacement induces a torque vector whose shoulder, T_S, and elbow, T_E, components are

$$T_S = R_{SS} d\theta_S + R_{SE} d\theta_E$$

$$T_E = R_{ES} d\theta_S + R_{EE} d\theta_E.$$

Here the four terms, R_{SS}, R_{SE}, R_{ES}, and R_{EE}, are the components of the joint-stiffness matrix, $\mathbf{R}$, which is the equivalent, in joint coordinates, of the hand stiffness, $\mathbf{K}$.

Not only are $\mathbf{K}$ and $\mathbf{R}$ similar physical entities, but the elements of $\mathbf{R}$ can be directly derived from the elements of $\mathbf{K}$ and the configuration of the arm. The transformations (see question 3.5) from hand- to joint-stiffness terms are

$$R_{SS} = x^2 K_{yy} + y^2 K_{xx} - xy(K_{xy} + K_{yx})$$

$$R_{SE} = xx'K_{yy} + yy'K_{xx} - xy'K_{yx} - x'yK_{xy}$$

$$R_{ES} = xx'K_{yy} + yy'K_{xx} - xy'K_{xy} - x'yK_{yx}$$

$$R_{EE} = x'^2 K_{yy} + y'^2 K_{xx} - x'y'(K_{xy} + K_{yx}).$$

Here x and y are the coordinates of the hand with respect to the shoulder, and x' and y' are the coordinates of the hand with respect to the elbow (that is, $x' = l_2 \cos(\theta_1 + \theta_2)$ and $y' = l_2 \sin(\theta_1 + \theta_2)$).

Two conclusions can be immediately drawn from these equations. First, if the hand stiffness is symmetrical ($K_{xy} = K_{yx}$), so is the joint stiffness ($R_{ES} = R_{SE}$). Then, if the postural behavior of the hand is springlike, the mechanical coupling between different joints must be balanced: the torque induced on the elbow by a unit displacement of the shoulder must equal the torque induced on the shoulder by a unit displacement of the elbow. The second observation is that a uniform scaling of the hand-stiffness matrix ($\mathbf{K'} = r\mathbf{K}$) corresponds to a scaling by the same factor of the joint-stiffness matrix ($\mathbf{R'} = r\mathbf{R}$). Hence, a change in size of the stiffness ellipse at constant shape and orientation is obtained by a uniform scaling of all the joint-stiffness terms.

To sum up, the experimental evidence indicates that the equilibrium position of the hand is established by the coordinated interaction of elastic forces generated by the arm muscles (Mussa-Ivaldi, Hogan, and Bizzi 1985). According to the equilibrium trajectory hypothesis, which was first tested in the context of single-joint movements, the multijoint arm trajectory is achieved by gradually shifting the arm equilibrium between the initial and final positions. In this control scheme, the hand tracks its equilibrium point, and torque is not an explicitly computed variable.

In the single-joint example in section 3.3, the condition that the joint stiffness must be different from zero for the virtual trajectory to be uniquely defined can be recognized as a special case of a more general theorem on implicit functions. Let

$$F_i(x_1, x_2, \ldots, x_M, u_1, u_2, \ldots, u_M) = 0; \quad i = e \ldots N \tag{3}$$

indicate a system of N equations in N variables x_i and M variables u_i. Let us also assume that the following conditions are satisfied:

1. The system has a solution at a point $P^0 = (x_1^0, x_2^0, \ldots, x_N^0,$
$u_1^0, u_2^0, \ldots, u_M^0)$; that is, $F_i(x_1^0, x_2^0, \ldots, x_N^0, u_1^0, u_2^0, \ldots, u_M^0) = 0$ for
$i = 1, \ldots, N$.
2. The functions $F_i(x_1, x_2, \ldots, x_N, u_1, u_2, \ldots, u_M)$ are continuous and
differentiable in a region W around P^0.
3. In the same region W, the determinant of the $M \times N$ matrix $\mathbf{J}$,
whose elements are the partial derivatives of the F's with respect to
the x's ($J_{i,j} = \partial F_i / \partial x_j$), is different from zero ($\det(J) \neq 0$).

Given these conditions, there exists in W a unique set of N functions

$$x_i = f_i(u_1, u_2, \ldots, u_M)$$

that satisfies the equations (3).

In particular, in the case of the two-joint planar arm the controllable
springlike behavior of the hand can be expressed by stating that each
component of the hand force is a function of the hand position (x, y) and
of M control inputs, where M is the number of muscles operating on the
arm:

$$F_x = F_x(x, y, u_1, u_2, \ldots, u_M)$$

$$F_y = F_y(x, y, u_1, u_2, \ldots, u_M).$$

Then the concept of a virtual position of the hand is equivalent to a map
from the M dimensional vector $(u_1, u_2, \ldots, u_M)$ to the two dimensional
hand location (x_0, y_0) at which both force components are zero; that is,

$$x_0 = x_0(u_1, u_2, \ldots, u_M)$$

$$y_0 = y_0(u_1, u_2, \ldots, u_M).$$

The theorem on implicit functions states that for this map to be defined
in a region of the workspace, the condition is that the determinant of the
hand-stiffness matrix, $K_{xx}K_{yy} - K_{xy}K_{yx}$, is different from zero in that
region. Note that this condition does not mention the joint-stiffness terms
or the length-tension properties of individual muscles.

Evidence supporting this hypothesis in the context of multijoint hand
movements has been obtained by combining observations of hand movements with computer simulation studies. A model developed by Flash
(1987) has successfully captured the kinematic features of measured planar
arm trajectories. As shown by Morasso (1981), planar hand movements
between pairs of targets are characterized by approximately straight hand-
paths. However, if the same movements are analyzed at a finer level of
detail, the paths present certain degrees of inflexion and curvature, depend-

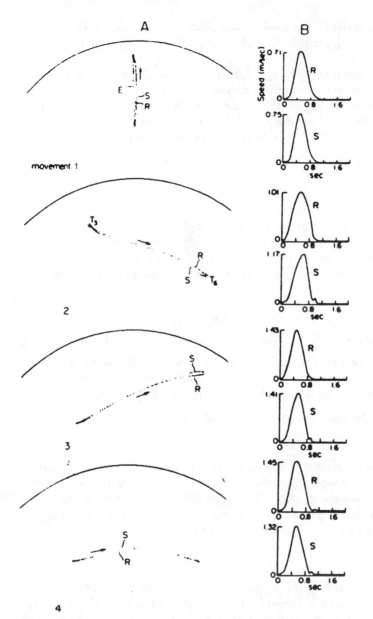

Figure 3.9
Comparison between measured (R) and simulated (S) hand trajectories. The real trajectories were obtained from three subjects. The simulated trajectories were derived with a straight virtual trajectory (E) from start to target position. (a) Trajectories. (b) Hand velocities versus time. (Reprinted by permission of the publisher and author from T. Flash, The control of hand equilibrium trajectories in multi-joint arm movements, 1987, *Biological Cybernetics* 57, 257–274.)

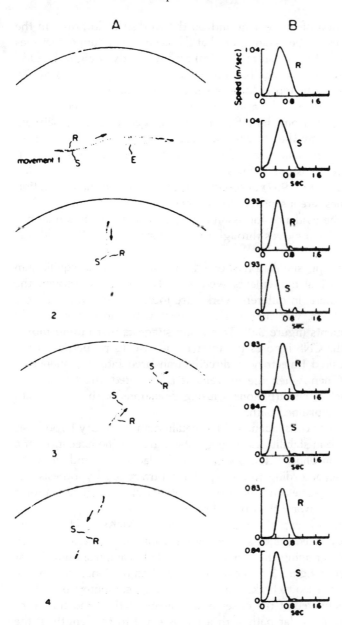

ing on the direction of movement and on the workspace location. In the simulation Flash made the assumption that the hand equilibrium trajectories (but not necessarily the actual trajectories) are invariantly straight. In addition, she assumed that the equilibrium trajectory has a unimodal velocity profile, regardless of the target locations in the workspace.

To test this hypothesis, the arm dynamics were simulated (section 1.4), obtaining torques, **T**, from the difference between actual and equilibrium positions multiplied by the stiffness. It must be stressed that the stiffness parameters used in the simulation of movements were derived from experimentally measured postural-stiffness values. In particular, Mussa-Ivaldi, Hogan, and Bizzi (1985, 1987) observed that the shape and the orientation of the hand stiffness are insensitive to changes in the net force output. This result provided the evidence for assuming that these parameters may not change when the hand moves through the locations at which the field was measured.

The results of the simulation showed that with straight equilibrium trajectories, the actual movements were slightly curved. Moreover, the direction of curvature, in different workspace locations and with different movement directions, was in good agreement with the experimentally observed movements (figure 3.9). This result suggests that during movement planning the CNS ignores the inertial and viscous properties of the arm, and the desired trajectory is directly translated into a sequence of static postures. Then, when the movement is executed, the inertial and viscous forces act as perturbations, causing deviations of the actual path with respect to the planned path.

A directly testable consequence of the equilibrium-trajectory hypothesis would be the built-in stability of movements: if, during the execution of a hand trajectory, an unpredicted disturbance displaces the hand from the planned path, then according to the equilibrium-trajectory hypothesis, the muscle's elastic properties and the proprioceptive reflexes generate a force attracting the hand toward the original path.

This prediction was experimentally confirmed by McKeon, Hogan, and Bizzi (1984). They asked subjects to perform pointing movements between two targets while gripping the handle of a two-link manipulandum similar to the one shown in figure 3.6. A clutch mounted on the inner joint of the manipulandum was used to brake the inner link under computer control. As the clutch was activated at the onset of a movement, the hand trajectory was restricted to a circular path with a radius equal to the length of the outer link of the manipulandum. While the clutch was engaged, the handle force was found to be always strongly oriented so as to restore the hand to the unconstrained path and not to the endpoint of the path.

The success of the simulation in capturing the kinematic details of measured arm movements is important as a step toward providing a new intellectual frame for understanding trajectory formation in the multijoint context. This work indicated a planning strategy whereby the motor controller may avoid complex computational problems such as the solution of inverse dynamics. According to the equilibrium-trajectory hypothesis, the muscle's springlike properties are responsible for generating the necessary joint torques, thus implicitly providing an approximated solution to the inverse dynamics problem. As the approximation becomes inadequate at higher speeds of acceleration, the stiffness can be increased and the equilibrium trajectory can be modified on the basis of the difference between the actual and the planned path. The task of the CNS is then to transform the planned trajectory into a different sequence of equilibrium positions and stiffnesses.

Suggestions for Further Reading

On general issues of motor coordination, see Bernstein 1967. This work has been reprinted, with commentaries by current motor control researchers, in Whiting 1984. McMahon 1984 provides detailed information on muscle properties. To pursue the study of reflexes, neural organization, and control systems, see Brookhard and Mountcastle 1981. On cerebral control of movements, see Brooks 1986, and on multijoint stiffness and virtual trajectory, see Hogan 1985.

Questions

3.1 Muscle spindles are sensitive to changes in muscle length. Their activity excites the motor neurons of the stretched muscle. In contrast, Golgi tendon organs detect changes of muscle tension and exert an inhibitory influence on the motor neurons of the loaded muscle. Show that this tension feedback effectively reduces the stiffness of a muscle. If g_T is the tension feedback gain ($g_T = \partial u / \partial f < 0$, u = motor neuron activity) and the muscle length-tension behavior is described by the function $f(l, u)$ with $\partial f / \partial u > 0$, find the factor by which the muscle stiffness is reduced at steady state.

3.2 Given a second-order linear system with a forcing input $f(t)$,

$$m\frac{d^2x}{dt^2} + b\frac{dx}{dt} + kx = f(t),$$

show that the forcing input maps into an equivalent virtual trajectory, $x_0(t)$, provided that $k \neq 0$.

3.3 Let the hand-stiffness matrix (in newtons per meter) be

$$\mathbf{K} = \begin{bmatrix} -100 & 0 \\ 0 & -200 \end{bmatrix}.$$

If the hand is displaced by $dx = dy = 0.5$ centimeter, what is the angle between this displacement and the resulting elastic force?

3.4 The stiffness ellipse associated to a stiffness matrix, $\mathbf{K}$, can be obtained by plotting the locus of the elastic forces corresponding to a unit displacement:

$$\begin{bmatrix} F_x \\ F_y \end{bmatrix} = \begin{bmatrix} K_{xx} & K_{xy} \\ K_{yx} & K_{yy} \end{bmatrix} \begin{bmatrix} \cos \omega t \\ \sin \omega t \end{bmatrix}; 0 < t < \frac{2\pi}{\omega}.$$

Assuming that **K** is symmetrical ($K_{xy} = K_{yx}$), derive the area, the orientation (the angle of the major axis), and the shape (the ratio of the major to the minor axis length) of the ellipse as functions of the hand-stiffness parameters.

3.5 Derive the transformations from hand- to joint-stiffness coefficients of a two-joint planar arm.

3.6 With a stiffness matrix **K**, the potential energy associated to a displacement vector, **dr**, is given by the quadratic form

$$E = \tfrac{1}{2}\mathbf{dr}^T\mathbf{K}\,\mathbf{dr}.$$

Hence, the equation

$$\mathbf{dr}^T\mathbf{K}\,\mathbf{dr} = \text{constant}$$

defines an elliptical curve at constant potential energy (isopotential line). How are these isopotential lines related to the stiffness ellipse?

References

Allum, J. H. J. (1975). Responses to load disturbances in human shoulder muscles: The hypothesis that one component is a pulse test information signal. *Experimental Brain Research* 22, 307–326.

Andersen, R. A., G. K. Essick, and R. M. Siegel (1987). Neurons of area 7 activated by both visual stimuli and oculomotor behavior. *Experimental Brain Research* 67, 316–322.

Bernstein, N. (1967). *The coordination and regulation of movements*. Oxford: Pergamon Press.

Berthoz, A. (1974). Afferent neck projection to the cat cerebellar cortex. *Experimental Brain Research* 20, 385–401.

Bizzi, E., N. Accornero, W. Chapple, and N. Hogan (1984). Posture control and trajectory formation during arm movement. *Journal of Neuroscience* 4, 2738–2744.

Bizzi, E., P. Dev, P. Morasso, and A. Polit (1978). Effect of load disturbances during centrally initiated movements. *Journal of Neurophysiology* 41, 542–556.

Bizzi, E., A. Polit, and P. Morasso (1976). Mechanisms underlying achievement of final head position. *Journal of Neurophysiology* 39, 435–444.

Brookhard, J. M., and V. B. Mountcastle (1981). *Handbook of physiology, section 1: The nervous system, vol. 1, part 1*. Bethesda, MD: American Physiological Society.

Brooks, V. B. (1986). *The neural basis of motor control*. New York: Oxford University Press.

Brooks, V. B., J. Hore, J. Meyer-Lohmann, and T. Vilis (1976). Cerebellar pathway for precentral responses following arm perturbations. *Neuroscience Abstracts* 2, 516.

Conrad, B., C. Matsunami, J. Meyer-Lohmann, M. Wiesendanger, and V. B. Brooks (1974). Cortical load compensation during voluntary elbow movements. *Brain Research* 81, 507–514.

Evarts, E. V. (1973). Motor cortex reflexes associated with learned movement. *Science* 179, 501–503.

Evarts, E. V., and J. Tanji (1976). Reflex and intended responses in motor pyramidal tract neurons of monkey. *Journal of Neurophysiology* 39, 1069–1080.

Feldman, A. G. (1966). Functional tuning of the nervous system during control of movement or maintenance of a steady posture. III. Mechanographic analysis of the execution by man of the simplest motor tasks. *Biophysics* 11, 766–775.

Feldman, A. G. (1974a). Change of muscle length due to shift of the equilibrium point of the muscle-load system. *Biofizika* 19, 534–538.

Feldman, A. G. (1974b). Control of muscle length. *Biofizika* 19, 749–751.

Flash, T. (1987). The control of hand equilibrium trajectories in multi-joint arm movements. *Biological Cybernetics* 57, 257–274.

Georgopoulos, A. P., J. F. Kalaska, R. Caminiti, and J. T. Massey (1982). On the relations between the direction of two-dimensional arm movements and cell discharge in primate motor cortex. *Journal of Neuroscience* 2, 1527–1537.

Georgopoulos, A. P., J. F. Kalaska, R. Caminiti, and J. T. Massey (1983). Spatial coding of movement: A hypothesis concerning the coding of movement direction by motor cortical populations. In J. Massion, J. Paillard, W. Schultz, and M. Wiesendanger, eds., *Neural coding of motor performance. Experimental Brain Research Supplement 7*, 327–336.

Gordon, A. M., A. F. Huxley, and F. J. Julian (1966). The variation in isometric tension with sarcomere length in vertebrate muscle fibres. *Journal of Physiology (London)* 184, 170–192.

Granit, R., B. Holmgren, and P. A. Merton (1955). The two routes for excitation of muscle and their subservience to the cerebellum. *Journal of Physiology* (London) 130, 213–224.

Grillner, S. (1972). The role of muscle stiffness in meeting the changing postural and locomotor requirements for force development of the ankle extensors. *Acta Physiologica Scandinavica* 86, 92–108.

Hogan, N. (1984). An organizing principle for a class of voluntary movements. *Journal of Neuroscience* 4, 2745–2754.

Hogan, N. (1985). The mechanics of multi-joint posture and movement control. *Biological Cybernetics* 52, 315–331.

Hogan, N., E. Bizzi, F. A. Mussa-Ivaldi, and T. Flash (1987). Controlling multijoint motor behavior. *Exercise and Sport Sciences Reviews* 15, 153–190.

Huxley, H. E. (1963). Electron microscope studies on the structure of natural and synthetic protein filaments from striated muscle. *Journal of Molecular Biology* 7, 281–308.

Huxley, H. E. (1969). The mechanism of muscular contraction. *Science* 164, 1356–1366.

Kelso, J. A. S. (1977). Motor control mechanisms underlying human movement reproduction. *Journal of Experimental Psychology* 3, 529–543.

Kelso, J. A. S., and K. G. Holt (1980). Exploring a vibratory system analysis of human movement production. *Journal of Neurophysiology* 43, 1183–1196.

McKeon, B., N. Hogan, and E. Bizzi (1984). Effect of temporary path constraint during planar arm movements. Abstracts of the 14th Annual Meeting of the Society for Neuroscience, Anaheim, CA.

McMahon, T. A. (1984). *Muscles, reflexes, and locomotion.* Princeton, NJ: Princeton University Press.

Matthews, P. B. C. (1972). *Mammalian muscle receptors and their central actions.* Baltimore, MD: Williams and Wilkins.

Morasso, P. (1981). Spatial control of arm movements. *Experimental Brain Research* 42, 223–227.

Mussa-Ivaldi, F. A. (1988). Do neurons in the motor cortex encode movement direction? An alternative hypothesis. *Neuroscience Letters* 91, 106–111.

Mussa-Ivaldi, F. A., N. Hogan, and E. Bizzi (1985). Neural, mechanical, and geometric factors subserving arm posture in humans. *Journal of Neuroscience* 5, 2732–2743.

Mussa-Ivaldi, F. A., N. Hogan, and E. Bizzi (1987). The role of geometrical constraints in the control of multi-joint posture and movement. Abstracts of the 17th Annual Meeting of the Society for Neuroscience, New Orleans, LA.

Nashner, L. M. (1976). Adapting reflexes controlling the human posture. *Experimental Brain Research* 26, 59–71.

Nichols, T. R., and J. C. Houk (1976). The improvement in linearity and the regulation of stiffness that results from the actions of the stretch reflex. *Journal of Neurophysiology*, 39, 119–142.

Rack, P. M. H., and D. R. Westbury (1969). The effects of length and stimulus rate on tension in the isometric cat soleus muscle. *Journal of Physiology (London)* 217, 419–444.

Rack, P. M. H., and D. R. Westbury (1974). The short range stiffness of active mammalian muscle and its effect on mechanical properties. *Journal of Physiology (London)* 240, 331–350.

Severin, F. V., G. N. Orlovsky, and M. L. Shik (1967). Work of the muscle receptors during controlled locomotion. *Biophysics* 12, 575–586.

Stein, R. B., and M. N. Oguztoreli (1976). Tremor and other oscillations in neuromuscular systems. *Biological Cybernetics* 22, 147–157.

Taylor, A., and F. W. J. Cody (1974). Jaw muscle spindle activity in the cat during normal movements of eating and drinking. *Brain Research* 71, 523–530.

Vallbo, A. B. (1970). Slowly adapting muscle receptors in man. *Acta Physiologica Scandinavica* 78, 315–333.

Vallbo, A. B. (1973). The significance of intramuscular receptors in load compensation during voluntary contractions in man. In R. B. Stein, K. G. Person, R. S. Smith, and J. B. Redford, eds., *Control of posture and locomotion.* New York: Plenum.

Whiting, H. T. A., ed. (1984). *Human motor actions: Bernstein reassessed.* Amsterdam: North Holland.

Chapter 4
Oculomotor Control
Henrietta L. Galiana

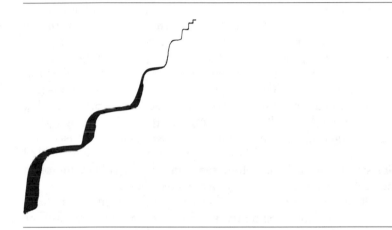

All species have as their primary objective survival, requiring the detection of potential danger and the search for food. Both of these tasks must rely on sensitive and mobile visual systems. Hence, it is not surprising that accurate control of eye movements is teleologically one of the first capabilities to appear in both vertebrates and invertebrates. The neural system responsible for this is called the *oculomotor control system*. It must continuously monitor and adjust the position of the eye in the head, taking into account the orientation of the head on the body and the body in space, in order to maintain the desired line of sight (gaze) in space. In this context, then, *gaze* is the sum of eye position relative to the head and of head position in space.

Because of their importance, the characteristics of eye movements in response to various stimuli have been the object of intensive study, especially over the last twenty years. As a bonus for scientists, the oculomotor system is structurally much simpler than those encountered in the

Work on this chapter was supported in part by the Medical Research Council, the Natural Sciences and Engineering Research Council of Canada, and the Fonds de Recherches en Santé du Québec.

control of body posture, or even in the movement of a single joint in a limb. Despite this apparent simplicity, however, it presents a complex repertoire of responses and offers the hope of deducing guiding principles or strategies used by the central nervous system (CNS). Hence, oculomotor control is an attractive model for general sensorimotor control systems.

Many factors contribute to the relative simplicity of oculomotor control:

1. The oculomotor system is a single-joint system, producing rotation of the eye globe in three dimensions. This is already a great simplification over the high-order dimensions encountered in segmental link control. Normally the coordinates of movement are referred to the head, in terms of horizontal, vertical, and torsional angles. The *direction* of the line of sight is actually fully defined by the horizontal and vertical components. *Torsion* (rotation of the eye about the line of sight) could be arbitrary, except for the findings described by Listing's law (1855): namely, that any eye movement is restricted to rotation about an axis lying in a plane fixed in the orbit (head), perpendicular to the line of sight in the primary (resting) position (Listing's plane). Helmholtz (1909) and Hering (1868) both proposed that Listing's law may be the result of an attempt by the CNS to simplify the processing of retinal images in a moving eye-world interface (see also Carpenter 1977, chap. 7). Though Listing's law is applicable only in limited cases, it illustrates the fact that other sensorimotor considerations often reduce the oculomotor system to only two degrees of freedom.

2. The pulling action (force vectors) of ocular muscles in a head-fixed coordinate system are not significantly affected by changes in eye position, at least up to 30-degree gaze shifts (Robinson 1985). This means that a relatively constant geometric relationship can be assumed between muscle torques and the resulting eye position relative to the head. This is a great simplification over the situation encountered in limb control.

3. Again, in peripheral motor control there is continuous modulation of CNS control signals in the spinal cord by sensory signals arising from muscle tendon organs and spindles. To date, such a "stretch reflex" has not been found to play any significant role in the control of ocular reflexes, despite the presence of spindles and tendon organs in eye muscles. Presumably, this is compatible with the invariant load (the globe itself) and the unlikelihood of external disturbances on the eye, since the stretch reflex is believed to serve as an automatic adjustment for unexpected changes in environmental factors (obstacles while walking, changing weights and torque arms while picking up loads, and so on).

4. Presumably for the same reason, pure cocontraction (simultaneous activation of opposing muscles across a joint) is never observed in eye muscles: movements are achieved through reciprocal activation of coplanar muscle pairs, where a gradual increase in tension in the agonist is matched with a decrease in tension in the antagonist. In peripheral limb control

cocontraction is often used to stiffen the joint and better resist destabilizing torques while lifting large weights. In brief, both the kinematics and the kinetics of eye movements, relative to the head, can be assumed constant throughout a movement.

5. Finally, all of the neural circuitry controlling eye movements is located in the brainstem or higher in the CNS, in the cranial cavity. At these sites modern microelectrode techniques allow the recording of neural responses along oculomotor pathways in alert behaving animals. As a result, it is possible to record simultaneously both behavioral factors, such as visual stimuli and resulting eye responses, and the control signals used by the CNS along different stages of the oculomotor system.

In summary, we now have access to a large amount of data on the anatomy, neurophysiology, and motor responses in a single system. Oculomotor research has reached the privileged position of being able to relate proposed models and control strategies to known neural networks and their responses. Hence, this chapter provides an example of model development tied to known physiology. In the sections that follow we will first consider the main components of the oculomotor system, together with their accepted mathematical representations. We will then examine alternative modeling strategies and compare them in the light of recent neurophysiology. In the interests of clarity, most examples and discussions will be limited to eye movements in one plane: the horizontal plane associated with temporally or nasally directed eye deviations (yaw).

4.1   Main Characteristics of Eye Movements

Records of eye movements in a human or animal are usually obtained with the head/body either fixed in space or rotated as a unit on a motorized chair. This allows testing of visual and vestibular responses, or any combination thereof, without involving more complicated postural mechanisms that would affect the ocular response (for example, eye-head coordination during active gaze shifts).

An example of a typical response in an ocular reflex is presented in figure 4.1. Here a time varying profile in head velocity (a) generates the associated eye position record (b) and its derivative, eye velocity (c). All types of ocular responses normally appear as seen in figure 4.1, namely, as a sawtoothlike pattern made up of *slow phases* and *fast phases*. Such patterns of slow and fast phases are called ocular *nystagmus*. This terminology was originally based on behavioral aspects, whereby "slow" phases normally appeared to have lower velocities and longer duration, on the average, than "fast" phases. However, such classification by speed is clearly not always sensible, as figure 4.1 illustrates. In fact, although the terms *slow* and

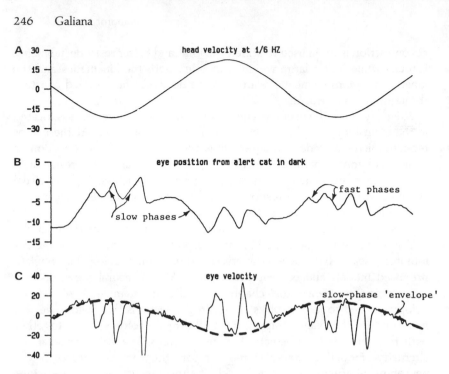

Figure 4.1

Examples of ocular nystagmus (cat) in response to head rotation at $\frac{1}{6}$ hertz in an earth-horizontal plane: the *vestibulo-ocular reflex* (VOR). Positive ordinates indicate movement to the right. Note eye position segments alternating between slow and fast phases, and the compensatory nature of ocular slow phases (that is, opposite to head movement).

fast have been retained for convenience, it is more appropriate to classify the two phases of nystagmus according to their function. These two phases appear to satisfy different criteria, or control strategies. Slow phases reduce velocity error between the stimulus and the eye—for example, to match eye *velocity* (the derivative of eye position) with the negative of head *velocity* during head turns (see figure 4.1 and paragraphs below). Fast phases, on the other hand, always reduce eye position error with respect to a desired target. This is true even in the case of nonvisual stimuli, such as head rotation in the dark: here the endpoints of fast phases have a very systematic pattern where eye *position* is now correlated with the time course of the head *velocity* pattern. In addition to sensory influences, both slow and fast phases are under the control of mentally imagined spatial targets.

As we will see, it appears that the CNS has opted for a strategy of switching between P-control and D-control modes in internal, central feedback schemes (P = position, D = differential, using the terminology introduced in section 1.5.2). This is an interesting alternative to proposed continuous PD schemes in limb control, though here the central commands are then used in a feedforward fashion to generate eye movements.

We now know that the two phases of ocular nystagmus reflect structural changes in the ocular control circuitry that will be discussed below. This is presumably due at least in part to the ocular motor limits, which would not allow sustained slow-phase responses unless stimuli were restricted to small peak angular deviations.

Eye movements have historically been classified according to the nature of the stimulus used to elicit them, so that observed nystagmus responses are assigned the names *pursuit, optokinetic,* and *vestibulo-ocular.* In addition, and again for historical reasons, the fast phases of nystagmus elicited by visual stimuli have been called *saccades,* and those induced by head movement have been called vestibular *quick phases.* These names were adopted in the original belief that the two fast-phase types were generated by different systems. However, recent neurophysiological data show that both types rely on the same pathways in the brainstem and that they differ only in their sensory drive.

There are three main types of *conjugate* eye movements, using parallel excitation/inhibition of agonist/antagonist muscle pairs for each eye on opposite sides of the head. Hence, here both eyes move in tandem, like a pair of horses yoked to a sleigh:

During *pursuit* nystagmus, the head/body can be stationary while the eyes attempt to track a moving visual target and keep it on the *fovea,* an especially sensitive area on the retina. During slow phases, eye velocity will approach target velocity; during saccades, the eye is nearly perfectly aligned on the target, nulling any remaining position errors.

During *optokinetic* nystagmus, the head/body are again stationary while a large textured visual field is made to rotate about the subject. The brain interprets the ensuing slip of images across the retina as resulting instead from rotation of the subject in a stationary world (the more naturally occurring condition). As a result, a human subject will report a strong perception of body rotation, and all species will produce a nystagmus pattern with slow phase velocities near those of the visual field, interrupted by quick phases in the opposite direction.

During *vestibulo-ocular* nystagmus, the head/body are rotated as a unit. Since during normal life it is important to maintain clear vision of the world, any head movement is reflexively associated with an opposite compensatory eye movement, even in the dark. This is the *vestibulo-ocular reflex* (VOR), whose main function is to stabilize the eye globe and hence the direction of regard (gaze) in space. Nystagmus patterns contain slow-phase segments of velocity opposite to head velocity, whereas quick phases redirect the eyes in the same direction as the head rotation ("look where you go").

One might surmise that nystagmus is the simple result of physical limits on the range of angular eye movements. A fast phase would be required whenever the target currently being tracked approaches the limits of eccentricity for the eye globe. This fast phase would bring the eye to a new target, more accessible to the eye's tracking range in the next slow phase. In fact, fast phases are triggered much earlier than required by eye plant limitations, so that some other central strategy must dominate (see section 4.5.3).

Though we will not examine it in detail, there is yet another type of eye movement, called *vergence*, which is stimulated by changes in target disparity or distance. Here the two lines of sight are misaligned so that they no longer intersect on the target, and corrective responses require opposite (*not* conjugate) movements in each eye—say, toward the nose—in order to acquire an approaching target.

4.2   Components of the Oculomotor System

To get an overview of some of the key points currently under discussion in oculomotor research, we will look at the approach of Robinson, who pioneered the application of systems theory and models to the study of the oculomotor control system and has written several excellent reviews on the subject (see, for example, Robinson 1981).

One of the main applications of systems theory is to break down a system into many simpler subsystems as possible and to attempt to describe each subsystem in a mathematical form that can relate its "input(s)" or stimuli to the observed "output(s)" or responses. The mathematical form describing the ratio of output to input is called the *system transfer function*.[1] The goal is to be able to make quantitative predictions concerning the behavior of the overall system, when all its subcomponents are recombined. This process produces a "model" or mathematical description of the physiological system under study, and if it is sufficiently accurate, it can serve as a diagnostic tool. For example, it might be used to show the effects of changes in any subsystem in the model, to help in localizing the site of a patient's injury or lesion.

We will briefly consider the main elements in the oculomotor system, together with their accepted transfer function representation. For the purposes of this chapter, the oculomotor system has three main subsystems

1. In the Laplace domain, the output of a linear system is simply the product of the input with the system transfer function. The output in the time domain can then be found by applying the inverse Laplace transform, which would correspond to the waveforms in the figures.

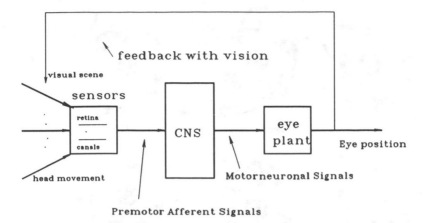

Figure 4.2
Main conceptual components of oculomotor control.

(figure 4.2) connected in series: *sensory transduction*, *central processing* (sensory/motor transformation), and the *eye plant*. This is a cascade with no interaction or feedback between the blocks except for vision. In the light, figure 4.2 should also have a *feedback* pathway from eye position back to the sensor box, since any eye movement would modify continuously visual variables such as the angular distance from the desired target.

In this section the properties of each major component of the oculomotor system will be described qualitatively, and an example of the form of typical input-output pairs will be given both graphically and as equivalent functions of time. The equivalent Laplace transforms of the input-output pairs and system transfer functions will appear in the text, set off by rules. A more detailed discussion of central processes involved in the generation of nystagmus will follow in later sections.

4.2.1   The Eye Plant

In all vertebrates rotation of the eye globe is achieved by stimulation of six external (*extraocular*) muscles, geometrically paired into three agonist-antagonist groups (figure 4.3). The action of these muscles is usually referred to geometric planes in the head: the midsagittal plane bisects the head vertically into symmetrical right and left halves; the horizontal plane, at right angles to the midsagittal plane, transverses the head at the level of the eyes; the frontal plane is perpendicular to the previous two, parallel to the face in man (see also figure 4.6). Of course, this coordinate system is simply one of convenience, chosen by general consensus. It is not necessarily the one chosen by nature in its sensors (see below).

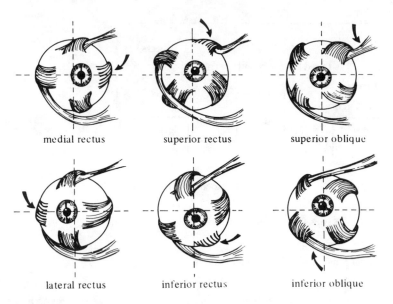

medial rectus   superior rectus   superior oblique

lateral rectus   inferior rectus   inferior oblique

Figure 4.3
Rotations of the eye globe caused by each extraocular muscle. The vertical and horizontal dashed lines represent the midsagittal plane and the horizontal plane, respectively, as viewed from the front. (Reprinted with permission from R. H. S. Carpenter, *Movements of the eyes*, 1977, p. 129, fig. 7.18. © 1977 by Pion Ltd.)

In humans the dominant contribution of each eye muscle pair is *naso-temporal movement* of the eyes (right and left) in the horizontal plane by the medial and lateral rectus, *elevation* and *depression* of the eyes in a plane parallel to the midsagittal head plane by the superior and inferior rectus, and *torsion* (rolling) of the eye about the line of sight in the frontal plane by the superior and inferior oblique. Of course, the terms *horizontal* and *vertical rectus* are only relevant when the head is in its normal erect position relative to the earth-horizontal plane. Also, it is clear that each pair will contribute to displacements in other head-fixed planes, albeit to a much lesser degree, since their planes of action are not exactly parallel to head-fixed planes (for discussion, see Robinson 1985). In the following sections head rotation and/or eye rotations in the horizontal plane will be assigned positive values for angular deviations to the right (clockwise, as viewed from above).

Because there is no feedback from eye position to the motor neurons (see section 4.1 and figure 4.2), Skavenski and Robinson (1973) were able to find a consistent and simple first-order relationship between observed motorneuronal activity and the resulting eye position. This would not be possible in the case of limb control, with complex peripheral feedback systems and variable cocontraction levels in the presence of varying loads. Hence, to a first-order approximation, we can write

$$R = R_0 + kE + r\dot{E}, \tag{1}$$

where

    R = motorneuronal firing rate (spikes per second)
    R_0 = resting rate on central gaze (spikes per second)
    E = eye position in the muscle's plane of action (degrees)
    $\dot{E}$ = eye velocity (degrees per second)
    k, r = proportionality constants, reflecting elastic and viscous properties of the muscles and globe ($r/k = T$, time constant; see below).

In the case of the horizontal system in monkeys, for example, $R_0 = 100$, $k = 4$, $r = 1$, so that $T = r/k = 0.25$ second. Equation (1) is an over-simplification of the biophysical events underlying muscle contraction. Given the accuracy of observed motorneuronal firing patterns and the statistical variation over a population, however, this simple model is remarkably useful in deducing required central processes in oculomotor control.

Therefore, we can express the eye plant dynamics in Laplace transforms as

$$\mathbf{E}(s)/\mathbf{\Delta R}(s) = G/(Ts + 1),$$

where $\Delta R = (R - R_0)$, $G = 1/k$, or 0.25 in monkeys, and $T = r/k$, or 0.25 second. This has the form of a low-pass filter with a gain of 0.25 and a time constant of 0.25 second. In figure 4.4 the input is $\mathbf{\Delta R}(s) = A/s$, so that the response in the Laplace domain is $\mathbf{E}(s) = AG/s(Ts + 1)$.

Figure 4.4 illustrates the eye plant dynamics. It exhibits the characteristics of a *low-pass filter*, where changes in eye position appear as a smoothed version of sudden changes in the motorneuronal firing rate. For example, if the motorneuronal input were a sine wave at any frequency below about 0.5 hertz and of amplitude 10, the eye position would appear as a sine wave of amplitude 2.5 (gain = $1/k = 1/4$). At the critical frequency defined by the time constant, $f_c = 1/(2\pi T)$, or here approximately 0.7 hertz, the response amplitude would be reduced to $2.5/\sqrt{2}$, and any inputs of progresssively higher frequency would cause smaller and smaller responses.

This is why the response to the step input in figure 4.4 shows only a gradual increase in eye position to the new level: the sharp corner in the

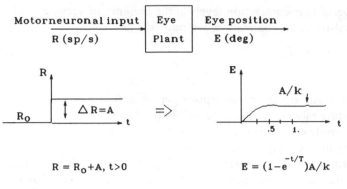

Figure 4.4
The eye plant- a low-pass filter. An example of the response to a step input of amplitude A is provided. Since $T = 0.25$ second, the response reaches its plateau within one second (sp = spikes).

onset of the stimulus has been smoothed out. As a consequence, in order to generate rapid eye movements with faster profiles than that seen in figure 4.4, additional stimulation is needed. The motor signals to the eye during fast phases, for example, must include a strong burst of activity, superimposed on the step appropriate for the desired endpoint (see section 4.4.3). Note that the *time constant* of a first-order filter can be measured from the exponential decay of *initial conditions*.[2] Similarly, time constants can be evaluated from responses to constant (step) inputs, as seen in figure 4.4.

4.2.2   The Sensors

Eye movements can be driven by both sensory and nonsensory stimuli (figure 4.5). For example, you can easily decide to change the position of your eyes in your head, even in the dark with your eyes closed. You need only imagine a desired target somewhere in the room. Such "cognitive" elements in the selection of targets and the generation of eye movements can also interact with the more "reflexive" responses to sensory stimuli. However, they lie beyond the scope of this chapter and in any case are still poorly understood. For sensory stimulation of eye movements, the two most important transducers are the vestibular system and the retina.

2. In the case of first-order systems an initial condition is the level of the response at time zero, when the input is either first applied or removed. With no inputs, this initial condition decays, following the time profile of an exponential, $E_0 e^{-t/T}$, where E_0 is the initial condition, t is time, and T is the time constant. Hence, the initial condition decays to $1/e$ of its initial value after T seconds.

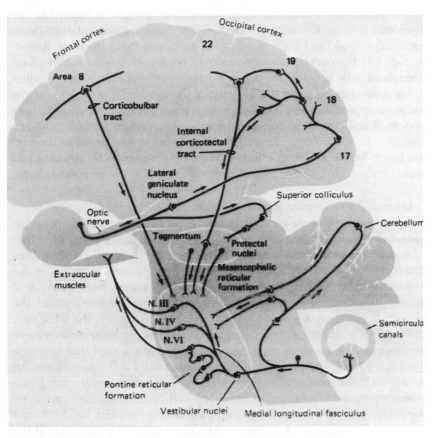

Figure 4.5
Convergence of cortical and sensory signals onto the common ocular motor centers in the brainstem. (Reprinted by permission of the publisher from E. R. Kandel and J. H. Schwartz, eds., *Principles of neuroscience*, 1981, p. 404, fig. 34.13. © 1981 by Elsevier Science Publishing Co., Inc.)

The vestibular system is a three-dimensional transducer located in the inner ear. It provides accurate measures of both angular rotation (from *semicircular canals*) and linear acceleration (from *otoliths*) of the head. Acoustic cues (via the cochlea) can also be used for target localization in space. Specialized cells in the retina provide measures of full-field *image slip* (that is, the difference between the velocity of the eye and the velocity of the surrounding visual scene). The selection of a particular target on which the eyes must align, from among a set of objects in a given field of view, is a complex cortical process. Given the chosen target, the distance (angular and linear) between each eye and the target (*position error*) is calculated and passed on as a motor error to the premotor circuits in the brainstem (figure 4.5).

Let us first examine the reference frames of the semicircular canals. There are three semicircular canals in each inner ear, arranged in a roughly orthogonal manner (figure 4.6). Each senses head rotation in the plane of its thin tube, due to inertial fluid effects bending sensitive hair cells. This in turn causes a change in the firing rate (spikes per second) observed in the vestibular nerve. The firing rate on the nerve arising from each canal normally operates at some relatively fixed background level, called the *resting rate*. Head rotation in any direction causes changes in the firing rate, and it is this modulation around resting levels that can cause reflexive eye movements. The orientation of the canals in humans is such that for those lying in the right inner ear, and with the head initially in the normal vertical position, (1) the nerve from the horizontal canal increases its firing rate during rightward head rotation about the vertical axis, (2) the nerve from the anterior canal increases its firing rate during forward head tilt in a vertical plane roughly 45 degrees from the midsagittal plane, and (3) the nerve from the posterior canal increases its firing rate during backward head tilt in a vertical plane roughly −45 degrees from the midsagittal plane.

These various head tilts can be used to selectively stimulate the canals. Rotation in directions opposite to those mentioned above would produce the opposite result—that is, a decrease in firing rates below the resting level in the right vestibular nerve. The canals on the left side of the head are arranged in a mirror fashion, so that opposite anterior-posterior pairs and the right-left horizontal pair are nearly coplanar. As a result, increased activity in a canal nerve on one side will always be associated with decreased activity in the nerve from the coplanar canal on the other side of the head (and vice versa).

All sensory signals relevant to oculomotor control eventually converge onto the same premotor neural circuits in the brainstem. This convergence is remarkable in two ways: (1) there is evidence that both vestibular and visual reference frames use the same preferred coordinate system, fixed on the head, and (2) these reference frames are very close to the planes of action of the ocular muscles (see figure 4.6). This is true in all species investigated so far (Simpson and Graf 1985; Ezure and Graf 1984a). The first observation means that visual and vestibular signals can be directly combined, since their information is related to common geometric planes. The second indicates that transformations from sensory to muscle coordinate systems are minimal and will be dominated by connections between most proximate sensory and muscle planes (for example, excitation from horizontal canal to ipsilateral medial rectus, or anterior canal to ipsilateral superior rectus and contralateral inferior oblique; Ezure and Graf 1984b).[3] These major connections form the basis of the so-called three-neuron arc in the VOR, as explained in section 4.3.

Because of this sensorimotor convergence, it is clear that an exploration of one reflex, such as the VOR, can lead to a general understanding of oculomotor control. Therefore, in this section we will examine mathematical descriptions only for the function of the semicircular canals, since only these are required for the scope of this chapter. The dynamics of the semicircular canals have been extensively studied (Goldberg and Fernandez 1982; Correia et al. 1981) by independently controlling angular head rotation profiles in a given plane while measuring the associated firing rate on the vestibular nerve. Both purely theoretical analysis of the fluid properties of the canals and experimental observations agree, in that the canals act as heavily overdamped accelerometers during head rotation. In fact, for head angular oscillations at frequencies below, say, 5 hertz, a simple first-order differential equation can quite adequately be used to relate the firing rate on the vestibular nerve to angular head acceleration:

$$\ddot{H} = k\Delta C + r\Delta \dot{C}, \tag{2}$$

where

$\Delta C = (C - C_0)$ is the modulation about the resting rate with
  C_0 = resting rate on the vestibular nerve, with no head movement (spikes per second)
  C = firing rate on the vestibular nerve during head turns (spikes per second)
$\Delta \dot{C}$ = rate of change (time derivative) of the modulation about the resting rate (spikes per second)
$\ddot{H}$ = angular head acceleration (degrees per second squared) in the excitatory direction; first time derivative of angular head velocity $\dot{H}$ (degrees per second) or second time derivative of angular head position H (degrees)

---

3. *Ipsilateral* refers to components lying on the same side of the head midline; *contralateral* refers to those lying on opposite sides.

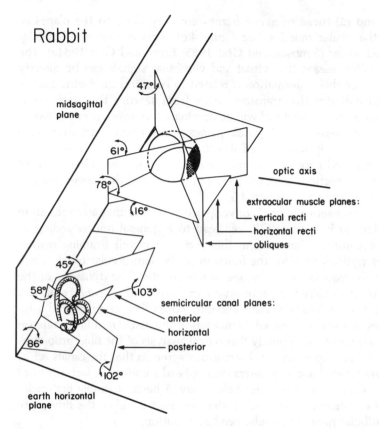

Rabbit

midsagittal plane

optic axis

extraocular muscle planes:
— vertical recti
— horizontal recti
— obliques

semicircular canal planes:
— anterior
— horizontal
— posterior

earth horizontal plane

Figure 4.6
Examples of canal and eye-muscle operational planes in rabbits and cats. (Reprinted with permission from K. Ezure and W. Graf, A quantitative analysis of the spatial organization of the vestibulo-ocular reflexes in lateral- and frontal-eyed animals. I: Orientation of semi-circular canals and extraocular muscles, 1984, *Neuroscience* 12, 85–93, fig. 1.)

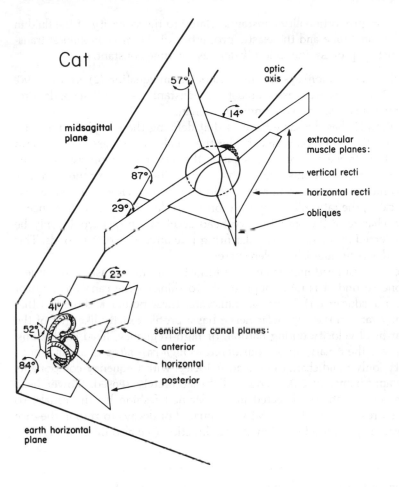

Cat

optic axis

57°

14°

midsagittal plane

extraocular muscle planes:

vertical recti

87°

horizontal recti

29°

obliques

23°

41°

52°

semicircular canal planes:

anterior

horizontal

84°

posterior

earth horizontal plane

r, k = proportionality constants related to the viscosity of the fluid in the canal tube and the elastic properties of the mechanoneural transduction process; the ratio r/k defines the time constant.

Typical values in monkeys for the parameters in equation (2) are $C_0 = 90$, $k = 0.43$, $r = 2.5$, with associated time constant $r/k = 5.7$ seconds. Presumably, similar values would hold in humans.

Equation (2) has the same form as that defining the eye plant dynamics (equation (1)). Hence, one can consider the canals as low-pass filters of head acceleration. In the case of the eye plant, the ratio r/k in monkeys is on the order of 0.25 second; this implies that eye position will respond to a new level in motorneuronal firing rate within one second. However, in the case of the canal, the ratio r/k is typically on the order of 5.7 seconds; hence, a sudden change in the amplitude of head acceleration $(\ddot{H})$ would only be fully reflected in the new vestibular firing rate after 12 to 20 seconds. This is indeed a very sluggish accelerometer.

Since natural head movements are in fact quite rapid, lasting much less than one second, it is more appropriate to think of the canals as angular *velocity* transducers $(\dot{H})$. Figure 4.7 illustrates these points, and the fact that the firing rate on the vestibular nerve has a profile exactly like that of the angular head velocity during natural, or high-frequency, head oscillations. In this case the canals can be considered as *high-pass filters* of angular head velocity: only rapid changes in head velocity, with frequency components above approximately 0.06 hertz, will be accurately sensed. Slower head movements cannot be detected in a sustained fashion by the canals, so that their response is either greatly attenuated or decays to zero in the case of constant speed head rotation in one direction (see also figure 4.11).

In terms of Laplace transforms, equation (2) translates into

$$\mathbf{C}(s) = C_0/s + (1/r)\dot{\mathbf{H}}(s)T_c s/(T_c s + 1),$$

where
C = canal primary activity (spikes per second)
$\dot{H}$ = head angular velocity (degrees per second)
$C_0 = 90$ is the background activity (spikes per second) in the stationary head
T_c = canal time constant (5.7 seconds)
$r = 2.5$, for monkeys.

Hence, the canals can be considered as high-pass filters of head velocity, with a time constant of approximately 5.7 seconds and a gain of 0.4 in monkeys. For example, in figure 4.7 the input in (b) is a step in head velocity, $\dot{\mathbf{H}}(s) = 100/s$, and the response is therefore

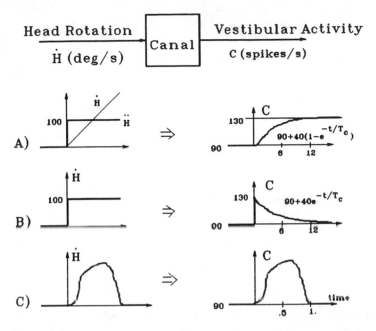

Figure 4.7
The semicircular canal: a high-pass filter of head angular velocity. (a) Using a step (constant) input in head acceleration equivalent to a ramp (increasing) input in head velocity. (b) Step input in head velocity. (c) Rapid pulse of head velocity. $T_c = 5.7$ seconds (compare (b) to figure 4.4).

$$C(s) = 90/s + 40T_c/(T_cs + 1).$$

This represents an exponential decaying back to the resting rate with initial value 130 and time constant $T_c = 5.7$ seconds, despite continued rotation.

Equation (2) should hold if firing rates remain positive and below some peak saturation level.[4] Similar results are now being found for the otolith organs, but we will not discuss them here. For more details, see Schor,

4. The activity on the vestibular nerve is restricted to positive values of impulses per second, since firing rates cannot be "negative" events. In addition, cells have maximal activity levels that cannot be exceeded, because of biochemical limits on the time and energy required to recover from each spike. This could be accounted for above by passing the results of equation (2) through a saturating rectifier. These factors limit the effective functional range of the vestibular sensor, but it turns out that the bilateral nature of the CNS structures can compensate nicely for this and provide large ranges for the perception of head rotation.

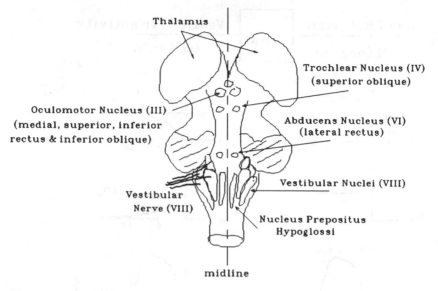

Thalamus

Trochlear Nucleus (IV)
(superior oblique)

Oculomotor Nucleus (III)
(medial, superior, inferior
rectus & inferior oblique)

Abducens Nucleus (VI)
(lateral rectus)

Vestibular Nuclei (VIII)

Vestibular
Nerve (VIII)

Nucleus Prepositus
Hypoglossi

midline

Figure 4.8
The major premotor and motor nuclei in the brainstem, controlling the extraocular muscles.

Miller, and Tomko 1984, Schor et al. 1985, and Fernandez and Goldberg
1976a,b,c.

4.2.3   The Central Processor

The neural circuits processing sensory afferent information into the required motorneuronal signals are located mainly in the brainstem (figures
4.5 and 4.8). These are actively monitored and inhibited by the cerebellum,
which is believed to play a key role in the adaptation of oculomotor
responses to changes in either plant dynamics (injury) or sensory conflict
(changes in optical magnification). Though it is clear that the cerebellar
pathways contribute to shaping the dynamics of responses (gain, time
constants), ocular nystagmus is still possible even after removal of the
cerebellum.

Thus, it is now generally accepted that the key elements of the central
processor in oculomotor control include the vestibular nuclei (VN), prepositus hypoglossi (PH) between the midline and VN, and surrounding
paramedian pontine reticular formation (PPRF). Cells in these areas that
respond during nystagmus for any one stimulus (say, head rotation) invari-
ably show the appropriate response correlated to eye movements, for any
other sensory stimulation (say, visual field rotation). In addition, many of
these cells project directly to the relevant motor nuclei of the eye muscles

(see figures 4.8 and 4.9). These pathways in the brainstem are shared by all oculomotor reflexes.

4.3 Introduction to Models of the VOR

General oculomotor control is a difficult multidimensional and multisensory problem. We have the advantage here that the sensory transducers and the eye plant dynamics can essentially be studied in isolation, and yet much remains to be done in order to refine models of the periphery. On the other hand, the most exciting discussions in oculomotor research now revolve around possible interpretations of a growing body of anatomical and neurophysiological data on the central processes.

Therefore, in order to clearly expose the key issues in central processing, we will concentrate specifically on the VOR, in the horizontal plane. In addition, we will simply assume that the relevant canal pair (right and left lateral canals) and muscle pairs (medial and lateral rectus) have the properties mentioned above (equations (1), (2)). The scope is then restricted to the processing of horizontal head velocity, as sensed by the canals, into appropriate stimulation of motor neurons in the abducens (VI) and medial rectus subdivision of the oculomotor (III) nuclei.

This is illustrated with a schematic of the *three-neuron arc* in figure 4.9. During rightward horizontal head rotation the right canal increases its activity, which increases activity on the vestibular nerve (VIII) and excitation on the contralateral abducens nucleus (VI). Simultaneously the left canal decreases its activity, which decreases its inhibitory effects on the ipsilateral abducens. Both result in an increase in tension in the left lateral rectus, so that the left eye rotates to the left. Conjugate excitation of the contralateral medial rectus is achieved via interneurons in the abducens nucleus (VI), whose axons cross the midline and project to the oculomotor nucleus (III): this forces the right eye also to rotate to the left. This is the most direct pathway in the VOR, containing three neurons: primary in vestibular nerve, secondary in vestibular nuclei, and motor neuron. Because of bilateral (across the midline) symmetry in the CNS circuits, the antagonist muscles undergo parallel and smooth reductions in their tension. Figure 4.9 represents the connectivity during slow-phase segments of the VOR. Signals controlling fast-phase behavior converge on this arc at both premotor (VN) and motor levels (abducens (VI) and oculomotor (III) nuclei).

In the following sections we will first consider the known dynamic characteristics of responses (neural firing rates) at different stages of central processing. We will then look at alternative views of oculomotor control and compare the models they propose.

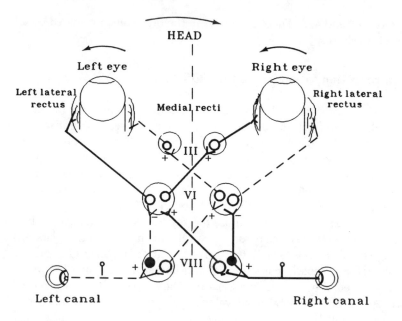

Figure 4.9
The three-neuron arc in the horizontal VOR. Excitatory cells are outlined; inhibitory cells are filled. The solid pathways carry increased activity, and the dashed pathways decreased activity, during rightward head rotation. Commissural connections carrying inhibition between left and right VN (VIII) have been omitted for clarity.

4.4   Required Characteristics of Models

All proposed models of the VOR must provide for certain key characteristics in observed ocular and neural responses. That is, the overall behavior of any model must include a neural integrator, velocity storage in slow phases, a mechanism to generate fast phases (saccades), and some sharing of the pathways used to generate slow or fast phases.

4.4.1   Central Neural Integrator

Mathematical integration of the vestibular signal must occur before projecting to the motor neurons, whereby sensory information on head velocity is transformed into an estimate of head position. There are two clear reasons for this.

First, the vestibular signal in the frequency range of normal head movements is in phase with head velocity. On the other hand, in order to stabilize gaze in space during slow phases, eye position must be modulated in a fashion equal and opposite to head position. This in turn requires a

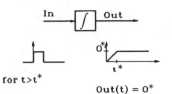
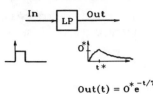

A) Perfect integrator

B) 'Leaky' integrator, or

low−pass filter

Figure 4.10
Schematic of input/output waveforms on idealized integrators. (a) Prefect holding power of an ideal integrator. (b) Slow discharge of a "leaky" integrator, which could be represented by a low-pass filter with the time constant of decay (here T').

motorneuronal signal in phase with head position, since the eye position will simply reflect the profile in motorneuronal activity (equation (1)).

Second, gaze deviations can be held even in the dark, typically for 20 seconds in humans. In this case there are no sensory inputs to maintain the required drive. This behavior implies the presence of a central "integrator," since an integrator has the essential property of "holding" or maintaining a response level in the absence of inputs.

For example, if the output of a perfect integrator is driven, say, to the level 10 (figure 4.10a), then it will hold this level indefinitely after the input is removed. If the integrator is "leaky," then the level will slowly decay to zero, following the time course of an exponential ($e^{-t/T'}$, t = time, T' = time constant). Thus, the central processor between canal and motor neuron appears to act as a leaky neural integrator with time constant of at least 20 seconds in normal adult humans or monkeys. A low-pass filter can be used to model such behavior (figure 4.10b), if its time constant is chosen to match the decay pattern.

In terms of Laplace transforms, the transfer functions of a perfect neural integrator, NI, or "leaky" integrator, NI', are

$$NI = 1/s; \qquad NI' = T'/(T's + 1), \text{ a low-pass form.}$$

Hence, the decay of any initial condition (O_0) on the output of such filters will be Out and Out', respectively:

$$\textbf{Out}(s) = O_0/s; \qquad \textbf{Out}'(s) = O_0 T'/(T's + 1).$$

The first represents a step function; that is, the initial condition is held indefinitely. The second describes a decaying exponential with initial value O_0 and time constant T' (see figure 4.10).

4.4.2   Velocity Storage

The term *velocity storage* has been coined to name an interesting property of nystagmic responses during head rotations at constant velocities. Under such conditions the canal signal must behave like a decaying exponential with time constant specific to each species (5.7 seconds in monkeys). Yet the nystagmic response lasts much longer. This is illustrated in the computer simulations of figure 4.11. The continuous solid curve represents the canal response profile to a step in head velocity, with a time constant of 5.7 seconds. The eye velocity profile, with truncated fast-phase peaks, has apparently very different dynamics, with approximately a 15-second time constant in the slow-phase envelope (dashed line). Somehow, the vestibular signal is accumulated or "stored" so that the eye velocity profile continues beyond the sensory input to the brainstem—hence the term *velocity storage*.

It has been proposed that velocity storage serves the purpose of improving on the dynamic characteristics of the vestibular sensor. It allows

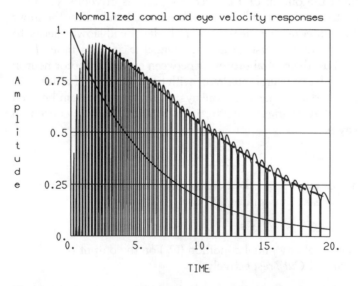

Figure 4.11
Simulation showing velocity storage in the VOR. The envelope of slow-phase eye velocity (dashed line) has longer time constants than that of the primary sensory signal from the canal (solid curve), during constant velocity (step) head rotation.

the perception of rotation to persist longer than the primary vestibular signal, in those cases where the canal would provide erroneous information. For example, during constant angular rotation, the canal would cease to measure head velocity within 10 to 15 seconds. The sensation of rotation, and nystagmus, can persist for 30 to 40 seconds.

4.4.3   Fast-Phase Burst Mechanism

The occurrence of fast phases (and saccades) is associated with the sudden activation of burst neurons in the PPRF, which project directly to ocular motor neurons and to other premotor centers (figure 4.12). These "bursters" are completely silent during slow-phase segments of nystagmus. The bursts are localized on the side ipsilateral to the direction of the fast phase; that is, a burst on the right side of the brainstem is normally associated with a fast phase or saccade directed toward the right side of the head. Furthermore, the rapid eye movement is achieved through strong activation of the

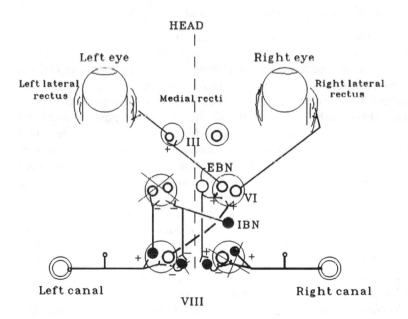

Figure 4.12
Schematic of central connections for a fast phase directed to the right side of the head. EBN are excitatory burst neurons; IBN are inhibitory burst neurons forcing pauses (silencing) in their target cells. Bursters project directly to the abducens nucleus (VI) and to vestibular cells that inhibit premotor cells in the VN (VIII). The result is strong activation of the left VN and right abducens nucleus. Their homologues on the contralateral side are silenced (indicated by cross). Compare this with the symmetrical functional connections during slow phases in figure 4.9.

agonist muscle and release of tension in the antagonist (by silencing motor neurons projecting to the antagonist). Only the agonist is under direct control; the antagonist contributes only passively to the response profile.

This behavior is in contrast to that observed in premotor circuits during slow phases of nystagmus. Here both premotor firing rates and muscle tensions are generally of a bilateral nature, with reciprocal activation of the agonist-antagonist muscle pairs for each eye. An increase in motorneuronal firing rate and muscle tension in the agonist is associated with an appropriate decrease in activation in the antagonist muscle. This allows simultaneous control over both muscles (compare figures 4.9 and 4.12).

This change in central connectivity during slow and fast phases of nystagmus presumably plays an important role in shaping the velocity and position profiles of behavioral responses. In fact, it might be interesting to see whether the CNS employs similar strategies in limb control, depending on the desired speed and precision of a movement.

4.4.4   Shared Processing between Slow and Fast Systems

The PH in the brainstem contains *tonic* cells whose firing rate is strongly correlated with eye position at all times, regardless of the nature or source of the eye movement (Cannon and Robinson 1987; see review in Galiana and Outerbridge 1984). That is, they provide an internal representation of the current eye position. As such, they can also be considered as the response of the postulated central integrator, since eye position and head position in the VOR should be in phase. Hence, the response of the neural integrator in models must also be updated during all types of eye movements, regardless of the source of the stimulus (cognitive, visual, and so on) or the nature of the response (for instance, slow-phase versus fast-phase or saccade).

Furthermore, the firing rates of all motor neurons, and several types of premotor neurons in the VN and PH, are modulated during all phases of nystagmus and hence must be shared by the slow- and fast-phase mechanisms. Their firing pattern reflects the activation of bursters in the PPRF, associated with fast phases in the ocular response. For example, some premotor cells in the VN on the right side of the brainstem will interrupt their slow-phase firing sequence to burst intermittently during leftward fast phases or to pause during rightward fast phases. Furthermore, the subsequent slow-phase activity resumes around a new level. This type of behavior is observed in all cells whose activity can be correlated with both vestibular signals and eye movement parameters (eye position, eye velocity), and such cells project directly to the motor neurons.

4.5   Modeling Approaches for the VOR

In the following models that have been proposed for the VOR, representations for the required processing of vestibular signals into appropriate oculomotor signals are derived from two approaches: (1) *parallel dedicated processes*: the use of linear networks acting in parallel, each using sequential (cascaded) processes, each specific for the slow and fast phase in the oculomotor response (see, for example, figure 4.9); and (2) *integrated feedback processes*: the use of feedback around linear networks with a two-sided symmetry to represent the bilateral nature of the CNS, together with structural modulation in a single system, to produce both slow- and fast-phase response segments.

4.5.1   Models Using Parallel Processing

Conceptually, it is easier to describe the VOR system as consisting of two parallel processes, each dedicated to a particular phase of the nystagmus response. For example, figure 4.13 depicts a slow-phase system that should account for the dynamics of the envelopes of slow-phase eye velocity segments, with a separate fast-phase system that will be activated according to some strategy only during fast phases. Interactions between the two pathways are not considered to be important. This is the approach used in many current models of the VOR, whereby the first task of the CNS is presumed to be the planning of the desired eye velocity profile in the movement trajectory. (In this section models refer to modulation about resting rates when dealing with central responses, or about zero when dealing with physical variables like velocity or position.)

Whether generated by the slow- or fast-phase mechanism, the desired velocity profile, $\dot{E}^*$, is then presumed to pass on through a shared neural integrator (figure 4.14). Robinson was the first to postulate that this inte-

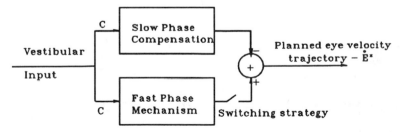

Figure 4.13
Postulated independent and parallel processes for the slow- and fast-phase segments of VOR reponses. Each is presumed to be shaping an internal estimate of the desired eye velocity profile, $\dot{E}^*$, derived from the canal's estimate of head velocity, C.

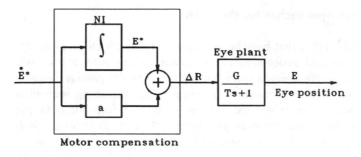

Figure 4.14
The central neural integrator in a proposed circuit to compensate for eye plant dynamics. $\dot{E}^*$ is the planned eye velocity from figure 4.13, ΔR is the motorneuronal firing rate about resting levels, E^* is an efference copy of eye position, and E is the actual response of the eye plant (see text).

grator could be used in parallel with a direct pathway, in order to provide the appropriate motorneuronal drive to the eye plant (Skavenski and Robinson 1973). This is easily shown, remembering that the integral of velocity is position. In figure 4.14, ΔR can be related to its inputs as the sum $(a\dot{E}^* + \int \dot{E}^*) = (a\dot{E}^* + E^*)$. Referring to equation (1), it is clear that the eye position profile, E, will match the profile E^* if the parameter a is chosen equal to r/k, the eye plant time constant. The result is that the neural integrator/direct pathways provide "compensation" for the eye plant dynamics, in a manner similar to the feedforward approaches discussed in chapter 1. This also guarantees that the behavioral eye velocity profile, $\dot{E}$, will follow the centrally derived profile $\dot{E}^*$.

In terms of Laplace transforms,

$$\Delta R(s) = \dot{E}^*(s)/s + a\dot{E}^*(s) = \dot{E}^*(s) \cdot (as + 1)/s.$$

Since

$$E(s) = \Delta R(s) \cdot G/(Ts + 1),$$

then

$$E(s) = \dot{E}^*(s) \cdot \frac{(as + 1)}{s} \cdot \frac{G}{(Ts + 1)} = G\dot{E}^*(s)/s \text{ or } GE^*(s)$$

if $T \simeq a$. The numerator (zero) of the compensation circuit cancels the denominator (pole) of the eye plant. (In the transfer function of a system, the roots of the polynomial in the numerator are called the *zeros* of the system, and the roots of the denominator are called the *poles*. Poles correspond to the time constants in a response.)

The parallel pathways independently process an internal representation of desired eye velocity ($\dot{E}^*$), and the eye plant compensation circuit provides an internal estimate of desired eye position (E^*). Such internal copies of motor behavior are termed *efference copies*, in that they are derived from information outflow rather than sensory feedback. Recall that the neural integrator time constant need not be infinite, and its function could be implemented by a low-pass filter with a large time constant.

To complete the schematic of oculomotor control, the problem is now reduced to postulating mechanisms that would generate the desired eye velocity trajectory, $\dot{E}^*$. It is tacitly assumed that $\dot{E}^*$ for the slow-phase process is observable as the trajectory described by the *envelope* of slow-phase velocity segments during nystagmus. Hence, the slow-phase process must duplicate *velocity storage* in the response to head velocity steps. The main purpose of velocity storage is presumed to be the extraction of an improved head velocity estimate from the inaccurate canal signal. Conceptually, this means that the rapidly decaying sensory signal during constant head rotations must somehow be replaced by a more accurate (slowly decaying) estimate of head velocity. Several approaches have been proposed (see, for example, Robinson 1977; Raphan, Matsuo, and Cohen 1979), but all rely on the same assumption that this storage is achieved at the level of the VN, before the neural integrator. Of the two approaches illustrated in figure 4.15, only one is discussed here. The other is equivalent and will be explored in the question section at the end of the chapter.

In the approach presented by Robinson (1977), positive feedback around the VN is postulated in order to transform the canal signal into the desired eye velocity profile. In essence, the feedback pathway is considered to contain an internal model of the canal dynamics. As a result, the slowly decaying signal from the canal (C) is boosted by a growing level from the storage pathway (S) so that the total activity on the VN now decays with a large time constant $T' \gg T_c$. The overall time constant achieved will depend on the gain of the feedback pathway (see question 4.3).

Since the canal response and the desired VN response are of the form

$$\mathbf{C}(s) = \dot{\mathbf{H}}(s)sT_c/(sT_c + 1) \Rightarrow \mathbf{VN}(s) = \dot{\mathbf{H}}(s)sT'/(sT' + 1),$$

it is clear that a transfer function of the form $G(sT_1 + 1)/(sT_2 + 1)$ must be interposed between the canal and VN responses: the velocity storage

A) Robinson Model

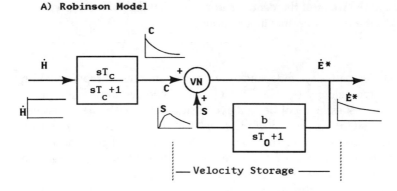

B) Raphan-Cohen Model

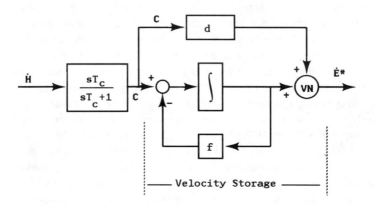

Figure 4.15
Two proposed realizations of velocity storage. In both (a) and (b): T_c, canal time constant; $\dot{H}$, head velocity; C, canal estimate of head velocity; $\dot{E}^*$, efference copy of eye velocity; b, d, and f, linear gains. Both approaches can provide the same equivalent transfer function between $\dot{E}^*$ and $\dot{H}$ (see question 4.3); VN signals will decay much more slowly than the canal activity during steps in head velocity.

process. A transfer function of this form is called a *lead-lag network*: it should cancel the pole in the canal transfer function and replace it with a pole closer to zero (that is, $T_1 \simeq T_c$ and $T_2 \gg T_c$). Of course, there are an infinite number of ways in which the desired cancellation can be realized. Two are illustrated schematically in figure 4.15 and analyzed in question 4.3.

Whatever the model for velocity storage, the resulting processed head velocity signal is set equivalent to the desired eye velocity profile, since one must equal and oppose the other in the VOR. Therefore, the model of velocity storage is cascaded with that of motor compensation in figure 4.14, to complete the modeling of slow-phase ocular responses. Envelopes of eye velocity are used to fit model parameters. Note that the efference copies of eye position (E^*) and eye velocity ($\dot{E}^*$) are then available for comparison with sensory or cognitive goals elsewhere in the CNS.

The above is an example of realizations for the slow-phase pathway in figure 4.13. Nystagmus is then generated by intermittently enabling the fast-phase system, according to the activity of bursters in the PPRF. The firing rate generated by such bursters has been shown to be highly correlated with eye velocity, and their axons indeed send projections to the motor nuclei (for a review, see Robinson 1981). Hence, it is generally accepted that they contribute a major component of the oculomotor drive during fast phases. The velocity content of their signal makes it reasonable to propose their projection to both the neural integrator and motor nuclei in the precompensation circuit, in exactly the same fashion as the velocity signal arising from the slow-phase system. That is, the bursters provide the desired eye velocity profile during fast phases. This satisfies the requirement that the neural integrator (and with it E^*) be updated during all movements.

Whether or not the slow system is disconnected from the eye plant during fast phases is still a point of discussion among researchers. So far the data appear to be contradictory, depending on the amplitude of vestibular stimuli and ocular responses (Guitton and Volle 1987). Nevertheless, it is always assumed that the slow-phase process itself continues unabated.

As first proposed by Robinson (1975), the fast-phase system is usually modeled as a position control servo. However, here the reference signal is the internal efference copy of eye position. This is an interesting variation on the external feedback schemes discussed in chapter 1. In the case of the VOR, some manipulation of the vestibular signal is presumed to provide an internally derived "target" (T in figure 4.16). The error (e) between this desired target and the efference copy of eye position is used to drive the

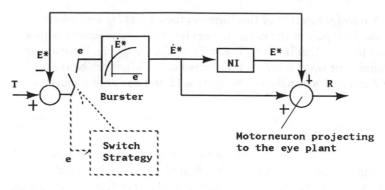

Figure 4.16
A simplified feedback model of fast-phase control. Initiation and termination of fast phases is implemented elsewhere through control of the switch status. The burster response represents the desired eye velocity profile during quick phases and thus projects to the same compensation circuit used by the slow-phase pathways (figure 4.14).

burster, which responds with a nonlinear relationship between its firing level, $\dot{E}^*$, and the input error, e. Figure 4.16 represents the simplest form of a fast-phase system most often used in the literature, though many refinements have since been proposed (see, for example, McKenzie and Lisberger 1986). Strategies to determine the timing and duration of the fast phases will be outlined in section 4.5.3.

4.5.2   Model with Structural Modulation in Feedback System

Anatomy and neurophysiology indicate that the bursters responsible for the activation of fast phases project not only to the motor neurons but also to premotor cells in the VN and PH. In forcing the silencing of cells in these areas, bursters essentially cause structural changes in the premotor circuits, which also contribute to the appearance of nystagmus.

In addition, VN and PH nuclei on both sides of the brainstem are strongly interconnected by (*commissural*) fibers crossing the midline.[5] Not surprisingly, the activity of these commissural fibers is also heavily modulated by bursts and pauses during fast phases. Furthermore, the integrity of processes such as the neural integrator rely on these nuclei and on intact commissural fibers (Cannon and Robinson 1987; Cheron et al. 1986). Based

5. There are several sites in the CNS where bundles of fibers interconnect homotopic areas on the two sides of the midline, between the two hemispheres. Examples are the corpus callosum in the neocortex, the posterior commissure between pretectal areas, and the vestibular commissure in the brainstem interconnecting the VN and PH. The last-mentioned commissure is the subject of this section.

on these data and other evidence, Galiana and Outerbridge (1984) have proposed an alternative approach to the modeling of ocular nystagmus.

Galiana and Outerbridge postulate that the bilateral nature of the brainstem and the presence of structural modulation are key components in the generation of vestibular nystagmus. A simplified schematic of their modeling approach is presented in figure 4.17. It relies on the facts that (1) symmetry in brainstem circuits and mutual inhibition between VN on each side must result in effective positive feedback across the midline, with associated repercussions on the dynamics of responses (see Galiana, Flohr, and Melvill Jones 1984; Galiana 1985), and (2) interruption of this positive feedback, as occurs during pauses in activity correlated with fast phases, must at least in part be responsible for nystagmus patterns.

In this approach, the CNS is presumed to be directly shaping the desired motorneuronal signals on the VN, rather than a desired behavioral pattern (eye velocity in previous sections). In summary, the model is symmetrical in the slow-phase mode, defined as those periods when the bursters are silent and the commissural fibers are active. Positive feedback around the VN on each side and across the midline can be shown to contribute to the realization of the required function of mathematical integration (neural integrator) between canal and motor neurons. Furthermore, if the filters H_R and H_L in figure 4.17 are treated as internal models of each eye plant, then their outputs will be internal estimates of right and left eye position. In addition, precompensation for eye plant dynamics can be achieved simultaneously on the VN signals projecting to the motor neurons (see question 4.4). In other words, the bilateral model during slow phases transforms the head velocity signal into appropriate motorneuronal signals, in a manner exactly equivalent to the models discussed above.[6] The only apparent deficiency is the lack of an expression for velocity storage. However, this is not necessarily the case, when the effects of nystagmus are taken into account (see section 4.6).

In the Laplace domain, if filters H_R and H_L are both equal to $K/(Ts + 1)$, then the bilateral model in the slow phase has the transfer function

$$\mathbf{R(s)/\dot{H}(s)} \propto [sT_c/(sT_c + 1)]^*[(sT + 1)/(sT' + 1)] \tag{3}$$

relating the motorneuronal drive to head velocity (see question 4.4), where T_c is the canal time constant, T is the eye plant time constant, and T' is the long time constant of the bilateral circuit. As in the block models

---

6. This can be verified by relating R to $\dot{H}$ in the cascade of figures 4.13 and 4.14 (see also questions 4.3 and 4.4) and comparing to equation (3).

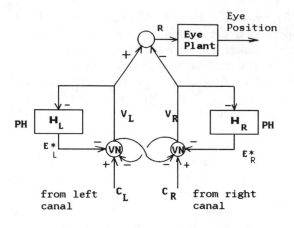

A — Symmetrical in slow phase

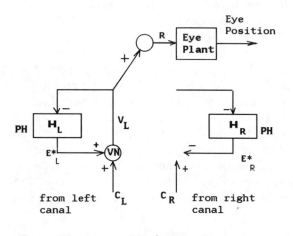

B — Nonsymmetrical in fast phase

Figure 4.17
Bilateral model of the VOR using structural modulation during nystagmus. The VN are interconnected by (commissural) inhibitory pathways during the slow phase. The fast-phase structure (b) applies for rightward rapid eye movements. Its mirror image would be used during leftward fast phases. E_R^* and E_L^* represent efference copies of the right and left eye position, respectively.

of the previous section, there is a term $(Ts + 1)$ in the numerator that can compensate for eye plant dynamics if T is chosen near the eye plant time constant, that is, if H_R and H_L represent models of the eyes.

Model eye position will respond as the "integral" of the canal estimate of head velocity and will modulate in phase with head position as required. In contrast to the cascaded models presented earlier, this approach implements all required processes through feedback, so that they already appear *at the level* of the VN. This means that any given characteristic of the ocular response will depend on distributed neural pathways, not on a specific site. For example, in figure 4.17 the function of gaze holding at the ocular level will deteriorate with loss of commissural connections, loss of a single VN or PH, or any combination thereof.

During fast phases the activity of bursters is postulated to alter the structure of the premotor circuits. However, the bilateral filters (H_R, H_L) are left unchanged since they are shared in both modes and represent invariant models of each eye. A potential strategy for switching between modes is outlined in the next section. In summary, during fast phases positive feedback is lost and is replaced with negative feedback around the filter on the side driving the fast phase. This negative feedback could be implemented via the bursters, for example, as above.

As in the slow-phase mode, the premotor signals drive both the eye plant and its internal models $(H_R$ and $H_L)$. Therefore, despite dynamic and structural changes, the efference copies of eye position are always updated, as required. However, there is an important difference here from the cascaded models using a specialized neural integration process. In the bilateral model, the function of mathematical integration, which would be equated with the neural integrator, is only implemented in the slow-phase mode with active positive feedback loops. There is no "neural integration" function during fast phases, though an efference copy of eye position is nevertheless maintained!

4.5.3   Potential Strategies for Generating Nystagmus

All oculomotor models must eventually address the question of a strategy to determine the timing of switching between slow and fast control processes. Unfortunately, this is one of the least understood aspects of oculomotor control. Most postulated strategies are based either on external, behavioral observations or on some internal variables derived from theoretical considerations.

For example, Chun and Robinson (1978) examined the parameters of eye responses just before and at the end of a fast phase during vestibular nystagmus. They concluded that current motor error from a desired mean eye trajectory played a key role, and they postulated that an internal representation of such a desired trajectory would be continuously derived by filtering of the incoming vestibular signal. This would drive the fast-phase process (T in figure 4.16) and cause the triggering of a fast phase whenever the error exceeded some threshold. Noise generators and a variable threshold had to be included in their model, in order to account for some randomness in nystagmus patterns.

On the other hand, completely theoretical considerations concerning the behavior of the bilateral model in figure 4.17 led to an alternative hypothesis: that nystagmus is part of an internal strategy to maintain linear responses in ocular premotor circuits. In the context of the bilateral model, it is clear that the required processing of vestibular signals during slow phases relies heavily on intact cross-midline signals. Hence, a very simple strategy for nystagmus has been suggested (Galiana and Outerbridge 1984; Galiana 1987). In order to avoid silencing of cell pools on either side (for instance, VN responses), fast phases in the appropriate direction would

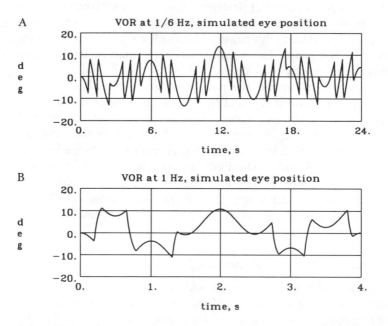

Figure 4.18
Examples of nystagmus patterns generated by the bilateral model during (a) $\frac{1}{6}$ hertz head rotation and (b) 1 hertz head rotation at identical peak head velocities. The vertical scales are in degrees. These profiles are very similar to those observed experimentally and were obtained from model simulations using identical parameter sets and automatic generation of nystagmus (see text).

be initiated by releasing bursters whenever premotor activity reaches a threshold near cutoff. In the bilateral model, interactions between slow and fast phases are strong, and each fast phase has the effect of resetting the operating point of the subsequent slow-phase segment farther away from nonlinearities. With this approach, variable nystagmus patterns appear without resorting to noise generators in the model. Examples are illustrated in figure 4.18.

It is generally accepted that the termination of fast phases can be modeled as a thresholding function operating on the difference between internal representations of the desired eye position (target) and an efference copy of actual eye position (E^* in all models described above). That is, fast phases, once initiated, are not ballistic but rather under the control of some internal servo mechanism. The problem here is deducing the internal target signal, when in most cases only behavioral ocular responses are available. This is a classical problem in state observability: the observations (eye position) reflect interactions between signals on the two sides of the brainstem, whereas the strategies for enabling and terminating fast phases depend on relevant signals (firing rates) on each side. This is surely one of the factors contributing to the apparent "random" aspect of fast-phase parameters (such as duration, size, and timing) measured at the ocular level.

4.6   Differences between Approaches and Model Testing

In general, the best test of any hypothesized model is whether it can (1) represent not only behavioral (ocular) responses but also central neural responses at various stages in the control process and (2) predict responses to new inputs, the effects of selective parameter modification (achieved, say, by reflex adaptation to new sensory conditions), or lesions. Several alternatives could be suggested using each of the two approaches in the previous section, but it is clear that the fundamental differences between them can themselves be tested. Some examples for future exploration are given below.

4.6.1   Steady-State versus Transient Assumptions

In models using separate, parallel systems for the slow- and fast-phase processes, it is tacitly assumed that the slow-phase segments of ocular nystagmus represent samples of an ongoing, continuous (*steady-state*), central process, only intermittently observed. Hence, the "envelope" of slow-phase eye velocity is presumed to exhibit the steady-state dynamics required of the slow-phase mechanism. Interactions between slow- and fast-phase responses are only possible downstream, at the level of the neural integrator in such models, and therefore can be neglected unless its time constant is abnormally small (say, 1 to 2 seconds; see question 4.1). Briefly, the characteristics of the slow-phase process remain independent of the nystagmus pattern itself (for instance, frequency and goal of fast phases).

In the approach using structurally modulated feedback, steady-state conditions can never be reached. It is accepted that all segments of nystagmus (slow and fast) represent short-lasting (*transient*) responses to stimuli, including sensory inputs and the new initial conditions introduced with each mode change. This means that the "envelope" of slow-phase eye velocity generated by the model can vary greatly, in spite of fixed transfer functions with respect to the canal input. For example, equation (3) predicts that a sustained slow-phase response to a step in head velocity would have two time constants. In the presence of nystagmus, on the other hand, each fast phase introduces a new endpoint in the direction of rotation, which becomes the new initial condition for the following slow phase. These initial conditions contribute an additional term to the slow-phase response segments, so that the "envelope" of eye velocity can exhibit a single time constant (as seen in figure 4.11).

This fundamental difference in the modeling approaches should be easily tested. For example, first-order models could be fit to an ocular response during a fixed testing protocol; parameters obtained by fitting the models to the envelope could be examined for consistency and invariance in the presence of varying nystagmus profiles, or even in the absence of nystagmus.

4.6.2   Lumped versus Bilateral Representations

Most models of the VOR use lumped (collapsed) representations for the bilateral CNS, on the premise that central responses on opposite sides of the midline are mirror images of each other about background resting activities. Nonlinearities such as positive-only firing rates and saturations are normally ignored.

With bilateral models, it is possible to consider that responses on the two sides may often differ from each other both in strength and in dynamics. The effects of CNS response asymmetries on oculomotor responses can be evaluated, sometimes leading to new insight into the interpretation of central mechanisms. For example, the simulation in figure 4.11 uses the bilateral model of figure 4.17. Velocity storage in the nystagmus response is possible, in spite of indications to the contrary in equation (3).

The shape of the envelope of eye velocity generated here depends heavily on the transient contributions of initial conditions and the fact that the bilateral model will in general respond with two components: one processing the sum of bilateral sensory inputs and initial conditions, the other processing the difference between inputs and initial conditions on each side (see, for example, questions 4.4 and 4.5). More succinctly, interactions between the slow- and fast-phase modes in this model are just as important as the direct processing of the vestibular signal (equation (3)). In order to achieve velocity storage here, it is sufficient to assume that central responses are not exactly symmetrical, especially during fast phases, and that the motorneuronal drive is a weighted (unequal) difference between premotor signals on the two sides. In this case producing a behavioral characteristic does not require a separate central process. Instead, interactions between slow and fast responses are sufficient to add an extra dimension to the dynamics observed at the peripheral level.

In order to validate block model approaches, the degree of symmetry in central and motorneuronal responses during nystagmus must be further quantified. In addition, the question now arises, Is velocity storage in the VOR an artifact of slow-fast interactions, requiring the presence of nystagmus?

4.6.3   Sequential versus Integrated Processing

If various apparent components in the behavioral responses are presumed to be due to sequential cascaded processes in the central system, this adds to model complexity. For example, in the VOR the canal sensor is followed by a "velocity storage mechanism" and then by the central "neural integrator" in Robinson's model. In the bilateral interconnected approach, the same result could follow from interactions between system mode dynamics and initial conditions, without necessarily increasing the required processing stages. Model structure can remain simple since structural modulation in itself can contribute to complex response dynamics.

Some experimental support has been found for a distributed, integrated approach to the modeling of oculomotor control. An example concerns the "neural integrator" required in oculomotor control. It was long believed to be a separate process that could eventually be located in the brainstem, if only the appropriate site were lesioned. Instead, recent lesion experiments indicate that the "integrator" function is actually a distributed process, not localizable, but instead relying on extensive interconnections between the VN and PH (Cannon and Robinson 1987). Also, if central processes were truly sequential, it should be possible to cause deterioration at one processing level independently (say, with lesions) without affecting another. So far any intervention destroying the function of the neural integrator is always accompanied by a concurrent deficiency in velocity storage.

Suggestions for Further Reading

The following references extend the material in this chapter beyond the one-dimensional VOR, toward multidimensional control of gaze in a free head.

Extensions of the oculomotor control system to three dimensions involve studies of eye plant mechanics (Miller and Robinson 1984), comparisons of sensory and motor reference coordinate systems (Simpson and Graf 1985), and detailed anatomical and neurophysiological observations on the neural connections responsible for slow-phase (Ezure and Graf 1984a,b) and fast-phase (Henn and Hepp 1986) components of the responses.

Since the general principles uncovered in horizontal ocular control have been found to be valid in three-dimensional conjugate movement, much work is currently being done on extending models using matrix or tensor theory (Robinson 1985; Pellionisz 1985; Raphan and Cohen 1985). However, much remains to be done to include in these models not only the anatomy of central connections but also the more recent observations on the dynamics of central responses. The potential for structural modulation and associated dynamic changes should especially be considered.

Goal-directed adaptation of oculomotor reflexes and observations during compensation for peripheral or central injury can both serve to explore the role of various elements in the oculomotor system. The results of such experiments have stimulated debate on the relative roles of brainstem versus cerebellar pathways in motor learning (Ito 1982; Miles and Lisberger 1981; Galiana 1985, 1986). They can also serve to test the adequacy of current models for slow-phase and/or fast-phase circuits (Optican 1985).

To date, very little has been done to integrate conjugate and vergent control systems in a cohesive model of oculomotor control. Certainly, access to data on neural activity in the bilateral brainstem is relatively recent, as is the use of bilateral models. The trend has again been to treat conjugate and vergent systems as separate parallel processes, independent of each other (Schor 1982; Miles 1985). This approach must be reexamined in the light of recent neurophysiological observations (Judge and Cumming 1986).

It is clear that oculomotor control is actually a subsystem of a more complex gaze control system. This brings us into the realm of multidimensional, multilimb control when the head is freed on the body, itself free to move in space. Important questions are again whether the systems controlling the coordination of eye and head movement are embedded in a single gaze control process or whether each is driven by different goals and pathways that could be treated separately. Perhaps the CNS uses both types of strategies, depending on the task. Their exploration will require combined behavioral and neurophysiological observations on animal models, of the type reported by Guitton and colleagues (Guitton, Douglas, and Volle 1984; Guitton and Volle 1987).

Questions

4.1 In figure 4.10, assume that the neural integrator is "leaky," with time constant 10 seconds. How long could an initial condition be held to within 80 percent of its initial value at time zero? Repeat for the case with time constant 1 second. Comment on whether the two cases could be distinguished during typical slow-phase periods of 0.5 second.

4.2 In figure 4.4, set $a = T$, but replace the neural integrator NI with a leaky integrator, so that its transfer function is now $NI' = b/(T's + 1)$, where T' represents the time constant.

   a. Find the expression for $\Delta R(s)/\dot{E}^*(s)$ in Laplace transforms (remembering that the output of any subsystem is the product of the input variable with the transfer function and that summations in the time domain remain summations in the Laplace domain).

   b. Find the condition on b so that compensation for eye plant dynamics is maintained; that is, $\Delta R/\dot{E}^*$ has $(Ts + 1)$ in the numerator to cancel the eye plant pole.

4.3 a. Verify in figure 4.15 that both models of velocity storage are equivalent in providing

$$\dot{E}^*(s)/C(s) \propto (T_1 s + 1)/(T_2 s + 1).$$

b. Find the conditions on the parameters such that $T_1 \simeq T_c$ and the new overall transfer function becomes

$$\dot{E}^*(s)/\dot{H}(s) \propto sT'/(sT' + 1); \qquad T' \gg T_c, \text{ the time constant of velocity storage.}$$

4.4 (difficult)

a. In figure 4.9, assume zero initial conditions on the filters H_R and H_L, with dynamics described by the Laplace transfer function $K/(Ts + 1)$ and a linear gain g in each cross-midline pathway. Show that the following transfer functions hold in the slow-phase structure:

$$V_R(s) + V_L(s) \propto [(Ts + 1)/(T''s + 1)](C_R(s) + C_L(s))$$

$$V_R(s) - V_L(s) \propto [(Ts + 1)/(T's + 1)](C_R(s) - C_L(s)).$$

That is, show that central responses are sensitive to both the sum and the difference of inputs.

b. Find the conditions on K and g such that $T' = 15$ seconds and $T'' = 1.3$ seconds if $T = 0.3$ second.

c. Verify that $E_R^* - E_L^*$ is proportional to eye position, when the eye plant dynamics are the same as those of H_R and H_L — that is, $\mathbf{H_R} = \mathbf{H_L} = K/(Ts + 1)$ and $\mathbf{E}(s)/\mathbf{R}(s) = G/(Ts + 1)$. Note that this implies an accurate efference copy of eye position independent of the neural integrator time constant (here T').

4.5 (more difficult)

Repeat exercise 4.3 with nonzero initial conditions on each filter output at time $t = 0$,

$$E_R^*(0) = E_R^0; \qquad E_L^*(0) = E_L^0,$$

and find the contribution of the sum and difference of the initial conditions on the sum and difference of the VN responses $(V_R + V_L)$ and $(V_R - V_L)$. (Note: An initial condition can be treated as a step input added to the output of an ideal integrator (E^0/s); in the case of a first-order filter the initial condition will contribute a decaying exponential on the output with the time constant of the filter, $(E^0 T/(Ts + 1)).$)

References

Berthoz, A., and G. Melvill Jones, eds. (1985). *Adaptive mechanisms in gaze control: Facts and theories*. New York: Elsevier.

Cannon, S. C., and D. A. Robinson (1987). Loss of the neural integrator of the oculomotor system from brainstem lesions in monkey. *Journal of Neurophysiology* 57, 1383–1409.

Carpenter, R. H. S. (1977). *Movements of the eyes*. London: Pion.

Cheron, G., E. Godaux, J. M. Laune, and B. Vanderkelen (1986). Lesions in the cat prepositus complex: Effects on the vestibulo-ocular reflex and saccades. *Journal of Physiology* 372, 75–94.

Chun, K. S., and D. A. Robinson (1978). A model of quick phase generation in the vestibulo-ocular reflex. *Biological Cybernetics* 28, 209–221.

Correia, M. J., J. P. Landolt, M. D. Ni, A. R. Eden, and J. L. Rae (1981). A species comparison of linear and nonlinear transfer characteristics of primary afferents innervating the semicircular canals. In T. Gualtierotti, ed., *The vestibular system: Function and morphology*. New York: Springer-Verlag.

Ezure, K., and W. Graf (1984a). A quantitative analysis of the spatial organization of the vestibulo-ocular reflexes in lateral- and frontal-eyed animals. I: Orientation of semicircular canals and extraocular muscles. *Neuroscience* 12, 85–93.

Ezure, K., and W. Graf (1984b). A quantitative analysis of the spatial organization of the vestibulo-ocular reflexes in lateral- and frontal-eyed animals. II: Neuronal networks underlying vestibulo-oculomotor coordination. *Neuroscience* 12, 95–109.

Fernandez, C., and J. M. Goldberg (1976a). Physiology of the peripheral neurons innervating otolith organs of the squirrel monkey. II: Directional selectivity and force-response relations. *Journal of Neurophysiology* 39, 985–995.

Fernandez, C., and J. M. Goldberg (1976b). Physiology of the peripheral neurons innervating otolith organs of the squirrel monkey. II: Directional selectivity and force-response relations. *Journal of Neurophysiology* 39, 985–995.

Fernandez, C., and J. M. Goldberg (1976c). Physiology of the peripheral neurons innervating otolith organs of the squirrel monkey. III: Response dynamics. *Journal of Neurophysiology* 39, 996–1008.

Galiana, H. L. (1985). Commissural vestibular nuclear coupling: A powerful putative site for producing adaptive change. In Berthoz and Melvill Jones 1985.

Galiana, H. L. (1986). A new approach to understanding adaptive visual-vestibular interactions in the central nervous system. *Journal of Neurophysiology* 55, 349–374.

Galiana, H. L. (1987). The implications of structural modulation in the vestibulo-ocular reflex. In *Proceedings of the IEEE Montech '87 Conference on Biomedical Technologies*, Montreal, Canada, November, 10–13, 1987.

Galiana, H. L., H. Flohr, and G. Melvill Jones (1984). A reevaluation of intervestibular nuclear coupling: Its role in vestibular compensation. *Journal of Neurophysiology* 51, 242–259.

Galiana, H. L., and J. S. Outerbridge (1984). A bilateral model for central neural pathways in the vestibuloocular reflex. *Journal of Neurophysiology* 51, 210–241.

Goldberg, J. M., and C. Fernandez (1982). Eye movements and vestibular nerve responses produced in the squirrel monkey by rotations about an earth-horizontal axis. *Experimental Brain Research* 46, 393–402.

Guitton, D., R. M. Douglas, and M. Volle (1984). Eye-head coordination in cats. *Journal of Neurophysiology* 52, 1030–1050.

Guitton, D., and M. Volle (1987). Gaze control in humans: Eye-head coordination during orienting movements to targets within and beyond the oculomotor range. *Journal of Neurophysiology* 58, 427–459.

Helmholtz, H. von (1909). *Handbuch der physiologischen Optik*. 3rd ed. Hamburg: Voss. English translation by J. P. C. Southall (1924) for the Optical Society of America.

Henn, V., and K. Hepp (1986). Pathophysiology of rapid eye movement generation in the primate. In H. J. Freund, U. Buttner, B. Cohen, and J. Noth, eds., *Progress in brain research*, vol. 64. New York: Elsevier.

Hering, E. (1868). *Die Lehre vom binocularen Sehen*. Leipzig: Engelmann.

Ito, M. (1982). Cerebellar control of the vestibulo-ocular reflex: Around the flocculus hypothesis. *Annual Review of Neuroscience* 5, 275–296.

Judge, S. J., and B. G. Cumming (1986). Neurons in the monkey midbrain with activity related to vergence eye movement and accommodation. *Journal of Neurophysiology* 55, 915–930.

Kandel, E. R., and J. H. Schwartz, eds. (1981). *Principles of neural science*. New York: Elsevier.

Listing, J. B. (1855). The first reference to Listing's law is apparently in Ruete's *Lehrbuch der Ophthalmologie*, 2nd ed., vol. 1, p. 37.

McKenzie, A., and S. G. Lisberger (1986). Properties of signals that determine the amplitude and direction of saccadic eye movement in monkeys. *Journal of Neurophysiology* 56, 196–207.

Miles, F. A. (1985). Adaptive regulation in the vergence and accommodation control systems. In Berthoz and Melvill Jones 1985.

Miles, F. A., and S. G. Lisberger (1981). Plasticity in the vestibulo-ocular reflex: A new hypothesis. *Annual Review of Neuroscience* 4, 273–299.

Miller, J. M., and D. A. Robinson (1984). A model of the mechanics of binocular alignment. *Computers and Biomedical Research* 17, 436–470.

Optican, L. M. (1985). Adaptive properties of the saccadic system. In Berthoz and Melvill Jones 1985.

Pellionisz, A. (1985). Tensorial aspects of the multidimensional approach to the vestibulo-ocular reflex and gaze. In Berthoz and Melvill Jones 1985.

Raphan, T., and B. Cohen (1985). Velocity storage and the ocular response to multidimensional vestibular stimuli. In Berthoz and Melvill Jones 1985.

Raphan, T., V. Matsuo, and B. Cohen (1979). Velocity storage in the vestibulo-ocular reflex arc. *Experimental Brain Research* 35, 229–248.

Robinson, D. A. (1975). Oculomotor control signals. In P. Bach-y-Rita and G. Lennerstrand, eds., *Basic mechanisms of ocular motility and their clinical implications*. Oxford: Pergamon.

Robinson, D. A. (1977). Linear addition of optokinetic and vestibular signals in the vestibular nucleus. *Experimental Brain Research* 30, 447–450.

Robinson, D. A. (1981). The use of control system analysis in the neurophysiology of eye movements. *Annual Review of Neuroscience* 4, 463–503.

Robinson, D. A. (1985). The coordinates of neurons in the vestibulo-ocular reflex. In Berthoz and Melvill Jones 1985.

Schor, C. M. (1982). Vergence eye movements: Basic aspects. In G. Lennerstrand, D. Zee, and E. Keller, eds., *Functional basis of ocular motility disorders*. New York: Pergamon.

Schor, R. H., A. D. Miller, S. J. B. Timerick, and D. L. Tomko (1985). Responses to head tilt in cat central vestibular neurons. II: Frequency dependence of neural response vectors. *Journal of Neurophysiology* 53, 1444–1452.

Schor, R. H., A. D. Miller, and D. L. Tomko (1984). Responses to head tilt in cat central vestibular neurons. I: Direction of maximum sensitivity. *Journal of Neurophysiology* 51, 136–146.

Simpson, J. I., and W. Graf (1985). The selection of reference frames by nature and its investigators. In Berthoz and Melvill Jones 1985.

Skavenski, A. A., and D. A. Robinson (1973). Role of abducens motorneurons in the vestibulo-ocular reflex. *Journal of Neurophysiology* 36, 724–738.

Chapter 5

Controlling Sequential Motor Activity

Charles E. Wright

5.1 Plans and Planning

To start thinking about the issues covered in this chapter, consider planning and then carrying out a sequence of actions. This might be a high-level plan toward a long-term goal, such as to ensure that you do well in school this semester, or it might be a much more limited and concrete plan, such as organizing a day involving several errands. In the second example, before setting out, you might decide on a tentative plan describing the order in which you will do the errands and how you will get from place to place. This plan is probably largely determined by the location of each errand and the layout of available transportation. As part of this planning process you

I thank my colleagues Ron Knoll at AT&T Bell Laboratories, Stephen Monsell at the University of Cambridge in England, and Saul Sternberg at the University of Pennsylvania for their permission to describe both work that we carried out jointly and, in some cases, work that they have done in which I did not participate. Nina Macdonald and Saul Sternberg provided useful comments on an earlier draft of this chapter. Writing of this chapter was partially supported by the National Science Foundation under grant BNS-87-11273.

will have explicitly made decisions about many details of your plan—what routes to take, where to stop for a break, and so on—while leaving others undecided. You may also have included some contingencies in your plan: for instance, what to do if the bookstore really doesn't open until ten o'clock.

Once the plan exists, you will need some way of recording it for future reference, as well as a mechanism to ensure that its steps are carried out. In a simple case you might just jot the plan on a piece of paper with the idea of referring to it at regular intervals. In a more complex case, such as planning for the semester, you might want to set up a timetable and goals, perhaps using a calendar to ensure that the plan stays on course.

Earlier chapters have examined the planning process for single, isolated movements in various domains. Here we will consider whether, when performing a task that involves sequences of these movements, we plan the sequence in anything like the way we plan a morning's shopping expedition. People often find this suggestion controversial, perhaps because this planning process, if it exists, is one we are rarely aware of. If movement sequences are not planned, however, it is hard to understand how and where we accumulate the information necessary to make them skillfully.

The mechanisms used by the brain to make, store, and carry out plans for sequences of movements have been an open issue for many years. Neurophysiologists, for instance, have only in the last few years begun to understand how, short of growing new physical connections, the nervous system can establish permanent (and/or temporary) links between preexisting pieces of information in the brain. If we are to combine preexisting specifications for unrelated, simple movements to produce more complex concatenations—for example, coordinated head and eye movements to track an object—then some mechanism for producing or simulating such connections or links must be necessary. Further, if the order of the component movements in a movement sequence is critical—a child learning to grasp after reaching, where both individual behaviors are well established—then these links must contain additional information specifying their coordination. This is the problem of *serial order* made famous by Lashley (1951). Finally, in some cases—for instance, playing a musical instrument—the precise timing of successive submovements may be important over and above the requirement that they be produced in a particular order. In this case a movement plan would need to be even more specific.

On the other hand, there are theorists who suggest that these "mental" links between successive actions do not exist. Classical behaviorists, for example, reject the explanation that internal, mental links are established that specify or control the successive components of a movement sequence. Instead, they theorize that sensory stimulation generated by the production of one submovement elicits, by strength of habit, the next appropriate movement as a response. In this conception, a plan for a movement sequence, rather than being a centralized, cognitive entity with an independent existence, is instead a result emerging from a distributed set of stimulus-response habits. According to this view, the notion that we engage in planning processes that result in independently existing mental plans is simply a misconception based on faulty introspective evidence.

One problem with the behaviorist perspective is that under such an approach, sequencing depends on a feedback process with moderately large delays. These delays establish the granularity of precise movement-sequence timing. In addition, the introduction of feedback delays can exacerbate control problems (see section 1.5.2); even if the stimulus for a response is the efference copy of the previous response—that is, a copy of the outgoing motor commands routed back as a stimulus—the loop delays would probably be on the order of 100 + milliseconds. These problems, along with widespread disenchantment concerning the explanatory power of the behaviorist viewpoint, crystallized for many by the criticisms in Lashley's (1951) article, were a major factor that generated interest in questions about the creation and representation of mental plans. This interest was one of the central themes in the early years of cognitive psychology; one influential monograph of that period was in fact entitled *Plans and the Structure of Behavior* (Miller, Galanter, and Pribram 1960). The nature of planning and plans has also been an important topic in many of the other disciplines that feed into cognitive science: computer science, linguistics, artificial intelligence, and robotics. In this chapter we will explore the nature of plans used to control sequences of simple movements as well as the cognitive mechanism involved in carrying out those plans.

5.1.1   Planning Movement Sequences: Motor Programs

Within the domain of motor control, plans are typically referred to as *motor programs*. Such programs, which take their name by explicit analogy to computer programs, are thought to be involved in activities as diverse as touching an object, hitting a ball with a bat, walking, running, pole-vaulting, driving a car, writing with a pen, and producing speech. They are often thought of as the mental representation that bridges the processes of planning and control (as discussed in section 1.1). More specifically, motor programs are seen as the repository for the accumulated information that underlies skilled, fluent activity. Clearly, a better understanding of the properties of motor programs for movement sequences as well as the planning and control processes that create and interpret them could have far-reaching implications for learning and ultimate performance in many areas.

This topic is also interesting because, although it shares many characteristics with other investigations of cognitive plans and planning—planning a shopping trip, a strategy to solve a physics problem, or a way to put an idea into words—it also differs from them in many important ways. Among other differences, executing a motor program results in overt, physical activity (movements) that can be measured precisely. These movements are usually relatively simple and repeatable. But, at the same time, unlike the way we view some other cognitive plans, we generally do not have the sense that motor programs can be the objects of introspection. The activities involved seem too automatic. For example, I can think about how to throw up a tennis ball and swing a racquet to produce a well-placed serve with top spin. I can read books on the subject or observe others who are experts. As part of this study process, I could learn exactly which muscles are activated, in which sequence, and at what level, as well as the ideal trajectory of the racquet, limbs, and so on. But simply learning this information will not allow me to duplicate the required movement. Thus, although I might somewhat improve my serve with all of this information, it is doubtful whether, without extensive, repetitive practice, I could ever master this movement sequence. In addition, although repetitive practice appears to be necessary for mastery of this skill, it is usually the case that we are unaware of what is changing or what things we are learning as we practice. I have more confidence, however, that I could improve my facility to write and speak more eloquently or to solve physics problems using just such processes of observation and reflection.

5.1.2 Representation of Motor Programs

The information contained in motor programs could potentially be specified at one (or, simultaneously, more than one) of several levels—high-level intentions, endpoint trajectories, joint angles, task dynamics, muscle force distributions, and so on—with necessary missing information presumably computed during the course of a movement. In particular, a number of theorists have proposed that motor programs are learned and organized hierarchically, much as subprograms of a computer program might be organized, and written, in a hierarchical fashion (Greene 1972; Rosenbaum 1985; Saltzman 1979).

Consider, for example, how an infant learns to reach through space and to grasp an object when it touches her hand. What might this learning consist of? How are these newly acquired movements represented so they can be repeated? Later, these activities are refined and combined so that reaching for and grabbing an object becomes a single fluid motion. Later still, this combination may be integrated with locomotion to grab objects that are out of reach. Finally, these same activities may be further refined and combined with other separately learned sequences to allow an infielder in baseball to instinctively (since, presumably, there is no time to create a new plan) and fluidly dive for a hard-hit ground ball, catch it, roll, and come up throwing the ball to first base. In what sense are these complex, learned activities made up of previously learned components? How does being integrated into a higher-level activity change the components?

In this chapter we will not specifically explore these questions of level representation and the hierarchical nature of motor programs. However, it is important to remain aware of these issues, since they will never be far below the surface.

5.1.3   Confirming the Existence of Motor Programs

Before attempting to study the structure of motor programs or the mechanisms used to sequence their elements, we need criteria that determine when the movements in a sequence are made according to a plan. The criteria we use must distinguish the intention to make a movement sequence, couched in terms of abstract, high-level goals, from a plan that is sufficiently detailed to control the neuromuscular system during the performance of that sequence—eventually directing muscles to contract and effectors to rotate about their joints. For example, a plan for typing a sequence of keys on a keyboard (one task that we will discuss extensively later) would presumably include motoric details about which fingers to use, which way they should move, and in what order their movements should be initiated, along with, or instead of, information about which letters are to be typed.

In addition to expecting a motor program to contain "motoric" details, we might also expect this representation to exist prior to the start of the movement.[1] In particular, given this chapter's emphasis on movement sequences, our criteria for performances controlled by motor programs should allow us to discriminate between these and performances produced without planning. One example of the latter would be response chaining, such as posited by behaviorists, where feedback from one action initiates the next action. In this scheme, the transition from one component action to the next depends only on local factors—that is, the particular previous action and the subsequent action that feedback from the first action elicits— not on any knowledge about other actions occurring later (or earlier) in the sequence.

Consider, for example, the sequence of movements required to draw a figure. If I draw this figure by making a stroke, stopping to compare the result with what I wish the overall result to be, choosing another stroke to

---

1. This expectation that "plans" exist prior to the beginning of a movement should not be taken to exclude the possibility of limited computations taking place during a movement that might alter the outcome.

follow the first, making this second stroke, and so on, an observer might be inclined to reject this as an example of a performance in which the sequence of movements (strokes) is governed by a motor program. And yet in this case there is clearly at least some high-level goal: I have an idea of the figure I wish to draw. To get a feel for the difference between these two processes, try writing cursively the words *motor program* first with your dominant hand (your right hand, if you are right-handed) and then with your nondominant hand. For most people, dominant-hand writing is fluent, quick, and almost effortless, whereas nondominant-hand writing takes much more time, is jerky, and requires substantial attention and concurrent visual feedback. And yet, the products of these two subjectively dissimilar processes are often quite similar and recognizably due to one person. This difference usually becomes more obvious if the movements are made without concurrent visual feedback, as would be the case if your eyes were closed.

From this distinction, we should not draw the conclusion that motor programs always proceed "open-loop," without making use of feedback. Instead, the role of feedback in performing a programmed movement sequence probably is to fine-tune the ongoing performance rather than to aid in the selection (or chaining) of subsequent submovements in the movement sequence. Another potential function of feedback is to allow the motor-system controller to gather information that can be used to update its model of the muscles and the load, allowing compensation for effects of muscle fatigue, poorly estimated load characteristics, and deficiencies in motor programs. Better information about any of these aspects of a movement should improve the performance during subsequent movement sequences.

Devising criteria to distinguish the various possible representations and processes that may underlie the production of a movement sequence is made more difficult by the layered nature of the motor system (see chapter 1). At the lowest level are the immediate, albeit passive, responses to changes in load that result from the stiffness of muscle itself or the non-linear relations between muscle force, neural activation, muscle length, and contraction velocity. Moving up through the neural control system, there is active feedback from spinal reflexes, pattern generators, and transcortical feedback pathways. Because of these and other mechanisms, there are, interposed between a plan and the resulting movement, myriad potential sources of movement modification and control. Though it may be, as some argue, that the actions of these peripheral layers of the motor system make high-level control feasible, from the perspective of studying the higher-level processes, these peripheral processes are a great source of complexity and confusion. In effect, these peripheral processes interpose unknown layers of buffering and filtering between us, as observers, and the central processes that plan or control movement sequences. Of course, this situation is hardly unique to the study of motor control or cognitive psychology in general. Unfortunately, there are no widely accepted rules that tell us what data will support particular inferences about motor programs.

In the search for movement-sequence regularities, some regularities will be more helpful than others in establishing the existence and nature of the movement-planning process. We should be especially interested in details of the performance at an early point in a movement sequence that depend on the nature of some later part of the sequence. Such observations are of particular interest since they fit well with our intuitions of a planned sequence of movements and would be difficult to account for in a sequence of movements that proceed without a plan. The longer the span of this influence, the more strongly it suggests that the influence results from a planning process rather than a local interaction of sequence elements.

The problem of local interactions would not be a concern if we could assert that one movement in a sequence does not begin until the previous movement has ended. It is possible that successive submovements in a sequence can overlap to some degree—that is, some commands related to a subsequent element in a sequence may be issued while an earlier sequence element still has primary control of the movement effector(s). These anticipatory (or perseveratory) commands will change the path of the movement effector(s) during the period of overlap. Looking from the outside in, it is difficult to distinguish whether these changes are the result of a mechanism, perhaps in the peripheral motor system, acting locally (in the terminology of chapter 1, an effect of the control process) or the result of a central planning process.

This overlap phenomenon and the interpretational difficulties associated with it have been particularly important in theorizing about the production of speech, where such overlap is often referred to as *coarticulation* (Kent and Minifie 1977). The speech sound stream is often represented as a linear sequence of abstract sound segments chosen from the small, discrete set of phonemes of a language. Attempts to locate the boundaries of these segments in articulatory events are usually confounded, however, by the fact that the articulatory movements appear to overlap one another in a complex fashion. This overlap also appears to make the details of the sound structure of a phoneme depend on its local context, especially at the beginning and end of the phoneme.

One possible source of coarticulation consistent with the idea of local interactions is that the paths of the articulators under the control of a particular phoneme are partially determined by the positions of those articulators at the end of the commands for the previous phoneme in the sequence. In this case the different paths of the articulators are not planned (in the sense of being determined by the system ahead of time); rather, the articulator trajectories result from the interaction of the current articulator positions and the commands for the next phoneme. Lenneberg (1967), on the other hand, has proposed an explanation for coarticulation that suggests a much stronger planning component. He proposes that for some phonetic sequences XY, part of the signal to articulate Y must leave the brain *before* the signal to articulate X.

One way to begin to differentiate between these alternative explanations for coarticulation, as well as others that fall between these extremes, is to look at the control signals to articulators. Even with this information, however, there will be cases where an instance of coarticulation cannot be classified definitively as a result of planning or local interactions. For our purposes, however, a useful heuristic is that the longer the time between an interaction and the following element that engendered it, the more confidence we can have that this interaction represents the result of planning.

Prior to the work that we are about to examine, speech researchers had interpreted various coarticulatory phenomena as support for preplanning and as evidence for what the unit of planning might be (Kent and Minifie 1977 includes a good review of these ideas). An illustration of these phenomena can be experienced in normal speech. Some vowel sounds such as /u/ (as in *you*) require protrusion and rounding of the lips to be produced correctly. Most other vowels (such as the vowel /æ/ as in *bat*) cannot be produced correctly with the lips rounded. On the other hand, many consonants can be produced acceptably with or without lip rounding, although the presence or absence of lip rounding will affect how they sound. It has been observed that if a series of consonants, which are "neutral" as far as lip rounding is concerned, is followed by a vowel requiring lip rounding, then the consonants are also produced with lip rounding. For example, in the word *construe* the final vowel /u/ is produced with lip rounding. The rounding is also anticipated in the production of this word, being present on the /str/ sequence that begins the second syllable. To see this, compare pronouncing *construe* and *constrict*.

In the case of *construe*, the anticipation of the lip rounding spans three segments, phonemes, in one syllable. Anticipatory effects of lip rounding have been cited that span up to six consonants in a syllable (Kent and Minifie 1977), although such constructions are not possible in English. Similar effects have also been reported that cross syllable and word boundaries (Moll and Daniloff 1971), although these effects seem less common.

Demonstrations such as these of lip rounding certainly satisfy the requirement for evidence to support a claim of preplanning that a specific, motor-related aspect later in a sequence influences performance at some distance earlier in the sequence. Although these demonstrations are impressive in themselves, there do not appear to be many other examples in speech that exhibit these properties. This raises the possibility that these anticipatory effects might be due to some special mechanism rather than to general preplanning. Such effects are also limited in their scope: they have only been observed to span several segments within a syllable or across a single syllable/word boundary. If, for example, the syllable rather than the phoneme is the unit of sequence planning in speech, then most of these coarticulation effects would be interpreted, because of their limited range, as within-unit effects rather than effects of planning across units making up a sequence.

5.1.4   A Plan for the Rest of the Chapter

In the rest of this chapter we will look at experimental results that support several inferences about the nature of movement sequencing and motor programs. We will first examine regularities in movement-sequence performance in the domains of speech and typing. We will then look at a parsimonious model capable of describing these regularities, as well as at research that proposes and rejects other plausible alternative models. Finally, we will use the model to generate novel predictions about new data—predictions that, when borne out, will strengthen our confidence in the validity of the model.

5.2   Regularities Observed in Speech

The work we will be considering began with experiments by Monsell and Sternberg (1981). In their pioneering studies they asked practiced subjects to recite lists of words as quickly as possible. Most of their results related the durations of the utterances produced to the number of words in a list.

5.2.1   Method

Figure 5.1 outlines the procedure used by Monsell and Sternberg. Most of these experiments involved only a few (four or six) highly practiced subjects, who participated in a large number of trials over many days. The sequence to be spoken on a given trial was displayed on a CRT screen. The sequence consisted of a word or series of words, usually monosyllabic, to be spoken as a single fluent utterance (for example, *five, three, one, two* or *track, bay, rum*). The display remained on the screen for several seconds, and then the subject was allowed 2 or 3 seconds more to prepare for a "go" signal. To maximize preparation, the duration of this preparation period was fixed, and it ended with two signals, rhythmically spaced, 750 milliseconds apart. To discourage anticipations, there were occasional "catch" trials on which the "go" signal did not occur and subjects were not to respond; this occurred on 10 to 20 percent of all the trials.

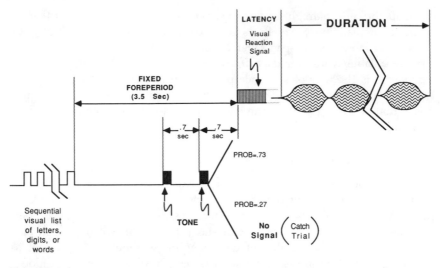

Figure 5.1
Procedure on one trial in a typical speech-production experiment. (After figure 1 in Stern-berg, Knoll, Monsell, and Wright 1983; by permission.)

Many of these details, although important for an understanding of the conditions studied, appear not to be critical for obtaining the results of primary interest in this chapter. For example, in another condition studied by Monsell and Sternberg and also reported by Sternberg et al. (1980), the foreperiod varied randomly from 2.6 to 5.4 seconds with no warning signals or catch trials, but the overall pattern of the results remained the same. What may be critical, however, is that instructions and feedback encouraged subjects to produce the sequence (1) *correctly*, with the specified words in the correct order, (2) *fluently*, without stumbles or pauses, and (3) *with minimal time from start to finish.* To ensure (1) and (2), an experimenter constantly monitored all of the utterances and counted those as errors that were incorrect or insufficiently fluent; subjects were penalized for these errors and data from these trials were excluded from most analyses. To ensure (3), subjects were given numeric feedback after blocks of 15 to 20 trials indicating the average duration of their utterances and the number of errors. Scores computed from these values were compared to target scores, which were set at levels designed to improve on previous performance, and subjects were given monetary bonuses for beating their target scores.

5.2.2   Latency Data

When Monsell and Sternberg began these experiments, their initial goal was to examine how the time to start saying a list, the *latency*, would vary

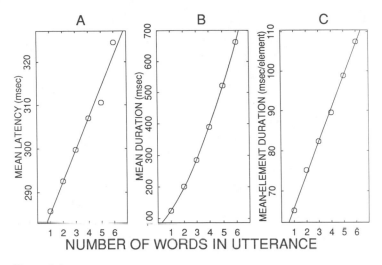

Figure 5.2
(a) Mean latency (b) utterance duration, and (c) estimated mean-element duration, as a function of the number of words for random sequences of digit names. The solid line represents a least-squares fit to the data in each case: for mean latency, $\hat{L}_n = 277 + 7.3n$; for mean duration, $\hat{D}_n = 40.9 + 55.0n + 8.6n^2$; and, for mean-element duration, $\hat{d}_n = 57.1 + 8.3n$. (Data taken from figures 3 and 5 in Sternberg, Knoll, Monsell, and Wright 1983; redrawn by permission.)

as a function of its length and composition. This interest stems from a long line of research based on the premise that, during the latency interval between the signal to respond and the beginning of the response, critical last-second computations are needed to construct the motor program for the upcoming movement (Henry and Rogers 1960). Much of this research has focused on the question of whether the latency to respond reflects the *complexity* of the upcoming movement (Hayes and Marteniuk 1976). In these experiments, changing the number of elements in the list was one way to vary the complexity of the material to be programmed.

Figure 5.2 shows data from one of Monsell and Sternberg's earliest experiments in which the utterances were made up of digits in random order. As figure 5.2a shows, Sternberg and Monsell found an effect of list length on the latency to begin reciting: mean latency increased approximately linearly with the number of words. The size of this *length* effect can be summarized by the slope of the fitted function in equation (1):

$$\hat{L}_n = \eta + \theta n. \tag{1}$$

Here n is the length of the list in words, $\hat{L}_n$ is the predicted latency for a list of length n, η is a constant intercept, and the slope parameter, θ, describes how the latency increases with list length.

5.2.3   Duration Data

Although these observations, in particular that of the functional form of this relationship, were important, Monsell and Sternberg also made another important observation. Along with the latency, the dependent variable in which they were primarily interested, Monsell and Sternberg measured the *duration* of the utterances: the time from when the subject began speaking until the utterance was complete. The results for duration are shown in figure 5.2b. These data show that mean duration, the average time to say the list of words, did not go up linearly with the list length, as one might expect, but rather increased approximately quadratically with the length of the list. This result is surprising since most intuitions about this performance suggest that durations should increase linearly with the list length.

To understand the implications of a quadratic duration function, consider the simpler, counterfactual case where the average duration of an item, in this experiment a digit, is roughly constant. We can represent this constant with the symbol d. In addition, we can use the symbol $\hat{D}_n$ to refer to the predicted duration of a list of length n. Using this notation, we expect the duration of a list of one word to be $\hat{D}_1 = k + d$, where k is a constant associated with the entire list. The value of k presumably is related to measurement error or "end effects," an issue we will discuss later. Similarly, we would expect the duration of a two-word list to be $\hat{D}_2 = k + 2d$, the duration of a three-word list to be $\hat{D}_3 = k + 3d$, and so on. We can generalize these equations for any value of n with the linear equation $\hat{D}_n = k + nd$.

As figure 5.2b shows, however, the actual durations that Monsell and Sternberg observed increased more than linearly with the number of items in the list. The upward curvature in these data is well described by the quadratic duration function in equation (2):

$$\hat{D}_n = \alpha + \beta n + \gamma n^2. \tag{2}$$

Here α, β, and γ are constants and n is, once again, the number of words in the list. The quadratic form of the mean duration function implies that the average duration of a single word in these utterances was not constant. If we assume that α represents measurement error or end effects on the entire list and correct for them, then the predicted average duration of an item in a list of length n, call this $\hat{d}_n$, is given in equation (3):

$$\hat{d}_n = \frac{D_n - \alpha}{n} = \beta + \gamma n \tag{3}$$

Equation (3) results by subtracting α from both sides of equation (2), since this is a value associated with the entire list rather than with an individual word, and dividing the result by n, since d_n represents the average duration of a single item obtained from the duration of a list made up of n words.[2] This algebraic manipulation makes it clear that, in Monsell and Sternberg's data, the average duration of *an individual word* rather than the *overall duration of the list* increases linearly with the length of the list.

Equation (3) suggests a useful form in which to examine the duration data from these experiments. Because the small degrees of curvature of the quadratic duration functions are hard to estimate and compare visually, often a set of observed utterance durations $(D_1, D_2, \ldots, D_n, \ldots)$ is transformed into estimates of mean-element durations $(d_1, d_2, \ldots, d_n, \ldots)$ using the formula in equation (3) so that the datasets can be compared more easily. To the extent that the utterance durations, D_n, are fit well by a quadratic function, the estimated mean-element durations, d_n, will be fit well by the linear function in equation (3). Figure 5.2c shows the mean-element transformation of the duration data and the best-fitting linear function.

5.2.4   Generality

The basic pattern of these results for latency and duration turns out to be robust. Sternberg et al. (1978) and Sternberg et al. (1980), for example, report similar patterns of data using utterances made up of

1. numbers in sequence like *two-three-four-five*,
2. weekdays in sequence like *Wednesday-Thursday-Friday*,
3. randomly ordered sets of weekdays like *Thursday-Monday-Tuesday-Saturday*,
4. reiterant sequences of weekdays like *Tuesday-Tuesday-Tuesday*,
5. randomly ordered lists of letter names,
6. novel and arbitrary lists of one- and two-syllable high-frequency nouns, and
7. lists of monosyllabic pseudowords like *vate-hane-vone*.

As we will see, a similar pattern of results for latency and duration is obtained for other complex, skilled movement sequences such as those produced in typewriting. In addition, Zingale and Kowler (1987) have observed very similar patterns of latencies and durations for sequences of

2. In equation (3), D_n is the observed duration of lists of length n and the value of α is obtained from fitting the model in equation (2) to the duration data. Note also that the parameters β and γ are mathematically identical in equations (2) and (3). However, the estimates obtained for these parameters using standard (that is, unweighted) least-squares regression procedures to fit equation (2) to the utterance durations or equation (3) to the mean-element durations will not necessarily be exactly the same. This occurs because error in the observations at each value of n is weighted differently when fitting the two equations. An exploration of why this is so and what to do about it makes an interesting exercise.

saccadic eye movements. Finally, the effects occur not only for the highly practiced subjects studied by Monsell and Sternberg but also for unpracticed subjects, indicating that they are not a result of general practice or a lack thereof. The latency and duration effects also survive specific practice. If the same utterance is produced three times in a row, the overall durations decrease, but the form and slope of the latency and mean-element duration functions remain unaffected. Similarly, there are nonzero slopes for the latency and mean-element duration functions in typing even after 20 consecutive repetitions of the same string.

5.2.5   Additivity of Utterance Length and Word Length Effects

We turn now to a more detailed examination of another experiment by Monsell and Sternberg (1981; briefly reported by Sternberg et al. 1978). This experiment was designed to allow a comparison of the latency and duration function for lists of one- and two-syllable words. To reduce the effect of as many extraneous factors as possible, lists of one to four words were constructed in which all of the words were either one-syllable or two-syllable nouns with a high frequency of occurrence in written English (Kučera and Francis 1967). The two-syllable words were all ones normally produced with stress on the first syllable. More important, the first syllable of each of these words was one of the one-syllable words used in the experiment.[3] Examples of such embedded pairs include *bay* and *baby*, *cow* and *coward*, *rum* and *rumble*, *track* and *tractor*. With these stimuli, Monsell and Sternberg intended to create a manipulation as close as possible to the addition of an unstressed syllable to a given stressed syllable. One reason for trying to create such a precise manipulation was to ask whether the "unit" or "element" in terms of which these effects should be measured is the word, the syllable, or something else.

Figure 5.3 shows the latency, duration, and mean-element duration data from this experiment graphed with number of words as the independent variable. Figure 5.4 shows these same data, but this time the number of syllables is the independent variable. Before examining the details of these data, it is worthwhile simply to compare the two representations. It is striking that the representation in figure 5.3 results in fitted functions that are much more nearly parallel for the latency and mean-element duration data. The simplicity of representation in this and other similar comparisons convinced Sternberg et al. (1978) that the proper unit for the analysis for these data was not the syllable but probably something more similar to the

---

3. The correspondence is not perfect, in some cases and for some dialects—a trained phonologist could discern and describe differences. For the purposes of this experiment, however, it appears to have been adequate.

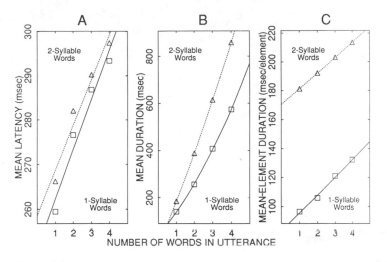

NUMBER OF WORDS IN UTTERANCE

Figure 5.3
(a) Mean latency, (b) utterance duration, and (c) estimated mean-element duration, as a function of the number of words for utterances composed of one-syllable words (squares) and two-syllable words (triangles). The solid lines represent the least-squares fit for the one-syllable words: for mean latency, $\hat{L}_n = 251 + 11.1n$; for mean duration, $\hat{D}_n = 45.0 + 81.9n + 12.6n^2$; and, for for mean-element duration, $\hat{d}_n = 83.3 + 12.3n$. The dotted lines represent the least-squares fit for the two-syllable words: for mean latency, $\hat{L}_n = 258 + 10.2n$; for mean duration, $\hat{D}_n = 2.8 + 171.8n + 10.5n^2$; and, for mean-element duration, $\hat{d}_n = 170.8 + 10.7n$. (Data taken from figure 15.3 in Sternberg, Monsell, Knoll, and Wright 1978 and figure 6 in Sternberg, Knoll, Monsell, and Wright 1983; redrawn by permission.)

word. Focusing first on the latency data, the slopes of the fitted functions for one- and two-syllable words are almost identical; the difference is 0.9 $\pm$ 1.1 milliseconds per word.[4]

As one might expect, despite its small effect on latency, the number of syllables in a word had a large effect on the duration function. This is best seen by looking at the mean-element durations in figure 5.3c. The intercepts of the fitted functions for one- and two-syllable words clearly differ: 83.3 milliseconds versus 170.8 milliseconds, respectively. An obvious interpretation of this is that the two-syllable words took, on average, 87.5 milliseconds longer to say. What is less obvious is that, although there was a large effect of the number of syllables on the *average* mean-element duration, number of syllables had little or no influence on the effect of list length or on mean-element duration. This is shown by the small difference

4. Here, as elsewhere in this chapter, the indication of variability, in this case 1.1 milliseconds per word, is the standard error of the mean based on the between-subject variability.

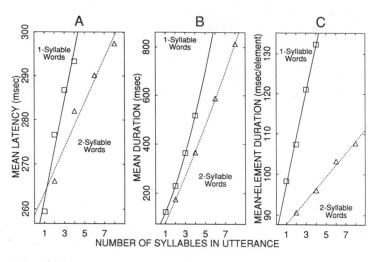

Figure 5.4
(a) Mean latency (b) utterance duration, and (c) estimated mean-element duration, as a function of the number of syllables for utterances composed of one-syllable words (squares) and two-syllable words (triangles). (Compare figure 5.3.) The solid lines represent the least-squares fit for the one-syllable words (these fits are identical to those in figure 5.3 for one-syllable words): for mean latency, $\hat{L}_n = 251 + 11.2n$; for mean duration, $\hat{D}_n = 45.0 + 81.9n + 12.6n^2$; and, for mean-element duration, $\hat{d}_n = 83.3 + 12.3n$. The dotted lines represent the least-squares fit for the two-syllable words: for mean latency, $\hat{L}_n = 258 + 5.1n$; for mean duration, $\hat{D}_n + 2.8 + 85.9n + 2.6n^2$; and, for mean-element duration, $\hat{d}_n = {}^*5.3 + 2.7n$. (Data taken from figure 15.3 in Sternberg, Monsell, Knoll, and Wright 1978 and figure 6 in Sternberg, Knoll, Monsell, and Wright 1983; redrawn by permission.)

between the slope estimates in these two conditions, 1.6 ± 1.2 milliseconds per word.

One summary of these results is that the effects of list length and number of syllables on mean-element duration and, perhaps to a lesser extent, on latency are additive; that is, the effects can be separated and their contributions added together to produce a good estimate of their combined effect. This is the simplest possible description for the combined effects of two factors on an observable variable. The fact that this is an adequate description in this case is a powerful observation with important theoretical implications that we will examine shortly.

5.2.6   Summary

Before we turn from speech to similar phenomena observed in typewriting, it may be useful to summarize the points made so far:

1. The latency to begin an utterance increases by a fixed amount θ for each element in the utterance.

2. The mean-element duration for an utterance increases by a fixed amount γ for each element in the utterance.

3. Although this is not documented systematically in the preceding discussion, the estimates of θ and γ tend to be quite similar.

4. The effects of number of elements and element size on latency are additive.

5. The effects of number of elements and element size on mean-element duration are additive.

5.3   Regularities Observed in Typewriting

5.3.1   Latency and Duration Data

Sternberg et al. (1978) have demonstrated in a number of experiments that *burst* typing of nonsense materials exhibits effects of list length on both the latency and the duration of the sequence. In burst typing, the subject is required to type a short sequence (one to six) of previously presented letters (usually all consonants) as quickly as possible. This task can be distinguished from *transcription* typing, in which a longer text is copied from another source. The burst typing paradigm has the advantage, for this work, that it has little or no perceptual (reading) component.

Figure 5.5 shows data from a typical typing experiment. The similarity of many aspects of these data to the speech data suggests that the phenomena in both modalities are the result of a general mechanism or strategy of motor control. Note that figure 5.5 also contains a comparison of between-hands and within-hand typing sequences. This manipulation is very similar in spirit to the one- versus two-syllable manipulation for the speech experiments. It is well known that the time between successive keypresses is longer if the keys involved are typed by the same hand rather than by different hands. Thus, for instance, the average time between keypresses for two letters typed by the same hand (for example, *J* and *K* or *A* and *D*) might be 200 milliseconds for a skilled typist, even though these keys are usually struck by different fingers. For comparison, the average time between two keypresses for letters typed by different hands (for example, *J* and *A* or *D* and *K*) might be 120 milliseconds for the same typist. As figure 5.5c shows, this difference, like the effect of one- versus two-syllable words, is reflected in the intercept, β, of the function relating mean inter-keypress time to the number of keypresses (equivalently, the linear parameter of the overall duration function), not the slope parameter, γ (the quadratic parameter of the overall duration function). Thus, once again there is clear additivity between the effect of sequence length and an element-size factor, in this case same-hand versus alternating-hands transitions, that has a large effect on the time to produce a single element.

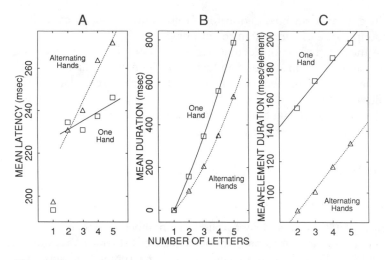

Figure 5.5
(a) Mean latency, (b) duration, and (c) estimated mean-element duration as a function of the number of letters in typewritten sequences of one to five letters. Sequences were typed either using all one hand (squares) or using a strictly alternating sequence of hands (triangles). The solid lines represent the least-squares fit for the one-hand condition: for mean latency (fit from $n = 2$ to $n = 5$ only), $\hat{L}_n = 223 + 4.1n$; for mean duration (constrained to pass through zero when $n = 1$), $\hat{D}_n = 142.9n + 14.3n^2$; and, for mean-element duration, $\hat{d}_n = 142.9 + 14.1n$. The dotted lines represent the least-squares fit for the alternating-hand condition: for mean latency (fit from $n = 2$ to $n = 5$ only), $\hat{L}_n = 200 + 14.9n$; for mean duration (constrained to pass through zero when $n = 1$), $\hat{D}_n = 72.7n + 14.7n^2$; and, for mean-element duration, $\hat{D}_n = 71.9 + 15.2n$. (Data taken from figures 15.5 and 15.6 in Sternberg, Monsell, Knoll, and Wright 1978; redrawn by permission.)

5.3.2   Inter-Keypress Time Data

Throughout this discussion of the effect of length on duration, we have been considering mean-element (word or inter-keypress) durations without ever considering the element durations themselves. An examination of speech or typing at this level requires measuring the duration of each element (word or inter-keypress time) as a function of the list length and the serial position of the item within a list. Although these measurements are hard to make for speech, they are quite straightforward to make for typewriting. The primary data collected for typing are the times and identities of a sequence of key-closures. From these data, it is simple to compute the intervals between successive keypresses.

Figure 5.6, a reanalysis of the data summarized in figure 5.5, shows typical inter-keypress time data for sequences made up of all same-hand transitions in one case and all alternating-hands transitions in the other. In graphing these data, Sternberg et al. (1978) chose to line up points for

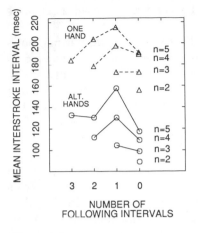

Figure 5.6
Data from figure 5.5 reanalyzed to show the time intervals between successive keypresses. Open triangles mark the data from the one-hand condition. Open circles mark the data from the alternating-hands condition. (Data taken from figure 15.6 in Sternberg, Monsell, Knoll, and Wright 1978, redrawn by permission.)

sequences of different lengths relative to the last keypress in each sequence. An alternative would have been to graph these data so that the first keypress in each sequence lined up. A priori there is no good way to choose between these and any of a number of other ways to establish (at least implicitly) correspondences between the various serial positions at each list length. (Are initial keypresses in sequences of different lengths necessarily more similar than the last keypresses in those same sequences?)

Two aspects of the data in figure 5.6 merit particular attention. First, the effect of sequence length is distributed fairly evenly across all of the keypresses in the sequence. To see this, consider first as an example the last inter-keypress times in the sequence for each length. These are represented by the points lined up vertically at the right side of the graph. Even though all of the other keypresses have been made, the time from the next-to-last keypress to the last keypress is longer when $n = 3$ than when $n = 2$, when $n = 4$ than when $n = 3$, and so on. This pattern of these data points is referred to as *dominance*. Looking at the other serial positions (vertical columns) in figure 5.6, it is clear that dominance holds for all of them. It is also of interest to consider the first keypress in each sequence. The data points representing these keypresses lie along a rough diagonal from the top-left to the bottom-right for the two sets of data. Again we find dominance according to list length; the time from the first to the second keypress increases as the number of keypresses to follow increases. Thus, even the interval between the first and second keypress in a sequence reflects the length of the entire sequence.

The overall increase in inter-keypress time with list length is not, however, the only factor determining the inter-keypress times in figure 5.6. A second interesting point about these data is that there are clearly strong effects of serial position within a list. The last keypress in lists of different lengths is one of the fastest, the second-to-last keypress in each list is always the slowest, and so on. These serial position functions cannot be explained by some simple artifact in the design of this experiment: Sternberg et al. (1978) were careful to ensure not only that each key occurred equally often at each serial position for each list length but also that the distribution of transitions between keypresses was consistent within conditions across serial position and list length. This makes it all the more interesting that, despite the apparent complexity of these serial position functions, we know from figure 5.5c that averages of these data across serial position lie on straight lines as a function of list length. Further, although the detailed shapes of the serial position functions differ somewhat for the alternating-hands and same-hand data, averaging across serial position for these two conditions results in parallel lines as a function of list length.

Sternberg et al. (1980) have reported similar serial position functions for the durations of spoken words within lists. As noted above, these measurements are quite difficult to make. The measurement process also appears necessarily to involve some degree of subjective human judgment or the imposition of largely arbitrary criteria. For these two reasons we will not dwell on them further here. The important point is that although there are systematic differences between the patterns of element-duration functions for speech and typing, dominance as a function of list length holds in both modalities. Put another way, in both cases there is a general slowing of all items in a list as a function of list length. This then is a case where a global property of a sequence affects performance at every point within the sequence. This is exactly the pattern of data that is taken as strong evidence for preplanning.

In addition, however, both domains reveal a complexity of data at the level of individual element durations that is absent when these durations are averaged to produce mean-element durations. This additional complexity in the lower-level measurements can be taken as evidence that the mean element is the best or most appropriate level for studying the mechanism underlying the regularities of the latency and duration data. Of course, this conclusion may be wrong, but it certainly defines an obvious starting point for model building.

5.4   Understanding the Regularities

So far we have concentrated on outlining a set of performance regularities in speech and typing, some of which were decidedly unexpected when they were first observed. This research required subjects to produce short action sequences, in a context that provided both the incentive and the opportunity to use advance planning. In this situation the sequence duration increased as a quadratic function of the number of elements in the sequence. This corresponds to a linear increase in the average element duration, an increase that is distributed over all of the elements in the sequence. Thus, a characteristic of the whole sequence influences the execution of each of its elements, precisely the type of evidence that suggests that a representation of the whole sequence—a motor program—exists before the sequence begins and is used to control the production of the sequence. If sequence length is measured as words for speech or keypresses for typing, then the size of the length effect is the same for words with different syllabic structure and duration and for keypress sequences made at different rates because of different hand combinations: the resulting mean-element duration functions are parallel and vertically displaced. This additive invariance suggests that these measures of sequence length may be theoretically significant.

5.4.1   The Subprogram Retrieval Model

Figure 5.7 sketches, in flowchart form, a model to explain the performance regularities just described. This model was first outlined by Sternberg et al. (1978) and has subsequently been restated and refined a number of times (Monsell and Sternberg 1981; Sternberg et al. 1983; Monsell 1986). The basis for this model is an attempt to describe one way a motor program might be used. The model incorporates a number of assumptions.

> 1. During the preparation interval the speaker or typist constructs a *program*, made up of *subprograms*, specifying the elements of the utterance to be spoken or the string to be typed and the sequence of those elements. Although we will not look at the evidence for this (see Monsell and Sternberg 1981 or Monsell 1986), this program is believed to be stored in a motor-program buffer distinct from short-term or working memory. Since little knowledge is currently available about the level of abstraction used for representing this information, the model is silent on this issue.
>
> 2. When the "go" signal is detected, the initial unit or subprogram is *retrieved* and then a *command* process initiates activity, ultimately resulting in the pattern of activity that is appropriate to generate the element specified by the subprogram. For speech, this would be vocal

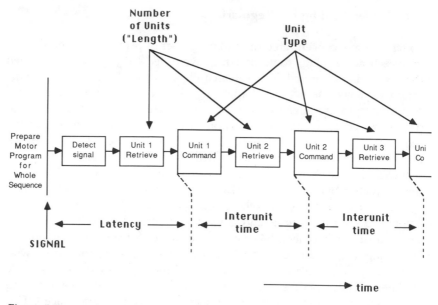

Figure 5.7
Subprogram retrieval model. (Redrawn, by permission, from figure 5 in Sternberg, Knoll, Monsell, and Wright 1989.)

activity; for typewriting, this would be hand and finger activity. The cycle of retrieval followed by command stages repeats until every element in the sequence has been executed.

3. The duration of the retrieval stage is a function of the number of subprograms that make up the program. The more subprograms that are simultaneously in a state of preparation, the more time it takes to "activate," "locate," "retrieve," or "select" each one. (These terms are all listed because any might supply an appropriate metaphor for this process. This process is meant to involve nothing more than gaining access to or passing control to the appropriate subprogram.)

4. The duration of the retrieval stage is influenced not by the composition of the subprograms but only by the number of subprograms. It is not known why the retrieval duration is a linear function of the number of subprograms. One possible mechanism is sequential *search* through a set of subprogram "directory entries" or "addresses." Under that proposal, linearity of retrieval time follows from simple properties of the search process. This mechanism can also be elaborated (see question 5.1) to explain the simultaneous simplicity of the mean-element duration functions and the complexity of element duration as a function of serial position. However, other mechanisms could un-

doubtedly account for these findings and as yet no compelling evidence has been found to support this particular proposal.

5. The duration of the command stage depends only on the composition of the subprogram being processed and not on the number or composition of the other subprograms, if any, in the sequence. This amounts to a claim that the actions of the command stage are purely local, made without reference to any information contained in the rest of the program.

6. The command and retrieval stages are "processing stages" in the strict sense defined by the assumptions of Sternberg's (1969) "additive factors" method. When subjects are required to complete the sequence as quickly as possible (and perhaps only under those conditions), the duration of a subprogram is the sum of the durations of its retrieval stage and its command stage.

5.4.2   Relating Model Stages and Equation Parameters

The structure of this model allows us to map various of its processes to the parameters in the fitted functions describing the latency and duration of sequences, equations (1)–(3). Examination of figure 5.7 may help to make these relations clearer.

Equation (1), describing the latency to begin a sequence, incorporates two parameters: the intercept parameter η and the slope parameter θ. The model posits two processes operating during the latency interval before the effects of the first command stage are reflected in output activity. The signal-detection process is posited to be independent of sequence length and element size. The time for signal detection is reflected in the intercept parameter, η, in equation (1). The latency interval also includes the time for the retrieval of the first subprogram. This time, according to the model, depends on the length of the sequence and is represented in equation (1) by the term θn.

Inevitably, the mapping of terms in the model to the elements in equation (1) is not completely straightforward. The intercept parameter η will additionally reflect a delay, which could be as long as 100 to 200 milliseconds, between the initiation of commands during the command stage for the first subprogram and the initiation of peripheral motor activity for the first element. The duration of this delay is assumed to be independent of both sequence length and element size. Unlike the time to detect the signal, this delay presumably would also not be changed by changes in the detectability of the "go" signal or the probability of catch trials. Of more theoretical importance, the latency interval may also include a chunk of the activity associated with the first command stage, suggesting that there could be an effect of element size on the latency. In speech, this contamination occurs because it is necessary to discriminate the onset of the speech signal from background noise; this process inevitably misses a little of the speech. The problem is probably worse for typing. Here, the keypress that terminates the latency interval occurs well into the movement trajectory that is controlled by the first command stage. These, or other similar effects, may be sufficient to account for effects of element size on latencies.

The processes posited by the model are also reflected in the parameters of the duration function. The duration of each element spans time taken by one command stage and one retrieval stage. Considering the mean-element duration function, equation (3), the intercept parameter, β, reflects the changes in command-stage duration associated with changes in the element size. Similarly, the term γn reflects how mean-element duration varies when retrieval time increases for sequences with more subprograms.

As discussed previously, the parameters β and γ have the same interpretations for the overall duration function, equation (2). The intercept parameter α in that equation reflects several factors that occur only once in the production of a list. For instance, it is likely that the criteria used to identify the beginning of the first element or the end of the last element in the external behavior systematically deviate from the points controlled by the beginning and end of the first and last command stages, respectively. This will lead to a systematic under- or overestimate of the duration of the performance, and this measurement error will be reflected in α. Similarly, any tendency of the subject to produce the first or last element in a sequence so that its duration differs systematically from what it would have been at internal positions in the sequence will be reflected in α.[5]

This model, along with the mapping of its elements to parameters in the fitted functions, describes all of the regularities we have discussed so far.

5.5   Predictions of the Model and Their Assessment

The descriptive success of the proposed model allows us to organize and make sense of a large body of data generated from two different response modalities. This should not be surprising, since the model was created to explain these data. A second approach to exploring a model such as this is to seek to confirm or disconfirm predictions made by the model that might

5. One example of this type of phenomenon from speech is phrase-final lengthening (Vaissiere 1983). This describes the strong tendency most speakers have to lengthen a syllable when it is the last syllable in a phrase, in some cases doubling the duration of the same syllable in a neutral context. This lengthening is often interpreted as a prosodic signal of the syntactic phrase structure of an utterance. This lengthening is also present under the conditions used in the experiments reported here, despite instructions that discouraged it, a reward system that penalized it, and the lack of a communicative purpose for it.

otherwise be unexpected or counterintuitive. We will explore two such predictions.

5.5.1   The Connection between Latencies and Mean-Element Durations

The model posits that two terms in the fitted functions, θn for the latency function and γn for the duration function, depend solely on the time required to retrieve one subprogram. Since there is no compelling reason to suspect that the value of n changes between the latency interval and the duration interval, the model implies that these two terms should have similar values and thus that $\theta = \gamma$.

Over the course of the many experiments done to explore the regularities captured by this model, only a few of which are described here, a large range of values for θ and γ have been estimated for many subjects under a large variety of conditions. These parameter estimates have ranged from low values, 3 or 4 milliseconds per element, to much higher values, on the order of 30 milliseconds per element. Since most of these experiments are not described here, it would be inappropriate to make a detailed comparison of the values of θ and γ across these experiments. However, it can be said that the correspondence is remarkably good, supporting this claim of the model.

5.5.2   Intermittency of the Effect of Length on Sequence Production

The sequences of activity controlled by the model are, in both speech and typing, relatively continuous. In typing, for instance, although the keyboard registers that a key has been pressed at one discrete instant when the key travels past a designated point on its path, the finger and wrist movements that cause the key to move are smooth. Similarly for speech: although we have the perception of hearing separate words in the speech stream, if we were to look at any of several graphical representations of the energy in speech, it would often be hard to decide where one word stopped and the next started. Against this background, the cyclic progression of nonoverlapping stages posited by the model seems distinctly unnatural.

According to the model, the time between the initiation of one element and the initiation of the next is filled first by a command stage and then by a retrieval stage. Of these two stages, the duration of only one, the retrieval stage, is lengthened as the length of the list increases. Taken together, these facts suggest that the influence of sequence length on the output activity should be *intermittent*.

Consider what this suggests about finger movements in typing or vocal articulator movements in speech. A command stage initiates and largely controls the trajectory for one element of the output sequence according to the directions contained in the most recently retrieved subprogram. Because the command process is not influenced by sequence length, it is possible that the corresponding portion of the trajectory for the element produced by this subprogram might also be independent of sequence length. This possibility depends on there being a strong moment-to-moment coupling between the command/retrieval processes and the observed trajectories. This coupling cannot be perfect, however, since the movements of speech and typing do not stop abruptly during the interval corresponding to the next retrieval process (it is effects of sequence length that the model suggests are intermittent, not the movement itself). One possibility is that activity initiated during the command process is carried forward under the control of lower levels in the motor system during the subsequent retrieval interval, a time when no further commands are being issued. If this is all approximately correct, then the extra time required for the retrieval process with longer sequence lengths should be *localized* within the production of each element of the sequence. To go even farther out on this limb, intuitively we might expect the localized effects of length to occur near the end of each unit, when the motor-sequence controller would need to retrieve the next subprogram.

The most interesting alternative to the prediction of localized effects is that the length effect is *distributed* throughout the duration of each output element. The empirical question has many similarities to that underlying the examination of the element durations as a function of serial position and sequence length. In both cases the primary question is whether the effect of length is localized at specific points or distributed across the entire activity. One difference between these analyses is that the model predicts the effects of length will be distributed across the elements in the sequence but that the effects of length will be localized within the segments of those elements.

This prediction seems counterintuitive and implausible. The measurements needed to confirm or deny this hypothesis are detailed and require either new analysis techniques or new instrumentation. Sternberg and his colleagues have, however, looked for evidence to confirm or disconfirm this prediction both in speech (Sternberg et al. 1980, 1983, 1989) and in typing (Sternberg et al. 1983); surprisingly, exactly the predicted pattern of results was found in both cases. Here we will consider only the procedure and results for the speech experiment.

To look for localization of the effects of sequence length in speech, Sternberg et al. (1980, 1989) had subjects produce sequences containing from one to five two-syllable words. The words themselves were chosen in an attempt to simplify the segmentation process. Both syllables of each word nominally began with a closure; all the words normally had stress on the first syllable (for instance, *copper* and *token*). Figure 5.8 shows the

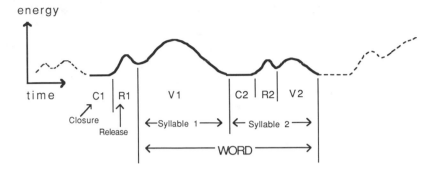

Figure 5.8
Schematic demonstration of the segmentation of a two-syllable spoken word (for instance,
copper or *token*) into six segments based on an idealized energy envelope. (Redrawn, by
permission, from figure 9 in Sternberg, Knoll, Monsell, and Wright 1989.)

idealized energy envelope for one of these words. Using a sophisticated
segmentation algorithm, which was developed for this research based on
techniques originally used for speech recognition, each word was decomposed into six segments roughly corresponding to the phonetic categories
of consonant-closure, consonant-release, and vowel for each syllable.

The upper panel of figure 5.9 shows the mean-element duration function,
which is similar to those found previously. The slope in this case is about
11 milliseconds per word. The bottom panel shows duration as a function
of length for each of the six segments identified in these words. Note that
these segment durations add up to the mean-element durations in the top
panel. Not surprisingly, the longest segment is the stressed initial vowel
(V1). Most of the effect of length is localized in the vowel of the unstressed
second syllable (V2) even though its duration is, on average, only about 40
percent of that of V1. There are also marginal increases in length for the
durations of the first closure (C1) and the first release (R1). Because the
second syllable of one word is followed by the first syllable of the next
word, these three segments are contiguous. This surprising observation of
localization in the effects of sequence length fits with the predictions
outlined earlier about the peripheral manifestations of intermittency in the
cyclic control process posited by the model to control the production of
these sequences.

5.5.3   Limits of the Model's Applicability

Although the generality and predictive success of the model are encourag-
ing, it is important not to overgeneralize from it. For example, it would be
wrong to expect that any response modality will exhibit the complete set

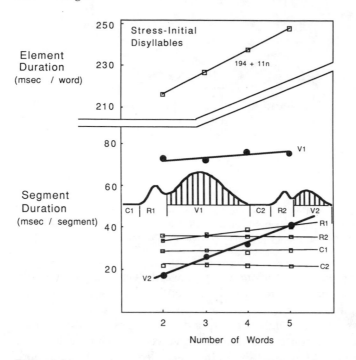

Figure 5.9
Mean-element duration and mean-segment duration of two-syllable spoken words. The
upper panel shows the mean-element duration data. The line represents the least-squares:
$\hat{d}_n = 194 + 11.1n$. The lower panel shows the decomposition of the mean-element durations into six mean-segment durations. (Redrawn, by permission, from figure 10 in Sternberg, Knoll, Monsell, and Wright 1989.)

of regularities outlined in this chapter. A counterexample to this generalization can be found in the work of Hulstijn and Van Galen (1983). They have reported that subjects rapidly producing prepared sequences of hand-written characters show a latency effect with increased sequence length but not a rate effect. This dissociation of the latency and rate effects might be troublesome for the model if handwriting were a domain in which movement timing is a free parameter. However, it has been shown that the control system for handwriting keeps stroke duration relatively constant despite changes in other factors such as writing size and pen-to-writing-surface friction that might be expected to cause changes in stroke duration (Denier van der Gon and Thuring 1965; Hollerbach 1981). Thus, even if a cycle of command and retrieval processes underlies the production of handwritten sequences, a rate effect would not be observed unless those processes limit the rate of production. An analogy has been suggested by Monsell: The rate at which a highway is constructed can be limited either by the efficiency of the bureaucrats responsible for obtaining permissions, purchasing land, and so forth, or by the work rate of the construction crews. Only in the former case would measurements of the rate of highway construction tell us anything about the performance of the bureaucracy (the planners).

Suggestions for Further Reading

The timing results for speech and typing described here are only selected highlights from a larger set of experiments undertaken to explore the properties of motor programs in these domains. Discussions of many of the important issues omitted can be found in the works cited. Among these topics is a more precise determination of the *unit* of programming for speech and typing. It turns out, after a more thorough investigation, that both the word in speech and the keypress in typing are only simplified approximations to the actual units in those domains. In particular in typing, immediate repetitions of a single character, *doublets*, appear to form a single unit. Sternberg and Knoll (unpublished research described briefly in Sternberg et al. 1983) test this hypothesis and use it to construct an ingenious test of the overall model by embedding single doublets in larger strings and then examining the implication of their presence for the effects on length of mean-element duration. It is also possible to explore, as Monsell (1986) has done, what the ultimate capacity of these programs is, how and where they are stored, and how they are maintained.

The findings described here might be explained from other perspectives or modeled using different techniques. Although a number of alternatives to explain pieces of the patterns described here have been proposed, tested, and, in many cases, rejected (see, in particular, Sternberg et al. 1978, 1980), no alternative proposals have been suggested to explain the broad range of these results. One alternative approach that has been explored for typing is that of using parallel activation-triggered schemas to control movement sequencing and trajectories (Rumelhart and Norman 1982; Norman and Rumelhart 1983). This particular simulation was developed to explain a different set of phenomena observed in transcription typing. Although this model has many appealing aspects and could certainly be usefully extended to cover other domains such as speech, it is not clear how it could be extended to explain the regularities described here.

A second approach that appears promising as a way to explain the data described here is the hierarchical editor model described by Rosenbaum and his colleagues (Rosenbaum 1985; Rosenbaum, Inhoff, and Gordon 1984; Rosenbaum, Hindorff, and Munro 1987). Using a model that represents movement sequences as hierarchical tree structures, they are able to explain, at least qualitatively, many of the results reported here for latency, duration, and element durations. In addition, this model provides a rational treatment of many often seemingly mysterious phenomena that occur when a choice must be made at the last instant between different but related movement sequences.

A third alternative is the class of explanations based on the notion of general-purpose processing capacity. Appeals to capacity-oriented explanations are not unusual in cognitive science. One major problem with them is that the notion of capacity is often poorly defined; almost any pattern of results can be interpreted post hoc in terms of heavy capacity demands here, light ones there, and so on. One experiment done originally by Monsell and Sternberg (1981) and repeated on a larger scale by Monsell (1986) seems to exclude most versions of this model as possible explanations for the results discussed here. In the more recent of these experiments, subjects with memory spans between 7.2 and 8.3 prepared and produced sequences of one to five ordered weekday names. In addition, during the production of the sequence, they were required to remember lists of zero, one, three, or five digits. Surprisingly, although Monsell observed the normal effects of sequence length on latency and duration, there was little or no effect of memory-load size on the latency or duration data; this despite the fact that the combined lists were well above the subjects' memory span in some conditions. This is not to say that the added load did not make the overall task harder (requiring more capacity). It is not easy to maintain a concurrent memory load, but doing so does not seem to interfere with the preparation or production of rapid utterances as we might expect from a general-purpose processing capacity account.

Questions

5.1 One possible mechanism to instantiate the retrieval stage described in section 5.4.1 is the process of search through a partially ordered list. The challenge in theorizing about the retrieval stage is to conceive of a process that simultaneously predicts the linearity of the mean-element duration function and the complexity of the interresponse times as a function of list length and position within the list. An appropriately defined search process can satisfy both of these requirements.

Consider a mechanism in which information identifying each item in a sequence of items to be performed (and only those items) is stored in a buffer. Once one item in the sequence has been produced, it is necessary to search this buffer for the information about the next item. We might assume that this search process is (1) *serial* (items in the buffer are considered one at a time), (2) *self-terminating* (the search process stops as soon as the next item is identified), (3) *minimal* (each item in the buffer is examined only once in a particular search), (4) *fixed-time* (each decision takes, on the average, the same amount of time), and (5) *unordered* (the order in which the items in the buffer are checked is random related to their order in the sequence to be produced). A search process defined this way would produce the required linear mean-element duration function. Why is this so? How is the comparison time of the search process related to the parameter γ described in equations (2) and (3)?

This search process does not produce the correct results for element duration as a function of serial position and list length. What functions does it produce instead? Now consider what happens if we relax the constraint that the search process be unordered. How might the search process now generate both the linear mean-element duration function and the correct predictions for mean-element duration as a function of serial position and length?

5.2 The model proposed in this chapter and the data presented to support it deal with planning movement sequences at the highest level. What if you wanted to look for evidence of sequence planning based on trajectories of your hand moving in space? What would you look for in these trajectories as evidence for planning? How would you distinguish planning effects from unplanned, local interactions? Do you have intuitions about what it means to "plan," other than those discussed in this chapter, that might be useful in this analysis?

5.3 Many theorists are intrigued by the possibility that motor programs are organized hierarchically (see, for example, Greene 1972; Rosenbaum 1985; Rosenbaum, Inhoff, and Gordon 1984; Rosenbaum, Hindorff, and Munro 1987). How might you distinguish a hierarchically organized motor program from one having a simple linear structure?

References

Denier van der Gon, J. J., and J. Ph. Thuring (1965). The guiding of human writing movements. *Kybernetik* 2, 145—148.

Greene, P. H. (1972). Problems of organization of motor systems. In R. Rosen and F. M. Snoll, eds., *Progress in theoretical biology*, vol. 2. New York: Academic Press.

Hayes, K. C., and R. G. Marteniuk (1976). Dimensions of motor task complexity. In G. E. Stelmach, ed., *Motor control: Issues and trends*. New York: Academic Press.

Henry, F. M., and E. E. Rogers (1960). Increased response latency for complicated movements and a "memory drum" theory of neuromotor reaction. *Research Quarterly of the American Association for Health, Physical Education and Recreation* 31, 448—458.

Hollerbach, J. M. (1981). An oscillation theory of handwriting. *Biological Cybernetics* 39, 139—156.

Hulstijn, W., and G. P. Van Galen (1983). Programming in handwriting: Reaction and movement time as a function of sequence length. *Acta Psychologica* 54, 23—49.

Kent, R. D., and F. D. Minifie (1977). Coarticulation in recent speech production models. *Journal of Phonetics* 5, 115—133.

Kučera, H., and W. N. Francis (1967). *Computational analysis of present-day American English*. Providence, RI. Brown University Press.

Lashley, K. S. (1951). The problem of serial order in behavior. In L. A. Jeffress, ed., *Cerebral mechanisms in behavior*. New York: Wiley.

Lenneberg, E. (1967). *The biological foundations of language*. New York: Wiley.

Miller, G. A., E. Galanter, and K. H. Pribram (1960). *Plans and the structure of behavior*. New York: Holt.

Moll, K. L., and R. G. Daniloff (1971). Investigation of the timing of velar movements during speech. *Journal of the Acoustical Society of America* 50, 678—684.

Monsell, S. (1986). Programming of complex sequences: Evidence from the timing of rapid speech and other productions. In H. Heuer and C. Fromm, eds., *Generation and modulation of action patterns*. Berlin: Springer-Verlag.

Monsell, S., and S. Sternberg (1981). Speech programming: A critical review, a new experimental approach, and a model of the timing of rapid utterances: Part 1. Unpublished technical memorandum, AT&T Bell Laboratories. [Available from the authors.]

Norman, D. A., and D. E. Rumelhart (1983). Studies of typing from the LNR research group. In W. E. Cooper, ed., *Cognitive aspects of skilled typewriting*. Berlin: Springer-Verlag.

Rosenbaum, D. A. (1985). Motor programming: A review and scheduling theory. In

H. Heuer, U. Kleinbeck, and K.-H. Schmidt, eds., *Motor behavior: Programming, control, and acquisition.* Berlin: Springer-Verlag.

Rosenbaum, D. A., V. Hindorff, and E. M. Munro (1987). Scheduling and programming of rapid finger sequences: Tests and elaborations of the hierarchical editor model. *Journal of Experimental Psychology: Human Perception and Performance* 13, 193–203.

Rosenbaum, D. A., A. W. Inhoff, and A. M. Gordon (1984). Choosing between movement sequences: A hierarchical editor mode. *Journal of Experimental Psychology: General* 113, 373–393.

Rumelhart, D. E., and D. A. Norman (1982). Simulating a skilled typist: A study of skilled cognitive-motor performance. *Cognitive Science* 6, 1–36.

Saltzman, E. (1979). Levels of sensorimotor representation. *Journal of Mathematical Psychology* 20, 91–163.

Sternberg, S. (1969). The discovery of processing stages: Extensions of Donders' method. In W. G. Koster, ed., *Attention and performance II. Acta Psychologica* 30, 276–315.

Sternberg, S., R. L. Knoll, S. Monsell, and C. E. Wright (1983). Control of rapid action sequences in speech and typing. Invited address given by Saul Sternberg to the 1983 Annual Meeting of the American Psychological Association. [Text available from the first author.]

Sternberg, S., R. L. Knoll, S. Monsell, and C. E. Wright (1989). Motor programs and hierarchical organization in the control of rapid speech. *Phonetica* 45, 175–197.

Sternberg, S., S. Monsell, R. L. Knoll, and C. E. Wright (1978). The latency and duration of rapid movement sequences: Comparisons of speech and typewriting. In G. E. Stelmach, ed., *Information processing in motor control and learning.* New York: Academic Press.

Sternberg, S., C. E. Wright, R. L. Knoll, and S. Monsell (1980). Motor programs in rapid speech: Additional evidence. In R. A. Cole, ed., *The perception and production of fluent speech.* Hillsdale, NJ: L. Erlbaum Associates.

Vaissiere, J. (1983). Language-independent prosodic features. In A. Cutler and D. R. Ladd, eds., *Prosody: Models and measurements.* New York: Springer-Verlag.

Zingale, C. M., and E. Kowler (1987). Planning sequences of saccades. *Vision Research* 27, 1327–1341.

Chapter 6

Action and Free Will

Alvin Goldman

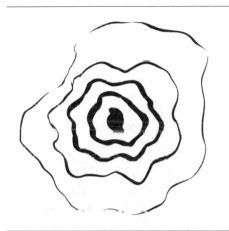

6.1 Two Images of the Behaving Organism

There are two ways of viewing human actors. The first is amply illustrated by the preceding chapters, which deal with locomotion, reaching and prehension, oculomotor control, and so on. As these chapters indicate, the activities in question are outputs of a highly complex physical system, ultimately to be understood in terms of its musculature and neurocircuitry. At a suitable level of analysis, persons are just physicochemical systems whose neurons are subject to the same electrochemical laws that govern wholly nonbiological systems. Although science has not yet identified all the relevant underlying principles, there *are* orderly, lawful patterns governing human behavior. Thus, the scientific image of human behavior is just a special segment of the general science of physical systems.

In at least apparent contrast to this scientific image of human beings is a second image: that of persons as freely choosing agents. Suppose you are deciding whether to go to a play tonight, and you weigh the pros and cons. The show is almost sold out, so you may get a poor seat; indeed, you may not get a ticket at all. You also have a paper due on Thursday, so perhaps you had better not squander the work time. On the other hand, the play got excellent reviews and this is the last night it is in town. The paper deadline can probably be met even if you go, and a night off would invigorate your thought processes. In this fashion deliberation ultimately leads to a choice; and it's a free choice. Nothing constrains or compels you to choose one alternative rather than the other.

As presented thus far, the agency image of the human actor is different from the scientific image but not obviously in conflict with it. Yet many philosophers think that the two images do conflict: they cannot both constitute accurate pictures of human nature. To understand the alleged conflict, we will need to look at some terminology, distinguishing different kinds of possibility and impossibility.

First, there is *logical* possibility and impossibility. A trillion-sided polygon is a logical possibility, even if there are no trillion-sided polygons in point of fact; whereas a square circle is a logical impossibility. Second, there is *nomological* possibility and impossibility, defined by the compatibility or incompatibility of an event with the laws of nature. (*Nomological* comes from the Greek root *nomos*, meaning 'law'.) Your traveling faster than the speed of light today is logically possible but nomologically impossible, because it contravenes a physical law that nothing travels faster than the speed of light. Third, there is *nomohistorical* possibility and impossibility. This type of possibility is defined by compatibility not only with natural laws taken by themselves but also with natural laws plus the actual history of the world up until the targeted event. Suppose a rock has been hurled from the top of the Sears Tower, and at time t it is halfway to the ground. Consider the event consisting in the rock's moving upward at time $t + e$, immediately after t. This event is both logically and nomologically possible. It is nomologically possible because the rock's rising at $t + e$ does not contravene natural laws *taken by themselves*. If we listed just the laws of nature, we could not deduce from them that the rock would not rise at $t + e$. However, on certain plausible assumptions, the event in question is nomohistorically impossible (henceforth *NH-impossible*). From the prior history of the world—indeed, from the entire state of the world just at time t—together with all physical laws, it can be deduced that the rock will fall, and hence will not rise, at $t + e$.

We can now see why some people hold that the two images introduced at the outset are not cotenable. If the scientific image of the world is correct, then it is plausible to infer that *determinism* is true—that is, that each succeeding state of the world is necessarily fixed by the preceding total state of the world together with the natural laws. Admittedly, the probabilistic laws of quantum mechanics belie strict determinism at a very microscopic level. Still, quantum-mechanical randomness barely impinges on the behavior of middle-sized, macroscopic objects, including the behavior of human beings. Thus, if the scientific image holds of human beings, it is plausible to say that human action falls under the sway of determinism. But if determinism is true in the sphere of human action (as well as in other macroscopic domains), then the only NH-possible actions are those that people actually perform. No action that is merely contemplated but ultimately rejected by a human agent is really NH-possible. For to say that determinism is true is to imply that any such nonactual bit of behavior is NH-impossible: its nonoccurrence is entailed by prior states of the world and natural laws. Indeed, we can go further. Any such nonactual behavior was precluded by (laws and) prior states of the world that obtained before the agent was born! If this is so, what becomes of people's vaunted "free choice"? If everything you do turns out to be NH-*required*—indeed, required by events that happened before you were born—isn't it an illusion to suppose that you ever make genuine choices? If all your movements are locked into a story that was written, as it were, long ago, aren't you merely a puppet acting out a preordained script? Isn't your supposition that you are a free agent just a pipe dream that is contradicted by the scientific facts? On this line of reasoning only one of the two images can be correct: the scientific image *or* the free-agent image. They cannot both describe reality.

Not all philosophers agree with this conclusion; indeed, they are divided into two camps. One group, whose conclusion we have just examined, defends *incompatibilism*. This is the claim that determinism and freedom are incompatible. The second group embraces *compatibilism*; they maintain that determinism and freedom might both be true. If the latter position is correct, we would not necessarily have to choose between the scientific image and the free-agent image of humankind. Both images might in fact be accurate.

It seems clear that cognitive science is wedded to a scientific image of humankind, whatever this implies or fails to imply about freedom. But the issue between compatibilism and incompatibilism is not centrally an issue for science to settle. It is not primarily an empirical question but a "conceptual" one, of the sort philosophers have traditionally addressed. Nonetheless, it is an important question *for* cognitive science, because it concerns the ramifications of this discipline's approach to human beings. We will therefore address this question in sections 6.2 and 6.3. As we proceed (in section 6.4), we will find that the psychology of choice can also shed light on the concept of freedom. Finally (in sections 6.5 and 6.6) we will turn to topics in the theory of action, planning, and execution, to which philosophy and various cognitive sciences have all made contributions.

6.2   The Compatibilist Account of Freedom

To understand compatibilism, we need to say what is meant by *freedom*. Only when we understand this term (at least roughly) can we decide whether freedom could exist in a deterministic world. Of course, *freedom* is a highly nuanced term, and giving strict definitions for any term poses severe difficulties. But even a crude and rough-edged account of the term's meaning should prove helpful.

Freedom is customarily opposed to bondage, imprisonment, or tyranny. What is gained when a slave is released from bondage, when a convict is released from prison, when a tyrant is overthrown? In each case an expanded range of choice is acquired: the agents have more opportunities to do as they please or as they wish, to act in accord with their true preferences. They are not constrained by shackles, edicts, or threats to confine their actions within a narrow compass, excluding what they most want to do. At a first approximation, then, freedom consists in the ability and opportunity to act in conformity with one's wishes, desires, or preferences. (Perhaps it is a comparative matter: having the chance to act *more* in conformity with one's wishes than in another, contextually indicated situation.)

Other common uses of the term *free* confirm this account. What is *free time* in school or business? A time when you may do as you please, where your course of action is not narrowly circumscribed by a teacher, a boss, or the management. The same theme accounts for the phrase *of your own free will*. To say that Eunice made a charitable contribution "of her own free will" indicates that she did so, not because her arm was twisted, but because she really wanted to. Once again, freedom or free will seems to consist in action, or opportunity for action, in conformity with desire.

How does this account of freedom bear on its compatibility with determinism? Let us address this by first considering a diagram depicting (part of) the causal chain of events leading up to an actually performed action, A_1. Figure 6.1 shows action A_1 being caused by (1) the agent's preference for A_1 (over its competitors), (2) the agent's (accurate) belief about how to perform A_1, and (3) the agent's possession of the ability and opportunity to do A_1 on the occasion in question. The arrows leading to a box indicate that the boxed event, or state of affairs, is causally necessitated by prior events. In other words, no other, incompatible event was NH-possible. Figure 6.1 thus purports to describe a deterministic sequence of actual events. For example, if you had really decided in the theater example to stay home, then A_1 might be interpreted in that case as the act of staying home. If so, the figure indicates that your preference, or decision, to stay home was causally necessitated by prior events.

Is it possible that you also had the ability and opportunity to attend the theater, despite the fact that it was causally necessitated that you decide to

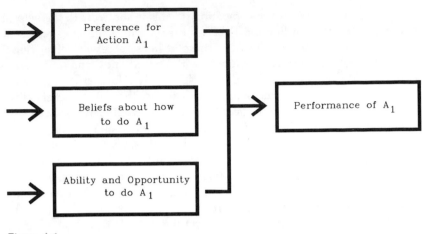

Figure 6.1
Actual performance of A_1.

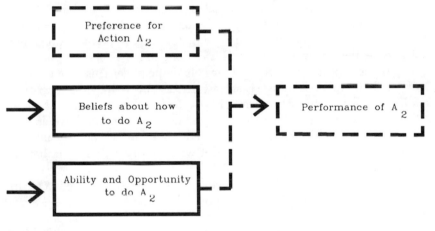

Figure 6.2
Hypothetical performance of A_2.

stay home? Yes, answers the compatibilist. This is shown with the help of figure 6.2. Here (as in figure 6.1) boxes drawn with solid lines represent actual events and arrows drawn with solid lines represent actual causal connections. Boxes and arrows drawn with dashed lines represent merely hypothetical events and connections, respectively. Now let A_2 be the act of attending the theater, and suppose that in fact there were tickets available, so that had you gone to the box office, you would have succeeded in attending the play. Then you did have the ability and opportunity to attend the play, as figure 6.2 shows. By hypothesis, you did not actually have a preference to attend the play (all things considered); hence, the preference for A_2 is drawn within a dashed box. If you had formed such a preference, however, this preference, in conjunction with the other boxed items, would have caused an occurrence of your attending the play. This hypothetical causal relation is depicted by the dashed arrow leading to the dashed box containing A_2.

Figure 6.2 is intended to show that people may actually possess the ability and opportunity to do actions that they are causally necessitated not to prefer and hence are causally necessitated not to perform. In other words, although your preferring or deciding to attend the play was NH-impossible, you still had the ability and opportunity to do the action. There is a sense, then, in which you *could have* done it; it was *open* to you to do, despite the fact that your doing it was NH-impossible. This different sense of possibility (or "openness") is at least partly expressed by the truth of the following subjunctive statement: "If you had wished to attend the play, then you would have done so." In other words, your action would have conformed to such a preference. You were *free* to attend the play although you actually decided against it—and it was causally necessitated that you would so decide.

The key to the compatibilist maneuver is the claim that there is a further sense of *possible* different from NH-possibility (and from nomological and logical possibility), that is relevant here. Let us call this *actional* possibility. The compatibilist contends that an act may be actionally possible for an agent at a given time even though it is not NH-possible for her at that time. How should this proposal be greeted? Is it plausible to hold that there is an additional kind of possibility, beyond the three kinds distinguished earlier?

Philosophers have discovered that numerous kinds of possibility are invoked in ordinary thought and speech. In addition to the ones previously mentioned, there is for instance the notion of *epistemic* possibility, which means 'possible for all one knows'—that is, 'not excluded by what one knows'. If Arnold says, "It is possible that Bacon wrote the Shakespearean corpus," he may only mean that Bacon's authorship is not excluded by his information. Even if Bacon's authorship never happened, even if its occur-

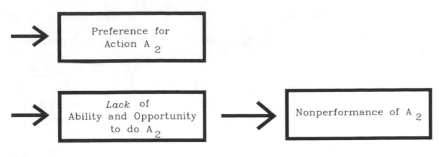

Figure 6.3
Nonperformance of A_2 necessitated by lack of ability and opportunity.

rence was NH-impossible, it may still be compatible with Arnold's information and hence be epistemically possible for him.

Epistemic possibility is introduced here only to illustrate the point that many senses of *possible* are at large in the speech community. We should therefore not assume that because an act is NH-impossible it must also be actionally impossible. The compatibilist claims that actional possibility is compatible with NH-impossibility. If determinism is true, then all unperformed acts are NH-impossible. Nonetheless, many of these are actionally possible. In that sense, freedom is compatible with determinism.

The compatibilist certainly concedes that many courses of action are closed for a given agent. Going to the theater is foreclosed for a jailbird; and if the show is sold out, it's closed for you as well. In these cases the nonperformance of the act is fixed *independently* of one's desire or pleasure. This is different from the earlier case, where non-theater-going is causally necessitated via the actor's preference. In the present case non-theater-going is causally necessitated by the absence of ability of opportunity, the basic form of unfreedom. This is illustrated in figure 6.3, where A_2 is the act of taking in the play. (For simplicity, the belief factor is omitted.)

If the compatibilist's attempt to reconcile freedom and determinism succeeds, there is no tension between the scientific image of humankind and the free agent image. Cognitive science can then retain its commitment to the scientific image without feeling that freedom, choice, or other such concepts are in danger.

6.3 Difficulties for Compatibilism

However, the case for compatibilism is not wholly secure; serious problems have been raised for it. In this section we will consider two such problems and some possible strategies for resolving them.

6.3.1   Choice Manipulation

A standard component of the compatibilist position is that actional possibility should be understood subjunctively: it was possible for the actor to do *A* if, *had* she preferred or chosen *A*, she would have succeeded in bringing it to fruition. But notice that this subjunctive statement could be true even if the agent was *unable to choose A*, or unable to prefer it to its competitors. Now if the actor is unable to choose *A*, she is not really free to do it. Hence, the indicated subjunctive statement does not really capture what is involved in freedom. To dramatize the point, suppose you are under the control of a scheming neurosurgeon, who has implanted electrodes in your brain and is bent on manipulating your preferences and choices. Then, although you *would* succeed in going to the theater *if* you chose, you *cannot* so choose. Under these circumstances you are not free to go to the theater.

In response to this criticism, the compatibilist can admit that the standard *if*-statement does not wholly capture the meaning of "It was actionally possible for the actor to do *A*." The compatibilist should concede that something additional must be said to rule out manipulation of choice, and any other impediment to choice. But why can't these further strictures come within a compatibilist mode? All the compatibilist need insist is that choice, or preference formation, be the result of purely "rational," unmanipulated processes. But surely such processes can be part and parcel of the causal order. Admittedly, the compatibilist has the burden of saying just what rational, unmanipulated processes consist in, and how they are to be distinguished in general from manipulated ones. This is no easy task. But there is every reason to expect that such a specification can be given within a deterministic framework.

6.3.2   A Paradox of Power

The following puzzle is due to Van Inwagen (1983) and others. Suppose that determinism is true, and that you actually stay home in the theater example. Then there was some world state P obtaining before you were born, such that from P and the laws of nature L it logically follows that you stay home. In other words, P and L jointly entail A_1. The compatibilist maintains that despite these assumptions, you still had the power (or "actional possibility") to do A_2, attend the play. But is this really so? If you did have this power, then you must have had the power to render it *false* that you stay home ($= A_1$). Did you have this power? Since P and L jointly entail A_1, not-A_1 must entail not-(P and L). (This is just a special case of the general logical truth that if Q entails R, then not-R must entail not-Q.) Thus, if you had the power to render A_1 false—to bring about not-A_1— then you must have had the power to render (P and L) false as well—to bring about the truth of not-(P and L). But how could this be so? P is some state of the world prior to your birth, and L is a set of laws of nature. Surely it was not in your power to render either of these false, or nonexistent! Nobody can change the past and nobody can change the laws of nature. It follows that the assumption of determinism is not really compatible with the notion that it was in your power to perform an action that you did not actually perform. Hence, compatibilism is mistaken.

Reflection on this puzzle indicates that it depends on the following principle: if one can bring about X, one can bring about anything Y that is entailed by X. In the case in question it is argued that if one can bring about not-A_1, then one can also bring about not-(P and L), because not-(P and L) is entailed by not-A_1. Unfortunately, the principle invoked here is incorrect. A person may be able to bring about a given state of affairs without being able to bring about everything entailed by it. For example, there being a party on your next birthday entails that you were born, because the simple fact of your having a birthday entails that you were born. But although you can bring it about that there is a party on your next birthday, you cannot bring it about that you were born. (Of course, you *were* born; but that isn't something you can *bring about*.) Or, to take another example, you can bring it about that you raise your arm while the sun is shining; and this action entails that the sun is shining. But you cannot bring it about that the sun is shining.

This response to the incompatibilist's puzzle consists in undermining a crucial principle to which the puzzle appeals. But an incompatibilist might try to reinstate the puzzle by modifying that principle, to produce a version that still supports the puzzle but is free from counterexample. There are also other puzzles, closely related to the foregoing, that incompatibilists have posed (see Van Inwagen 1983). Thus, compatibilism is not yet out of the woods. On the other hand, it is not clear that any insuperable problems have yet been raised for it. Hence, compatibilism remains an eminently defensible position, and so is the scientific image it helps to bolster.

6.4   Freedom and Choice

However, the compatibilist account sketched thus far is not fully satisfactory, for reasons yet to be considered. The account presented in section 6.2 suggests that freedom is primarily a matter of having a choice, of having options or alternatives, so that if you want to do one thing, that option is open to you, but if you want to do something else instead, that option is equally open to you. Is this the whole story of freedom? Surely not. The victim of an armed robbery is confronted with a choice, "Your money or your life." Two options are fully open to him. If he wants to surrender his wallet and escape with his life, he can effectuate that alternative. If he wants to sacrifice his life but retain the cash, he may be able to effectuate that alternative as well (his wallet, let's suppose, is in a well-hidden pouch). Nonetheless, we would hardly say he is free. Certainly we would not say, if he chose the first alternative, that he "freely" handed over his wallet, or did it "of his own free will." But nothing in our discussion thus far explains why this is so. Whence his unfreedom?

One possible explanation is that his choice situation has been shaped by the robber, an external agent. But it cannot be supposed that whenever an external agent influences your choice situation, you are thereby rendered unfree. A woman who offers you her yacht in exchange for your wallet influences your choice situation but does not make you unfree. Perhaps the difference lies, then, in the difference between a threat and an offer (see Nozick 1969). The robber's threat worsens your choice situation from what it was antecedently, whereas the yacht owner's offer improves your choice situation. But this distinction also fails to cover all the ground. Consider a Robinson Crusoe case. A man on a desert island develops gangrene in his injured leg and is confronted with the choice of amputating it or risking death. He performs the amputation, but this action is not fully free. It is something he is forced to do, not something he does willingly. Yet he certainly has a choice, and one that no external agent imposes upon him.

To explain these differences, what we seem to need is a suitable set of subjective value categories: negative value, positive value, and neutral value. In the robber case it is intuitively plausible to say that both of the victim's options have negative value. The same holds of the injured Crusoe. Although he prefers amputation to nonamputation, he certainly dislikes both prospects. That is why even the preferred option is viewed as forced, or contrary to what he ("really") wants. In the yacht case, by contrast, neither alternative is negative in value, or at any rate not both. A yacht for your wallet sounds like a good exchange, and even if yachting doesn't appeal to you, there is the option of simply declining the offer, which is at least neutral in value.

But what is this talk of negative, positive, and neutral subjective values? Are we entitled to appeal to these sorts of notions? Do they have any psychological validity? Here a look at cognitive science, specifically the psychology of choice, is essential.

Under standard *utility theory*, a person's preferences are not taken to reflect any (nonarbitrary) zero point of utility. But *prospect theory*, a theory of choice advanced by Kahneman and Tversky (1979), does postulate that cognizers in choice situations commonly establish neutral reference points, or points of zero value. In this theory, outcomes judged better or worse than a (subjectively established) zero point are viewed as gains or losses, respectively, and people's attitudes toward gains and losses are markedly different.

To illustrate the point, consider consumers' readiness or reluctance to use a credit card for purchasing gasoline. There is commonly a four-cent difference between cash and credit prices; but should the difference be labeled a "cash discount" or a "credit surcharge"? Credit card companies strongly urge the former, in the plausible belief that foregoing a discount is more acceptable than incurring a surcharge. A surcharge is conceptualized as a loss and is therefore more aversive than simply passing up a possible gain.

In an experimental illustration of this point (Tversky and Kahneman 1981), a choice was presented to two different groups of subjects with slight changes in the formulation so as to produce different reference points. Here is the choice as presented to the first group (p 453):

> Imagine that the U.S. is preparing for the outbreak of an unusual Asian disease, which is expected to kill 600 people. Two alternative programs to combat the disease have been proposed. Assume that the exact scientific estimates of the consequences of the programs are as follows: If Program A is adopted, 200 people will be saved. If Program B is adopted, there is $\frac{1}{3}$ probability that 600 people will be saved, and $\frac{2}{3}$ probability that no people will be saved. Which of the two programs would you favor?

This formulation of the problem implicitly adopts as a reference point a state of affairs in which the disease takes a toll of 600 lives. The outcomes of the programs include this reference state and two different possible *gains*, measured by the number of lives *saved*. Under this formulation, 72 percent of the subjects preferred Program A, saving 200 lives for sure. Now consider the following formulation of the problem, preceded by the very same cover story (p. 453):

> If Program C is adopted, 400 people will die. If Program D is adopted, there is $\frac{1}{3}$ probability that nobody will die, and $\frac{2}{3}$ probability that 600 people will die. Which of the two programs would you favor?

Although the options presented in the second formulation are indistinguishable in real terms from those presented in the first formulation, the second suggests as a reference state, or neutral point, one in which no one dies of the disease; any deaths are then viewed as *losses* relative to this state. Under this formulation, 78 percent of the subjects preferred Program D, apparently being unwilling to accept the sure loss of 400 lives.

It seems clear that people view losses and gains from a judged status quo asymmetrically. In light of this, it should not be surprising (to return to our original problem) that people take a particularly negative view of choice situations in which all their options are below the conceptualized status quo—that is, in which all their options are losses. This is precisely the situation of a robbery victim given the alternatives of surrendering his wallet or surrendering his life, or of a gangrene sufferer confronting the alternatives of amputation versus a death-incurring risk of nonamputation. In such situations all the prospective choices are losses, and whichever choice one selects is naturally viewed as less than fully accepted or "willed." With this in mind, we might return to our original account of freedom as the ability to do as one pleases. If we now restrict the term *pleases* to actions with (subjective) positive value, or at least not negative value (not net losses), we will have a substantially improved account of freedom. The mere multiplicity of alternatives does not guarantee freedom; only if some of the alternatives are "pleasing"—that is, not negative in value—is an agent genuinely free.

6.5   Action and Executability

Until now we have listed four main types of determinants of action: preferences, beliefs, ability, and opportunity. But how exactly are these factors (and perhaps others) interwoven in the production of behavior? To answer this question, we need an integrated theory of behavior production. In this context *behavior* does not mean merely movements of limbs or vocalizations. Human behavior commonly takes place in complex environments and is endowed with much social significance. Behavior is standardly conceptualized, both by actors and by observers, in terms of complex situations and social conventions. Thus, we need a theory that integrates these dimensions of behavior with the production of movement and sound. We also need to reflect on how the choice of behavioral outputs is guided by reasoning about the enviromental and social ramifications of actions. In turning to these issues, we will be addressing action theory as an autonomous subject, but this will also shed further light on some of the key concepts invoked in our account of free will, such as ability and opportunity.

Let us begin with a theory about the units and structure of action proposed by Goldman (1970) and reformulated and elaborated by Pollack (1986). When people perform actions, they instantiate or realize various *act-types*, such as moving a pawn, checkmating an opponent, turning on a light, tying their shoes, requesting the salt, and so on. Of course, a single act-type can be instantiated by different agents, and by the same agent at different times. Instantiations of the same type by different agents are different actions (*act-tokens*), and realizations of the same type at different times are different actions. Furthermore, let us assume that instantiations of different act-types count as different actions. Thus, a single action can be represented as a triple consisting of an act-type, an agent, and a time-interval. For example, George's jumping in the air during a specific time-interval t can be represented as the triple $\langle x, G, t \rangle$, where x is the act-type of jumping in the air, G is George, and t is the time-interval in question.

Strictly speaking, a triple such as $\langle x, G, t \rangle$ represents a *possible* action, which may or may not be actual. Possible actions should be included in a theory since they are objects of an agent's deliberation, whether or not she ultimately decides to perform the act-type or succeeds in doing so. To represent actual actions, let us introduce the ternary relation *OCCURS*. $OCCURS(x, G, t)$ will be true if and only if agent G performs act-type x during time-interval t. A similar treatment of nonactional states of affairs is also in order. For example, let s be the possible state of affairs of the sun's shining. Then if the sun actually shines on Tuesday, this state of affairs *holds* on Tuesday. Using *HOLDS* as a binary relation, we write this as $HOLDS(s, t)$. Both *OCCURS* and *HOLDS* could be defined as being satisfied just in case they are realized throughout the interval in question, or alternatively during any segment of the interval. We will adopt the former convention.

An agent can perform many act-types at the same time. Some simultaneous actions are independent. A pianist can simultaneously play one chord with the right hand and another chord with the left. A cheerleader can simultaneously leap, clap hands, and shout a cheer. But even focusing on a single movement or utterance, more than one act-type can be performed thereby. Consider a chess player Helen who, grasping her queen, moves it to square king-knight-seven (K-Kn-7). Helen may well instantiate each of the following act types at the same time: move-right-hand, move-queen-to-K-Kn-7, checkmate-opponent, and win-match. Corresponding to each act-type, there is a (distinct) particular action that occurs.

What is the relation between these several actions? We often describe agents as performing one act-type *by* performing another: *by* flipping a switch, an agent turns on the light, or *by* winking, an agent signals acceptance of a proposal. Let us express this by-relation by saying that the action of flipping the switch *generates* the turning on of the light, and that the winking generates the accepting of the proposal. Similarly, the four indicated chess actions are related by the (transitive) generation relation. $\langle$Move-right-hand, Helen, noon$\rangle$ generates $\langle$move-queen-to-K-Kn-7, Helen, noon$\rangle$, which generates $\langle$checkmate-opponent, Helen, noon$\rangle$, which generates $\langle$win-match, Helen, noon$\rangle$.

There are several species of the generation relation. One is *causal* generation, which obtains when the generating action produces an effect that is partly constitutive of the generated action. If $\langle$flip-switch, $G, t \rangle$ causes the light to go on, then it causally generates $\langle$turn-on-light, $G, t \rangle$. Similarly, if $\langle$growl, $G, t \rangle$ gives the cat a fright, then it causally generates $\langle$frighten-cat, G, t⟩. A second species of generation is *circumstantial* generation, which obtains when the generated action arises from some attendant circumstance in which the generating action is performed. For example, in the circumstance that Henry has promised to come home before midnight, ⟨come-home, Henry, 12:30⟩ circumstantially generates ⟨break-promise, Henry, 12:30⟩. A third species of generation is *conventional* generation, where the generated action is the upshot of (1) the generating action, (2) some rule or convention that is in force, and possibly (3) some attendant circumstances. For example, given the rules of chess and the particular configuration of the board at the time in question, ⟨move-queen-to-K-Kn-7, Helen, noon⟩ conventionally generates ⟨checkmate-opponent, Helen, noon⟩.

As these examples amply illustrate, the generation of one act by another characteristically depends not simply on the performance of the generating act but on surrounding factors as well. The environmental conditions, including the social environmental conditions, have to be ripe in order for one action to generate another. Moving your queen to K-Kn-7 does not in general suffice to checkmate your opponent; the rest of the pieces have to be suitably configured. Flipping a switch does not in general suffice to turn on a light; the switch has to be wired to a light fixture, and the latter must have a functioning bulb in it. Giving an argument does not by itself suffice to persuade your audience; the audience needs to be capable of understanding the argument and disposed to accept your premises.

Let us call all antecedent or concomitant conditions that are requisite for enabling one action to generate another *enabling conditions*. C is an enabling condition for ⟨x, G, t⟩ to generate ⟨y, G, t⟩ if and only if, given C, ⟨x, G, t⟩ would generate ⟨y, G, t⟩, but without C, ⟨x, G, t⟩ would not generate ⟨y, G, t⟩. (We will ignore complications arising from the possibility of alternative enabling conditions.) The presence of suitable wiring and a functioning bulb are enabling conditions for your flipping the switch to generate your turning on the light.

Restricting attention to prospective generational action pairs, it often happens that in order to perform act-type z you need to perform y, in order to perform y you need to perform x, and so on. Does such a hierarchical series come to an end? Are there some act-types that you can perform without needing to perform other act-types to generate them? Presumably yes. You can raise your hand, wiggle your toes, utter various sounds, blink your eyes, and so on, without having to do anything else to generate them. All these act-types will be called *basic acts*. (Is it true that you don't have to do anything else to perform a basic action? Don't you have to send messages to relevant motor neurons and innervate the relevant muscles? Yes, but these are not *actions*.)

Each human being has a repertoire of basic act-types. These are act-types one is able to perform more or less at will, as long as minimal boundary conditions are satisfied (your hands are not bound, your mouth is not gagged, and so forth). Although there are some interpersonal differences in basic act repertoire—some people can wiggle their ears and others cannot, for instance—there is extensive overlap in the human basic act endowment and its complement. All ordinary people can raise their hands at will but nobody can raise his hair at will. Repertoires can expand with training and can decay, erode, or become impaired through age, disease, or injury. But repertoires normally remain quite stable over time, at least after maturation.

The notions of basic acts and enabling conditions can help us be a little more concrete about two notions invoked earlier in the chapter: ability and opportunity. Ability, at least "primitive" ability, consists in having appropriate act-types in one's basic act repertoire. Opportunity consists in the satisfaction of suitable enabling conditions, which permit appropriately chosen basic actions to generate the action in question. Combining the notions of ability and opportunity, we can speak of the *executability* of actions.

Let us divide executability into *simple* and *sequential* executability. Simple executability holds of an act when the agent can perform it via a single basic act-type, not a succession of basic acts. In other words, act-type y is simply executable by G at t if and only if either (1) y is a basic act for G at time t, or (2) there is some other act x in G's basic act repertoire at t, and some suitable enabling conditions C hold at time t so that if $\langle x, G, t \rangle$ occurred, it would generate $\langle y, G, t \rangle$. Simple executability will be represented by the relation $EXEC$. For example, we can write $EXEC(y, G, t)$.

Sequential executability is a bit more complicated. At this moment Oscar cannot grasp a certain book in his study because it is on the very top shelf, and Oscar cannot reach the top shelf. So $\langle$grasp-book, Oscar, now$\rangle$ is not (simply) executable. But Oscar can execute a *series* of acts that would include grasping the book as its final member. He can fetch a stool, place it on the floor beneath the book, climb on the stool, extend his arm, and grasp the book. All of this might take him 30 seconds. Thus, although Oscar cannot execute the act of grasping the book right now, it is true of him that, starting now, he could execute it within 30 seconds from now. To express this, let us introduce a four-place relation $EXECQ$, which has two arguments for times, and where the second time argument is understood as a time *by which* the action can be performed. For example, we may write: $EXECQ(\text{now, grasp-book, Oscar, now-plus-30-seconds})$. In general, $EXECQ(t, y, G, t')$ is true if and only if (1) there is a set of acts $x_1, \ldots, x_n$, each of which is in G's basic act repertoire, such that (2) there is a series of successive time intervals between t and t' such that $x_1, \ldots, x_n$ can all be performed by G during these intervals, and such that (3) if x_1,

..., x_n are performed by G during their appropriate intervals, then G's performance of x_n at its appropriate time (at or before t') would generate G's performance of y at that time.

In action sequences of this type the early members typically have the function of creating enabling conditions that allow the final member to generate the target action. Fetching the stool, placing it beneath the book, climbing on the stool, and extending his arm toward the book jointly create conditions that enable Oscar's basic act of making a hand-grasping motion (at the right time) to generate the target action of grasping the book. (Of course, fetching the stool is not really a *basic* action; nor is placing the stool beneath the book; and so forth. But in each such case there must be a basic action to generate the listed action.)

Thus far we have been discussing what it takes for an action to be executable, that is, in the terminology of section 6.2, "actionally possible." However, the mere fact that an action is executable for an agent does not imply that she will execute it. She will normally execute it only if she actually *desires* the target action, or desires the state of affairs that it might achieve. But even if an action is executable and the agent desires to perform it, it does not follow that she will even try to perform it. Achieving that desire might involve foregoing other things she values even more. In short, people are often forced to choose between incompatible actions or outcomes, each of which independently is somewhat desirable.

Suppose that an agent chooses to perform (or try to perform) a desired action, an action that is actually executable for her. Does it follow that she will succeed in performing it? No. The fact that an action *is* executable for an agent does not guarantee that she *knows* how to execute it. Even though the action is executable for her (simply or sequentially), she may fail to design an adequate *plan* for its execution. Her plan may be ineffectual.

Ineffectual plans standardly arise from the agent's false beliefs about enabling conditions, either false beliefs about the enabling conditions that already hold, or false beliefs about the enabling conditions that would be created by certain initial steps in a sequential plan. Helen may believe that the current configuration of the chess board is such that her moving her rook to Q-R-8 would generate her checkmating her opponent. This belief, however, may be false: rook to Q-R-8 may still leave the opponent a legitimate response. This may be so despite the fact that checkmate is currently executable by Helen via some other move (say, queen to K-Kn-7). Sequential plans can be poorly designed for analogous reasons. An agent's calculations about the upshots of intermediate steps can readily misfire.

Clearly, effective planning requires effective reasoning about the results of possible actions. Workers in the field of artificial intelligence have addressed this topic in the specific context of trying to design robots that can make effective plans and execute them. What formal reasoning mechanisms should such an automaton be endowed with? An illustration of the difficulties encountered in devising such mechanisms is the *frame problem* introduced by McCarthy and Hayes (1969). In their formal framework, an action was conceived as a transition from one situation to another. For example, the action Paint (House17, Red) is such that if this action is taken in any situation s_1, the result is a situation s_2 in which the color of House17 is red. But now consider taking the action Rearrange-Furniture in s_2, which results in a new situation s_3. What is the color of House17 in s_3? One would like to say that it is still red, since rearranging the furniture should not affect the color of the house. But should we then add an "axiom" to the Rearrange-Furniture frame that the color of the house remains unchanged? The problem is that to use this strategy one would need a tremendous number of axioms, because rearranging the furniture doesn't clean the floors, doesn't change the president of the United States, and so forth Since each action concept would be represented by a huge number of axioms, it is not clear how these could be retained in memory or how the relevant ones could be retrieved when needed. Even if the axiom approach is abandoned, we are left with the general problem of how an intelligent agent can feasibly keep track of all the changing and unchanging states of affairs that flow from an action's performance. (Notice too that the axiom approach has other problems: the proposed axiom would simply be wrong if concurrent actions are allowed. Someone might paint your house while you are busy rearranging your furniture. So we cannot have it as a fixed rule that rearranging furniture results in no change in house color.)

It seems likely that cognitive scientists will not solve the problem of how intelligent reasoning about plans can be accomplished, whether by humans or artificial systems, until there is an adequate theory of causal inference. But this topic goes beyond the scope of this chapter.

6.6   Plans, Execution, and Misexecution

Let us therefore set aside the question of *how* agents form plans. Granted that a plan has been formed, we will inquire into how it is executed or misexecuted. The first question we will address here is what *counts* as execution or misexecution of a plan. In particular, what is it for a plan to misfire?

Before answering this, we need to say more about what plans are (see Bratman 1987). A plan can be thought of in two related ways: either as a mental phenomenon of some sort, or as the content, or data-structure, represented by the relevant mental phenomenon. Focusing first on the mental phenomenon aspect, a plan can plausibly be construed as a set of *intentions*, or perhaps intentions and beliefs. To have a plan is to have a set

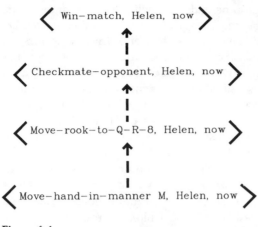

Figure 6.4
A simple action plan.

of actions one *intends* to perform. Since plans can be either simple or sequential, the content of a plan can take one of two forms: either a set of actions that are related by the generation relation (a simple plan), or a set of actions related both by temporal succession and by generation (a sequential plan). For the moment, let us concentrate on simple plans.

Suppose Helen believes that she can checkmate her opponent by moving the rook to Q-R-8—in other words, that ⟨move-rook-to-Q-R-8, Helen, now⟩ would generate ⟨checkmate-opponent, Helen, now⟩. She also believes that, having grasped the rook in her hand, ⟨move-hand-in-manner-M, Helen, now⟩ would generate ⟨move-rook-to-Q-R-8, Helen, now⟩, and she believes that ⟨checkmate-opponent, Helen, now⟩ would generate ⟨win-match, Helen, now⟩. Since she has it as a (dominant) *goal* right now to win the match, she forms an intention to perform the basic act of moving-hand-in-manner-M, with further intentions that the other actions should be generated in the indicated fashion. Helen thereby forms a simple plan, the content of which is shown in figure 6.4.

Suppose now that Helen executes the basic act element in her plan: she moves her hand in manner M. This action indeed generates moving the rook to Q-R-8, but since that still leaves the opponent a legitimate response, the latter action does not generate checkmating the opponent; nor is winning the match generated. In short, the only portions of her plan that are successfully executed are the first two actions. This is one way, then, in which a plan can misfire: not all of its components actually occur. In particular, a plan misfires when its *goal-element* fails to occur. (Plans can have more than one goal-element, which complicates matters. But this issue can be ignored in the interest of simplicity.)

A plan can also misfire if an action is generated that was not included in the plan. A parent who is teaching a child how to play chess might be intending *not* to checkmate the child very early. The parent might intend to make a certain move precisely because he thinks it would not generate a checkmating action. If, to his surprise, it does generate a checkmate, this is a kind of misfire: an unintentional action. So one kind of misexecution is the nonoccurrence of an intended action; another kind is the occurrence of an unintended action. A third kind of misexecution is for an intended action to occur but not in the expected generational position. This is a less common and less serious type of error, and need not detain us.

The topic of sequential plan execution and misexecution is much more complex. Here it is especially important to take into account the cognitive aspects of a plan—in particular, whether and to what extent the initial mental plan retains its status over the whole course of the planned sequence. For initial discussion of this topic we will draw on Norman's (1981) treatment of action errors or *slips*. Norman proposes numerous categories of action errors, but let us concentrate on three: (1) *capture* errors, (2) *data driven* errors, and (3) *mistiming* errors.

Capture errors occur when a familiar habit substitutes itself for an intended action sequence. The basic notion is simple: Pass too near a well-formed habit and it will capture your behavior. One example of a capture error is William James's (1890) undressing example. James reported that very absentminded persons have been known to go to their bedroom to dress for dinner, but then take off one garment after another and finally get into bed, merely because that is the habitual issue of the first few movements when performed at a later hour. Another example is this: After finishing your day's activities at the university, you usually drive straight home. But today you wish to stop by the post office, the drive to which has the same initial segment as the route home. So you plan to drive that initial segment and then deviate from the customary route and go to the post office. When the time comes, however, the old routinized plan "captures" your initial plan, and you wind up going straight home.

In these sorts of cases an earlier plan is displaced by a later plan, or the earlier one is at least forgotten and replaced. As a result, there is some ambiguity about whether the final course of action should be categorized as unintended. Relative to the earlier plan, the terminal action segment (undressing completely and getting into bed) is certainly unintended. But relative to the belatedly formed plan, the terminal action phase is perfectly intentional.

Data-driven errors occur when there are intrusions from the environment. One of Norman's examples is the well-known Stroop phenomenon. In a classic demonstration experiment in psychology, names of colors are printed on a page in colors that differ from the names. For example, the word *blue* might be printed in red ink. The subject's task is to look at each word and say as rapidly as possible the name of the ink color in which it is printed. However, the intrusion of the printed names causes extreme difficulty. Although the subject should say "Red" on seeing the word *blue*, since the word is colored red, it is difficult to avoid reading the word normally.

Another example of a data-driven error is this: A department chairman is assigning a visitor a room to use. Standing in front of the room at a telephone in an outside alcove, she decides to call the department secretary to tell her the room number. Although she knows the department telephone number well, visual sighting of the room number intrudes into the plan and she dials the room number she is looking at.

There clearly are components of misexecution here. The chairman intends to reach the department secretary, and intends to dial the department telephone number; she does neither. But there is a component of successful execution even in the dialing. The number the chairman does dial—say, 3486—is one she presumably has (belatedly) formed a plan to dial. The real trouble is not that her performance of this action fails to conform with *any* plan of hers; rather, the plan with which it does conform is improperly linked to the originating plan or goal, namely, to call the secretary.

Mistiming errors are easily illustrated by verbal slips, such as the Spoonerism "You have tasted the whole worm" instead of the intended "You have wasted the whole term." The initial *t*-sound of *tasted* and the *w*-sound of *worm* are indeed intended elements of the action sequence, but they do not occur at their (originally) intended times.

Now some of these action errors can be interpreted as resulting from false beliefs, a diagnosis of misexecution that we considered earlier. For example, the department chairman somehow comes to believe (momentarily) that dialing 3486 will generate the action of reaching the secretary, which is false. And *perhaps* the agent guilty of the Spoonerism comes to have false beliefs at critical moments concerning where the indicated *t*-sounds and *w*-sounds belong. But not all these slips can plausibly be understood or explained in terms of false beliefs. Let us look at the model Norman proposes to account for them.

Norman's model is an *activation-trigger-schema* (ATS) system. A schema is an organized memory unit, of the sort some theorists have proposed for perception and other domains of cognition. An action schema is a unit that can control a specific overlearned action skill such as drinking from a container, doing long division, making breakfast, or finding one's way home from work. It is an organized body of representations that can direct the flow of control of motor activity. Typically action schemas are linked into an ensemble of related schemas, organized in a heterarchical control structure. Norman calls the highest-level schema a *parent* schema. Subschemas can be initiated by the parent schema to control each of the component parts of a complex action sequence; these subschemas are called *child* schemas.

In the course of planning and deliberation, a variety of possibly competing action schemas can be *activated*, or brought into operational readiness. But no schema actually engenders behavior unless it is *triggered*. The model provides each schema with a set of specific conditions that are required for its triggering. When the current conditions match the conditions associated with the schema, then the schema is triggered. Exact match is not required; but there is assumed to be a trade-off between level of activation and the goodness-of-match to the trigger conditions. A weakly activated schema may be triggered if its conditions are matched exactly; a highly activated schema may be triggered if its conditions are only approximately matched.

This ATS model might explain a variety of different slips. Many verbal slips can be explained as resulting from the mistiming of trigger conditions. Suppose someone says, "Financed by the Rockebrothers, uh, the Rockefeller Brothers Foundation." Clearly, the component *brothers* had been activated and was in readiness for speech; but somehow the trigger conditions for this utterance occurred at too early a juncture.

The model might also explain capture errors. In the post office example, the post office route plausibly gets mentally specified as a deviation from the better learned home route schema. This new schema is intended to be triggered at a critical location along the usual path. However, if the relevant schema for the deviation is not in a sufficiently activated state at the critical time for its triggering, it is apt to be missed, and the more common home route followed. To put it otherwise, an old habit tends to have a high activation level, so it is easily triggered even by a partial match. For these reasons, it is easy for the old familiar action schema to be triggered, contrary to one's original intention.

Although Norman's model of action errors is slightly different from the model we articulated earlier, there is no necessary conflict between them. If we assume that what Norman calls an action-schema is something like the content of a plan, and if the activation of an action-schema corresponds to acceptance or endorsement of a given plan, then the models are quite close. Only the trigger-conditions concept, the levels-of-activation concept, and possibly the partial-matching concept introduce fundamentally different ideas, and these are best seen as *additional* to the earlier model, not incompatible with it.

Other research on motor control suggests different ways in which the framework sketched earlier should be supplemented. Many researchers have suggested that movement sequences are executed by means of a *motor program* and that there is a special motor program *buffer* distinct from ordinary short-term memory. This might suggest that in addition to planning that takes place in short-term memory, special motor plans are prepared in the motor buffer just prior to execution (see chapter 5 and Sternberg et al. 1978).

Suppose, for example, that an agent is asked to perform a rapid sequence of actions, such as reciting a sequence of words or typing a sequence of keystrokes, after a start signal. Experimental results on such tasks suggest that the agent prepares a motor program consisting of a set of linked subprograms, one for each unit of the response. Then, once the start signal occurs, a sequential search process takes place to retrieve each appropriate subprogram as the time for its execution unfolds. The longer the length of the sequence (the more units in it), the greater the delay in beginning its execution (latency), presumably because the retrieval process is longer the greater the number of units in the sequence. For the same reason, the longer the sequence the slower the *rate* of execution.

Although Sternberg et al. do not examine the question of response errors, the idea of a motor program buffer and a process of search through the buffer could certainly help explain the mistiming errors discussed by Norman. These would be particularly easily explained if partial matching is allowed in the model. As the buffer is searched for the next unit to be selected, units originally slated for subsequent performance might be selected too early. (This is compatible with either sequential or parallel search.) This could yield the Spoonerism "You have tasted the whole worm," as well as the error "financed by the Rockebrothers."

As we see, the sorts of models of planning and execution that have been sketched by philosophers can complement those of planning and of motor execution that are under investigation by workers in artificial intelligence and in psychology. This illustrates the convergence of disciplines that so frequently transpires within cognitive science.

Suggestions for Further Reading

On the topic of free will, two useful collections of articles are Watson 1982 and Honderich 1973. Rigorous arguments for incompatibilism are given in Van Inwagen 1983; a recent lively defense of compatibilism is Dennett 1984. A discussion of determinism and the predictability of human action appears in Goldman 1968.

On the topic of choice, the influential papers by Kahneman and Tversky (Kahneman and Tversky 1984; Tversky and Kahneman 1981) should be consulted. The former is reprinted in Elster 1986, which also contains selections on choice from other behavioral sciences. The article on coercion by Nozick (Nozick 1969) is an intriguing philosophical piece.

Detailed development of the theory of actions and generation presented in this chapter appears in Goldman 1970. A recent adaptation of this theory for purposes of artificial intelligence is Pollack 1986. Davidson 1980 contains many influential essays, some of which articulate a contrasting position on the ontology of actions.

The topic of planning is addressed from an artificial intelligence perspective in chapter 9 of Charniak and McDermott 1985 and in Georgeff and Lansky 1987. Bratman 1987 is a sustained philosophical treatment of plans, intentions, and rationality. Brand 1984 integrates philosophical and cognitive science approaches to action theory.

On the topic of execution and action slips, see Norman 1981, as well as literature cited in the previous five chapters.

Questions

6.1 Some people believe that determinism is essentially the same thing as fatalism: if an action is determined, then it is fated to occur. Compatibilists generally deny this. How might a compatibilist go about distinguishing between determinism and fatalism?

6.2 How should a compatibilist spell out the sorts of constraints on preference or choice that conflict with freedom? Suppose that commercial advertisements create tastes for certain products that people did not previously have. Does this violate their freedom of choice? What forms of advertising (if any) would constitute "manipulations" of preference? Suppose you have a certain desire but deplore your having it; you wish you didn't have the desire , but it persists nonetheless. Is this a constraint on freedom? Is it necessary, in order to be free, that any higher-order desire will automatically spawn its lower-order object?

6.3 Do all generationally related sets of actions form a single series or hierarchy? If not, give examples where a more complex structure is realized.

6.4 Why are neural signals or muscle innervations not considered actions? What in general distinguishes basic acts, for example, from muscle innervations?

6.5 If you plan to do action A, must you believe you are going to do A? Must you believe you are at least going to try to do it? Can you believe beforehand that you will do an action without planning to do it?

6.6 Is the construct of schema-triggering in Norman's model the same thing as the construct of a motor unit being "retrieved" in the model of Sternberg et al.? Does the latter model have anything that corresponds to "activation"? If not, does it need such a construct?

References

Brand, M. (1984). *Intending and acting.* Cambridge, MA: MIT Press.

Bratman, M. (1987). *Intention, plans, and practical reason.* Cambridge, MA: Harvard University Press.

Charniak, E., and D. McDermott (1985). *Introduction to artificial intelligence.* Reading, MA: Addison-Wesley.

Davidson, D. (1980). *Essays on actions and events.* Oxford: Clarendon Press.

Dennett, D. (1984). *Elbow room: The varieties of free will worth wanting.* Cambridge, MA: MIT Press.

Elster, J., ed. (1986). *Rational choice.* New York: New York University Press.

Georgeff, M., and A. Lansky, eds. (1987). *Reasoning about actions and plans.* Los Altos, CA: Morgan Kaufmann.

Goldman, A. (1968). Actions, predictions, and books of life. *American Philosophical Quarterly* 5, 135–151. [This appears in slightly revised form as chapter 6 of Goldman 1970.]

Goldman, A. (1970). *A theory of human action.* Englewood Cliffs, NJ: Prentice-Hall.

Honderich, T., ed. (1973). *Essays on freedom of action.* London: Routledge and Kegan Paul.

James, W. (1890). *The principles of psychology,* vols. 1 and 2. New York: Holt.

Kahneman, D., and A. Tversky (1979). Prospect theory: An analysis of decision under risk. *Econometrica* 47, 263–291.

Kahneman, D., and A. Tversky (1984). Choices, values, and frames. *American Psychologist* 39, 341–350.

McCarthy, J., and P. Hayes (1969). Some philosophical problems from the standpoint of Artificial Intelligence. In B. Meltzer and D. Michie, eds., *Machine intelligence*. New York: American Elsevier.

Norman, D. (1981). Categorization of action slips. *Psychological Review* 88, 1–15.

Nozick, R. (1969). Coercion. In S. Morgenbesser, P. Suppes, and M. White, eds., *Philosophy, science and method*. New York: St. Martin's Press.

Pollack, M. (1986). *Inferring domain plans in question-answering*. Technical Note 403. Menlo Park, CA: SRI International.

Sternberg, S., S. Monsell, R. L. Knoll, and C. E. Wright (1978). The latency and duration of rapid movement sequences: Comparisons of speech and typewriting. In G. E. Stelmach, ed., *Information processing in motor control and learning*. New York: Academic Press.

Tversky, A., and D. Kahneman (1981). The framing of decisions and the psychology of choice. *Science* 211, 453–458. [Reprinted in Elster 1986.]

Van Inwagen, P. (1983). *An essay on free will*. Oxford: Clarendon Press.

Watson, G., ed. (1982). *Free will*. New York: Oxford University Press.

Contents of Volume 1

Language: An Invitation to Cognitive Science *edited by*
Daniel N. Osherson and Howard Lasnik

Contents of Volume 3

Thinking: An Invitation to Cognitive Science *edited by*
Daniel N. Osherson and Edward E. Smith

Index